GERRARD

MY AUTOBIOGRAPHY

BANTAM BOOKS

LONDON • TORONTO • SYDNEY • AUCKLAND • JOHANNESBURG

TRANSWORLD PUBLISHERS
61-63 Uxbridge Road, London W5 5SA
A Random House Group Company
www.transworldbooks.co.uk

GERRARD: MY AUTOBIOGRAPHY
A BANTAM BOOK: 9780553817331

First published in Great Britain
in 2006 by Bantam Press
a division of Transworld Publishers
Bantam edition published 2007

Addresses for Random House Group Ltd companies outside the UK
can be found at: www.randomhouse.co.uk
The Random House Group Ltd Reg. No. 954009
The Random House Group Limited supports the Forest Stewardship Council®
(FSC®), the leading international forest-certification organisation. Our books
carrying the FSC label are printed on FSC®-certified paper. FSC is the only
forest-certification scheme supported by the leading environmental organisations,
including Greenpeace. Our paper procurement policy can be found at
www.randomhouse.co.uk/environment

Typeset in 11/14pt Sabon by
Falcon Oast Graphic Art Ltd.

Printed and bound by
CPI Group (UK) Ltd, Croydon, CR0 4YY

19

Contents

Acknowledgements

This book is for the people who make my world go round: for my wonderful partner Alex, and my precious daughters Lilly-Ella and Lexie, for my loving parents Julie and Paul, who have always been there for me, and for Paul, the brother I idolize. Struan Marshall has always been a good friend as well as my trusted agent, and his assistant, Kathryn Taylor, has been fantastic.

I'm eternally grateful to everyone at Liverpool Football Club for giving me the chance to live my dream. I know I'll never walk alone.

I'm grateful to Henry Winter of the *Daily Telegraph* and Paul Joyce of the *Daily Express* for listening to my story and recording it so faithfully. The Transworld team have been terrific, led by editor Doug Young and his assistant Emma Musgrave. I'd also like to thank other members of the Transworld team: publisher Bill Scott-Kerr, copy-editor Daniel Balado-Lopez, publicist Alison Barrow and jacket designer Steve Mulcahey. Many thanks also to Ged Rea and Dave Ball for supplying the statistics of my career with Liverpool and England.

Picture Acknowledgements

All uncredited images are © Steven Gerrard.

FIRST SECTION
Page 1
Portrait: © Alan Clarke.

Pages 4 and 5
Dave Shannon and Liverpool youth team; training at Melwood; SG and Dave Shannon; SG with Liverpool trainees and Steve Heighway, Dave Shannon and Hughie McAuley; SG in changing room with Dave Shannon, Hughie McAuley and Michael Owen: all courtesy of Liverpool Football Club Academy. SG and Michael Owen in England blazers: © Steven Gerrard.

Pages 6 and 7
SG with Lilly-Ella at Anfield: © Empics.

Page 8
SG and Lilly-Ella in Germany and SG with Alex Curran and Lilly-Ella: © Empics.

SECOND SECTION
Page 1
SG and Gérard Houllier: © Empics.

Pages 2 and 3
SG and Jamie Carragher; SG and Jose Mourinho; SG and Rafael Benitez; SG and Stan Lazaridis; SG with referee Barry Knight and Paul Ince; SG tackles Garry Naysmith: all © Empics. SG, Danny Murphy and Robbie Fowler with FA Cup: © Action Images/Darren Walsh. SG scores against Alaves: © Empics, Robbie Fowler, SG and Sami Hyypia during a parade: © FP/MC Reuters, picture supplied by Action Images.

Pages 4 and 5
SG in Basle; SG scores against Olympiakos; scoreboard at Champions League final; SG scores first goal against AC Milan;

SG brought down by AC Milan's Gennaro Gattuso: all © Empics.

Pages 6 and 7
SG lifts Champions League trophy; SG waves from tour bus; SG and Rafael Benitez carrying the Champions League trophy; SG scores his side's 3rd goal against West Ham United during the FA Cup final: all © Empics.

Page 8
SG lifts FA Cup: © Empics.

THIRD SECTION
Page 1
SG and Kevin Keegan; SG and Sven-Goran Eriksson; SG and Michael Owen: all © Empics.

Pages 2 and 3
SG scores against Germany; SG and Wayne Rooney training; SG plays a backpass England v. France; SG and Carlos Paredes of Paraguay; SG scores his side's 2nd goal against Trinidad and Tobago; SG and Wayne Rooney in Germany: all © Empics.

Pages 4 and 5
SG replaces Wayne Rooney: © Phil Cole/Getty Images. SG scores his side's 2nd goal against Sweden: © Empics. SG celebrates his goal: © Stephane Reix/For Picture/Corbis.

Pages 6 and 7
SG at England v. Ecuador: © Action Images/Reuters/Alex Grimm. David Beckham celebrated by his team-mates after scoring against Ecuador: © Empics. SG and Ecuador's Luis Valencia: © Empics.

Page 8
SG and Portugal's Cristiano Ronaldo: © Action Images/Tony O'Brien Livepic; SG with dejected Rio Ferdinand, Gary Neville and Jamie Carragher: © Empics; SG dejected: © Action Images/Tony O'Brien Livepic.

Dedication

Every time I drive into Anfield, I slow to a crawl as I pass through the Shankly Gates. My eyes are drawn towards the Hillsborough Memorial. I see the tributes to the ninety-six Liverpool fans who never returned from that FA Cup semi-final in 1989. I see the scarves left by visiting fans, signs of respect that lie alongside wreaths placed by families whose tears will never dry. I see the flame that burns always, reminding the world that the ninety-six will never, ever be forgotten.

As my car inches past the Memorial, I look down the names of those who fell on the Leppings Lane End, never to rise again. My eyes stop at one name. Jon-Paul Gilhooley, ten years old, the youngest of those who never came home from Sheffield. A fan who died following the team he loved. A boy whose life was snatched away just as it was starting. Crushed to death in a stand unfit for human beings. I knew Jon-Paul. He was my cousin. A shiver runs down my spine. I make the sign of the Cross and drive on.

I park the car and step into Anfield still thinking of Jon-Paul, his parents, and how lucky I am. I was nearly nine when Hillsborough took Jon-Paul from us. We were separated by a year and a bit in age but united in a passion for football. Jon-Paul adored Liverpool with the same fervour that fills me whenever I pull on that red shirt. We were so alike. Similar Merseyside estates, similar interests. Jon-Paul joined in the kickabouts on the street outside my house in Huyton on the edge of Liverpool, proudly wearing his Liverpool strip. The club meant the world to Jon-Paul.

As with all people across Merseyside, Saturday, 15 April 1989 is forever scarred in my mind. Liverpool FC was a religion in the house I grew up in so the moment we heard something had happened at the game we quickly gathered around the television to watch the news. Me and my dad Paul, my mother Julie and brother Paul sat there, staring disbelievingly at the pictures. We listened, shaking, to the grim details emerging. I couldn't take it in, the sheer horror of Hillsborough. None of us could comprehend the carnage. Why? How? Who? So many questions. The atmosphere was bad in our house that night, really bad. Each of us kept repeating the same anxiety: 'I wonder if anyone we know went to the game. God, please let there be no-one.' Eventually, I went to bed. I climbed the stairs and threw myself down on the bed, hoping for sleep to banish my thoughts. No chance. The images from Hillsborough kept me awake. Finally, in the early hours, I slipped into an uneasy sleep.

At half-eight the following morning, there was a knock at the door. I ran downstairs and undid the lock. Granddad Tony stood there. Without a word, he walked into the front room. The rest of the family began stirring, and soon we were all in the front room waiting for Granddad to talk. We all knew something was wrong. Granddad lives over the road and is not the type to be out and about at 8.30 on a Sunday morning. 'Our family has not escaped Hillsborough,' we thought. The look on Granddad's face told us something terrible had occurred.

'I've got bad news,' he said. 'Jon-Paul is dead.'

Tears, anger and confusion tore through all of us. We hadn't known Jon-Paul was at the game. He went to Anfield all the time, but an FA Cup semi-final was a special treat. Granddad explained: Jon-Paul's mum, Jackie, had somehow managed to get a ticket. She knew how much it meant to Jon-Paul to see his heroes in such an important match. It was only in Sheffield, barely seventy miles away. And he so wanted to go. A friend of the family took Jon-Paul. They set off from Liverpool that Saturday morning, all buzzing with excitement, but Jon-Paul never returned. Never returned from the match. Those words will haunt me for ever.

The bleak process of post-mortems meant that Jon-Paul's funeral was quite a while after Hillsborough. I didn't go to the funeral because of school. Well, that was the reason I was given. Actually, I'm sure Dad didn't want me to attend the funeral. My parents wanted to protect me. I was just a kid, struggling to understand that my cousin had died supporting the team we both adored.

I had just started at Liverpool's Centre of Excellence and training was cancelled for a while after Hillsborough. When we finally resumed, I could tell from the shocked look on the coaches' faces that this was a disaster that affected a whole club and a whole city. Hillsborough was the talk of my family for months afterwards. Even now, seventeen years on, we still touch on a subject that remains raw and painful.

Whenever I saw Jon-Paul's parents during my Youth Trainee Scheme days at Anfield, it gave me an extra determination to succeed. Just before I made my Liverpool debut, they said, 'Jon-Paul would be so proud of you.' During that match, I felt Jon-Paul was looking down on me, pleased I was fulfilling a dream we both shared. In the thrill of victory, I always think of Jon-Paul and about how buzzing he would be over a Liverpool win. It breaks my heart every day just to think Jon-Paul is not here any more.

Liverpool were brilliant with Jon-Paul's family. They were so caring and helpful towards all the people who lost loved ones at Hillsborough. They still are. Liverpool are a compassionate club with roots that go deep in the community. I remember Jackie once telling Dad how well the club treated them. Every year, on the anniversary of Hillsborough, Liverpool hold a service at Anfield. It's compulsory for players to attend. Rightly so. The team must show their respects to the ninety-six. In 2005 I felt really fluey, but I went. No way would I miss the Hillsborough service. It is part of my life.

The players normally meet up at our Melwood training ground and take the team bus to Anfield. During the journey, I talk to the foreign lads who don't understand. 'Where are we going?' they ask. 'What are we doing?' They have heard of the Hillsborough disaster, but don't know the full story. I fill them in, and they sit there, speechless with shock. I explain that there was a lot of anger over what got written after Hillsborough, which is why the worst offender, the *Sun* newspaper, will never be seen at Melwood, Anfield or in my house. Every Liverpool fan is completely against the *Sun*. I'm a Liverpool supporter so I respect their views, and I also lost a member of my family at Hillsborough. I won't touch the paper. The foreign players are very respectful. I have never known any of them not to want to pay their respects. They always go to the service. That's a credit to them and to Liverpool, a sign of the deep respect even new players feel for the club.

The trip is strange for me. I travel with the team yet when I arrive I see my family and all the thoughts about Jon-Paul come flooding back. For me, it's not a professional duty going to the Hillsborough service; it's desperately personal. I stand there, my head bowed, as a grieving relative as well as the team captain. Liverpool usually open the Kop, where Jon-Paul and many of those who died used to spend their Saturday afternoons. The service lasts a couple of hours. We sing hymns, say prayers and mourn for the ninety-six. In 2006, I did the reading, which I found incredibly emotional. Occasionally at the services, I speak to Paul Harrison, who used to be Liverpool's reserve keeper. Paul lost his dad at Hillsborough. Terrible. I cannot imagine being without my parents.

The families are very good at supporting each other. At Liverpool, You'll Never Walk Alone. Our famous club song is more than a string of words and a great tune; it is a pact between people. We stand together in good times and bad. The people who run the Hillsborough Families' Group deserve so much praise. They want justice and they just won't give up, which is completely right. There are families across Liverpool with an empty seat at their table, an untouched bedroom upstairs. These families deserve justice. I fully support the campaign because I want it myself. We should know exactly what happened at Hillsborough, and who was to blame. Action should be taken against those in authority who let ninety-six innocent people die. My cousin died at Hillsborough, and he has not had justice. When I warm up at Anfield, I see the 'Justice for the 96' banner and I nod passionately in agreement. The government should hold a proper inquiry. Only then can the families of the ninety-six sit at home and mourn, knowing justice has been done. Only then can they tend their loved ones' graves knowing someone has been brought to account for this terrible tragedy. A tragedy that could have been avoided.

Hillsborough must never be allowed to happen again. No-one should lose a life or a relative at a football match. Every time I see Jon-Paul's name cut into the cold marble outside the Shankly Gates, I fill with sadness and anger. I have never let anyone know this before, but it's true: I play for Jon-Paul.

1
Born to be Red

Cut my veins open and I bleed Liverpool red. I love Liverpool with a burning passion. My determination to reach the heights at Anfield intensified when poor Jon-Paul passed away. Also fuelling my drive to succeed was an accident I suffered during my school days. My career was nearly destroyed before it started. All my dreams of starring for Liverpool and England, of lifting European Cups and shining in World Cups, rested on the skill of a surgeon when I was only nine.

Anfield was already my first love and my second home. I'd been there a year, training with Michael Owen at the Vernon Sangster Sports Centre, learning my trade, when a calamity hit me that left me in hospital fearing for my future. Even now, I shudder at the memory of what took place on a patch of grass near my house on the Bluebell Estate of Huyton, Merseyside.

It was just a field, surrounded by bushes, a mess really. The type of place where people threw their rubbish without a second thought. Me and my mates didn't care. All that mattered to us was the grass was half-decent for a game of shootie. We were on it night and day, summer and winter. To us kids, that scrap of wasteground was Anfield, Goodison and Wembley rolled into one – a heaven on earth. One Saturday morning, early doors, I was kicking about on the strip with a kid from our street, a boy called Mark Hannan. We'd sorted out the pitch. It wasn't exactly the Bernabeu, but it was home. A mate nicked some nets from his Sunday League team, cut them in half, and rigged up two seven-a-side goals. Perfect.

So there was me and Mark, having a dead good kick-about, when the ball flew into some nettles. No problem. I ran across to fetch it. 'I'm not putting my hands in there,' I shouted to Mark. 'I'll get stung.' I couldn't see the ball. The nettles were too thick. 'I'm going to have to kick it out.' So I pulled my footy socks up and put my leg into the nettles to kick the ball out. It wasn't coming. I gave it a really good welly with my right foot, my tin-opener, the one I shoot and pass with. I kicked fast and deep into the nettles.

Agony. Total agony. My foot hit something. Jesus, the pain was merciless. I nearly had a heart attack. I fell down, screaming for help. In my career I've had smashed metatarsals and torn groins, but honest to God, I have never felt pain like this. Like poison from a needle, it shot up my shins. Mark sprinted over. 'I don't know what it is, Mark,' I yelled. 'I can't see it. My leg won't come out of the nettles.' Mark looked. Christ. All the blood drained from his face. He's going to throw up, I thought. How bad is it? I looked down and couldn't believe my eyes. A garden fork was embedded in my big toe. Straight through my trainer and into my foot, no stopping. Some nugget tossed this rusty fork away, and it got lodged in the nettles. The handle wasn't there, just the metal prongs, and I had kicked right into them. I felt the prong go in, burrowing into the bone.

'Go and tell someone!' I shouted, and Mark ran off to get my mum and dad.

A neighbour, Neil Weston, heard me screaming, and came running up. He dragged me out of the nettles, the fork following like an extra limb.

'Shall I pull it out?' asked the neighbour.

'You can't, you can't!' I shouted.

'I've got to try,' he said. The fork wouldn't shift. 'I'll get an ambulance,' he said, and disappeared.

I just lay there on the grass, tears spilling down my face and fears spinning through my head. Would I ever kick a ball again? Shit.

Mum and Dad arrived sharpish. Immediately, Dad realized how serious this was. 'He's going to lose his foot,' I heard him tell Mum. Amputation? Jesus Christ, no. My Liverpool career was being buried in a bed of nettles.

Finally, the ambulance from Alder Hey nosed its way into the field. It had taken only ten minutes but it felt like ten hours. The medics took one look at the foot and even they understood they couldn't yank the fork clear. 'We'll have to sort this out back at the hospital,' one of them said. Four people lifted me into the ambulance and off we went, bells and lights going crazy, racing to Alder Hey.

The journey was torture. I never realized how many bumps there were on the roads of Liverpool. Every time we drove over a bump, I screamed at the ambulance driver. Whenever I moved, I took the load of the fork in my bone, a stone in weight bending my toe. Tears followed every movement. I was shaking. One of the medics tried to hold the fork to stop it digging further in. The pain was horrific. I kept shouting at the driver. 'It's not his fault,' Mum and Dad told me. I just wanted the pain to stop. Stop. Please stop. As we sped through the streets, they pumped me with gas and air.

At Alder Hey, I was rushed straight into Accident and Emergency on the trolley – straight through, no waiting. Everyone could see how bad it was. And hear. Mum was hysterical, and I screamed the hospital down.

Only when a painkilling injection took hold did my howling stop. I was all dazed and weak but not quite unconscious. Through the clouds, I heard the doctor say, 'The fork is rusty, there's a chance of gangrene. We might have to take the toe off to stop any gangrene spreading.'

'Wait,' Dad intervened. 'Steven plays football, you must speak to Liverpool before you do any operation. They must know what is going on.'

My dad quickly called Steve Heighway, Liverpool's Academy director, who drove over sharpish. Steve's the strong type, and he immediately took control. 'No, you are not bloody well taking his toe off,' Steve told them.

The doctor replied, 'We have to operate. The decision will be made by the surgeon.'

Steve was adamant. 'No. Don't take his toe off.'

Steve won the argument. Thank God. The surgeon numbed the whole foot and tugged the fork out. The hole was huge, as big as a 20p coin and an inch and a half deep. It was a mess, but at least the surgeon saved my toe and my career. 'You are a very, very lucky young man,' Steve said. The doctors all agreed. 'We have never seen anything like this before,' they said. Even my brother, Paul, looked worried when he came to see me, and Paul usually winds me up over anything.

The one half-decent thing about the accident was that I missed three weeks of school. The doctors insisted, so who was I to argue! School sent homework round but it never got done. No chance. I was too busy milking my injury. My family spoiled me rotten. I lay there on the couch, being waited on hand and bandaged foot, and watching Liverpool videos. Fantastic. All my heroes parading their skills on the screen: John Barnes, Kenny Dalglish and Ian Rush. This was my sort of medicine, guaranteed to quicken recovery. Every day, a nurse came round to clean the hole with antiseptic, pack it with cotton wool balls, put a mesh around it. She then bandaged the foot up to the ankle. As the wound healed, the nurse put less and less cotton-wool in. Soon I could go to school on crutches. But I was not able to play in the yard. Nor could I go to the Vernon Sangster to train with Liverpool. For the first time in my life, I was prevented from doing what I love most.

That accident, and the weeks of recuperation, reminded me how important football was in my life. I started watching football seriously on the telly. I sat on the couch juggling the ball on my head, or with my left foot. I held the ball tight, almost for reassurance. I never wanted to be apart from a ball again. I was still getting twinges of pain, but after five weeks I was able to kick the ball cleanly. Thank God. Without football, my life would have been empty. I never forget that utter desolation of being separated from a ball.

As well as Alder Hey's permission to bunk off school, the doctors sorted out another bonus. The surgeon took one look at the rusty garden fork and said, 'That shouldn't have been there on the back-field.' So Mum and Dad showed the trainer and the fork to a solicitor and he knew we had a case. We claimed off the council because it was their wasteland. You're going to, aren't you? I've only made two claims in my life: one was a crash in a taxi which got us £800, and then the fork in the foot. We got £1,200 for that. That wasn't bad! Mum took me to town, got me new kit, two trackies, loads of stuff. 'All that pain was well worth it!' I kept laughing with Mum.

When I think back to the accident, the pain still goes right through me again, like an electric shock. I still see the fork sticking out of my trainer, still sense it grating against the bone. Once or twice, I spoke about the incident with my dad. Like Steve Heighway, he wasn't the type to take credit. Dad would never boast 'I made sure they didn't take your toe off'; he just says, 'You were fortunate, Steven.' We all knew if I had lost the big toe of my right foot, any chance of Liverpool and England would have ended right there, impaled on a rusty garden fork on a council wasteland in Huyton.

Bungalows cover that patch of land now. No nettle-beds will ambush any innocent schoolkids now. My earliest pitches disappeared under concrete or cars. They park all over the cul de sac where I grew up, Ironside Road on the Bluebell Estate. Back then, that tarmac area in front of my house, No. 10 Ironside, was My Pitch. No cars allowed. Unless the weather was good, when we'd dash round to the grass back-field, we'd be on Ironside. Straight out the front door, into a game, full throttle. Brilliant. Someone put that concrete area there for a reason, I'm convinced of it. Someone was telling me to make football my life, showing me the way ahead. It was so strange. That was My Pitch. If anyone was there when I came out of my house, they had to go. We used it for five-a-side, ten-a-side, twenty-a-side, rounders, shootie, catch, and a great game called Bare Arse. That was hilarious! If you got a certain amount of goals scored past you, you had to get your arse out. Everyone then got a free shot at your bare arse. Bare Arse is a Scouse tradition that produces brilliant goalkeepers and really accurate shooters. Fifteen years on, when Peter Crouch struggled to get off the mark at Liverpool, Bare Arse came in handy. We played it in training to help me and Crouchy with our shooting. I dropped my shorts and got Crouch to aim at my Bare Arse. Someone looked over the wall, sneaked a picture, and me and Crouchy both got our arses in the papers! The papers never said we were just playing Bare Arse! Games picked up on Ironside have stayed with me for life.

Ironside was known as the Happy Street. I arrived there on 30 May 1980, straight out of Whiston Hospital and into a football-mad house on the Happy Street. Bluebell's quite a big estate, a warren of roads with four pubs, one on each side: the Swan, Bluebell, Rose, and Oak Tree. Quite a few famous people come from around here, comedians like Freddie Starr and Stan Boardman, and the old actor Rex Harrison. The actress out of *Sex and the*

City, Kim Cattrall – the lively one – lived on Whiston Lane for a while. Bands like The La's, Space and Cast grew up in Huyton. Characters were on every corner.

I loved life on the Bluebell – my kingdom, my playground. Two youth clubs offered the usual attractions, but mostly we were outside, playing two-man chase on the River Alt, hide and seek, and you'd better be quick. Me and my brother Paul would come home filthy with mud. Mum went crazy, Dad just smiled. Ironside was always alive with activity. In the summer, families sat out, chatting away, sharing a drink while the kids played. Ironside had many distractions. Two girls my age, Lisa and Caroline, lived either side of No. 10 and I knocked about with them, crawling around the square, playing in the mud. Girls fascinated me. I had no sisters myself. I thought Lisa and Caroline were well fit. I flirted with them. Lisa and Caroline had one fault, though: they couldn't play football.

Didn't matter really. I never had far to look for a game. Bluebell was full of lads up for some footy action, always has been. Huyton is famous for producing decent pros, like Steve McMahon, Joey Barton, Lee Trundle, Peter Reid, Tony Hibbert, Craig Hignett and David Nugent. The town is crammed with Sunday League sides. Football is the local religion. On the Bluebell, I joined forces with seven or eight lads my age and we all became good mates, playing football every hour until our mums shouted us in. One problem bugged me: I never got a really decent game out of them. I was better than them, simple as that. I preferred games with Paul, three years my senior. Paul had around fifteen mates and their matches were full-on brilliant. At six, I could hold my own with Paul and the other nine-year-olds. Most of Paul's mates wanted me on their side. I loved competing against them. They accepted me because I didn't look out of place. Paul's mates were good players as well. Paul himself had trials at Bolton Wanderers. A kid called Danny Walker turned down a YTS at Tranmere Rovers. Paul's gang played in a local league for an U-10 team called Tolgate, run by two fellas from the Huyton area. One day, I followed Paul down to a Tolgate match and asked the organizers if I could join in.

'How old are you?' they asked.

'Seven,' I replied.

'Too young,' they said.

I burst into tears. 'You're wrong, I'm good enough,' I said. Still no joy. That feeling of rejection burned hard inside.

That concrete patch outside Ironside and the back-field on the Bluebell were breeding grounds for competitive players. A good touch and a tough streak were needed to survive, and I quickly developed both. I had to. Paul and his mates never held back in tackles on me, even though I was three years younger, just a scrap of skin and bones. Bang. Knock me over. No mercy. That's how I liked it. Do it again. That's why they used to let me play. I hobbled back into No. 10 all the time, covered in cuts and grazes from slide tackles on the concrete. I still have a scar on my face after being shoulder-charged into a fence. A nail nicked my skin. No fuss. No bother. I went in to see Granddad Tony across the road at No. 35 Ironside. He put three butterfly stitches in, neat ones, and I charged back to the game. 'Hurry up!' they shouted at me. Bang. Back into battle.

I have since bought 35 and 10 Ironside. Those houses will always be in our family. My brother lives in No. 10. There will always be Gerrards in Ironside. Granddad Tony was my dad's dad. My mum's granddad, Sidney Sullivan, was disabled so he lived with us for eight years, throughout my time at school. When Sidney was released from hospital after his first stroke, we got an unbelievable letter from the authorities. The message was brutal, the gist being that if someone in our family didn't look after Granddad, the council would stick him in a home. My nan lived in Mosscroft, a couple of estates away, and she wasn't capable of taking all that responsibility on herself. If Nan needed to pop out, Sidney couldn't be left on his own. 'He's not going in a home,' Mum said. So Sidney moved in with us. We built an extension on No. 10, giving Sidney his own en-suite shower and disabled facilities. He had a big living-room area that doubled up as his bed-room. Sidney rarely left this room. Occasionally, he wandered into our living-room to watch TV with us. Otherwise he was just happy being in that back-room.

He endured four strokes in all. I hated seeing what the strokes did to him, disabling him down one side. Paul and I could talk to him really good after his first stroke because he was quite clear then. Communication became more difficult after his second, third and fourth strokes. His deterioration really distressed us. He was a lovely man worn away by the strokes. I preferred remembering him the way he was before he got sick, smiling and chatty. If Mum noticed Paul and I hadn't been in to see him for a bit, she was on to us sharpish. 'Take Granddad's tea in,' Mum would say. 'Go and have your tea with him.'

Granddad was dead good with me and Paul. He made sure we got all the boots and kits we needed. 'Give the boys this money, make sure the boys get those football things,' he kept telling Mum. 'No,' she replied. 'Go on!' Granddad insisted, pushing some money across the table at Ironside. Granddad was the most generous man. 'Make sure the boys have everything,' he ordered Mum. He wasn't rich. Nothing like that. But Granddad had a bit of money from his sick pay and pension. He worked hard all his life in the Forces and on the ships.

Mum got paid a few quid for looking after Granddad. Paul and I could see the selfless job she did for him. We were a really close family anyway, but Sidney actually tied the bonds even tighter. Me and Paul realized we had to chip in as Dad worked only part-time. He was wary of a full-time job. He needed to be around the house, keeping an eye on Sidney when Mum went to the shops or picked Paul and me up from school. Dad was a labourer. His mates from the pub might find him some foreigners, as extra work on the side is called in Liverpool. Dad would be busy for a few weeks here and there in a gang.

Paul is my best mate. Always has been. Always will be. He had the bigger bedroom at Ironside, which pissed me off big-style. A midget couldn't have swung a tiny cat in my room. Paul had the heater, the biggest bed, all the trimmings. I didn't really mind. Paul was my hero. I just wanted to hang around with him and his mates. 'Get away,' Paul shouted at me, 'go home.' He didn't mind me joining in his football games, but didn't want me about when he and his friends were sitting around, talking. Fists flew. Me and Paul had some real toe-to-toe fights, steaming into each other, no holds barred. 'I hate you!' I'd shout at Paul after another scrap, rubbing my face or ribs where he whacked me. 'I want to kill you!' My anger soon subsided. Even if Paul gave me a real hiding, or wouldn't let me play with him and his mates, an hour later he would come back in and say, 'Stevie, do you want a game on the computer?' 'Yeah,' I'd reply enthusiastically, grateful to be back in Paul's world again. We'd then play a computer game as if no punches had been thrown. Storms passed quickly between Paul and me. I worshipped my brother. Looking at Paul now, he seems younger and smaller than me. No-one would ever cotton on he was my older brother. Strange.

Paul was a decent player, but short of aggression – a trait I have never been accused of lacking. Paul never wanted to be a footballer. He played for a laugh with his mates. 'Get more involved,' Dad yelled at Paul. 'It's cold,' Paul responded. 'I'd rather be at home.' Paul would never have made a living out of football, but if you put him in a gym for a game of five-a-side, he wouldn't look out of place. My brother knows tactics, and can spot a good player. I speak to Paul after matches and we are on the same wavelength.

Family friends and relatives tell me Dad was a good player. So does he! 'That's where you get your football skills from, Steven!' Dad laughs. Sadly, he damaged his knee as a kid playing on Astroturf. That did him. Bang went any dreams of being a pro. He stopped playing. Dad's brother, Tony, was meant to be decent, and played

Huyton Boys. Between ten and fifteen, people thought Tony had a chance of making it as a professional. Football runs deep in my family. I've got loads of cousins, who often came down Ironside for a game. One of them, Anthony Gerrard, was good enough to be signed by Everton. He's at Walsall now after being released by Goodison. Sunday League football around here has always been packed with my cousins and uncles.

A love of football ran through my family like letters through a stick of rock. Anfield and Goodison were regular weekend haunts. Walk into any of my relatives' houses and I guarantee there is a match on. Everyone crowds around the telly. Grab a drink, pull up a chair, watch the game. It's brilliant. On Saturday nights, Dad headed down the pub, but he was always back for *Match of the Day* on the BBC. You could almost set your watch by Dad, stepping back through the door of Ironside in time for *Match of the Day*. Dad, me and Paul squeezed onto the sofa for our Saturday-night ritual. I'd be buzzing with excitement as the programme came on. All of us sang along to the music. The Gerrards never missed *Match of the Day*. Never. It was the high point of the week.

Football ruled No. 10 Ironside. *Coronation Street* and *EastEnders* stood no chance if they clashed with the football. My dad wouldn't have it any different. It was always murder in our house if Mum wanted a soap ahead of the footy. Now and again, as a treat, Dad took me and Paul down the local to watch the live Sunday match on a big screen, or for a game of darts. I'd have a glass of Coke, chuck a few darts, and watch the match. Dead grown-up, I felt. Shortly before six p.m., the fun was over and we headed home with heavy hearts. School loomed in the morning like a dark cloud on a sunny day.

Still now I hate Sunday nights. Still! It's impossible to blank out the memory of getting ready for school, a ritual torture that ruined the final moments of a glorious weekend. According to the calendar most people use, a weekend lasts two days. Not at No. 10 Ironside. Not with Mum. A weekend is a day and a half with her. She demanded we be home by six p.m. to be scrubbed, bathed and ready for school the next morning. We ran in at six and the uniform was there, on the ironing board, all pristine and pressed, glaring at us. Just seeing the uniform made me sick. They resembled prison clothes after the freedom of the weekend. It was not that I hated school; I just loved my weekends roaming around Bluebell. Mum took school more seriously than Paul and I ever did. A proud woman, she made sure our uniforms were absolutely spotless. She polished our shoes so hard you could see your grimacing face in them. Poor Mum! She had her work cut out. If I left the house with a clean uniform, it was guaranteed to come home dirty. The same with shoes. Scuffed and muddy. Every time. Mum went up the wall.

My journey through the Merseyside school system was straightforward and undistinguished. I looked on schools as fantastic playing fields with boring buildings attached. My first stop was St Michael's, which became Huyton-with-Roby Church of England Primary. Though only a short walk from Ironside, Mum still insisted on driving me to St Mick's and picking me up. I enjoyed the infants and junior school, just messing about. When I was naughty, the teachers made me stand by the wall, looking at the bricks for five minutes as punishment. I never bullied anyone. I never hurt anyone or swore. I was just cheeky and mischievous. My crimes were petty ones: answering back or going on muddy grass when we were told to stay on the yard. Usual kids' stuff.

School held limited appeal. I sat in class, longing for play-time because there was always a match on in the playground. I loved dinner-time because it lasted an hour, which meant a longer match. I abandoned hot dinners because they wasted precious minutes. Queuing for my meal, I'd shout, 'Come on, there's a big game going on out there.' Eventually, I asked my mother for packed lunches. 'You should be on hot dinners,' she screamed, 'or come home if you don't like school food.' We compromised on packed lunches: sandwich, bar of chocolate and drink. And some fruit. The fruit always came home untouched. Apples, bananas and oranges weren't me. Butties weren't even me at that age. It would be bread off, meat out, quick bite, on with the game. 'Stevie, you haven't eaten your butty,' Mum would say, 'you've only eaten your chocolate.' Mum didn't understand. Speed was vital at dinner-time. I ate the packed lunch while playing or wolfed it down running back into class. Same with my tea. If there was a match going on outside Ironside, a game of chase, or my mates were waiting for me, I slipped my food in my pocket, sprinted out the door, threw the food to the neighbour's dog and raced on to the match. I returned home starving, picking at biscuits, crisps and chocolate.

Back at St Mick's, the teachers watched me scribbling

away busily in my school-book. Steam almost rose from my pencil I wrote so furiously. The teachers must have thought I was focusing really hard on the lesson. I'm sorry. I wasn't. Lessons were spent working out the teams for dinner-time. In the back of my school-book, I wrote down the names. When the bell for break rang, I dashed out to organize all the boys – and get the girls off the playground. 'You can watch,' I'd tell them generously, 'but that's the pitch and you can't go on it.' The pitch was marked out with bags and tops for goals. They were right serious battles at St Mick's. Wembley Cup finals have been less intense. My face still bears the trace of a scar collected in the playground after I collided with a fence, tussling for the ball. Defeat was unthinkable. The winners milked it loudly while the losers got caned for the next lesson.

Me and Barry Banczyk were the best players at St Mick's. Barry and I were good mates, but our playground rivalry was something else, real physical. We picked the sides, Barry's team against mine, always dead competitive. Barry was a decent player. He turned out for Denburn U-13s, a side my dad helped run. Denburn were good: Michael Branch and Tony Hibbert played for them. I turned out for Denburn briefly, helping them win the Edgehill Junior League, until Liverpool stopped me playing. Barry and I were the main men in the school team. One year, we helped St Mick's win a local cup which gave us a chance of playing at Wembley. First we had to beat sides from different districts in a tournament. The prize was huge. Wembley! Just the thought of the famous old stadium had me lying awake in bed, thinking of what it would be like to step out onto the best-known pitch in all the world. Wembley! What a dream come true that would be! I was certainly up for the tournament. In one match I went in for a slide tackle with my usual determination. I caught my knee on the sharp ring-pull of a Coke can, which sliced open my leg. It was only five stitches but it cost me my chance of joining the team at Wembley. I cried my eyes out. That was typical of my luck. My mates were off to Wembley and I was off to hospital. The scar on my knee faded but the pain of missing that trip to Wembley remains.

The time came when I had to leave St Mick's. For secondary school, a difficult choice awaited. Most of my class were going either to Bowring Comprehensive School or Knowsley High. Paul was at Bowring so I wanted to go there, just to be with my brother. Bowring and Knowsley High had serious problems, though: football was not high on the agenda. Everyone knew I was mad keen on football so only a school which improved me as a player would do. My teacher at St Mick's, Mrs Chadwick, gave me some sound advice. 'You should go to Cardinal Heenan, Steven,' she told me. 'It will be better for your football.'

Cardinal Heenan Catholic High School was well known to me. It had a really good name for football, probably the best in the area. Mrs Chadwick's husband, Eric, taught PE at Cardinal Heenan. 'Have a look at Steven Gerrard,' she told him. 'He's dead good at football. He'd make a great pupil for Cardinal Heenan.' Some people were not keen on me moving, though. The Bluebell Estate was outside the catchment area and I wasn't a

Catholic. But who cares? Football won. Cardinal Heenan wanted me. Along with a reference from Mrs Chadwick that I was half-decent in class, my ability on the ball carried me through the gates of Cardinal Heenan. My career demanded I go there. Enrolling at Cardinal Heenan brought eligibility for Liverpool Boys rather than Knowsley Boys, and that was key. Liverpool Boys teams were better run. The scouts at Liverpool and Everton knew that and always went talent-spotting at Liverpool Boys games. Cardinal Heenan was the only place for me.

Having picked my secondary school for footballing reasons, I still had to endure lessons there. Cardinal Heenan was massive – more than 1,300 boys. I didn't want to go at first, even with the knowledge that the football would be good. Night after night, I cried. The idea of moving among so many strangers horrified me. Cardinal Heenan was three miles from home – another country in my mind. But Mum and Dad persuaded me it would be best for my football. Reluctantly, I went. I needed time to settle, for it to become a familiar scenario in my life.

By the third year, I was on the back of the bus from the Bluebell with the boys, the whole atmosphere buzzing, loving it. For this was the first time Mum let me go to school on my own. I was thirteen and it was brilliant. Christ, I felt grown up. I left Ironside with my bus money and dinner money jangling in my pocket, feeling like a king, strutting down the Bluebell streets. I'd knock on the door of a couple of mates, Terry Smith and Sean Dillon, and the three of us would head on to the bus-stop, striding along like the top gang in town. Sean was a nightmare, late every day. Terry and me chucked stones at Sean's bedroom window to get him up at quarter to nine. Sometimes we got so annoyed we threw the stones really hard. A few shards of broken glass around Sean's bedroom would sort out his lousy time-keeping. When we finally got Sean out of his house, there would be a mad dash to the bus. All three of us, school-bags dangling, legs racing, sprinting down the road, laughing our heads off. Great times. Sean is a bricklayer now, doing well. I see Terry often. He's a huge Everton fan. So we have some banter.

When Sean, Terry and I reached Cardinal Heenan, the day revolved around waiting for the two play-times of 25 minutes each and the hour-long dinner-time. I spent all day thinking about football. I loved PE with Mr Chadwick. Unfortunately, we never did football all the time and I used to get a cob on if it was rugby, gymnastics or cricket. I wanted football, indoor or on the field. Or tennis. I was quite warm at tennis. At Cardinal Heenan we played short tennis, with a smaller net and these wooden bats. We decorated our bats with the Nike Swoosh or Adidas stripes to see who had the tastiest bat. But football remained the main subject on my personal curriculum.

Cardinal Heenan wasn't rough. Just a few fights in the playground now and again, a few big boys who were the so-called Cocks. I had my own gang and we looked out for each other. The odd fight erupted and I would be in the midst of it, throwing punches, standing my ground. No-one was going to push me around. Older boys, bigger boys, no-one. I suffered the occasional split lip from a punch I failed to dodge, but my uniform tended to be more spattered with mud than blood. I was always throwing myself around on the pitch, covering myself in dirt. I lived for those moments. Lessons were just the dead time between games.

When it came to class-work, though, I wasn't thick. All the way through Cardinal Heenan, I was in the middle academically. Different subjects provoked different moods. If I wasn't doing well at maths, I despised it and hated going to the lesson. But if I was flying in English, and our brilliant lady teacher helped me, I wouldn't mind it. I enjoyed creative writing, making up stories. I wrote about how one day I'd win the World Cup. I liked messing about with words. Reading, too. My favourite book at school was *Of Mice and Men*. It's quite a sad story when you get to know the characters. I read *Of Mice and Men* from cover to cover so many times the book almost fell apart. We watched the story on video, did a project on it, and an exam on it. When GCSEs arrived I got a C in English, six Ds and two Es.

But above all this I had only one ambition, one dream, one target – football.

2
Growing Up and Toughening Up

I never bunked off school. Never. Dad wouldn't have any of that. The consequences of bunking off, sneaking a ciggy, or fare-dodging, were unimaginable. Dad gave me a few clips round the ear and bollockings, but nothing too damaging. He never hit me. Dad showed his disappointment in a different way. He had a stare that could break my heart. What stopped me messing about was I feared losing the great relationship we had. Dad didn't need to use violence or to raise his voice to teach Paul and me right and wrong. Dad would not have his kids disrespecting anyone or doing wrong. He wouldn't tolerate having police coming round to Ironside. Loads of people banged on the door to complain about Paul and me throwing stones at their windows, but we never had the police round. Never.

I screwed up once. Just once. I went robbing and got caught. Me and a mate were mucking about in the centre of Liverpool, as eleven-year-olds do, just being stupid in Woolies. We had five quid between us to get home and grab a Maccies or Wimpy at Lime Street on the way. The problem was I needed some stationery for homework, just graph paper and pens – usual school nonsense. The plan was sorted with Woolies the target. We snuck in and went up and down the aisles putting pens in our pockets and paper up my coat. Confidently, we walked towards the exit. The plan seemed to be working. Brilliant. I could feel the money in my pocket for a burger and a Coke at Lime Street. Easy, easy. Step through the door, onto the pavement, turn left, ready to leg it . . .

A shout stopped us in our tracks. 'Oi!' came a voice that froze our blood. 'Stop!' Shit. The Woolies security man was standing there. I couldn't move, I was so scared. He grabbed us both by the collars. Fuck it. It was the worst day of my life. 'That's it,' I thought, my heart and mind racing. 'I have blown everything. Liverpool is finished. The club will go crazy. Dad's going to disown me. Shit.'

This security guard marched us back into Woolies, into an office, and took the stationery off us. He then gave us a right bollocking. 'What school are you at?' he screamed. 'Where do you live? Give us your phone number now.'

My head was spinning. 'We've not got a phone,' I lied.

The security guy went red in the face. 'Give me your address then.'

I couldn't mention Ironside. Dad would go mental if the bizzies went round. Think. The guard asked again, so I gave the address of my auntie's house. He wrote that down, gave us another rollicking, and kicked us out of Woolies.

My head in a mess, I ran to Lime Street. Woolies would

phone school, then get hold of Dad, and that would be it, me grounded, no football for ages. Fuck. When I jumped off the train at Huyton, I couldn't face Ironside. 'Dad will definitely kill me for robbing,' I thought. Home was out of the question, so I sprinted round to my auntie Lynn's. She let me in, sat me down, and listened me out. 'Will you go and see Dad?' I pleaded with her. 'Please? Make sure he's all right.'

Auntie Lynn went round to Ironside and explained to Dad how terrible I felt. Too late. Dad already knew about my shoplifting. Bad news travelled fast. Woolies had been on to St Mick's, who phoned Dad, and he was on the warpath. Dad came round, dragged me back home and slaughtered me, big-time. He looked me in the eye and just massacred me. 'Why did you do that?' he shouted. 'Why go robbing? Why didn't you pay for it? Why didn't you ask me or your mum for money? Why? Why? We can't tolerate stealing in this family. You'll get another bollocking at school. They'll want to know why you were nicking things.'

On the train back from Lime Street, in a rare clear moment, I had thought this bit through. 'Dad,' I replied, 'if the school have a go I will say I needed the stationery for my homework. I was doing it for school. It wasn't sweets I took. It was graph paper.'

Dad looked at me and went, 'I'm not having that.'

As excuses go, it was pretty feeble. Nothing could save me from the doghouse.

Dad then hit me with another killer thought: 'If Liverpool find out, you are in even more trouble, Steven,' he said. 'What the hell is Steve Heighway going to think of you? You might have screwed up everything at Liverpool. They could kick you out.'

Those words smashed into me like a wrecking ball. I felt so small. I love Dad. I hated letting him down. I love Liverpool. The idea of them giving me the elbow horrified me. Football was all I dreamed about. Why had I gone robbing? Jesus, what a mess. Robbing was stupid. I had money, and if I hadn't, I could have just done without. Our parents always told Paul and me: 'You don't have to steal. If you want anything, by hook or crook we will try to get it for you.' Idiot that I was, I went robbing and now faced the consequences.

As Dad slated me, Mum stood in the doorway, watching and listening. Mum wanted Dad to stress how serious the situation was, but she was also behind him making sure there were no belts. Me and Paul were mummy's boys, and she protected us. I could always blag Mum. 'Oh, Mum! Shut up!' I'd say, if she were on at me. A smile would flicker across her face as she gave in. Her love for us meant me and Paul got away with murder. Mum was more laid-back than Dad. He was enraged by the Woolies incident, but Mum made sure he didn't hit me. A lot of kids who got caught smoking or robbing got leathered by their dads. My accomplice in Woolies certainly suffered an almighty hiding when he got home. Dad just sent me to my room and grounded me for three nights. It felt like six months.

I got no sympathy off Paul. Just the opposite. My brother laughed his head off at me being incarcerated in my room. There'd be a knock on my door and I'd hear Paul whispering, 'Stevie, I'm going into town. It's going to be brilliant. Come on.' Thanks. He wound me up something rotten. 'The computer's on downstairs,' Paul said through the door, 'do you fancy a game?' Paul knew I couldn't come out. It was only banter but it cut me to pieces. I heard Paul running outside and organizing a game of football. He called out to all the other Ironside boys in a really loud voice, 'Who wants a game? Let's go.' It was torture. I heard the game going on, listened almost in tears to the screams of delight, the jokes, the noisy celebrations. I couldn't escape. My room was in the front. My mates shouted up to my window, 'Stevie, Stevie, this is a brilliant game, it's such a pity you can't join in. You'd love it.' Cruel laughter followed their words up to my window. My mates! My bloody brother! They knew I could hear. They knew it would kill me. When they stopped calling up, I sneaked a look out the window to watch them enviously. It was my fault. I deserved my spell in solitary confinement.

Normally, I behaved myself, certainly by the standards of some boys I knocked about with. Mates of mine robbed shops and garages, nicking sweets and drinks, when I was with them. I never got involved, but I was there. I watched friends pull ciggies out of pockets at playtime at school. They'd light up and blow smoke in people's faces. They didn't care. A few were on the road to nowhere, but I enjoyed hanging out with them. I could have gone off the rails. Temptations abounded, dangerous ones. Fortunately, Dad kept me straight. Without his guidance, I wouldn't be where I am today.

Dad was always the boss of No. 10 Ironside. Dad's word was law, but he was never a dictator. Me and Paul have never been scared of our parents. Sometimes we were spoiled brats wanting more – too much more, given our modest circumstances. But Paul and I had unbelievable respect for our parents. We are a very close family – as close as it gets. We ate breakfast together, tea together, sat in every night, watching telly and chatting. The atmosphere was class. Paul and I couldn't have asked for more loving, caring parents. Mum is very proud. Hunger never knocked on the door of 10 Ironside. The Gerrards always had enough food on the table. The cupboards were always full. If Paul and I weren't allowed something, or were short of money, Mum told us, 'It's because the cupboards are full. That's the number one priority. The cupboards must always be full.' We were free to help ourselves from the biscuit tin. 'But you are not to go anywhere near that cupboard until you've eaten your meal,' Mum would say.

Money was tight. Holidays abroad were a distant dream. Every year we went to Butlin's, in Skegness, or to a holiday park in Devon. My auntie and uncle would come with their kids, Nan and Granddad too. The whole family. What an adventure! The trip dominated my thoughts for months in advance. Mum was always planning, always squirrelling away money throughout the winter to pay for the holiday. She knew how much Skegness meant to the family, and particularly Paul and me. Sometimes, if Paul and I were lucky, a mate was allowed along. I let Paul pick the lucky guest. I would be buzzing to be with them, to hang out and play football with older boys. Skegness was great. 'Make sure you do the soccer schools,' Dad told me on the drive to the

Lincolnshire coast. As if I needed reminding! Even when we mucked about on the beach, hitting balls around with bats or bombing down the slides in the water park, one thought occupied my mind: when can I get to the soccer school? Even when I was on the go-karts, chasing Paul round the track, I was thinking about getting to the soccer school. 'Is it time to go now?' I'd ask Dad. 'Come on. Must be time.' Skegness was luxury. Of a night, we would go into the local club where there would be singers on, bands, and karaoke. The next morning, I would wake early and say, 'When can I get to the soccer school?' Skegness felt like heaven.

Me, Paul and Dad talked football all the time. Dad was daft about Liverpool. He bought me Liverpool videos and we watched them together, admiring the way Graeme Souness thundered into challenges, Alan Hansen's coolness and Kenny Dalglish's class around the box. One day, Dad came home with a massive picture of Dalglish. He climbed the stairs to my room and handed over the picture. 'Kenny Dalglish is the best player who ever played for Liverpool,' Dad said. 'He's The Man. Get him up on your wall.' Dalglish's picture was up on my wall for years. It was like a shrine. I was lucky enough to see King Kenny live at Anfield when I was very young, only about six or seven. I even have one of Kenny's shirts in my trophy room at home now. Back then, I loved standing on the Kop, bewitched by Kenny, Ian Rush, John Barnes and Steve McMahon. Great players. I saw some amazing championship moments. I was on the Kop in 1989 when Michael Thomas broke Liverpool hearts with that amazing last-minute goal for Arsenal. It denied us the title. I remember the following year when Hansen lifted the title. What a brilliant sight. I set my heart on following Hansen and bringing that trophy back to Anfield again.

Only when I began training with Liverpool at the age of eight did I become a hard-and-fast Kopite. Before then, I didn't understand who to support. I would be in the Panini enclosure at Goodison Park one week, singing and swaying on the Kop the next week. My heart was taken by football, not by one tribe. Other people didn't see it that way. With Dad, you were either Red or Dead. 'Liverpool, Liverpool, Liverpool,' he drummed into me, like a religious chant. As with many families on Merseyside, there were mixed loyalties. Mum's brother, Leslie, was crazy about Everton – season-tickets, scarves, flags, the lot. Leslie was always coming back from games with Everton kit for me, trying to turn me into a Blue.

A quick search on the Internet will reveal a photo of me as a schoolboy in a full Everton strip. Blue shirt, shorts, socks, the works. When I became big news with Liverpool, some enterprising Everton fanzines discovered the picture and printed it. They must have loved that! The *Mirror* heard about it, tracked down the picture and published it when I was becoming famous at Liverpool. A huge debate broke out. Was the picture real or not? Many people thought it was a fake. It isn't. It's a genuine photo-graph, taken in 1987. That is me, dressed as an Evertonian, and it wasn't at a fancy-dress party or for a bet. Leslie took me to Goodison when I was six and I saw some of Everton's games on the way to their league championship. I won a programme competition to have my picture taken with the league trophy and Charity

Shield at Goodison. Uncle Leslie was buzzing. He knew it would send Dad through the roof, and it really did. Dad went ballistic at the thought of his son, all in blue, standing proudly in the Goodison trophy room. 'He's not going,' Dad kept telling Leslie. 'You're not going,' Dad kept telling me. But I did. I was so keen. I was seven by that time, mad about football, not that clued-up in those days about the intense rivalry between Everton and Liverpool. It didn't seem wrong at the time. Leslie came over to Ironside with a brand-new kit. All excited, I ripped open the wrapping, put the crisp blue strip on and headed off for Goodison with Leslie, leaving an enraged Dad behind. Disowning me must have crossed his mind. Leslie guided me into the trophy room at Goodison, all smiles, and the photographer snapped away. Now that my heart belongs to Liverpool, I look back on the incident and wonder what the hell I was doing. Put it down to the naivety of youth. We all make mistakes.

Everton, Liverpool or whoever – at the time, just the chance to own a new football kit thrilled me. Collecting different strips became a massive hobby. Every Christmas I got two kits. Every birthday, more kits. I had a face like thunder if I never got replica gear for presents. Mum and Dad were superb. They knew how much shirts from different clubs meant to me. With Granddad's help, and the money Mum got for looking after Granddad, they saved up to buy the kits. I had Tottenham, Man City and, of course, Liverpool and Everton. Panini sticker books were scoured intensively. Every page checked out, every kit assessed. 'Mum,' I'd shout downstairs, 'I want this new Spurs top. Please?' Catalogues and sports-shop windows were not the only ways of feeding my addiction. *Match of the Day* was a catwalk for kit. What a parade! It became an obsession. If Tottenham met Everton on the TV on a Sunday, I would be out on the street after the final whistle, wearing the kit of whoever won, imagining myself to be the hero of the game. I had stars in my eyes, and the star's shirt on my back.

That jersey was often Neville Southall's. His Everton goalie kit was a real favourite. Days went by when I never took it off. I copied Southall perfectly: socks rolled down, so you could see the top of his Sondico shin-guards. Big Nev wore Hi-Tech boots so I badgered Mum and Dad for a pair of those. I loved Southall. When I didn't fancy playing out, I donned my goalie kit and pretended I was the great Neville Southall, throwing myself around on the grass, diving at my mates' feet, making brave and athletic saves like the real Everton master. Neville was a real character and I loved his committed approach to football. It was always a special moment when I opened a Panini sticker and found Neville Southall. Fantastic. I would be buzzing for hours. Running around Ironside, holding the sticker aloft like some great trophy.

Stickers, kits, going to games, playing matches – my life, as I said, revolved around football. And that passion was channelled through Liverpool Football Club.

3
Clocking on at the Dream Factory

Joining Liverpool was like starting a love affair you know will never, ever end. It's true: You'll Never Walk Alone at Anfield. Of course, I could have gone to another top club. Loads pursued me: Man United, West Ham, Everton, Spurs, you name it. Nice letters dropped through the letter-box, detailing how much they wanted me and how I would flourish under their care. 'We'll make you great,' they said, 'rich and famous.' Flattery got them nowhere. Only one destination beckoned – Anfield. Dad insisted. He was spot-on, as usual. Anfield just felt right, going to the club I adored and being coached by people whose trademark is trust. Good, honest footballing men ran the Liverpool School of Excellence, which eventually became the famous Academy at Kirkby. Meeting Steve Heighway, Dave Shannon and Hughie McAuley for the first time, I instinctively knew they would look after me. Even aged eight, I knew. Steve, Dave and Hughie inspired me from the first handshake and conversation. Steve is a Liverpool legend, a fantastic player from the seventies. Dave was friendly with Ben McIntyre, the manager of my Sunday League team, Whiston Juniors, and it was a simple step from there to Anfield. I carried on with Whiston, and got my first international experience in an U-12 competition against teams from all over the world, but my main focus was Liverpool.

I couldn't wait to get started. Come on! Give me the ball! Let me learn. Let me show you what I can do. My dream was gathering pace. Heighway, Shannon and McAuley held these brilliant training sessions down the Vernon Sangster Sports Centre every Tuesday and Thursday – special times of the week. I counted down the hours, minutes and seconds before we burst out into that sports hall – our Anfield, our Wembley. As well as being in good hands, I was also in good company. Michael Owen and Jason Koumas were in my year at Liverpool and we quickly fell in together. Talent attracts.

The three of us soon realized how to get the best out of the Vernon Sangster. On arrival, we shook hands with the staff, all very respectful – the Liverpool way. Skills, drills and possession work occupied us for an hour. The best bit was yet to come. Michael, Jason and I knew there would be half-an-hour at the end of five-a-side. 'All those in Liverpool tops this end,' Dave Shannon would shout, 'and all the rest put bibs on.' Kids wore all types of tops. But me, Michael and Jason came prepared: we agreed in advance which strip to wear. Come the five-a-sides we were always in the same team. 'Right,' Michael said, 'let's all wear the Liverpool away kit next week.' Jason and I made sure we came in with the right Liverpool top on. If my extensive collection of strips did not contain the proposed outfit, I'd be on Mum and Dad's case in the car all the way back home. 'Mum, Dad, I must have this kit. If I don't, Jason and Michael will be on a different team. Please?' Poor Mum and Dad. I pressured them badly. I sat in the back of the car and explained the humiliation if I didn't have the right kit. Mum and Dad usually relented and got me sorted. Thank God. The thought of letting Michael or Jason down made me almost sick.

Jason was a good player. Really good. He was always going to make it as a pro. But Michael stood out most. Even aged eight he was obviously special, a star in the making. Everyone knew it. Michael was put on this world to destroy goalkeepers. Those five-a-sides in the Vernon Sangster was the first time I ran into Michael and I was gobsmacked by his unbelievable talent. He played his schoolboy football over the Mersey, ripping up the record-books on Deeside. When he breezed into the Vernon Sangster, it was like a whirlwind visiting. The moment I saw him running at the keeper, killing him with his pace and touch, I appreciated his extraordinary gifts. Michael's talent didn't just talk; it shouted. From first glance, I understood his game was goals. A natural. Michael realized I was a good passer, so we quickly teamed up. Everyone thought we wanted to be on the same side because we were best mates and wanted to talk. Rubbish. Michael and I just wanted to win. Simple as that. That's always been the way with Michael and me. We have a hatred of losing. We chatted after the game, but the main line of communication was footballing: me transferring the ball to Michael in places where he could inflict most damage. Michael and I still joke about our days in

Liverpool's U-12s when we battered teams. Michael always says, 'Every time Stevie got the ball he would pass to me.' To which I reply, 'And every time I did, Michael scored!'

Back in those days, Liverpool's first team seemed a far-off dream. At such a young age I just concentrated on developing under Steve and Dave. I was gutted if I wasn't the best at training. In the car on the way to the Vernon Sangster, Dad drummed into me the need to be disciplined. 'Make sure you're ready,' he stressed, 'make sure you're not talking when training starts. Always try your hardest.' Dad's support has been unstinting. When I started out, Dad never, ever spoke about Liverpool's first team. He focused only on the game ahead, or the next training session. One night I was knackered and didn't fancy training. Dad sat me down in the front room at Ironside. 'Why don't you want to go?' he asked. 'If you want to give it a miss, I will phone Steve Heighway up and say you have done too much at school today.' Dad never pressured me. Encouragement was his line of attack. 'Steven, go to training, it's good for you,' he added. 'You'll love it, you're doing well.' Dad had great belief in me, and in coaches like Steve and Dave. 'If you keep learning and improving, the coaches will make you a very good player,' he said. 'If you miss training, all the other kids are getting an advantage because you are missing out. I won't pressure you to go. But the more you go, the more you'll learn and the better you'll get.' I went.

My parents were very aware of the qualities Liverpool sought in a player. One day, I heard Dad tell Mum, 'Steve Heighway and Dave Shannon are always checking on how their players present themselves. Steven must represent Liverpool well.' Standards count at Liverpool. Be tidy. Be on time. Mum and Dad wouldn't let me go to training or do any activity associated with Liverpool Football Club unless my hair glistened, my face shone and my clothes were spotless clean. Sometimes I wanted to go to the Vernon Sangster in my comfy shoes, a pair of trainers full of holes, battle-hardened from games on Ironside. I loved them. 'You are not going in those,' Dad would insist. 'We'll get you a new pair.' Mum even ironed my kit for training. Ironed! I watched in amazement as she put creases in the shirt with her iron. Those neat lines in an uncrinkled shirt summed up Mum's desire for me to look smart always. No-one irons football kits! My mum did. The kit had to be all matching as well. I couldn't wear a Liverpool home top with away shorts. Or Spurs shorts with a Liverpool shirt. Mum would not let me. 'You must show respect for Liverpool,' she said. My parents were so proud their son was involved with Liverpool Football Club. They wanted to make sure I gave it my best shot. I wasn't turning up Rag-Arse Rovers or giving lip.

Under the guidance of Steve and Dave, I rose steadily through the Liverpool ranks. Towards the start of every season, I worried whether I would be kept on by Steve. Impatiently, I waited for the letter of confirmation from Liverpool. 'Tell Steven not to worry,' Heighway always told Dad. 'He will be in. Here's a pair of boots for him.' I was doing well, building a reputation, enjoying the training. At fourteen, Steve called four of us into his office: me, Michael, Stephen Wright and Neil Murphy. Wrighty eventually played for Liverpool before joining

Sunderland. Murphy was a very good right-back who made the reserves and now coaches at the Academy. Steve had big news for the four of us: 'You've all been invited to trials for Lilleshall.'

Lilleshall! The National School! I couldn't believe it. Lilleshall was the business, the place to be if you wanted to make it as a footballer. Only the very best got in. Jesus, hellfire, this was serious. Lilleshall meant everything, a springboard to success. The trials would be incredibly competitive, I knew that. Everyone wanted to go to the National School. At the first trial there were hundreds of hopefuls, good players drawn from across England, all dreaming of a place at Lilleshall. A series of trials gradually reduced the numbers and destroyed the ambitions of many. Soon there were only fifty boys left, then thirty, then twenty-four scrapping for recognition. It was brutal. Few survived. Every time I got through a trial, a letter popped through the door at Ironside saying 'Congratulations . . . you have been selected for the next trial'. I was flying. Lilleshall beckoned.

The quality was high, the competition intense. As well as Michael Owen and me, there were good players like Michael Ball, the left-back who did so well at Everton before heading up to Rangers, and Kenny Lunt, the midfielder from that impressive youth set-up at Crewe Alexandra. I still fancied my chances of getting the final call from Lilleshall. I looked around the pitches during the trials and checked out my rival midfielders. No-one was better than me. Honestly, no-one. I never hid in the trials. I was right in there, hard in the tackle, clever in the pass. Lilleshall's officials must have been impressed. I was my normal self: driven by a will to win so powerful it almost hurt. I had the ability. No doubt. No-one could pass the ball better. Liverpool were my club, and Liverpool took on only the best kids. Lilleshall must pick me. The one nagging doubt in the back of my mind was that my rivals were bigger. I was really small and facing some tall, strong units in my position. Michael Owen was tiny as well, but he had so much pace he made big fellas look like dustbins. Midfield is different.

It did not seem to matter. I progressed to the penultimate trial and an invitation to Lilleshall seemed inevitable. I thought of the two years there, learning to become an even better player, on the fast-track to fame and fortune. Every morning, I pissed the postman off as I ambushed him outside Ironside. 'Where is it? Where's my letter from Lilleshall?' The final trials were just around the corner, so I knew the letter was imminent. Family life almost stopped as we sweated on this one letter. One morning, it fell through the letter-box. I was upstairs, still in my room. Dad was first to the post. He picked up the letter which he knew from the writing came from the National School. He opened it, knowing how much it meant to me. I could hear him downstairs by the door, shuffling the letter and envelope in his hands. The silence killed me. Why the pause? Bad news? Must be. If I had been accepted, my old fella would have shouted 'YES!' by now. Instead, Dad just called up, 'Post's here.' The disappointment in his voice rang like a church-bell at a funeral. As I walked downstairs, I saw him standing in the hall with the letter in his hand, a crushed look on his face. Lilleshall had rejected me.

I tore straight back upstairs. Tears? Christ, they never stopped. It felt like the end. It was bad. Bad. Dad climbed the stairs slowly. He knew I was beyond consoling. He knew how much I wanted the chance of going to Lilleshall. He walked into my room and saw I had the pillow over my head. I was completely gone, in floods of tears. My dream of a life in football seemed wrecked. I felt I was not good enough. Me! Captain of Liverpool Boys! Rated by Liverpool Football Club! Big clubs like Manchester United chased me. If those people from Lilleshall had been there in that room, I'd have killed them. How could they do this to me? I knew I was good enough. Never before had someone dared tell me I was not up to scratch. Never. My first setback hurt like hell. I dreaded the news circulating within Liverpool. Michael was a dead cert to go to Lilleshall. Jamie Carragher and another Liverpool kid, Jamie Cassidy, were already there. So was Tommy Culshaw, a midfielder on Liverpool's books. I just wanted so much to join them.

Dad attempted to make me feel better. I lifted the pillow from my head, stared at him through the tears, and said, 'I can't carry on. That's me finished with football.' Dad was superb, as usual. He dried my tears and soothed my pain. 'Listen, son, you've done well to get where you are,' he told me, sitting on the side of my bed. 'I watched all the trials and you were as good as anyone there. Maybe Lilleshall turned you down because you lack a bit of height. Maybe they spoke to Cardinal Heenan and think you can't hack two years away from home. It doesn't mean you're not a good footballer. You are good. I know it, you know it, and most importantly Liverpool know it.'

In my devastation, I seized on Dad's words. Maybe it really was nothing to do with my football. In their letter, the Lilleshall people gave a vague explanation. 'You are a great player, don't give up,' they wrote. 'Sometimes it is not just on football why we select certain people to go further than you. It's for other reasons.' Bloody well tell me then.

I heard the whispers: Huyton was looked down on by those smart blazers from the National School. Did Lilleshall feel I might be a jack the lad and disrupt life at their nice school? That wasn't me, though. Honest. At the trials I was quiet, well behaved and well presented. I always did the right thing. Before the trials, Steve Heighway warned us the Lilleshall staff watched how we ate, whether or not we were polite. I tried my best.

What were these 'other reasons'? I knew Lilleshall held meetings during the trials and Mum and Dad were quizzed about me. 'What's Steven like? Is he doing well at school? Could he handle being away from home?' Mum and Dad spoke well of me. I know that. They always backed their sons 100 per cent. Maybe Lilleshall felt I couldn't cope away from home, being separated from the family I adore. I certainly hated being away from home. Even now. In my heart, I don't know whether I would have gone to Lilleshall anyway. Maybe I would have done simply through Dad forcing me. But, for all the whispers about Huyton and homesickness, I still feel it was my lack of height in those days that brought rejection from Lilleshall.

No reason could ease the grief, though. My anger at Lilleshall's cold shoulder has never subsided. The insult was personal, one that remains in my mind, needling away at me. It never dims, that memory of rejection. Of course, I never chucked football in. Dad talked me round. He was all compassion and common sense. Still, for all Dad's tender words, the sense of frustration, humiliation and bitterness lingered. But life went on. 'Prove them wrong, son,' said Dad.

With a heavy heart, I resumed Liverpool training. Steve Heighway was waiting for me. He pulled me into his office, sat me down, and went behind his desk. 'I am absolutely ecstatic you didn't get into Lilleshall,' Steve said. 'I am so made up.'

I was astonished. 'You prick,' I thought.

'I didn't want you to go to Lilleshall,' Steve explained. 'I don't want Michael to go. I'm selfish. I want you here at Liverpool. Steven, I know you are upset but, trust me, I can make you a better player than Lilleshall can.'

At the time, I didn't believe him. Michael was packing his bags for a new adventure, and supposedly the best coaching in the country. Michael deserved it. Good luck to him. 'I'm buzzing for you,' I told him when he came to say goodbye. Secretly, I was gutted. I just wanted to be setting off to Lilleshall, walking in there shoulder to shoulder with Michael. I didn't want to be left behind, staring at Michael's empty place in the dressing-room. I loathed the taste of failure. I thought that if Steve had pushed me, I could have got into Lilleshall. It took me a long time to understand Steve's motives.

Lilleshall's rejection slowed my climb up the England ladder. Bias rules in schoolboy football, no doubt about it.

Players at the National School were always selected for the England U-15s. Always. The advantage was huge, obvious and deeply unfair. It really pissed me off. The midfielders who got into Lilleshall ahead of me were players like Kenny Lunt, Jamie Day of Arsenal, and Richard Keller of Scarborough. They were also ushered into the U-15s. Go on, straight through, there are your England shirts, help yourselves. I seethed with resentment at their fast-track treatment. I sat at Ironside, just thinking of those midfielders running out onto those beautiful pitches at Lilleshall, enjoying daily coaching and being handed the key to the England U-15s dressing-room. These England games were on Sky. I fancied some of that, being broadcast to the whole country. Watching the games was torture. I sat there with Dad, looking at midfielders who were my age but not my equal. I screamed at the TV, bollocking the commentator when he praised one of the midfielders with Three Lions on his shirt. I would have walked out in disgust but for one person. I loved seeing Michael do well.

Lilleshall screwed up, and I hoped and prayed every day they would recognize their mistake. Shit, we left out that brilliant kid from Liverpool. What's his name? Gerrard. Let's get him in, sharpish. I dreamed of a letter coming through with a Shropshire postmark apologizing for their terrible oversight and telling me to get down there now. The door seemed to open briefly when a youth attached to Arsenal left Lilleshall. Michael called to tell me. 'There's talk of them bringing in a replacement,' he said. I couldn't sleep that night. I lay in bed thinking of Michael's words. Mentally, I was already packing my bags for

Lilleshall. They had to call me in. But no. The call never came. My dream died again.

Seven months later, my anger with Lilleshall found a fantastic outlet. The National School came to Melwood, where us Heighway kids were based at the time, for a fixture. Thank you, God! I prepared an ambush. I was steaming for this game like nobody's business. Honest to God, the night before the game I was cleaning my boots, making sure the studs were nice and sharp for those pretty boys from Lilleshall. Dad realized how pumped up I was. He wound me up relentlessly. 'You'll shit yourself against Lilleshall,' he said. 'You will. I know it. Those National School boys are better than you.' I went, 'Yeah, yeah.' I was burning inside. I felt like having a fight on the Friday evening. I stayed awake all night, as if I feared sleep might soften me, lessening the fury inside. In the morning, I stormed into Melwood on a wave of adrenalin and resentment. Steve could see the fire in my eyes.

'Be careful,' he warned. 'You'll get injured.'

'These lot are getting it,' I replied. 'They are all getting booted everywhere. I am going to show Lilleshall they got it wrong. All of them.'

Steve tried to reason with me. No chance. I was on a mission.

And when I saw those Lilleshall boys marching into the pavilion at Melwood, all smart and smiling in their England blazers, the fire raging within me turned into an inferno. I was more than a man possessed. Even now, I don't know how I restrained myself from nailing them in the corridor. 'Let's have it now,' I thought. 'Come on, in your spotless blazers and cocky smiles. Huyton v.

Lilleshall, now. We'll see who's better!' God, I couldn't wait.

I sprinted out of the pavilion and towards the pitch. Good, I thought, as I realized which pitch we were on. Liverpool had done me proud. Normally we played on the B team pitch; for Lilleshall's visit, Liverpool gave us the A team pitch, a surface as good as Anfield. Someone at the club knew how much this game meant to me. Thank you. I warmed up, went through the pre-match formalities as captain and kept staring at the ref to hurry him up.

The first whistle made the same impression on me as a bell in a prize fight. A call to arms, the signal for battle. I smashed Lilleshall's midfield to pieces. Absolutely shredded them. No mercy. Into every tackle I poured all my frustration at being ignored by the National School. I loved the thought of their coaches standing helplessly on the Melwood touchline as I tore into their chosen ones. 'This will show them what they rejected,' I thought as I crunched another set of shin-pads. 'This will make them see how wrong they were,' I told myself as I sent another of their precious boys flying. 'Calm down,' the ref kept shouting at me. No chance. Those Lilleshall boys were getting it big-time. Nothing was going to stop me. How could a referee understand my pain?

Lilleshall fielded some good players, like Michael Ball, Wes Brown and, of course, my mate Michael Owen, who inevitably struck his usual hat-trick. The score was 4–3 to Lilleshall, but I settled a personal score. My performance was so good that all their players ran over at the end to shake my hand. I had battered them, but they still wanted to show their respect. Fair play. I admired them for that.

'How you never got into Lilleshall was a joke,' Michael remarked as we walked off, the battle over. 'You are well better than these.' The England staff all strolled across to congratulate me. I just turned and ran to the dressing-room. I was so upset inside. There was no way I could shake hands with those who gave me so much heartache. They snubbed me. Here was some of their own medicine. Take that.

Even now, I still fume at them all. I cannot stand set-backs. The manager who never picked me for the U-15s, John Owens, is now a coach at the Liverpool Academy. I love walking past him now. Love it. I see him coming, compose myself and say 'All right?' as we pass. Owens thinks I have forgotten about the Under-15s. I haven't. Whenever we bump into each other, Owens is so nice. I talk to him, all polite on the outside, all angry on the inside. I feel like pulling him in a room and asking, 'Why didn't you pick me? You're wrong. Tell me the reasons to my face now, because I know the reasons you put on that letter were a load of shit. Was it really to do with my height? OK, the other midfielders might have been a bit bigger and stronger than me but none were better than me. None of them.'

Sod it. Heighway was right anyway. Would I rather have gone to the National School for two years or had two seasons of Steve's expert training? Steve and his coaches just loved me, and I loved them. Their sessions were class. Steve and Dave Shannon did all the things I adored: possession, crossing and shooting, passing. At the end we played games that felt as important as the World Cup final. If you made a mistake, Steve and Dave had you doing press-ups, your face going in and out above the grass as boots chased the ball around you. I raced through my press-ups and steamed back into action. I wanted to win so much, wanted to impress. This was my life. This was everything. Liverpool training meant the world. Academy football was so far removed in quality from kickabouts with schoolmates at Cardinal Heenan or friends on Ironside. Team-mates at Liverpool were on my wavelength; they could read my passes. If someone at Cardinal Heenan failed to make the right run or mis-controlled the ball, it annoyed the hell out of me. 'They might not be as good as you, but they are your friends,' my teachers at Cardinal Heenan told me. 'So get on with it.' At Liverpool, everyone was on my level.

Lilleshall's rejection deepened my love for Liverpool. They wanted me, and I was determined to deliver for them and prove Lilleshall wrong. In the long run, failing to get into the National School worked in my favour. In my opinion, those national coaches would never have developed me as well as Steve Heighway did. Steve used to come round Ironside, see how we were, or call on the phone. Steve always had Mum and Dad into the Academy, checking everything was OK. Steve gave me boots on the sly. 'How's your family?' he often enquired. 'What's the money situation?' He knew we never had much. He used to help. Steve likes to bond with families, assist people. He's a top guy. Genuine. Obviously, it was in Liverpool's interests to keep me happy, but Steve's commitment to me was not merely professional. He really cared. I was not a piece of meat, or an investment opportunity, to Steve and Liverpool. I was flesh and blood, fears and dreams, and Steve looked after me like a son. I will never forget Steve Heighway's immense involvement in shaping me as a man and as a footballer. Fuck Lilleshall. I had Liverpool.

Steve wasn't stupid. He knew how many clubs circled around me. Those fools at Lilleshall might not have realized it, but I was rated everywhere else. Manchester United kept sending letters to Ironside, far nicer letters than the ones from Lilleshall. The postman also brought regular offers from Crystal Palace, Manchester City, Everton and Spurs. One day, Dad spoke to Steve. 'Look, Steven is getting all these offers,' he said. 'Can we sort out his future here?'

Steve was laid-back, perhaps deliberately so. 'If Steven wants to go and have a look at what Manchester United and the rest have to offer, then let him,' he said. 'If he wants to have a look at the facilities at Spurs or City, no problem. We won't think anything different of him. We won't fall out with Steven.'

So I did. Everton showed me around, attempting to woo me. I played a trial game for Tranmere Rovers. I wore the claret and blue of West Ham when we took Cambridge United apart 6–2. At fourteen, the red of Manchester United even enveloped my small frame in two trial matches. After doing well in those games, United offered me a three-year pro contract. I even met their legendary manager, Sir Alex Ferguson. A group of us triallists had dinner with Mr Ferguson, as he was then. Michael Owen was meant to be at the meal, but he didn't turn up. Michael Ball was there. We sat and listened in awe to one of the managerial greats. Mr Ferguson was top man. I knew all about him, obviously. He was master-minding United's re-emergence. He had heard about me and desperately wanted me to sign. Mr Ferguson told us how well we would do at Old Trafford and that he was committed to promoting good youngsters. Ryan Giggs and the David Beckham generation were beginning to break through around then. I enjoyed the meal, and listening to Mr Ferguson, but I was never going to sign for United. No chance. I looked around other clubs partly to pressure Liverpool into giving me a YTS contract.

When I returned to Liverpool after those games, I sought out Steve Heighway. 'I really enjoyed playing for those teams,' I said with a smile. I soon got a promise of a Youth Trainee Scheme contract out of Liverpool! Towards the end of the U-16 season, all the schoolboys went one by one into this room at Melwood to learn whether a YTS place was on offer from Liverpool. I never went in. I already knew. I couldn't click on to anyone that I had this deal with Steve, all in black and white. But it was there: £50 a week. Michael Owen had one off Steve as well.

Steve always looked after us, like getting us tickets for the Kop for me, Paul and our friends. He took me to Wembley three times to watch FA Cup finals and Coca-Cola Cup finals. We travelled south on the train, with Steve, Hughie, Dave and their wives looking after me like a son. We saw Liverpool's 2–0 FA Cup defeat of Sunderland in 1992, and that brilliant Steve McManaman performance against Bolton Wanderers in the Coca-Cola Cup three years later. Michael was also in the party heading down to Wembley. Michael was Liverpool's prized junior, so I thought I must be the second best if I was also being taken down to Wembley.

Steve was always good to me. I will never forget receiving a phone call from him early one morning in May 1996. I was just about to head out of the door to catch the bus to Cardinal Heenan when the phone went. Steve came quickly to the point. 'Steven, we've got the FA Youth Cup final against West Ham in two days' time and we have one or two injuries, so we need you on stand-by. Be on your toes.' I was buzzing, floating on a cloud all the way to Cardinal Heenan. Injuries and illnesses had plagued the youth team, but I never dreamed they might turn to me. I wasn't required in the end – a real pity. Liverpool had some youth side, with David Thompson, Jamie Carragher and, of course, Owen, the real star of the show. They won the final against the likes of Rio Ferdinand and Frank Lampard comfortably. But I was grateful to Steve simply for considering me.

Steve even organized it so I did my work experience at Liverpool. I sat in the classroom at Cardinal Heenan, listening to all the boys talking of where they were going on work experience. Stacking shelves at Asda or Kwiksave was not for me. As the forms were going round, someone mentioned that a few Cardinal Heenan boys wangled work experience at Melwood in the past. That was me sorted. No chance was I going to a supermarket. Not with a chance of Melwood. Sharpish, I was into Steve Heighway's office. 'I will mop as many floors, clean as many boots as you want, so long as I can do my two weeks' work experience at Melwood,' I told him. Steve agreed, and set it up with Cardinal Heenan. Liverpool obviously thought a lot of me. While the rest of my year worked with their dads, brick-laying, labouring or helping out in shops, I joined Liverpool's first team for a fortnight. I could not believe my luck. Nor could my schoolmates. I was the envy of everyone at Cardinal Heenan.

Those boys who had done work experience at Melwood just trained with the ressies. When I reported for duty, I was informed I would be training with legends like John Barnes and Jan Molby. My idols! The pair of them, I swear, were so good. It was a privilege just to watch them at close quarters. Standing on the touchline at Melwood, my mouth open in amazement at their skills, seemed the closest I would get. Work experience involved washing floors, cleaning boots, pumping balls up, putting cones out, and collecting balls. But Roy Evans, the manager at the time, invited me to join in the five-a-sides. I was sixteen and passing a ball to John Barnes and Jan Molby! They kept passing to me, making me a better player. They made me look like Diego Maradona.

Those two weeks deepened my passion for football and my desire to make it as a pro with Liverpool. I never changed with the first team those two weeks. I was put in with the young pros like Jamie Carragher, Jamie Cassidy, David Thompson and Gareth Roberts. Their banter was just pure quality. So funny. So wicked. God, I was jealous of them. Carra and the rest were in at Melwood every day, having the time of their lives, and I was heading back to a boring classroom after a fortnight. I was spewing. It was not for long. I had that promise of a YTS. That last term, I did most of my homework and had a go in my exams, but I wasn't really focused. I knew two months down the line was Liverpool.

On my last day at Cardinan Heenan, I faced a two-hour RE exam. I sat in the exam hall thinking hard over one important question: exactly how I would burn my uniform. The clock showed barely an hour before I sprinted out the room. I have never run so quick to a bus-stop. I wanted to get back to Ironside, get into my normal clothes, ditch my uniform, have six weeks off and then start football full-time.

'How did your exams go?' Mum asked.

'Yeah, fine,' I replied, knowing I had done shite. I handed her my uniform. 'Just pop that in the bin, please, Mum.'

A new uniform awaited me: Liverpool FC.

4
Teenage Kicks

And so began the best days of my life, my two years as a Liverpool apprentice, a time of banter and dreams, dressing-room fights and glorious wind-ups. Laughter all the way. As I swapped the dour school uniform of Cardinal Heenan for the bright red strip of Liverpool Football Club, my character changed as well. Gone was the shyness that accompanied me through school. At Cardinal Heenan, I always avoided getting into trouble. I hated bollockings, being sent out of classrooms, or being ordered home to face Dad. I loathed the thought of getting a telling-off or a little belt. So I behaved at school. A mischievous streak emerged the moment I set foot in Melwood as an apprentice.

At Cardinal Heenan, I never had many mates. Liverpool was different. Everyone was a friend. We all shared this unbelievable passion for football. My partners in crime were known as Boggo, Greggo, Wrighty, Bavo and Cass. John Boggan was a year below me with his own firm, but he soon became a close ally in the wind-up business. Boggo, a real funny character, could talk for England; he's now training with Accrington Stanley after losing a couple of stone. Neil Gregson was another real character, and like Stephen Wright and Matty Cass, he was always up for some banter. Ian Dunbavin, a Knowsley lad, was also in the group; Bavo now keeps goal for Accrington Stanley and to this day is a really good friend of mine. And of course there was Michael Owen, the Boy Wonder who mucked in brilliantly with us mortals. None of us could believe our luck. After the drudgery of school we were actually getting paid to live the dream of becoming footballers. It wasn't riches. As an apprentice, I got only £50 a week; Mum was paid £160 a month to feed me. Compared to what I make now it was peanuts, but I felt on top of the world every day. The sun seemed to shine just on us Liverpool apprentices.

Because the new Academy at Kirkby was not ready until my second year on the YTS, we spent the first twelve months at Melwood, seeing all the stars. We heard the banter bubbling around the first-team dressing-room at Melwood, so we copied them. So this was the way to become a Liverpool professional: work hard, train hard, laugh hard. Jesus, did we muck about. Liverpool's staff slaughtered me for all kinds of minor offences, but it was completely different from being coated by the teacher or Dad. I made amends in the next training session.

Pure madness reigned in the apprentices' dressing-room. As soon as I came through the door, I started wars simply by flicking the lights off. That would be the signal for all the lads – Greggo, me, Bavo, Wrighty, Cass, Michael and everyone – to batter each other with towels in the dark. That room staged many an ambush. Liverpool had this caretaker called Don; he was in his late forties but the fittest man ever. Don was in the gym all the time, pumping iron. Arm-wrestling was his forte. He would charge into the dressing-room and challenge the bravest apprentice to wrestle him. Elbow on the physio's table, right hand gripping Don's, try to muscle him over. I never could. Don was so strong. He could fight us all. Sometimes when Don entered the room, the lads gave each other the nod. Bang, lights off. 'Let's get him!' We'd thrash Don with towels or throw boots at him. One day, Greggo hit Don in the head with a pair of Reebok studs. 'LIGHTS!' Don screamed. Nervously, I turned them back on. Jesus, Don was a mess. This huge lump rose above his eye. Don was raging. 'I'm going to kill you!' he shouted. He was old enough to be our granddad, and there he was, roaming angrily around Melwood with a black eye and steam coming out of his ears. 'What have we done now?' I said to the lads as Don charged out the room. 'He's off to get Roy Evans.' Fortunately, Don didn't go to the manager. After getting his eye sorted by the doc, Don was ready to sort us out. He rushed back into the dressing-room like a maniac. 'He's going to blame me,' I whispered to Wrighty. I was not in Don's good books at the time. 'He's going to kill me with his bare hands. If he gets into me, Wrighty, you had best help me.' Luckily, Don just wanted to rant and rave. The storm passed.

Along with torturing innocent caretakers, us YTS boys had another favourite dressing-room game. Again, the lights went off. This time the maulings were verbal not physical: Chinese Whispers. We'd sit around in a gang, the lights extinguished, and the whispers began. I might quietly tell my neighbour, 'Greggo's got some shocking gear on.' Caning people was the aim of the game, and I was a master. Whispers went round the room, everyone trying to remember all the abuse. The last man switched the lights back on and recited every whisper. 'Tell Stevie to sort his trainers out. Tell Greggo he dresses like a tramp.' I loved Chinese Whispers. It was a brilliant chance to slaughter someone without them knowing.

No-one was safe. Even tough guys like me were targeted. Whenever I came in with a new pair of trainers on, the other apprentices plotted their demise. The moment I headed off to the showers, the lads would cut right through the laces or tie them in unbelievable knots. One time, it took me an hour to get my trainers back to normal. Frequently, I pulled a sock on and my foot went straight through the end, which my team-mates had kindly cut off. I sat there in the dressing-room, with my toes sticking out the sock, as all the boys fell about laughing. They were so bloody sneaky. I never knew they had planned any skit against me until it was too late.

Revenge was had, though, big-time. I was one of the ring-leaders, inflicting loads of grief on others. Sometimes it stepped over the line. Fights broke out in training through bad tackles, pushes and snarls. The changing-room was no different. If someone couldn't take the banter or a prank, arguments would erupt. Rucks were part of my daily life. If I ruined someone's trainers and they weren't happy, I reacted. Pushing and shouting broke out. 'Can't you fucking well take a joke?' I'd scream at Greggo or Wrighty as they stood there, steaming, holding a pair of wrecked trainers. Emotions ran high at times. Training was so exhausting, I would be knackered, short-tempered, my head gone. A confrontational streak occasionally seized me in the dressing-room, but I never, ever got nasty violent.

Any small room packed with competitive teenage lads will spill over. Sometimes, even the kickabouts in the changing-room got heated. We'd put one footy sock into another, twist it and push it through to make a solid ball, which we'd ping around. Michael and I always played it, belting this sock from one end to the other. Two-a-side matches were always going on, with benches for goals. Michael had the ball once, and gave me the nod that he was going to blast it at someone. His target was Roy Naylor. Michael jumped up, smacked this sock-ball across the room and sat down quickly. For once, Michael missed. Instead of Roy, Michael hit one of the goalies, Adriano Rigoglioso, on the back of the head, almost decapitating him. Michael carried on tying his trainers. Adriano turned around, his face like thunder. Matty Cass started laughing so Adriano went for him. Full-on fight. Blood everywhere. Michael sat there, shitting himself, thinking, 'I've caused murder!' As soon as we could, Michael and I scarpered. 'You are going to have to own up,' I told Michael when we reached somewhere safe and quiet. 'Adriano will kill Cass.' The next day, Michael admitted to Adriano that he was the guilty man and it was all forgotten about.

Loyalty was an unbreakable code in Liverpool's YTS dressing-room. Whatever happened, however ruined your trainers were, nobody complained to the staff. If there was a fight, it would be split up. 'Shake hands,' came the order from all the other boys. If two lads wrestled and one got cut, everyone else shouted, 'So what? Get on with it.' Adriano was never going to tell on Michael. Everyone respected a team-mate clearly heading for greatness. When Michael first came in, after Lilleshall, people looked up to him because he was so good as a footballer. Michael had his own sponsorship, and soon his own car. All the other apprentices knew it was only a matter of time before he was off with the first team. Michael was a class apart, we all realized that, but he was never aloof. He was one of the lads. He could have said, 'I'm Michael Owen, fuck all youse.' But he never did. There were no airs and graces with Michael, none of this England school-boy superstar crap. All the banter and wind-ups often had Michael bang in the middle of it. He was clever about it, though. Michael hated getting caught. He was just focused on reaching the top.

Greggo and Boggo were different. They were always being cheeky, and being moaned at by the staff. They were just thick, really! All Greggo and Boggo were interested in was getting in the betting shop after training, or playing on the fruit machines. I loved hanging out with Greggo and Boggo. We'd play snooker or go shopping. But when they went gambling, I kept my money in my pocket and just watched them. But I loved their company.

One day, the management announced that us YTS boys were moving to Liverpool University's grounds, before we eventually settled at the new Academy at Kirkby. Liverpool's staff almost had to drag us kicking and screaming from Melwood. We loved it there, but Liverpool decided it would be best if the YTS lads and first-year pros were kept separate from the first team. Shit. I wanted to be at Melwood, showing what I could do in front of the Liverpool management. Melwood was the gateway to Anfield. Instead, we were packed off to some student pitches. I came back from the university on the first day and Dad immediately asked what the set-up was like there. 'Shite,' I replied. 'The pitches and facilities are shite.' It was only for six months, before Kirkby opened, but I felt like I had stepped on a snake after climbing so many ladders.

The university offered some attractions, though. The pavilion had this dead-long corridor with all the changing-rooms facing each other. One of them Liverpool turned into the physio's room. Once, maybe twice a week, this hilarious chiropodist called Jeremy visited and held court in the physio's room. Jeremy was a bit different, to say the least. He was obsessed with purple. His house is purple – front door, walls, carpet, the lot. I know. I've been there. I've seen Jeremy's Purple Palace with my own eyes. One day, Jeremy drove up to the university in his purple car and stepped out, head to toe clad in purple gear. He was unbelievable. Jeremy had his own business, but Liverpool paid him good money, and he loved the wit and chitchat.

One day, Jeremy's banter was so poor the lads decided to lock him up. He was in his special room as normal, gabbling away, goggles on, as he did a mini-operation on someone's foot. 'Jeremy's a tit,' I told the lads. 'All that purple is a crime in need of serious punishing. He's staying in that room all day.' Imprisoning Jeremy was easy. All the rooms in the corridor could be locked from the outside. So when his patient came out, we turned the key in Jeremy's door and sprinted away, laughing our heads off. 'Help,' Jeremy shouted. Training was almost ruined because we kept smiling at each other, thinking about Jeremy. 'Help, help.' No-one could hear his screams. The Liverpool staff were already out on the training pitch, laying out the cones for our arrival.

When we came back in, I rushed down the corridor and jumped up at Jeremy's door to look through this small gap at the top. Jeremy was inside, going mental. I ran off laughing. All the boys were in hysterics. No-one could keep a straight face as we trooped into the canteen for dinner. We sat down and began eating. The next thing we knew, the doors burst open and Jeremy stormed in. He charged over to the staff table. Steve Heighway, Hughie McAuley and Dave Shannon looked at him in amazement. 'This gang of bastards locked me in that room for three hours,' Jeremy said, pointing at us. 'Why didn't you come and look for me?'

Steve was the first to say something, probably because Hughie and Dave were struck dumb at Jeremy's entrance. 'Sorry, Jeremy,' he said, 'we thought you had gone home at ten.'

Jeremy was raging. I have never seen someone so aggressive in my life. His face turned as purple as his shirt. He marched over to my table. Jeremy knew I was heavily involved. My reputation for pranks was well established. 'Youse have cost me so much money,' he shouted. 'I have lost out on six or seven patients in these three hours. Liverpool are going to have to pay.' He was like a madman, shuttling back and forth between the tables. He raced back across to Steve. 'The club must compensate me for your players' locking me up.' Hughie and Dave couldn't restrain themselves any longer and burst out laughing.

Jeremy never came back. We had to get a brand-new chiropodist. Steve caned us. He called a meeting of all the YTS boys and read the riot act. But as he was lecturing us, Hughie was behind him, laughing away. That was great. The staff found it funny. Liverpool liked their players to have character.

Jeremy wasn't finished with football, though. Everton took him on. When Boggo was released by Liverpool, Francis Jeffers got him a trial at Everton where he ran into Jeremy again at their Bellefield training ground. Boggo walked into the treatment room, saw Jeremy and immediately started trying to have some banter with Mr Purple. The treatment room was really quiet, which Boggo didn't understand. Jeremy had been dead loud at Liverpool. Jeremy quickly took Boggo to one side. 'These don't know I am like that,' said Jeremy, 'so keep your voice down and quit the banter.' But there was no chance of Boggo being quiet. He carried on leathering Jeremy in front of the Everton first XI. Apparently the team at Everton all slaughter Jeremy now. It's important to keep traditions going in football.

All clubs have banter, but people say the atmosphere at Liverpool is unique. When Boggo's firm came in, we taught them the ropes and they kicked it all off again. The dressing-room games of sock-ball and Chinese Whispers and battering each other with towels was passed down the generations. It was a Liverpool thing. Sadly, that special spirit may be going. I look at the current YTS boys when they come over from the Academy to Melwood and they seem quiet and shy. They don't have the banter we did. I wish everyone was together, as we were for that first wonderful year at Melwood, Liverpool's first team and apprentices living side by side.

Back then, Liverpool's first team were known as the Spice Boys. People used the tag as a derogatory one for the likes of Jamie Redknapp, Robbie Fowler, Steve McManaman, Jason McAteer and David James. I never considered the label offensive. I was steaming to be a Spice Boy. Let me be in your team! Let me be your mate! Every day, I went out of my way to be nice to Redknapp, Fowler, McManaman, McAteer and Jamo. After every encounter, I told myself, 'Hopefully, I will be in with these one day. Some day, we will be on the same level.' I am not a Spice Boy type, certainly not flash or obsessed with fashion, but I admired Jamie, Robbie and the rest. The image was false anyway. Nobody used to say, 'Oh, we're the Spice Boys. Let's all go off on modelling assignments.' No chance. The Spice Boy label was a media creation. Jamo, McManaman and the boys didn't take any notice of it. Those 1996 FA Cup final suits, where the players looked like ice-cream salesmen, didn't help, but the perception that the Spice Boys weren't professional is a myth. During my work experience and YTS, I trained with the Spice Boys and played with some of them in Liverpool's A and B sides. They worked their bollocks off. None of the Spice Boys took the piss out of training. None of them eased off. It wouldn't happen.

People claimed Roy Evans wasn't strong enough, but

that's rubbish. Roy and Ronnie Moran, his assistant, had a relationship with the players where they could have a real go at them. Some managers were stricter than Roy and Ronnie, but the standard of training was really good. John 'Digger' Barnes was an absolute joke in training; I couldn't get the ball off him. It was pointless closing Digger down. Redknapp too. When I was a YTS and invited to train with the seniors, I couldn't get near any of them. If I gave the ball away, Ronnie or Roy were immediately on my case. 'Look after the bloody ball!' Everyone else did. Possession was the Liverpool creed. All the Spice Boys treated the ball as their best friend. They never surrendered it cheaply. When I got bollocked, I just wanted the ground to open up and swallow me. 'God, this is real pressure,' I thought as I chased McManaman or Digger around Melwood. It did my head in. I walked off the pitch at the end having looked a fool trying to tackle some of the Spice Boys. They had so much skill. I would sit in the changing-room, heaving with frustration. 'How am I going to get to this level?' I would ask myself. 'Some of these players are fucking frightening.' Even when our YTS sessions finished, me, Boggo, Greggo, Wrighty and Cass would sit spell-bound watching the first team doing shooting or pattern of play. The Spice Boys were so talented. Forget all the bullshit about Jamie and the rest being playboys first, players second. These were proper professionals.

Fowler and McManaman were my main heroes. Part of my YTS duties involved standing outside the first-team dressing-room and getting shirts, balls and pictures signed by the first-team stars. These items were then sent to hospitals, schools or charity auctions. Whenever Fowler and McManaman walked past, I was in awe. They were local heroes. Some banter went on between the YTS and first-teamers, but I made sure I never said the wrong thing or was too cheeky. I was not intimidated, but I looked up to Fowler and McManaman so much. I never wanted them to think I was a tit. If they had caned me, I would have been devastated. The sad truth is that they probably were not even aware of me, Steven Gerrard, an unknown kid with a huge desire to copy them.

In contrast to Robbie and Macca, Paul Ince wasn't dead helpful to the young lads. He ordered us about. 'Do this, do that.' Not nasty, but you didn't let Incey down. One morning I was hanging about on the stairs to the gym at Melwood, knocking about with Wrighty, Cass and Bavo. We were always glued to each other. The first team were coming in and we were getting a few things signed. Incey bounced in, driving his big, boss Audi. He got out, trackies pulled up to his knees, jabbering on the phone. 'He's got to get fined,' I told the lads. Mobiles were banned at Melwood, but Incey couldn't be arsed. He was so high up. Life under Roy Evans was not that strict.

Incey walked past us, turned around and shouted, 'Do any of you drive?'

None of us could. I was only just seventeen, one driving lesson to my name. But that was more than the rest combined! Wrighty, Cass and Bavo went, 'Yeah, Stevie can drive. No problem.'

Incey threw me the keys and a piece of paper, and said, 'Get down the shops. Get all the things on this list – plus ten ciggies. Don't miss any or I'll fucking kill you. Crash the car and I'll definitely kill the four of you.' He must have noticed my hesitancy as I looked at the keys. 'Have you passed the test?' he asked.

'Yeah,' my mates shouted. 'He can drive.'

I went all red. 'Fucking hell,' I thought as I cradled the gleaming Audi keys in my hand. 'Where do I start here?'

As Incey walked away, he shouted back, 'Ten minutes. Hurry up.'

'Come on,' shouted Wrighty, Cass and Bavo as they dashed outside, 'we've only got ten minutes. Let's get into the car.' I followed, reluctantly. The four of us climbed into Incey's Audi. I could hardly see over the steering wheel. As the lads mucked about with the seat-belts, I panicked. Incey's motor was the fastest thing I had ever been in – as a passenger. Now I was about to turn the key and unleash a beast of an engine without a licence and only an hour's tuition from an instructor. I couldn't stop now, though. The shop was only round the corner, maximum 300 yards. Quick spin? Yeah. Go on. No harm. Risk it.

'OK, let's get to the shop and get back,' I said.

'Fuck off,' said the other three. 'Get the tunes on, let's go somewhere. We're off!'

So away we went. The hardest part was getting out of the Melwood car-park because it was chocka. I inched Incey's Audi past all these other expensive cars, praying I wouldn't hit anything.

As we were about to pull out on to the road, the gate-man asked, 'Where are you going?'

'Incey sent me to the shops,' I said.

He nodded and walked back.

I was shitting myself. If I got stopped by the police, got caught speeding or bumped this expensive Audi, there would be a long line of people queuing up to strangle me. Incey would be first, then my dad, then Steve Heighway. Roy Evans would fuck me off from Liverpool. But as I drove, admittedly only at 20 mph, I loved it. I was always begging Mum and Dad for a go with their car. I was buzzing. I was in a huge Audi, with the lads, singing and shouting. We had the windows down and 96.7 on the speakers. We drove to the newsagent via Alder Hey, West Derby, all over town. If Incey's car had been fitted with sat-nav, it would have gone into meltdown. We were all over the place, following our noses. Half an hour we were on the road.

'Where the fuck have you four been?' yelled Incey as we eventually returned and handed over his ciggies and change.

'The local shop was shut so we had to find another,' I lied.

'Fucking half an hour?' said Incey. He caned the four of us for taking so long. Thank God he never checked his milometer.

Far more laid-back than Incey was John Barnes, the skipper, and a legend. England international. Twice Footballer of the Year. Awesome. Talking to Digger scared the life out of me. If I walked into a room at Melwood and Digger was there, I tried to get out quickly. When I did pluck up the courage to speak to him, though, he was incredibly friendly, putting his arms around me, giving me advice. We used to have pretend fights, with John shaping up to punch me, shadow-boxing with me, sometimes wrestling me. Just mucking around with stars like John Barnes was the business. I was being noticed! Suddenly my dream of playing for Liverpool did not seem so unreal.

I had so much to prove to myself, and to everyone at Liverpool. I never thought established stars like Jamie Redknapp realized I existed until one day after training. 'You are a player,' Jamie said to me. 'I love the way you pass and shoot. Keep doing that.' I went home on cloud nine. Jamie Redknapp, England international, spoke to me! Not only that, Jamie Redknapp rated me. He only talked to me for a few seconds, it was only a few words, but they meant the world. Jamie was different class with the young lads. Unbelievable. After the first few words of encouragement, he was always offering advice. I will never forget how Jamie helped me climb the ladder to Liverpool's first team. When he came back from injuries, Jamie regained his sharpness in the A or B teams and I was lucky enough to play alongside him. What a privilege. I felt like a king being named on the same team-sheet as Jamie Redknapp. He talked to me, more and more. In games, he explained which positions I should take up, when to make runs. I was an apprentice learning from a master. What an education. He often called me over in the dressing-room and said, 'How are you? What have you been up to, Stevie?' Jamie Redknapp knew my name! Jamie talked to me as if I had played with him in the first team for five years! God, I felt so honoured just to be in the same room with him, let alone talking to him. Maybe because I played in the same position as Redknapp was why he took me under his wing. Maybe it was because he was simply a nice bloke who cared about other people.

'Hey, Stevie, what size are you?' Jamie shouted one day.

'Same as you,' I replied. I cleaned Jamie's boots, so I knew his size. He was actually a size bigger, but I pretended to be the same.

'Well, these will fit you then,' said Jamie, throwing me some boots.

Christmas came flying through the air in the shape of those beautiful boots. Jamie often gave me boots, moulded and studs, brand-new Mizunos. They were *the* boots at the time.

The British players in the first team were so generous. Me and all the YTS boys loved Redknapp, McManaman and Fowler. We would leave training, swapping stories of which star had given us what. 'Top man, that Robbie, he gave me these new boots, still in the box, unopened!' said Cass as we walked out of Melwood one day. No YTS boy in the country could have been kitted out as well as us lot at Liverpool. Dom Matteo, the defender who played for Scotland, was brilliant as well. Looking after Dom's boots was also my job, and he really looked after me. Before Christmas one year, Dom walked past me, stopped and turned round. 'Stevie, come here,' he said. He put his hand in his pocket, handed me what seemed like small bits of folded paper, and strolled off. I couldn't believe it. I looked at the paper and counted out £200. Some Christmas tip! I worked hard for Dom and Jamie. They massacred me if their boots weren't done properly. I would sometimes come into training knackered and think, 'Shit, it's ten o'clock, I haven't done Dom's boots.' So I'd get busy, washing and brushing all the shite off his boots, making sure they were polished properly. I knew how I liked my boots, so I made sure Dom's and Jamie's boots were perfect. With their big tips and helpful advice, Dom and Jamie were worth the extra effort.

Certain first-teamers, namely the foreigners like Oyvind Leonhardsen, weren't arsed about being nice to young lads like me. They would always have a go if the boots weren't spot-on. Stig Inge Bjornebye, the Norwegian full-back, was all right. He had been at Liverpool quite a long time, so he appreciated the apprentices. Stig gave me boots now and then. He wasn't a bundle of fun or a boss laugh, he was just OK. At least Stig showed us respect. Others didn't. That pissed me off. We were working and training hard to become professional footballers like them, cleaning the shite off their boots, doing all sorts of menial jobs around Melwood, and it infuriated me when some of the foreign players looked down at us. Patrik Berger wasn't really good with the apprentices. The dismissive attitude of the majority of the foreign lads irritated me, though I understood in a way. 'If I go to a foreign country, am I going to be bothered with the kids?' I wondered. I was on quite good terms with Fowler, Redknapp and McManaman, and that was all I was arsed about. I knew Carra and Michael Owen, too. I was OK.

The English players were brilliant with us. David James was such a character. As soon as I walked into the dressing-room, bang, Jamo caned me! If I had dodgy clobber on, or my hair wasn't right, Jamo was straight on to it. 'Where did you get those clothes?' Jamo would ask. 'A jumble sale? Have the police caught your tailor yet? Is the guy who cut your hair back inside?' Jamo modelled for Armani at the time so it was difficult to criticize his style. Anyway, us YTS boys knew the drill. 'Never, ever answer Jamo back' was the unwritten rule. We all whispered it to each other when he gave one of us some stick.

One day Greggo and Boggo, two lads from Croxteth who talked back to anyone, were cleaning the first-team dressing-room. They had to make sure the floor was spotless and put all the kit out. I came through, on my way to the boot room, and found an extraordinary scene. John Barnes, Robbie, Macca and all the first-teamers were on their backs, laughing, tears rolling down their faces. They pointed towards the corner of the room where a bin stood. And in the bin was Greggo with his arms stuck down inside! Greggo has red hair, floppy like McManaman's but red, and there he was jammed into this bin, looking hilarious.

'What happened to Greggo?' I asked Boggo.

'He answered Jamo back,' Boggo replied. 'Jamo picked Greggo up, folded him in half and shoved him in the bin.'

Only when the players stopped laughing, about ten minutes later, did someone pull Greggo out. Greggo could hardly walk. He was doubled up like an old man. Brilliant. That was classic Jamo! Never give him any lip. He's tall, strong, and he leaves YTS boys stranded in bins.

Only one thing pissed down on me as an apprentice at Liverpool: injuries. In my first year, I was plagued with them. A vicious circle trapped me: one step forward, play-ing really well; strain a muscle, hobble one step back. My ankle always played me up. When my back was wrong, I didn't look forward to training or playing because I knew it would be only a matter of time before something else would be sore. Injuries first began impeding my development towards the end of my time at school. If I played two or three games in a week, my back would be really stiff. The medical term for my problem was Osgood-Schlatter's, a bone disease tied up with the growth spurts that took me from a fifteen-year-old the same height as Michael Owen to a gangly six-footer. My back hurt. My knees were sore. Every physio and doctor I went to see just examined me and said, 'It's because you are growing.' I wanted to be tall, but it was a pain getting there.

Fortunately, I was in the down-to-earth hands of Liverpool manager Roy Evans. Whenever I look back now, I thank God I had such a caring person as Roy helping me in the early days of my career. One day, Roy called me into his office. His assistants, Doug Livermore and Ronnie Moran, were already in the room. 'How are you, Steven?' Roy asked kindly. 'How are the injuries?'

'It's so frustrating, boss,' I replied.

He knew. Roy had picked up signals that I was gloomy. 'Steven, keep your chin up,' he said. 'We've noticed you are down. Steve Heighway thinks so highly of you, and you are definitely going to play for the first team. Get your injuries right. Keep working. Don't be getting involved in messing around. We think the world of you here. As soon as you are right, you will sign your first pro contract.'

I was really grateful to Roy. But that's the way Liverpool are as a club. They look after players. We're family to them.

My development was still stop-start. At seventeen, and back from a broken wrist, I went flying into a tackle in training and damaged my ankle. Typical me, never holding back. I was told to calm down millions of times by Liverpool coaches. Ronnie Moran pulled me aside once and said, 'Steven, the staff are telling me you are getting injured because you go into stupid tackles. You try to kill people in training. These are your mates, Steven. Relax. Save it for the games.' I couldn't help it. It's the way I train, the way I play. Full on. No pulling out. No messing. Of course, I was also trying to impress, to catch the eye of the coaches. But it's my nature to go in hard. I couldn't go into a session thinking, 'I'll take it easy today, I'm not going to tackle.' It's a waste. Pointless. I got loads of warnings off Dave Shannon and Hughie McAuley. Actually, Hughie loved it. If you tackled hard, you were in Hughie's Academy team, especially against Everton and Man United! Because of the rivalry, those matches were like blood sports. Boys tackled like men. When the final whistle blew, I felt like a boxer who had been the distance – bruised, and sometimes bloodied.

For all my passion for big, bruising matches against Everton and Man United, my body struggled to withstand the pressure. Injuries held me back. I soon arrived at the age when pro contracts were being handed out. Lads younger than me were going in to see Roy and coming out with pro contracts. Naturally, I got the hump. Roy promised me a contract but it never came at the right time because of injuries. Liverpool were clever. They wanted me back fit a while before giving me the contract. That made sound financial sense to Liverpool. They did not want to give someone a three-year deal and then see his body pack up. So Liverpool delayed. It drove me mad with anxiety. Roy told me I was in his long-term plans but the doubts kept crowding in with every passing week without a hint of a contract. I lay in bed at night at Ironside, staring at the ceiling with one thought bouncing around in my head: 'Do Liverpool think these injuries are never going to go away?' Doubts affected me as much as the injuries. I felt my whole career was on a knife-edge. My dream was to make it with Liverpool. Did they really believe my body was too frail? I felt my head was about to explode.

One day, after training, I'd had enough. I stormed home, mind all over the place. 'Dad,' I said, 'you had best get in to Liverpool and talk to Steve and Roy. I can't go on with this uncertainty. Do they really want me?'

Dad was brilliant, as usual. 'Don't worry, Steven, we know they rate you,' he said. 'I'll go and talk to them.'

That calmed me down a bit. 'Dad, just tell them I want to sign pro because I am not having fucking lads in the year below signing pro before me.' Dad got the message!

He went to see Steve. 'Look,' said Dad, 'Steven's head has gone. He needs that deal. He's sick with worry.' Dad had a bit of a moan. Steve listened and appreciated how important the contract was for me. He realized it would give me peace of mind about my future. I soon had my deal. Three years – £700 a week for the first year, then £800, then £900! It was some jump from my apprentice cash of £50 a week. I thought I had won the lottery! I could not believe my luck. For Steve to offer me that deal, to go to Roy and say, 'I am going to offer this Gerrard kid this amount of money,' meant Liverpool thought something of me.

Anfield's appreciation of my potential was more important to me than the money. I was so grateful to Roy, Steve and Dad for sorting it out. It was like emerging from a dark tunnel. I could see the way ahead now. I was nearing my first-team destination.

5
Liverpool Heaven

Gérard Houllier turned me from a boy into a man but he can't take all the credit for the player I am today. This belief that I was destined to remain in the shadows at Liverpool if Gérard had not come along is just wrong. Liverpool had always backed me, giving me a six-year contract taking in schoolboy forms and YTS, and then that fantastic three-year pro, before Gérard even arrived, so how can he say he pinched me from the Academy? His claims are an insult to Academy coaches Steve Heighway, Dave Shannon and Hughie McAuley. They were the ones who worked so hard at improving my game from an early age. They helped shape me as a player from the moment I set foot in the Vernon Sangster. Steve has been a massive influence on me. He still is. Even now, when I get the chance, I talk to Steve and he makes useful points about my game. For Gérard to state he saved me from the Academy is disrespectful to Steve. It's like Gérard saying, 'Steven Gerrard wasn't doing well at the Academy and the people at the Academy weren't telling me Gerrard was good.' They were. They informed Gérard about me. I knew that.

What Gérard says about rescuing me from the reserves is also unfair on Roy. Roy was aware of me long before Gérard arrived at Anfield to be joint-manager with Roy in the summer of 1998. After the Frenchman took full charge, he did a lot for me, I know, and I am incredibly grateful. He looked after me, protected me and built up my game. But everyone at Anfield assisted my development into an England international. I have a good relationship with them all – Steve Heighway, Gérard and his coaches Phil Thompson and Sammy Lee. I never fell out with any of them. Gérard was definitely brilliant for me, but I must attack this impression that I would never have made it without him. I was not Gérard's invention. I made it because of my own efforts, because of fantastic coaching at the Academy, and because of the love and support of my parents. Gérard opened the door to the first team, but I had been banging loudly on it.

I was hardly unknown at Anfield. Gérard's suggestion that I was a no-mark at the Academy is plain wrong. I captained England U-18s before Gérard even turned up at Anfield. When Peter Robinson, who was Liverpool's chief executive back then, spoke to the Frenchman about joining the club, he mentioned that the future was bright because Liverpool had young talent like me. Rick Parry, who succeeded Peter, subsequently talked at length about me to Gérard. I know this sounds cocky, blowing my own trumpet, but I'm annoyed. Roy thought enough of my future at Liverpool to award me that three-year contract.

I was rising up through Liverpool's age-group teams way before the French showed up.

People talked about me at Melwood, Anfield and outside. Premiership clubs tried to buy me. When I played my first game for Liverpool U-19s, against Tottenham Hotspur in August 1998, Spurs certainly knew all about me. The match was at Spurs' Chigwell training ground in Essex and we were buzzing. Me, Boggo, Wrighty and the other lads felt like proper pros, proudly wearing our Liverpool tracksuits. We travelled south the night before, doing it in style, like the first team. The whole trip was quality. Luxury coach. Smart hotel. I roomed with Wrighty, and we almost didn't get to sleep we were so busy discussing what our first U-19 match would be like. I loved everything about the whole experience. Before the game, we ate a proper meal with all the right food: pasta and chicken. Tottenham fielded a good side at Chigwell. Peter Crouch and Luke Young both played; they went on to represent England, and Crouchy is now my team-mate at club and international level. So it was a tough old battle. Quite a few people were watching, including Alan Sugar, then the Spurs chairman rather than the TV firer of apprentices. I played really well, and smacked one in from long-range. The game finished 1–1, and as I walked off the pitch I noticed Sugar in conversation with Steve Heighway. Sugar even put his arm round Steve's back as they chatted. When I got into the changing-room, Boggo said, 'They were talking about you.'

'How do you know?'

'Because I heard them mention your name. I don't

know exactly what they said, but Alan Sugar was talking a lot about you.'

I didn't think anything more of it. I got showered, changed and jumped on the bus back to Liverpool. A week later, I heard Sugar tried to buy me. For £2 million! Not bad for an 'unknown'. Liverpool turned Spurs' offer down. 'Don't be ridiculous,' Steve told Alan Sugar. They obviously did rate me.

A month or two after that Spurs game, I got fined for messing about by Dave Shannon. As crimes go, it was a minor offence: not taking my plate back after a meal. Trivial. It was only a fiver, but I had just come off YTS money and it felt a decent sum – plus I was innocent. I was raging. I went in to see Dave, one-on-one. Straight in. Slammed the door.

'What's the fine for? I'm not happy.'

'You never took your plate back.'

'I did take it back.' I had. Some of the lads I was with, lazy bastards, left their plates everywhere. Not me. Mum and Dad brought me up to show respect. I was upset Dave didn't believe me. 'You are not taking a fiver off me.'

Dave refused to budge. 'No, it's done. You're fined, and I want it Friday.'

I knew I'd lost. 'I'll take the fine, but you are out of order, Dave.'

Everyone bantered with Dave. He was a terrific bloke, the one who got the team spirit going. Anyway, while he was screwing that fiver off me, we got talking about football and the season. 'Dave, do us a favour, give us another fixture list for the reserves and nineteens,' I asked. 'Someone has nicked mine.'

Dave looked at me and smiled. 'You won't need those fixtures. You'll be needing these.' He put his hand into his bag and pulled out the fixtures for the first team.

The firsts! I was stunned. I walked out of Dave's office thinking he would not have given me the first-team list without the coaches considering I had a chance. That gave me the biggest boost I ever needed. My fury over the fiver disappeared immediately.

Gérard said he came down to watch me training at the university one afternoon, but it wasn't him. It was his number two, Patrice Bergues, a top fellow. Patrice checked me out before Gérard did. I will never forget that day. In the morning, Steve Heighway pulled me into his office. 'Steven, we've got company today,' he said. 'Gérard Houllier, Phil Thompson, Sammy Lee and Patrice Bergues are coming down from Melwood to look at you in training.' Steve didn't need to say any more. I knew. This was it. This was my chance to force my way into the first-team squad.

Before training started, the whisper went round the dressing-room that only two were coming down from Melwood. It didn't matter to me how many; it just mattered to me that I was being assessed by the management. I must take this chance to impress. I always trained hard, but this session was my ticket to fame. I was itching to get cracking. I sprinted out of the door, onto the pitch, and looked around. No-one there! Shit. Maybe Gérard and his coaches decided they weren't coming after all. Maybe they felt I wasn't ready. Sod it. I got on with training.

After a while, I became aware there was someone

walking around. They stayed well back from our pitch, but they were definitely watching us. I looked closer. It was Patrice and Sammy. Brilliant. Time to step up a gear. We trained for an hour and forty-five minutes, doing possession, then had a game. I was everywhere. First to every ball, hardest in the tackle, strongest in the shooting. I treated it as a trial for the first team. I sweated buckets. I could see them looking at me. Sammy did the pointing, and wrote little notes. Patrice just studied me and the other lads.

When the session ended, Steve introduced us to Sammy and Patrice. We all knew Sammy anyway. He was superb with the young lads. Everyone liked Sammy. Sammy certainly appreciated who I was. 'Well done,' he said. I was buzzing to hear those words. As the group broke up, Patrice strolled across. I had never met him before. None of us had. Gérard had only just taken over fully with Patrice. It was a big moment. Patrice shook my hand. 'You are looking sharp,' he said. That was it. He strolled away. I walked away on air.

Another audition needed passing. Gérard had not seen me yet. The story of Gérard 'discovering' me came about because a couple of weeks after that training session watched by Patrice and Sammy we had an U-19 game against Man United. It was a November Saturday, and I was dying to play. By then I was starting to push for a reserve-team place full-time, but there were special reasons for wanting to start that U-19 fixture. The opponents were United and I love piling into them, always have done and always will do. It was also my first game back after an injury. I broke my wrist and had been playing with a cast on. I was meant to play in a reserve/YTS match against the first team, but the doc stopped me. He took one look at the cast and said, 'You're not ready.' I was devastated, particularly as the word was that Patrice was going to watch me again. The wrist got better by the time Man U were in town. I couldn't wait to launch myself into them.

All my U-19 mates were playing, boys like Boggo and Greggo. A decent crowd gathered, around 200, which is good for an Academy match. Dad was there, giving me the support I prize so highly. All our normal staff were present, too, like Steve and Dave, and I spotted Gérard standing near them. Little did I know then he had initially come down to run the rule over Ritchie Partridge, our Irish winger. I assumed Gérard was there just for me. So I took control. I bossed the game from start to finish, smashing into United players left, right and centre-midfield. I really should have been shown the red card for bad tackles. 'One more and you're going off,' warned the ref. 'One more and you are coming off,' warned Steve. I ignored them both. I just wanted to rip Man United to pieces. They were a good team, as well, with players like John O'Shea in their ranks. It felt similar to when the Lilleshall boys swanned into Melwood. I wanted to crush them. We drew 1–1, but I scored, and I knew I had shone. As I walked off the pitch, feeling like a king, I glanced around to check Gérard's reaction. He'd gone. Shit. But he must have been impressed. When I reached Ironside, Dad was already home.

'The manager was there, you know,' Dad said.

'I know,' I replied with a smile. 'I saw him.'

Dad's next comment filled me with pride. 'You never did yourself any harm there, Steven.' That was lavish praise from my dad. I went up to bed feeling on top of the world.

Sunday passed slowly. My impatience for Monday was massive. I wanted to get into training to find out if there had been any word from Gérard. Nothing happened on the Monday. Nor Tuesday. But on the Wednesday, I was walking down a corridor in the Academy and there, coming towards me, were Gérard and Roy Evans. Roy had called time on 12 November, and was going round saying his goodbyes. Typical Liverpool – even dismissals are done in a civilized fashion. Roy stopped me. I didn't know what to say. I shifted from one foot to the other, slightly embarrassed. Here was Roy Evans leaving as joint-manager standing next to the man who was taking over fully, my new boss whom I'd never met before. Bloody weird, I felt.

Roy was brilliant. 'How are you, Steven?' he asked. 'Keep going, you've got a great chance of making it.'

Gérard then interrupted. 'You've got a very good chance,' he said.

I looked at him, looked at that face that was to become so familiar to me over the next few years.

'Keep doing what you are doing,' he added. 'I watched you last week against Manchester United and you were very good.'

'Thank you,' I said to Gérard, and turned back to Roy. 'Sorry to hear about what happened.'

'Don't worry, Steven, I'll be OK. You just make sure you keep doing what you are doing.'

I felt sorry for Roy. I wanted him to stay manager. He

was always first-class with me, and I knew how much he wanted me in the first team. Whenever I saw Roy, he always said, 'Just get rid of your injuries and you will be with me.' Now that the French were in charge of Liverpool, I wondered what would happen. Would Gérard really want me in the first team? He didn't really know who I was. Roy had known me since I was twelve. Roy leaving really felt like a huge blow. I heard from people at Melwood that the French changed everything and that no-one enjoyed training any more. Gérard was really strict. A lot of negative vibes came down from the reserves, too. On first impressions, Gérard seemed a nice guy. But I was shitting myself because of the language. I didn't know how good his English was. I was scared of him. Definitely. He was the boss, the man who could decide whether to keep me or bomb me out. I was just terrified of this French set-up. I wanted it to be English, to be people I knew and understood. It seemed inevitable under Roy that I would progress to the first team. It was a matter of when, not if. But then Roy got shown the door. Now I had to prove myself to a foreigner.

Two days later, on the Friday, Steve Heighway called me and Wrighty into his office. Dave Shannon was already there. 'Important news, lads,' Steve announced. 'Gérard and Phil want you at Melwood now.' Wrighty and I looked at each other. Fantastic. This was it, the news we'd craved. 'You start on Monday,' Steve added. 'Gérard wants to put you on a programme, and get you to train with the first team. Go on, lads, this is your big chance to leave us behind.' Steve paused, and then gave us some really important advice. He knew our Academy days were over. 'Never forget where you've come from,' he told me and Wrighty. 'Never forget what we've done for you and that we are still here for you. We don't want you to change as people. Keep your feet on the ground. Blank out all the big-heads. And you are leaving good mates behind, so make sure you come back and see them.' It was good advice, as usual from Steve, but he need not have worried. I would never have raced out of the Academy, glanced briefly over my shoulder and never again looked back. I know my roots. I know the names of those who guided me along the road to the first team: Steve Heighway, Dave Shannon and Hughie McAuley.

I drove home, parked up outside Ironside, and nodded to the young lads kicking the ball about, as I used to. My world was spinning fast, faster than even I had dreamed of when it was me playing shootie out there. I walked through the front door, my head still in a daze. Dad was sitting in the front room, flicking through the paper. He looked up and saw the glint in my eye.

'What is it?' he asked.

'I'm at Melwood now!' I said.

Dad was so proud. 'This is where it starts,' he said.

That weekend passed by in a blur. All I could think of was Monday and Melwood. That Sunday night, as the clock ticked towards our move towards the big time, Wrighty stayed at Ironside. The two of us were really close, and spent a lot of time together off the field. We were both buzzing and could hardly sleep. Me and Wrighty just talked and talked. We felt as if we had made it as pros. But before I left the house and embarked on the next stage of my career, Dad pulled me aside. 'This is the beginning,' he reminded me. 'You are going into a room full of England players. Full of internationals. Remember, Steven, you've achieved nothing yet. Know your place, but take your chance.' Dad's words acted like a wake-up call. I was very focused.

And fucking nervous. Going into Melwood that day, I was shitting myself. Wrighty and I arrived ridiculously early. Those big steel gates were open, but few cars were inside. We went in, and walked cautiously towards the pavilion. Wrighty and I knew where the dressing-room was, but we stood outside it for a few minutes, plucking up courage. Eventually, I turned the handle and went in. The room was empty. The kit-man had been in, laying out each player's training stuff. Wrighty and I looked along the pegs to see if there was any spare kit for us. None. Our hearts dropped.

'Fuck it, Wrighty, they don't know we're coming,' I said.

'Shit,' he said.

We felt like trespassers.

I looked at Wrighty and said, 'The first team are going to come in and say, "What the fuck are youse doing here?"'

We were just about to make a break for it when the door opened and the stars began rolling in. Robbie, Macca, Jamie. Thank God for friendly faces. Wrighty and I knew them and they had always been brilliant with us.

'You down here for good now?' said Jamie. 'Well done.'

Macca laughed. 'About bloody time!'

Robbie joined in. 'Bit late, aren't you?'

Wrighty and I relaxed. Maybe they were expecting us

after all. 'Get your kit, and get in next to me,' said Jamie. Christ, I've arrived, I thought, as I sat down next to one of the country's most famous footballers. But then one of the coaches came in and signalled for me and Wrighty to sit down at the far end, with all the shite, the fringe players and the old guys. No pegs, hardly any room. We folded our clothes up and bundled them together on the bench. So what? I didn't care that my spot in the dressing-room was cramped. This was it, lift-off, time to train with the first team. Get on with it. Get out there.

On the training pitch, Gérard called us all together in a circle. He stood in the middle and pointed at me and Wrighty, the new boys. 'These lads are here now,' said Gérard. 'I have moved them up from the Academy.' That was it! Introductions over. On with training.

For all my fears about what training would be like under Gérard, I loved it. It wasn't as strict as I expected. The pattern-of-play work was enjoyable. The practice games were brilliant. Afterwards, as Jamie, Macca and the others were heading off to the dressing-room, all laughing and shouting, Gérard kept me and Wrighty back. Neither of us had had a proper one-on-one with him yet. This was the first time he had addressed us. 'You are here now,' Gérard began. 'This is where it starts. We are not happy with how you look. We want you bigger and stronger. You are very thin. Look around the first-team dressing-room and they are a lot bigger than you. You must get to their level. We are going to put you on a different training regime from them. Don't complain. Get on with it. If you are told to stay back, or get in early, make sure you do as you are told. Eat what we tell you. Drink what we tell you. We want you physically ready for the first team. You are not far away.'

Things moved fast. A dietician spoke to us. He checked me over and ordered me to cut out fast food. My eating habits weren't too bad before, but I knew I had to get fitter. No more burgers. 'Live like an athlete' became my motto. A fitness guy worked hard on me and Wrighty, keeping us in the gym four afternoons a week for two hours of weights. I sweated loads, pushing myself to the limit to inch closer to the first team. Every time I bench-pressed some more iron, I told myself the effort hastened the date of my Liverpool debut. I imagined touching the 'This Is Anfield' sign as I ran out to the roar of the Kop. That image made the pain worth it.

Gérard often put his head around the door to check on my progress. After one afternoon in the gym, I was called into his office. 'Steven,' he said, 'you've got a great chance. You have the ability. It is whether you have the mentality. We are going to watch you closely.' Gérard really cared. 'I want to have a meal with your mum and dad,' he added. So we went for a quiet meal, somewhere nice on the Allerton Road. Gérard didn't talk much about football. He wanted to know my background, so we all just chatted. My parents came away very impressed, pleased that their son was being looked after by a genuine guy.

Football had suddenly become big-time serious for me. All my banter from the YTS days was gone. Now I was just a little gobshite in the first-team dressing-room. Joining in with the banter was impossible – I was that scared. I would have died if I had got hammered by

Robbie, Jamo or any of the established boys. I just looked up to them all and shat myself. Keep quiet, work hard, I told myself. Gérard had introduced so many rules so I had to be on my toes the whole time. There were fines for everything. I was fined a few times for being late, for turning up in the wrong T-shirt through being nervous. I knew from the first day not to piss about with the French regime or with Gérard. He made it very clear that anyone who didn't abide by the rules would be out. Simple as that. Some players found it hard because Liverpool had been more relaxed under Roy Evans. Some couldn't adapt. Macca was going on a free to Real Madrid. Phil Babb was training on his own, seeing his contract out. Everyone understood: don't mess with Gérard.

Despite my trepidation, I began to win favour with Gérard. On 23 November, Liverpool flew out to Celta Vigo for a UEFA Cup third-round first-leg tie. Wrighty and me were on the plane! We had not been at Melwood a month and there we were, checking in for a flight to Spain with the first team! I was awestruck, travelling with the other players, the coaches and directors. I sat next to Wrighty on the plane and told him, 'We are just here to help with the kit. We'll not get a kick.' Wrighty agreed. The lack of pressure made the trip even more enjoyable. I was just buzzing to be there: sitting with the first team during meals, getting changed with them for training at the stadium that night, mingling with them around the hotel. I was a kid fresh out of the Academy talking to players who had graced World Cups. Awesome.

When it came to sorting out the hotel rooms, Gérard

split me and Wrighty up. I shared with Jamie. 'Watch him,' Gérard advised me. 'Watch how Jamie behaves around the place. How he eats, trains, conducts himself, how he plays. You can learn off him.' Jamie was, as usual, first class. He treated everyone the same. He talked to me as if he were talking to Jason McAteer, Phil Babb or anyone he had played with for years.

I still didn't expect to get closer to the pitch than the stands. But then I walked into the dressing-room and found a shirt with my name and number on, 28. My own shirt. I belonged. I was now part of the fabric of Liverpool FC. It hit me then that I had crossed the threshold into an exclusive new world. Gérard named me and Wrighty as subs. European ties allow seven on the bench, so Wrighty and I had our chance.

We sat there that night and watched Liverpool being given a lesson in possession. Celta were a useful side with players like Claude Makelele, who went on to prove such a formidable player for Real Madrid and Chelsea, and the clever Russian attackers Valeri Karpin and Alexander Mostovoi. Celta were too good for Liverpool and we lost 3–1. Neither me nor Wrighty made it off the bench. No problem. It was unbelievable simply to experience European combat close up, in a noisy stadium containing 24,600 fans, scarcely a month after playing in an U-19 game at Liverpool University in front of 200 people. Some change.

When we got back to England, I was dying to find out whether I had kept my place in the match-day squad. I was at full throttle in training. In our first session back from Vigo, I absolutely took the piss out of Paul Ince. He couldn't get near me, I was that up for training. Incey was only interested in matches, not practice, but he could turn it on when he wanted. A lot of people claimed when Incey came to Liverpool from Inter Milan that he wasn't as good, but there were certain training sessions and games when he was awesome. I swear it. I never knew there was any tension between him and Gérard, but I did know Incey was one of the main men in Liverpool's dressing-room. Everyone knew it. Incey made sure we all knew it. Rule number one at Melwood: don't get on the wrong side of Incey. Training was different. I was busting to make a point, to prove myself. Towards the end of the session, Incey started to step it up, but he still couldn't touch me. The players wound Incey up something rotten. 'That's the end of you, Incey,' Fowler shouted. 'Fuck off,' he yelled back. The banter was only starting. 'Watch your back!' Redknapp teased Incey. I wasn't showing off. I was just doing everything right. Deep down, I thought, 'I want Incey's place. End of story.' I was on fire that session.

Gérard obviously noticed. He named me in his eighteen-man squad for Liverpool's next Premiership game, against Blackburn Rovers, on 29 November. My heart went out to Wrighty, who wasn't included, but privately I was overjoyed for myself. 'I have a chance of being on the bench here,' I told myself. Two got left out of the squad, but I was picked among the subs. Gérard selected his subs on covering positions and he appreciated I could do a number of jobs: central midfield, right mid-field or at right-back. 'The boss must have an idea of putting me on,' I thought.

Magical is the only way to describe the whole

experience that day at Anfield. The memory is so strong it feels like yesterday. I left the dressing-room, lined up in the corridor and religiously touched the 'This Is Anfield' sign on the steps leading to the pitch. This is Anfield. This is it. I came out and heard the noise of the 41,753 fans. Bloody deafening. During the game, Gérard sent the subs down the touchline, towards the Kop, to warm up. All the subs were applauded. Well, nearly all. When I ran towards the Kop, did they clap me? Did they fuck! Nothing. Nerves filled every part of my body. I could see the doubts on the fans' faces as they watched me warm up. I could almost hear them say to each other, 'Who's this skinny little twat? Who the fuck's he? I hope he doesn't come on.' I was shitting myself.

With five minutes left, I thought, 'I'm not coming on. I'm sound. I'm safe. Just relax.' Liverpool led 2–0, with goals from Incey and Michael, and the lads were just seeing out the game. It was all over. Then Phil Thompson turned round and said, 'Go and do a warm-up.' I put in a big professional warm-up, actually believing I might now get a minute or two. I was sixty yards away from the dug-out, doing my stretches in front of the Kop and waiting for Phil to wave at me. I didn't want to look back, as if I was being busy. I leant down to do some stretching and blagged a glance back. Phil was standing up and beckoning to me. Me! Breaking Anfield's touchline record, I sprinted back to the dug-out. Sammy Lee leaned over, steaming for me to come on. 'Good luck,' he shouted. I saw Sammy's face. He was delighted, completely made up for me. A local lad, Sammy served Liverpool so well as a player and then as a coach.

Sammy knew how much this moment meant to me.

So this was it. My Liverpool debut was seconds away. All the hard work, all the dreaming, all the fight-backs from disappointments and injuries would be made worthwhile with one step over a white line. All the batterings I took on Ironside. All the fears about losing my toe and my career. I'd survived. Now, my debut awaited. I nearly dropped a load.

Veggard Heggem, our Norwegian right-back, came off and I was told to slot in there. 'Keep the ball for us,' Gérard ordered, 'keep the position, see the game out.' My heart beat crazily fast. I tried to keep my cool. 'Get on, get the job done, get off,' I told myself as I ran into the fray. Despite my nerves, I was desperate for the ball. I didn't want to come on and not get a touch. Touching the ball just once would feel like I'd arrived. The ball soon came my way. I controlled it, looked around and passed to another red shirt. Nothing fancy, nothing risky. Thank God. I didn't want to see the ball again. My job was done. I looked at the ref. Blow the fucking whistle!

Then the ball got switched and I was down the right. Incey played me in, the ball gagging to be crossed into the box. It was set up perfectly. Jesus, I had been in this situation so many times before and always delivered. As I brought my right foot down into the ball, one aim raced through my mind: 'Just whip it in, put it in the danger area.' But the occasion got to me. I must have been too keen. With 41,000 pairs of eyes burning into me, I overhit the cross disastrously. The ball went twenty yards over the last defender's head and almost cleared the Centenary

Stand. Incey gave me a little snarl. 'Shit,' I thought. I was gutted, fuming with myself.

Liverpool won, so the atmosphere was good in the dressing-room afterwards. Everyone shook my hand, patted me on the head and gave me hugs. Wrighty came over and said, 'Well done – you've now played for Liverpool.' I really appreciated that, because it must have been hard for Wrighty. For all his frustration at not yet getting a game, Wrighty was buzzing for me. Everyone was. I just wanted to get my clothes on and go and see my family in the players' lounge. That was another massive thing. Mum, Dad and Paul mingling with the other players' families. It was a long way from shivering on the touchline at Liverpool University.

Games kept coming. On Friday, 4 December, I was down at Melwood getting ready with the rest of the squad for the journey down to White Hart Lane. It was a big game, and I was hopeful of a place. Carra walked past as I talked to a local reporter, Paul Joyce, now of the *Daily Express*. He caned me: 'Fucking hell, Stevie, youse have only played one fucking game and you're doing big-time interviews already! And don't pretend you don't know the team.' But I didn't. Gérard gave me no indication I would play against Spurs. Carra stitched me up!

As Liverpool had been hit by some injuries and suspensions, though, I had an idea I might be involved. After dinner at our hotel on the edge of London, Gérard called me to his room. 'Steven, you are starting,' he said. My first start! I floated out of Gérard's room, thinking, 'Fucking hell.' I got back to my room, lay down on my bed but never slept a wink. 'I'm so nervous,' I told

Wrighty, my room-mate. 'I will be up against Allan Nielsen. He's useful.' I was convinced I was starting in the middle so would be facing Nielsen.

The next morning, Gérard ran through the formation: 3–5–2. 'Steven, you're on the right,' the boss said. The implication sank in like a dead weight. Starting on the right meant one thing: David fucking Ginola. As we left the meeting-room, all the lads said, 'Ginola! All the best.' I knew Ginola was good. I'd seen him on TV many times, but he couldn't be that good, could he? French international, darling of the Spurs fans, on his way to being voted Footballer of the Year. Fuck it, get on with it. Just give it your all. Adrenalin will get you through. I looked again at our team line-up and saw Incey was playing. If I had a shocker against Ginola, Incey would slaughter me all game.

Before leaving the dressing-room, Gérard took me to one side. 'Get fucking stuck into Ginola,' he ordered. 'Don't let him do his turns.' Gérard never swore, but he really wanted me to nail Ginola. There was history between the pair. Make that bad blood. He and Ginola were not the best of friends after their falling-out when Gérard coached France. Gérard claimed a mistake by Ginola cost France the chance of qualifying for the World Cup in America in 1994. He wanted Ginola sorted out here.

No chance. Ginola was on fire. He took the piss out of me. He was so strong. 'Go away, you little boy,' Ginola seemed to be saying, 'you are not good enough. Get away. Come back when you can live with someone as brilliant as me.' I stumbled through a nightmare. Ginola was awesome that afternoon. Within five minutes, he had done seven step-overs running at me and put six crosses into the box. He was just knocking balls into Steffen Iversen and Chris Armstrong for fun. It was an onslaught. I was a bag of nerves, terrified when the ball came near me. I panicked. I gave a few passes away, and Incey was on to me straight away. 'Get a fucking grip!' he screamed. 'How can this get worse?' I wondered. 'Incey is on at me. Fucking Ginola is taking the mickey. I am out of position, and out of my depth. Get me out of here!'

Liverpool got battered first half. I actually had a half-chance to score but couldn't take it. What a disaster. Players I really respected rallied behind me. Thank God for good team-mates. Fowler was on to me all game, help-ing me. Jamie said, 'Carry on, you are doing all right, keep the ball for us.' Incey, though, was on my back big-time. 'Get tight to Ginola, keep the fucking ball, come on!' I was fuming with him. Hated him big-time. The words 'fuck off' formed on my lips as I looked at Incey, but I never said them. Christ, how much did I want to confront him. Why pick on me? I never had his respect early on. As I got to know Incey better through the season, I realized that non-stop moaning was his way of getting players going. Incey was not having a go at me to put me down. He felt this was the best way to help me. Now, if Incey said something really nice to me on the pitch, I would think, 'You don't mean that.' If I played with him now, I would prefer him to be on my case. That's his style. Always aggressive. Always demanding. That's why Incey's career has lasted so long.

In the first half, I was on the far side of the pitch from

the bench, so I got no encouragement or advice from Gérard, Phil Thompson or Sammy Lee. Actually, that was probably a blessing. That far away, maybe Liverpool's coaches couldn't tell the excruciating level of my discomfort. Still, every second I expected my number to go up. I could imagine Gérard's thoughts: 'Gerrard, you're off. Sharpish. You've been found out.' I wouldn't have blamed him for the early hook. All the Spurs players were miles too good for me. On the day, Ginola was The Man, but even when I was bumping into Iversen and Armstrong, they were just so much bigger and stronger.

My first start ended in a 2–1 defeat for Liverpool and humiliation for me. Everyone was polite enough afterwards. 'You did OK,' said Gérard. 'Well done,' said Thompson. All the lads were all right with me, yet I knew deep down I hadn't done myself justice. Some words of my dad's crept into my head: 'Just take your chance, Steven, just take your chance.' I hadn't.

The trip home was long. I sat next to Wrighty but couldn't bring myself to say more than a few words. Family and friends phoned and enquired, 'How did it go? How long did you play?' I gave them the bare details, and hoped they would be out when *Match of the Day* came on. Dad called. I could be honest and open with him. 'It was really hard, Dad. I hope I haven't blown it.' Sammy Lee knew I would be hurting. He came down the bus and was brilliant with me, trying to lift my spirits. But my depression was beyond even Sammy's motivational powers of curing. When the bus arrived back in Liverpool, I didn't want to get out. I thought it wouldn't be long before I was out permanently, sent back to the U-19s with a note marked 'Not Good Enough'.

Somehow, I survived. Liverpool's next game was the return with Celta Vigo at Anfield on 8 December – a big game, even though we trailed from the first leg. I was surprised to discover I was actually starting – amazing, given that I was convinced Ginola had dug a grave for me in North London soil. Incey was suspended in Europe after getting sent off against Valencia, so Gérard turned to me. A rumour gathered pace that I would be used in my normal position. The stories were right. I started in the middle, and immediately felt comfortable. I played a couple of nice balls early doors and confidence flooded through me. This was it! I was showing people what I could do, thumping into tackles, pinging balls about. Back on the dirty old tarmac of Ironside, I had dreamed of this. The fans' songs and applause lifted me higher. Liverpool supporters have always loved home-grown players and they were right behind me, cheering whenever I did something right. I was even voted Man of the Match.

In a way, there was no pressure. Everyone knew Liverpool were up against it that evening, because of what happened over in Spain. Our team was really weak, too. Injuries and suspensions took their toll, claiming important players like Incey, Redknapp, Heggem and McManaman. People could see our defence was suspect at that time. No-one really gave us too much hope of over-turning the deficit against Celta. The Spaniards were a tidy outfit. For their goal, by the Israeli Haim Revivo, me and Danny Murphy got turned inside out, embarrassingly so. We were made to look like schoolboys. But that mistake never got mentioned in the changing-room afterwards. Everyone came over and congratulated me. Gérard was made up. Liverpool had lost 1–0, but the look in the manager's eyes told me how pleased he was with me. All the staff and players were going, 'Fucking hell, your first home start and you did really well.' When I first entered the dressing-room that night, my mind was racked with doubts about whether I could cut it as a top player after my Trial by Ginola. When I walked out of the dressing-room at the end of the evening, I knew I belonged. 'I can handle this,' I told myself as I left Anfield.

First thing next morning, I almost broke the world 100m record getting down the newsagent's. I bought all the papers to see what they had written about me. I checked the player ratings. Only nine out of ten. Fuck off! Where's my picture? Back page. Fucking magic. I craved being recognized. Walking down the street and having people asking for my autograph was such a buzz. Having my family make a fuss over me spread my smile even wider. Fame was new to me, and I couldn't get enough. More please! In the Liverpool programme, there were pages on Steven Gerrard – 'the new kid on the block'. I must have read the piece a thousand times. Arrogance wasn't the reason; I just loved all this recognition. If I got noticed in the street or written up in the papers, I was delighted because it meant I was doing all right on the pitch.

The praise didn't go to my head. I had the right people around me. Dad was brilliant, always making sure my new-found celebrity did not soften me or make me slacken off in training. 'Don't fucking read all that,' Dad said when he saw me lounging around on the settee, flicking through newspapers. 'You've got training tomorrow. Make sure you play three or four games. You have done nothing.' Dad had one special piece of advice, which he kept reminding me of: 'Don't copy those players who have played 300 games and are starting to relax. Train and play as if it's your first ever game. Train and play as if it's the World Cup final. Learn. Never ease off.' Established players like Incey, Redknapp and Fowler would never have let that happen. If this new boy fresh from the Academy had got above his station, Incey would have hammered me straight back down.

I began to receive more and more attention in the papers – 'The local lad in the Liverpool engine room', 'Huyton's Hero', that sort of thing. Jamie, Robbie and Michael helped me handle the fame, and gave me tips on how to deal with dodgy questions in interviews. I just kept stressing how much I had to learn. Gérard deliberately made me room with Steve Staunton for the remainder of that season. He knew I would learn about being a proper pro from being around 'Stan'. We called him Stan because he looked like Stan Laurel. Stan watched me closely in training, in games and around the place. He picked up on little things like the importance of being polite to everyone, from hotel staff to fans, everyone. Stan was such a nice fellow and had done so much in the game. A young pro can take so many wrong turnings, but Stan pointed me in the right direction.

Everyone at Anfield assisted me. Even Incey. I had some one-on-one chats with him, and got to know him. My perspective on him changed. I started to really like him. The memory of being terrified by him as a YTS disappeared, replaced with a feeling that he was all right. What had really altered was his view of me. After a few games, particularly the Celta Vigo match at Anfield, Incey realized I wasn't just a lightweight from the Academy. I could handle life among the heavyweights. Conversations with Incey really lifted me. Imagine it. Me talking to Paul Ince! One of my England heroes!

Life at Liverpool just got better and better. Being part of such a lively dressing-room was brilliant. The lads all really got on with each other, and I listened eagerly to their plans for the Christmas party. Liverpool's Christmas parties have always been legendary, with fancy dress and epic nights out. I wanted some of that. A few drinks and a few laughs with my new friends, the superstars of Liverpool Football Club. I couldn't wait for the big night. Every day at training, when the banter was banging around the dressing-room, the talk would be of the Christmas party. As it drew closer, the excitement level rose to almost fever pitch. Players were discussing what fancy dress they were wearing. I knew Michael was going as Harry Enfield's Scouser. I couldn't decide what to wear. I was more distracted by a fear about what might happen to a new boy like me. I was actually shitting myself, because Robbie, Macca and Jamie would walk past and whisper, 'You're singing, aren't you? It had better be some decent music. Don't worry, there's no pressure. You'll be up there, on stage, with the microphone, on your own. Don't let us down. Sing your heart out for the lads.' And they'd walk on, laughing their heads off. Jesus Christ. What was coming my way? I also noticed in the sneaky smiles of the older players that I was heading for an ambush. Pints over the head. Bombarded with food. Bring it on!

Suddenly, my social arrangements were rearranged by the manager. A week before the big date, Gérard summoned me into his office at Melwood. 'Steven, you are not going to the Christmas party,' he said. I desperately tried not to show my disappointment, despite being ripped up inside. 'If I find out you went, you are fined. Keep away. It's not for you.' I was gutted. Wrighty was also banned from attending.

Thank God we didn't go. The party got infamously out of hand. The players began at a local hotel for some drinks and then hit a club. Outsiders and friends turned up who couldn't be controlled. People got carried away with the drink. A stripper turned up, and it all got ugly. The *News of the World* had somehow got in and taken pictures, and they ran a story. Certain players got set up and looked bad. A depression fell over the team. I remember sitting at the dinner table with the lads and they were all shaking their heads in frustration. The mood was bleak. The camp was down for weeks and weeks. The team realized it was a mistake.

Gérard stormed into the dressing-room and gave the players a monster caning. I had never seen the manager so incensed. He felt Liverpool's good name had been dragged through the gutter. He was right. It had. The players let the club down. No question. No excuses. After Gérard's rant, he pulled me and Wrighty. 'That's the reason why you got told you were not going,' he said. 'You guys are innocent. But just you learn from the others' mistake.' Even though I hadn't gone to the party, we were all in it together and I felt for the lads. It was unlikely to happen again. Not just because the players all felt so bad, but because all parties were banned by Gérard.

Still, the season seemed like one long celebration for me. Liverpool were not enjoying the best of fortunes but I was loving just being part of the drama, good or bad. I was living the dream, playing against boyhood idols like Paul Gascoigne. I first bumped into Gazza when Middlesbrough visited Anfield in February 1999. More accurately, he bumped into me. There were thirty-six seconds on the clock and Gazza elbowed me. A full-whack right elbow straight in my left eye-socket. Off the ball. Bang. No reason at all. A gift from Gazza, my hero! Thanks, mate. I'd love to know the reason from Gazza. Fucking hell, why? Maybe he heard I was doing all right, that people were talking about me as future England material, and he wanted to put me in my place. Maybe that elbow was a welcome to the big time. Bang. Clobber. My eye was throbbing. Boom, boom. I hadn't even touched the ball. It was a bit harsh.

'Right,' I shouted over at Gazza, 'is that how you fucking want it?'

The next time he had the ball, I went in hard and fast like a steaming bull. I wanted to send him flying. No chance. I never got near him. He just turned sharply, like a matador, and swept the ball away, leaving me tackling thin air. Chasing Gazza was like trying to catch a ghost. Back I went again, this time winning the ball. Now it was Gazza after me. A game broke out within the game. Gazza closed me down dead quick, and I tried to slip the ball through his legs. What the hell was I playing at? Trying to nutmeg one of the most skilful midfielders ever to play for England? I must be mad. I was so fired up by the challenge of taking on Gazza. 'Behave!' Gazza said. 'What the fuck are you up to?' Gazza stared at me and then added: 'You little cunt!' Gazza was loving it. He knew he had wound me up.

After the game, Gazza strolled over, ruffled my hair and put his arm around me. 'You are a fucking good player,' he said. 'Keep going.' Unbelievable. I was still no-one at the time, third choice, a young kid fresh from the Academy. And there was Gazza going out of his way to congratulate me! Deep down, I think Gazza was happy with the way I reacted to his elbow. I never complained. I never hid. I just went looking for him. Unfortunately, I couldn't get near him. Back in the dressing-room, I told the other players about my run-in with Gazza. Like the ref, most hadn't seen the elbow. 'Don't worry about it,' Jamie said. 'Gazza probably knew he was going to do that even before the game. You will get more of them off Gazza!'

I wore my black eye from Gazza like a medal won in battle. It meant the world to me to encounter him, however painfully. I wanted another memento, his shirt, but I was that intimidated. Because he elbowed me, I probably thought he would tell me to fuck off. I was terrified of asking him. It must sound strange being in awe of someone you have just spent ninety minutes trying to smash to pieces, but that was the way I was with Gazza. I grew up on his brilliance. I read his book. I bought his England shirt. So did Paul, my brother, who used to look like Gazza. Bit heavy. Chubby cheeks. 'Hey, Gazza,' I used to shout at Paul. He went off his cake! We both loved Gazza. His video, *Gascoigne's Glory*, was my prized possession. I must have watched it a million times. I used to watch that tape thinking, 'Oh my life, what a player.' It was a wonder the tape never wore out. Gazza at Italia 90. Gazza taking on the world. Skill, determination, love of the shirt, cheeky smile. The whole package, the real deal. Gazza summed up everything I worshipped about football. He was the David Beckham of his day. I looked up to him so much. In my early days at Liverpool, people considered me a defensive midfielder, but in training I was always trying to be Gazza. I play more like Gazza today than when I first started. I am nowhere near as skilful as him, but I have things he never had, like endurance.

When we collided at Anfield, I knew his career was on the downward slope. Of course, it was sad to see someone once so special on the decline. But just think about the career. Remember the good things about Gazza, the turns away from his marker, the dribbles and the fantastic goals. That free-kick in the FA Cup semi-final at Wembley in 1991 was like a fucking rocket. His control and finish against Scotland at Euro 96. Gazza was a genius. Everyone said he was a wayward genius. I never used to believe the bad things I read about Gazza because I loved him so much. Black eyes apart, he was so good to me. I was fortunate enough to have some conversations with him when he was at Everton, living nearby, and he was top-class. On the pitch, he was always at it, slyly digging me in the ribs or trying to intimidate me. Off the pitch, Gazza was such a nice fella. He filled me with confidence. He praised bits of my game, and always asked me how things were going. I thought, 'Let me talk about you! I want to hear about Italia 90, Lazio, Spurs, everything!' When I was younger, Gazza's was the only autograph I craved. You see, Gazza lived the life I wanted: fame, fortune and England.

6
England Calling

England obsessed me from my earliest days. Running around Ironside in my Gazza shirt, weaving past Huyton lads and sticking the ball between two dustbins, I imagined it was the winning goal in the World Cup final. I pictured all the England fans leaping up, punching the air and screaming my name. 'Gerrard, Gerrard!' I saw myself mobbed by my England team-mates, celebrating the goal that brought the World Cup home. Pulling on the white shirt. Looking down and seeing the Three Lions crest over your heart. Walking out into a packed stadium, knowing the eyes of the country are on you. The adrenalin, the noise, the sweat, the glory. All of it. I wanted it big-style.

Countless obstacles were strewn across my path to senior international recognition. I had to fight my way to the top. First up, those idiots at Lilleshall ignored me at U-15 level. England realized their mistake when I tore into the National School at Melwood. The season after that, when the England get-togethers started, I was straight in (no apology, though). I was soon involved with England U-16s, coming off the bench in a 4–0 rout of Denmark on 3 February 1996. That was me finally going, on the road to the England first team.

I will never forget my first U-16 start, seventeen days after that thrashing of Denmark. The stage was Lilleshall, of all places. The opposition, the Republic of Ireland, a good team with future stars like Richard Dunne, a tough defender with Man City, and Stephen McPhail, who made his name at Leeds United. England put out a tidy XI as well. Wes Brown and Michael Ball stood out in defence. My area, midfield, quickly became a battle zone against the Irish. I was up against McPhail, who was streets ahead of me. This was during my teenage years when I started growing fast. I needed to because I was really too small to compete in such daunting midfields. Apart from scoring England's first, I was awful. McPhail was a class apart. At least we won 2–1, with Phil Jevons netting the second. My first England start was a winning one. I was up and running.

I watched Euro 96 at home on the Bluebell Estate, cheering on Gazza, Alan Shearer and Teddy Sheringham. Wembley looked and sounded fantastic, packed with people waving banners and singing 'Football's Coming Home'. England treated the fans to some fabulous football, particularly in the 4–1 defeat of Holland. I so wanted to be there. I had just turned sixteen and I was desperate to reach the top.

I carried on up through the England age-groups, growing physically and developing technically. Come France 98, I sat transfixed in front of the TV at Ironside as my mate Michael took on the world. Go on, Michael! Jesus, what a sight that was. A tireless trainer and relentlessly ambitious, Michael deserved his shot at World Cup glory. There had been a lot of speculation that Glenn Hoddle, the then England manager, might take Michael to France. His name was all over the press and on the telly. I was really buzzing for Michael to go. In April, I talked to him about his chances of getting the nod from Hoddle. 'That's my aim,' Michael told me. 'I would love to go.' Michael was on the fringe of a few squads. Then he scored against Morocco in Casablanca in one of the warm-up games. Suddenly, everyone talked about him starting. I so wanted him to be picked. Not only because he was a mate, but also because of what it meant for me. I played with Michael for so many years. If he was in with the England big boys, I must have a chance. 'Look how well Michael is doing,' Dad said as we sat on the sofa glued to France 98. 'It might be you the next World Cup.'

Those match nights were magical, extra special when Michael started, against Colombia and, famously, Argentina. I grabbed a bite of dinner and jumped on the sofa in front of the telly. I couldn't wait for kick-off, I was that excited. The Argentina game in St-Etienne was awesome. When Michael picked the ball up and began accelerating towards Carlos Roa's goal, pandemonium broke out in our front room. 'Trouble!' I shouted. 'If Michael gets you one-on-one with space behind you, you're history,' added Dad, almost as a warning to the Argentina defenders. Jose Chamot and Roberto Ayala had no chance. Too slow, too late. Michael was off and past them, racing into the history books and the hearts of a nation. I leapt up and down, screaming my head off, hugging Dad and Paul. I almost went hoarse shouting Michael's name. Yes! Get in! Brilliant, Michael!

When the TV replayed the move, Dad said, 'Paul Scholes looks like he is about to nick it just before Michael shoots.'

'No chance,' I replied. 'There's absolutely no chance in the whole wide world that Michael was going to leave that ball.'

I fell back in my seat and just tried to imagine how Michael's world was going to change. I looked across at Dad, who still had this massive smile on his face. He liked and respected Michael. Everyone did. 'What has Michael just done there?' I exclaimed. The camera focused on Michael, but he was concentrating on the game, as if he hadn't just struck one of the greatest goals in the history of football. 'That's him finished!' I laughed. 'That's his life changed. It's over for him now. He won't be able to do nothing. Imagine what it will be like when he comes back. It will take him days to get out of the airport there will be so many press and fans there.' I was so happy for my mate.

Michael's success made me believe even more I could make it. My own journey towards the England shirt I craved was assisted by Howard Wilkinson. During his time as technical director of the Football Association, Wilkinson looked after the U-18s and the U-21s and picked me regularly for both. He had a certain reputation. I knew that. Wilkinson was often slated for some of his management skills. True, he was a bit long-winded in team-talks. We wondered occasionally what the hell he was going on about. He often sounded like a school teacher addressing very young children. Howard also called team meetings when he didn't really need them. I don't care. People can snipe at Wilkinson if they want, but he was good to me and knew his football. I liked Wilkinson because he liked me. He always spoke well of me, always included me in his squads, always suggested things to improve my game. He even made me captain of England U-18s – a massive honour. All my family were so proud. We will always thank Howard for that. When I heard he got the U-21 job, I had half an idea that sooner or later the call would come for me to step up.

Throughout 1999 I was steadily making a name for myself in Liverpool's first team. One day in the late summer, a letter arrived from the FA. Finally calming my shaking hands, I ripped open the envelope. Inside were instructions to report for U-21 duty against Luxembourg on 3 September. Another rung up the ladder! Wilkinson must really have rated me because he started me in midfield. I repaid his faith by scoring after twelve minutes. We won 5–0, and there was a real buzz about the team.

Every English player knew the new season ended with Euro 2000. Every ambitious young player wanted to force himself into the thoughts of Kevin Keegan, the England manager. Whenever Keegan took his seat in the directors' box of a Premiership ground, all the English players on the pitch were aware of his presence, and determined to parade their abilities. I certainly felt under scrutiny. When Liverpool beat Coventry City 2–0 a week before Christmas, Keegan was there, watching me. When the U-21s then saw off Denmark, Keegan was there again, appraising me. I knew that. Howard marked my card. 'Do well and Kevin may call you up,' he told me. I never stopped running against Denmark.

I impressed for Liverpool in 1999/2000, scoring against Sheffield Wednesday and filling in all over the place. Right-back, left-back, right midfield, central midfield – no problem. Every challenge made me a better player. When Liverpool beat Leeds United 3–1 on 5 February, I bust my lungs stifling Harry Kewell, a real tricky winger. A week later I set up Titi Camara's winner at Highbury – a huge result for Liverpool. Arsenal are a class side, and Freddie Ljungberg almost scored. He rounded our keeper, Sander Westerveld, but I managed to get a tackle in to stop him. Victory came at a cost for me: I damaged my groin and had to walk off for some ice treatment.

About a week after that, Dad called. He could barely speak he was so excited. 'Get on to Steve Heighway and Gérard Houllier quick,' he said. 'They have something to tell you.'

What the hell was going on? I rang Steve immediately. He had big news. 'Kevin Keegan wants you to go down to England to train with the squad before the game with Argentina,' Steve said. I couldn't believe my ears. Training with England? Gérard confirmed the news. England wanted me! 'Now, Steven, you have not been named in the squad, but you will be working with them,' warned Gérard. Fuck that. I felt I was in the squad. This was my chance. England! I was going to have a right go in training and convince Keegan to pick me for the friendly against Argentina on 23 February. Wembley. Full house. Argentina. Brilliant! Michael made his name against them, so why not me? Officially in the squad or not, I wasn't going down to England's base at Bisham Abbey just to train. I meant business.

The FA contacted Liverpool and offered to chauffeur me down to the team hotel at Burnham Beeches, a few miles from Bisham. But Dad lent me his Honda and I made my own way south because I was that nervous. I was shitting myself big-time on the journey. At one point I thought there was something wrong with the car. I almost got out to check the noise until I realized it was me rattling. Getting so close to something I wanted so much filled me with self-doubt. Was I good enough? Shit. Let's turn round. Get back to Liverpool. Steve Heighway can call Keegan. Apologize. Gerrard's too nervous. Not ready. That would save me the embarrassment of looking a dick in training. But I kept going. I had to conquer my insecurity, kill the panic attack. Go on. Drive through the gates of Burnham Beeches. Park the Honda. Don't hit the smart cars. Into reception. Up to your room.

Made it. Thank God. I sat on the edge of the bed, knowing I had to report downstairs to Kevin in the dining room. The players were all eating. What do I do? I couldn't face the thought of walking into a room crammed full of my heroes. Alan Shearer, Tony Adams, David Beckham – world-famous names. How could this newcomer at Liverpool stroll calmly into the middle of the England dining room and coolly sit down next to Beckham? Shit. I had another panic attack. I phoned Jamie Redknapp, who was downstairs with the squad. 'Jamie,' I pleaded, 'I'm upstairs shitting myself. Come and get me, please.' Jamie was brilliant. He quietly left the dining hall and sprinted to my room. 'Come on,' Jamie said. 'Keegan wouldn't have called you here unless he really rated you. Let's go.' The other Liverpool lads also came out, so we were all able to walk in together. Without the support of Jamie, Robbie, Macca and Michael, I would have spun on my heels and raced back north, back home, where I felt safe. With my club-mates by my side, I found the strength to enter the dining-room of Burnham Beeches.

Stepping through that doorway was still one of the most intimidating things I have ever done. Looking around the room, I caught my breath. Top players were everywhere; it was an autograph-hunter's paradise. 'What the fuck am I doing here?' I thought. 'Get me back to my room!' Somehow, I negotiated my way to the staff table.

Kevin Keegan looked up and smiled. 'Hi, Steven, welcome to England,' he said. He shook my hand, then stood up.

Bloody hell. He was only going to address the whole fucking room.

'Lads, stop eating and talking for a second,' Keegan said. A host of household names looked up. Keegan pointed at me. 'This is Steven Gerrard. The kid will be training with us. He's a player. Don't be going easy with him because he certainly won't be going easy with you. He is going to be with you full-time very shortly.'

I squirmed from one foot to the other, my face as red as a Liverpool shirt. Fucking shut up now, Kevin. Let them carry on eating. Forget about me. I'm nothing compared to all these superstars. They know of me, but these are heroes who have played in World Cups and had hundreds of career games. And Kevin Keegan was talking to them about me! I thought, 'What the fuck is going on here?' I felt every England player staring at me.

Thankfully, Keegan did stop. I retreated to a table with familiar Liverpool faces and sat down to a fantastic meal, but I couldn't eat. No chance. My stomach had space only for butterflies. Just the thought of food stirred a nausea inside. All I wanted in that England meal-room was an escape route. At least I was surrounded by club-mates. I heard and read about these cliques with England, how the tables were split up along club lines. Being in that meal-room confirmed it was true: tribal rivalry ruled.

The Liverpool boys took me round to all the other tables and introduced me to the rest of the squad. To David Seaman. 'David, this is Stevie.' To Sol Campbell. 'Sol, this is Stevie.' I was in a daze, shaking hands with some of the greatest footballers ever to represent England. God, I was nervous. I have sweated less in games. The last table I visited belonged to Manchester United. Phil Neville, David Beckham, Andy Cole and Paul Scholes looked up and smiled at me. What the hell was going on? Shock-waves ripped through me. These people were supposed to be my enemy. I'm Liverpool. They're United. We don't smile at each other. We snarl. Growing up in Huyton, I was taught to loathe Manchester United, their fans, players, manager, kit-man, mascot, megastore workers – everyone associated with Old Trafford. But almost twenty years of being conditioned to hate Man U went up in smoke that day at Burnham Beeches. There I was, shaking hands with Beckham and Scholes, thinking, 'But they hate me and I hate them.' But they didn't hate me. They were brilliant at putting the new boy at ease. The United lads couldn't have been more welcoming. In fact, they were so nice I began to wonder about all this long-standing hatred.

Before coming down to Burnham, I talked to my mate Boggo about what it would be like seeing the United players. 'I am convinced in training the United lads will have a pop,' I told Boggo. 'They'll wind me up. Kick me. I'd love it to go off. United don't like Scousers, so they might kick me. I'll be on my toes.' I was ready to kick all of them. Scholes, Beckham, the lot. That misconception also disappeared in a flurry of handshakes and smiles. I ran out at Bisham the next day for practice, looking for any sign of an ambush. Surely this would be normal United v. Liverpool, just in a neutral venue? No. Again, the United lads were fantastic. I chatted with Boggo on the phone that night. 'Becks, Scholesy and the rest are top lads,' I said. He was amazed. Liverpool fans slaughter United players without realizing they are human beings. Rivalry clouds their judgement.

I spoke to Gary Neville about the tension between his United and my Liverpool. At the time, Gary was getting some stick for something he was supposed to have said about Liverpool supporters. He got misquoted. What Gary actually said was, 'I have been brought up in my area to hate Scousers.' The same way Liverpool fans are raised to hate Mancs. But the newspapers printed it as 'I Hate Scousers'. I don't know whether Gary was telling me to get the message across! He certainly got on with this Scouser.

Whether United or whoever, all Keegan's players

greeted me really kindly. They treated me as if I were actually in the England squad and was in contention for the Argentina friendly. They couldn't do enough for me. After that first meal, I returned to my room at Burnham and flicked the telly on to kill some time before bed. After ten minutes, there was a knock at the door. Arsenal's huge centre-half Martin Keown stood there. 'I'm rooming next door,' said Martin. 'I know it's difficult with all the times for meals and trainings and meetings. People are always late. If you get stuck for the right time, just phone me. I know you are with the Liverpool lads, but I am next door. Just give me a knock if you're bored.' How good was that? Martin had won Premiership titles, he'd been to big tournaments, yet he was kind enough to help a new boy. I got to know Martin dead well straight away. What a top fella. Honest to God, Martin is probably one of the funniest men I have ever met.

Keegan gave us all an afternoon off, so Martin said, 'Do you fancy London for a few hours, go round the shops?' None of the Liverpool lads were going out, they were staying in with their DVDs, so I was grateful for Martin's offer. 'Do I!' I smiled at him, and rushed off to get some money. I don't know why Martin did it. Maybe he was lonely or bored. Maybe he just took pity on me. Who cares? I was buzzing that I was in London with Martin Keown, England centre-half. I laughed at his jokes, even if they weren't funny. What a character! Because he was so serious, the England lads enjoyed teasing him, knowing he could explode. They loved lighting Martin's fuse and then running for cover. Climbing on the bus for training, one of the players warned me, 'If Martin's head goes, get out of the way! It's very funny, but watch out.' An intense man, Martin treated training like the last minutes of a World Cup final. In one of the practice games at Bisham, he even left a few stud-marks on me. 'Take it easy on him, Martin,' the players shouted. Martin didn't know how to go easy. He trained with studs every day, never mouldies. He had those red Pumas, long studs in, and he wasn't scared to show them. If someone upset Martin, nutmegged him or just wound him up, a red mist would grip him and he'd start topping people. The other players fell about laughing. Real ding-dongs erupted between Martin and Michael Owen – classic centre-half against centre-forward stuff. No love lost. No quarter asked or given. Martin and Michael flew into each other, going to work on each other's legs like tattooists. Michael is as competitive as Martin and is prone to the old red mist as well. It was brilliant watching the two of them piling into each other. A proper dust-up!

I wasn't the only new boy at Bisham that week. Jonathan Woodgate, the young centre-half, had been doing really well at Leeds United so Keegan brought him down as well. Woody was the same as me on the bus going to Bisham, dead nervous, quiet and intimidated. Neither of us could believe we were on the England coach, heading off to practice with all our heroes. Keegan was so good to us on the way to Bisham. He stood up again and sang our praises to the players. Keegan talked about me again. 'Just wait till you see this little prick play!' The Liverpool players shouted back: 'We are fucking with him every day!' When we arrived at Bisham, Keegan treated me and Woody like we were the best two players in the

squad. How unreal was this? I was on the England training field, keeping a ball up in the air with Beckham and
Shearer, and the media were out in force, filming us. I had
a sneaky look to check where the cameras were to let the
lads back home see me! Get on that telly! We then went
into possession straight away, and that's when Keown
began to put it about. I thought there would be some fireworks between the Liverpool and United lads, but it was
physical all round. No chance of anyone taking it easy
with a big match like Argentina coming up. People were
getting right stuck in.

The possession was lightning quick, far quicker than at
Liverpool. I never got anywhere near anyone. The session
was too fast for me. 'Keep the ball, keep on your toes,' I
kept telling myself. 'Concentrate.' I did one turn on
Keegan, dragging the ball away from him, and Keegan
raved about it. So did some of the other players. 'Ahh, did
you see that, lads?' Keegan shouted. 'Steven will be
with you soon. Watch your places.' I laughed. The trick
was nothing special, more luck than judgement. It was
tough, though. The skill and speed levels were nothing I
had experienced before. Whenever I gave the ball away,
everyone screamed, 'Fucking keep it!'

Afterwards, I rang home. 'Dad, I'm nowhere near this
level,' I told him.

'Just keep going, keep trying,' Dad replied.

'I've no chance of playing for England, Dad. I did one
half-decent turn, but it was hard. This lot are different
class. But I'm enjoying it. I can't wait for the next session.'

It was true. I was loving it, even though I felt out of my
depth. I wanted afternoon sessions, anything to get back

out on the training ground. The next day, the training was even more incredible. I couldn't believe some of the things I saw at Bisham that day when we did some crossing and finishing. Shearer in the finishing – my life! Every one, top corner, keeper no chance. Bang, take that. All around, the quality was frightening. This was the first time I had seen Beckham cross a ball close to. 'Fuck me!' I said to Michael. 'How does he do that?' When it was my turn to run in to finish one of Beckham's crosses, it was a goal before I touched it. Honestly. He was that accurate. Beckham puts his crosses in just the right place; it is in fact harder to miss. We had a game after the crossing and finishing, and Beckham was again sensational. After only a couple of hours' training with England it was obvious who the top players were.

A couple of weeks earlier, Michael and I had been at Melwood, chatting away. 'Just wait till you get to Bisham and see how good Paul Scholes is,' said Michael. 'Wait till you see with your own eyes.'

I looked at him. 'Well, I've watched Scholes loads of times and I know he's good.' Michael just smiled. That set me thinking. Michael was going on as if Scholesy was different gravy, streets ahead of everyone else. During that shooting session at Bisham, I realized where Michael was coming from. Scholes was just so sharp, so clever. He was banging goals in from anywhere. Crossing, finishing, volleys, the power in his shots, the dip and movement. 'Fucking hellfire,' I said to Michael. 'How do I get to this level?' The Man United players were just brilliant. I swear it. 'Just watch the United boys,' Keegan told me. 'Just watch the way they are around the place and in training.

Learn off them.' The United lads gave a master-class. Bisham was heaving with top players, like Shearer, but Beckham and Scholes seemed to be just on a different level.

Back at Burnham after our first session, I counted down the hours and minutes until we returned to Bisham. I was so wired into training that I stupidly ignored a few little niggles in my back. On the bus going back to Burnham, I felt it stiffen a touch. If I had been at Liverpool, I would have mentioned it to the physios. But I was that scared to go to England's physios and tell them, 'Look, my back's sore.' The main England physio, Gary Lewin, is a top guy, but I just couldn't admit my problem, and there was no way I would have told Keegan. 'Fuck it,' I said to myself. 'I'll just take a painkiller when I get back to the room.' I took two. Before the second practice, I gulped down another one.

I survived that second session, but the pain deepened. I called Dad.

'What shall I do?' I asked him.

'Just make them aware of it,' he replied.

'Dad, I can't, because they might send me home.'

I sat in my room, in tears of frustration. I had to make a decision. Eventually, I went in to see Lewin. He called Kevin down to the medical room and explained the situation. 'Listen, Steven,' said Keegan. 'We have got to be careful with you because of Liverpool. If we let you continue, it gets worse, and you miss games, we would get into trouble with Liverpool. Let the physio and doctor have a look, miss the session, and we'll see how you are.' Keegan then went off and phoned Gérard Houllier.

'Get him back here,' said Gérard.

Keegan came to my room and broke the news. My England dream was on hold. 'Listen, I am under strict orders to get you back to Anfield,' Keegan said. 'But you have done well. Keep doing what you are doing. I will be watching you. Hopefully, next time when you come back it will be as a proper squad member.'

When Keegan left the room, I collapsed in tears. A sense of devastation overwhelmed me. I returned to Anfield with a sore back and a heavy heart and they immediately sent me off for a scan. My back really troubled me from then on. Now, if I feel something in training, I go straight off. I don't take risks. Missing Argentina was frustrating, but the media have always made too much of my injuries. Press speculation about my fitness never helped me at all. My injuries have never been career-threatening, as some people wrote.

The problem having eased temporarily, I launched myself back into games. England still occupied my thoughts: the door remained open to Euro 2000. The biggest U-21 international that season was the Euro play-off against Yugoslavia on 29 March, in Barcelona. This was serious stuff, with qualification for the European U-21 Championship at stake. England had to win. The papers were full of talk about the tie. Everyone speculated over who would be in Wilkinson's party, as if it were the senior squad. I have never needed any additional moti-vation to work my bollocks off for Liverpool, but I really bust a gut in the build-up to the Yugoslavia game. I was desperate to be selected. For me, it offered a short-cut to the seniors. That was my ambition: climbing the ladder as fast as possible. Keegan announced he would be watching the Barcelona game closely for any likely young lads to take to the big show in Holland and Belgium that summer. Some incentive.

Good as gold, Wilkinson picked me in the squad. When the list of names came through the post, I thought, 'This is a proper U-21 squad.' Players like Rio Ferdinand and Jamie Carragher had racked up loads of Premiership games. The squad was packed with names who wouldn't have looked out of place in Keegan's full squad. All of us youngsters who flew out to Spain felt this was a ninety-minute audition for Euro 2000. After settling into our Barcelona hotel, we engaged in a final training session that was sharp and full-on. Everyone was up for this. And the quality of the players there was frightening. Sitting down for dinner that night at a table with Lee Hendrie, Kieron Dyer, Frank Lampard and Ferdinand, I was too scared to talk. These lads were serious players. I felt an apprentice in comparison. My experience of top-level football ran to a few first-team outings for Liverpool and a handful of U-21 matches. I knew my place. Be seen and not heard. 'Just shut up and listen to the banter, new boy,' I told myself. I was intimidated by confident West Ham lads like Lampard and Ferdinand. I didn't really mix with anyone except Carra. My shyness was compounded by the U-21s being really cliquey. Club-mates stuck together. I just wanted to train and get back to my room dead sharp.

The mood mellowed a bit as the trip went on. My nerves began to disappear. I became increasingly involved in the banter, while guarding against appearing cocky. In my heart, I still didn't feel I belonged with England. I knew I had done well against Luxembourg and scored, and I'd played in U-21 wins against Poland and Denmark, but a play-off against Yugoslavia was a proper game. Everyone was talking about it. I never expected to start. So I was shocked when Wilkinson told us the team after dinner. My name was among the eleven chosen ones.

As the meeting broke up, Howard sat me down for a quick chat, basically to mark my card. 'Tomorrow is a very important game for you,' he told me. 'The top people are going to be studying you. This is the game to perform in. Kevin Keegan is particularly looking to see how you do. He's watched you before. There's a possible place up for grabs in the Euro 2000 squad. Go get it, Steven.'

Music to my ears! A ticket to Belgium and Holland!

Wilkinson hadn't finished. 'If you do well tomorrow, don't think that's it,' he continued. 'In the Premiership games after this, there will be people watching you every game – England scouts, probably Kevin himself. Always have it in the back of your mind you are being watched, not just by the people at Liverpool but also the FA. So make sure you perform.'

I walked back to my room, lay on the bed and tried to get my head around the size of the challenge hurtling towards me. My mobile rang. It was Dad. As usual, he called to wish me good luck and to remind me to seize my chance.

'I'm starting tomorrow, Dad,' I told him.

'Well, Steven, this really is the game you've got to deliver in.'

It sounded like a warning. The stakes were that high. Sky's cameras would be rolling live. Keegan would be taking notes and looking for names. Could I handle the pressure? But then I remembered a saying Dad loved to tell me: 'Big players come into their own in big games.' And I wanted the big time.

I smiled to myself. I couldn't wait to get to the stadium.

I almost ran there the moment morning dawned. The game was held next door to Camp Nou, at Barcelona's reserve-team ground. Wilkinson fielded a strong team, lining up 3–5–2 in front of Richard Wright. At that time, Wright was doing brilliantly for Ipswich Town and everyone was raving about him. He was the hottest young keeper around. Everyone predicted he would be David Seaman's successor for England. When I travelled down from Liverpool for U-21 get-togethers, Carra always went on about how naturally brilliant Wright was. Great shotstopper, terrific anticipation. Wright's career has gone a bit downhill since, but he was the main boy about then.

Glancing around the dressing-room, I was thrilled by the wall-to-wall talent. Defenders of the quality of Carra and Rio were slipping their shin-pads on, ready for battle. Juggling a ball in one corner was Kieron Dyer, buzzing with energy; he was an amazing performer in training out there. Midfield comprised me, Lampard and Lee Hendrie. We all knew how good Lampard was. Everyone had seen him shine for West Ham. And Hendrie was probably the best young midfielder around at the time. In training, he was the busiest, the cleverest, a good kid as well. Up front, Andy Campbell was very quick. I thought he might play at a higher level, but things never really worked out for him at Middlesbrough. We also had Emile Heskey, who copped a shit-load of racist abuse off the sick Yugoslav fans. What morons. Their monkey chants just made us doubly determined to stick it to their team. And we did them good and proper. We won 3–0, and the game went brilliantly for me. Dad told me later that on Sky, Ray Wilkins said I played really well, which was a great compliment coming from a former England midfielder. The press lads all gave me decent write-ups, too. My career started moving quicker after that game.

Keegan watched me more and more. One day, in the middle of May, I was walking through Liverpool city centre with Dad when my mobile went. 'Private Number' came up on the screen. I pressed the green answer button.

'Steven? It's Kevin Keegan,' came a voice.

I didn't believe him. 'Yeah,' I replied, 'good one, whatever. Go on then.'

I was convinced it was mates stitching me up. Probably Boggo. But the bloke on the line kept talking, and I got a bit worried. Oh my God, if it's not Keegan, they have got his accent in the bag, absolutely spot-on. How do I play this? Christ knows!

'I am calling you up for the game against Ukraine,' the voice said.

It was possible. I had been playing well for Liverpool, and I remembered the last words Kevin said to me: 'It won't be long before you are in the full squad.' So I decided to go with the flow – act normal; don't let on any suspicions – even if I eventually had the piss taken out of me. Dad looked at me, wondering what the hell was going on. I walked away. If it was a wind-up, I didn't want him witnessing my embarrassment.

Two minutes into the conversation I was sure it was

Keegan. It couldn't be a hoax. This bloke knew too much stuff about the squad and about the FA staff who organize the travel. It had to be Kevin. But even when the caller signed off with a cheery 'see you at Bisham', I still wasn't 100 per cent certain. Fortunately, a couple of hours later someone from Melwood phoned to say they had an FA fax confirming I was in the squad. Until then, I had been waiting for a mate to ring, laughing. 'Ha, ha, it was a wind-up!' The next day, I got a text off the England team administrator, Michele Farrer, giving me details about meeting up. Keegan then announced the squad officially. That phone call had been a call-up, not a wind-up.

Stories stating I would start against Ukraine on 31 May kept appearing in the newspapers. 'Don't believe none of that,' Dad urged. 'Just keep doing what you are doing in training. Until you're told, keep playing for a starting place.' On the Monday, two days before the game, Keegan pulled me during training at Bisham. We were doing some shape work, tactical pattern-of-play stuff. 'Come Wednesday, don't do that, do this,' said Keegan, indicating a position he wanted me to keep. His words stopped me in my tracks. Had Keegan just dropped a big hint there that I might be involved? I pretended I never heard it. Me? Starting for England? The possibility still seemed unreal.

I phoned Dad the moment I got back to my room at Burnham. 'I might be playing some part, Dad, for England!' I said. 'The gaffer talked me through a move he wanted me to do on Wednesday!'

Dad got a bit buzzing, but then played it down. 'Take no notice of it. Keegan might just have slipped up, or not meant it.'

So I got on with training the next day, giving my all.

Distractions blew into Burnham on the Tuesday. It was my twentieth birthday, and I certainly got given the special treatment by the England lads. The day started off nicely. Burnham's chef did a cake. I got up and blew the candles out as all the lads shouted 'Speech, speech!' I went red and sat back down sharpish. It was all really friendly. Afterwards, we all went off to Bisham. With England, you leave your doors open. We have the hotel to ourselves, so no problem. No-one would break in. So I just wandered out of my room and didn't think twice about locking the door. When I came back from training, I almost died. My room had been trashed good and proper. It looked as if a hundred kids had enjoyed a wild birthday party in there. Toothpaste was everywhere, over the mirror, my bed, the table. 'Happy birthday – you soft-arse' was smeared in toothpaste on the wall. When I read that, I began to detect the mischievous hand of Robbie Fowler and Michael Owen.

My bag had gone, too. Shit, this was serious. I ran into the bathroom and found it lying empty on the floor. The entire contents – clothes, kit, everything – had been tipped into the bath and the taps turned on. The bath was over-flowing. My blood boiled. I leant down and picked my trainers out of the bath – sodden through. If I had tossed them on the bathroom scales, they would have touched four stone each. I couldn't believe it. Brand fucking new as well. I wanted to look the part coming down to England so I went to a top clothes shop and bought some really good gear – trainers, shirts, trousers, a whole classy wardrobe. All of it was now soaking or ruined. 'You big, lanky, stupid tit,' I screamed at myself. What have I done leaving that door open? Happy fucking birthday. Must be Fowler.

Sadly, no punishment was possible. I couldn't report to Kevin Keegan that a so-called team-mate unleashed chaos and a ton of Colgate in my room. I cleaned it up myself. No choice. The trainers went out on the window ledge, almost breaking it. They had dried out by the time we went home two days later! I wiped the floor, removed all traces of toothpaste with a towel, and hung up my dripping clothes above the bath. Lunch was about to be served so I had to hurry. I realized I had nothing to wear, apart from the training kit I stood up in. Sod it. It would have to do. If I smelled, the others deserved it. But I had nothing on my feet. I had taken my boots off downstairs and walked up in my socks. Embarrassed, I picked up the phone and rang the England kit-man. I had only met him once or twice before in my life. I was terrified. 'Listen, I have nothing to wear on my feet,' I explained. 'You'll understand when you come and have a look at my room.' He came up, gave me a pair of Umbro flip-flops, and walked off down the corridor trying to suppress his laughter.

I dashed down to lunch, turning up late because of the salvage operation. As I walked into the meal-room, I was sick. Gutted. 'Go along with the banter,' I told myself. 'Don't look as if you have the hump.' I strolled into lunch and looked around to see if I could work out the offender. Bloody Sherlock Holmes wouldn't have known. All the players looked up from their meals, nodded at me, and then carried on eating as if nothing had happened. I was livid inside, furious they were all secretly laughing at me. I was late, and still in my sweaty training kit, so they bloody well knew what was up. No-one let on, though. I just encountered a sea of straight faces. More than one had to be involved in the actual crime. Given the mess they made, there was definitely a firm at work in there.

Fowler had to be guilty. It was a classic Fowler stunt. If I were a betting man, I would have put good money on Fowler as the mastermind and Steve McManaman as chief accomplice. When news got out that something had happened to my special trainers, Fowler was asked by the press whether he was responsible. The papers reported that Fowler was the prime suspect but that the only offence on his charge-sheet was cutting the laces on my trainers. Fucking hell! And the rest! They should have seen my room! Anyway, Fowler swore on his daughters' lives that it wasn't him. But he never had any daughters at the time! It was definitely him, and not just the trainers. My wrecked room was a Robbie Fowler production. One day, his conscience will get to him and he will confess.

That afternoon, I climbed aboard the bus to training, stood at the front and looked down the aisle. 'Anyone owning up for this room then?' I asked. Silence. The players carried on reading their papers, or jabbering on their phones. They pretended they never heard me. I sat down next to Shearer. 'Alan, do you know anything about it?' I enquired. He looked at me dismissively. I could read his mind thinking, 'Shut up, tit. As if I am going to tell you that. Dickhead. Go away.' Shearer never gives anything away. He's got a poker face. He definitely knew something about it though. They all did. Everyone on that coach –

guilty. I should have cornered Fowler. But I couldn't. I was just a puppet in the squad then. To this day, I still don't know for sure who ruined my room. I swear I want someone to own up for it, though, because they absolutely destroyed my clothes. My lovely trainers never recovered. They had a sad burial in the garbage. I will never forgive Fowler!

My twentieth birthday was certainly memorable. After training, Keegan tapped me on the shoulder and said, 'Are you looking forward to tomorrow night?'

'Yeah, I can't wait.'

He then looked me in the eye and said, 'You're starting.'

I almost fainted! These were the words I had dreamed of hearing. Starting! For England!

'Thanks, boss, I won't let you down.'

Keegan went off to announce the news to the media. They immediately demanded to see me in the big press tent outside Burnham. Interest was massive in the England new boy. I couldn't escape. I was terrified. I nearly had to put a nappy on to do that interview. We spoke to journalists at Liverpool, but usually local guys we knew and trusted, or a few guys from the national newspapers whom the club felt would not turn us over. England was a different ball-game. A whole media army had set up camp in the grounds of Burnham Beeches. As I went through hotel reception, a few of the England lads shouted, 'Good luck.' Christ, that tightened the knot in my stomach even more. I felt like a condemned man as I walked towards the press marquee. I was rattling. Interviews have always scared the shit out of me. Even now, as an established player, I am still not 100 per cent comfy talking to the media. Basically, I just don't like speaking to people I hardly know. Back then, I was even more tongue-tied.

Burnham was torture that day. The FA's press officer, Adrian Bevington, told me not to worry as we headed towards the battery of cameras, microphones and note-books. Don't worry? A bit fucking late! 'They'll go easy on you,' said Adrian. It was like being led to the wolves and told to relax because they had already eaten once today. Jesus, I couldn't believe how many journalists were waiting for me. More than a hundred, I guess, although I didn't really want to look up and count properly. I sat down and tried to handle the questions as best I could.

'What are your strengths?' someone asked.

'In what position?' I replied.

Everyone there thought that showed how confident I was, but I was just being factual. Keegan spoke as well, and told the journalists I wasn't arrogant. 'His confidence comes from his ability,' he said. I was full of gratitude to Kevin for being close by in the tent and taking some of the pressure off me. Facing the press was not an experience I enjoyed.

I managed finally to slip out but immediately ran into another ambush, this time by photographers. They swarmed around me, clicking away. Eventually, Bevington imposed some order and me and Keegan posed for a picture with an England cap. My first cap. In fact, I learned later that it had been borrowed for the photo-shoot. The cap actually belonged to Paul Madeley, the old England all-rounder from the seventies. In a way, wearing something of Madeley's was really appropriate. I just wanted to show everyone, and particularly Kevin, that I could do a job anywhere for England.

I couldn't wait for the game to start. All the fannying about and official stuff in the build-up to an international pissed me off. I was relieved to get back from the media village. I had only been out of my room for ten minutes but I had ten missed calls and a load of text messages. The word was out. I was starting. Sorting out tickets for family and friends was a nightmare. So many people wanted to come to Wembley. It broke me up having to tell a few I couldn't get them tickets. 'Hopefully, there will be another time,' I said, crossing my fingers. I didn't want to go over the top, promising there would be another game. And I was too unsure of myself to ask the FA girls for more tickets. 'Who does he think he is, asking that amount?' I could imagine them saying. 'He hasn't even played a bloody game yet, cheeky sod.' So I just took the complimentary tickets made available by the FA and those I was able to buy. Some players do trade, but again, I was too scared to badger anyone for tickets. Newcomers can't walk up to England stars and demand, 'Are you using your spares?'

Ukraine's visit was a night match, so the lads killed time before kick-off sleeping in their rooms at Burnham. That shocked me. How could players calmly kip hours before going into battle for England? I sat in my room, rattling, on the phone, trying to pass the time away. Eventually we were on the coach to Wembley, people shouting messages of good luck and sticking their thumbs up as we passed. Christ, this was just a friendly. Just imagine the atmosphere for a full-on World Cup tie. Kick-off was more than

The Future is Red I'm staying with Liverpool.

Above, **Digging for victory** Here I am, aged two and a half, playing with my brother Paul, five.

Left, **First team bib** me at six months.

Below, **Blond ambition** I loved being in Paul's company.

Smart lad Me in my school uniform, aged seven.

Opposite page from the top,

In the middle of it Dave Shannon (*back left*) was there from the beginning, I'm right at the centre of the middle row. Frank Skelly from the Academy is on the far right.

On the ball training at Melwood was a dream come true.

Raising the bar Dave Shannon made me want to be the best.

Surrounded by class Steve Heighway (*on the left*) with Michael Owen, Dave Shannon (*with me in the middle*) and Hughie McAuley (*on the right*) took care of the Melwood lads.

That winning feeling When the older lads were winning Dave Shannon (*left*) and Hughie McAuley (*right*) let me and Michael Owen soak up the atmosphere.

Young dreams Me and Michael Owen, looking good in our England Under-15 blazers.

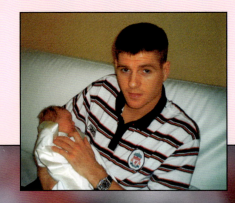

Left, **Holding role** Here's me cradling Lilly-Ella on the day she was born.

My Two Loves, Family and Liverpool Lilly-Ella meets the Anfield crowd in 2004.

Home fixture my mum loves looking after my girls.

Next generation My brother Paul's boy Louie was born last year.

Beautiful my life changed when Lilly-Ella was born.

Sweet It was a wonderful moment when Lexie was born.

Above, **Three lionesses** Alex Curran has changed my world, settling me down and giving me two beautiful daughters.

Right, **Side By Side** Alex and the girls make me so proud.

Below, **In Safe Hands** Having my family close by during the World Cup was a real help.

two hours away, but the fans were flooding into Wembley, tens of thousands of them. Groups of blokes. Fathers and sons. All chanting 'England!' Young boys, eyes shining in anticipation, had their faces painted with the flag of St George. Their exhilaration intensified my own excitement. It was only Ukraine, only a friendly, but the sense of expectation was incredible. England have always mattered to me, and as I looked through the coach window at all the fans, I began to realize how much the England team meant to the nation. These people loved England with a passion. I resolved then never, ever to let them down.

'Just wait till you get in the dressing-room,' Michael told me with a smile a week earlier. 'You'll love it. It's awesome. Just watch everyone – and listen.' Michael's words didn't make much sense at the time, but they rang loud and true when I crossed the threshold into the home dressing-room at Wembley. Nothing could have prepared me for the atmosphere inside. Of course, I had experienced the Liverpool dressing-room where determination hung in the air, an emotion so real you could almost stretch out a hand and touch it. But with England, Jesus Christ, I couldn't believe the atmosphere. The mood stepped up big-time over Anfield. What a special place! Some of Keegan's players, like Sol Campbell, sat there quietly, undergoing familiar pre-match routines that have served them so well for so long. Others, like Robbie and Macca, were chatting and laughing, behaving as if it were a normal game at Liverpool. For a while it was pretty restrained, just a few words from Keegan and his assistants Derek Fazackerley and Arthur Cox. But as kick-off approached, the players talked louder and louder, the mood rising to fever pitch. Battle-cries began. Each player was made to feel that nothing else in his life would ever matter as much as this. Club affiliations and expectations were irrelevant. Shout after shout. This is England. Our country. Millions watching. Don't let them down. Don't miss a tackle. Don't give the ball away. Every eye is on us. Fucking deliver.

The noise was unbelievable. In the middle of the dressing-room stood Alan Shearer and Tony Adams, whipping up the storm. Changing-rooms are always loud, but Adams and Shearer cranked the volume up to a different level. Shearer was getting everyone going, standing there like a warrior preparing for combat, screaming at his fellow soldiers. Adams was going around the room bawling at players individually. He fixed each of us with a stare and then spat one question in our faces: 'Are you fucking ready for this?' Jesus, hellfire. He got closer to me, and soon he stood in front of me. 'And are you fucking ready?' A coward would have felt his blood run cold. I returned his gaze, unflinching. 'You bet I'm fucking well ready.' And I was. I felt ready for anything. Satisfied, Adams moved on. Behind him, Shearer barked out orders. 'Get stuck in. Don't let them settle.' Keegan had a few words, but the real rallying calls came from Shearer and Adams. It was a shock to me. I was so hyped up I almost couldn't tie my laces. Fucking let me at Ukraine. Where are they? Bring it on.

Ukraine must have heard us. Christ alive, the racket coming out of the England dressing-room was so loud it could have been heard in Kiev, let alone down the corridor. Even Gareth Southgate, such a calm, cultured individual by day, stirred up the players, sending the decibel level rocketing higher. My admiration for senior pros like Southgate, Adams and Shearer doubled that day. I knew they were great players, but this showed me why they ascended to the pinnacle of their trade. Commitment. Will to win. Teamwork. Men like Adams, Shearer and Southgate boasted all these important qualities. Leaders all. I idolized them even more than before. Martin Keown didn't play that night but he was another who was incredibly aggressive in the dressing-room, yet constructive with it.

The referee, Lubos Michel, rang the bell to call us to the tunnel. Walking up the Wembley tunnel was special. I saw the light at the end, heard the crowd going crazy, and was almost knocked over by the wall of noise as I emerged onto the pitch. Wembley is the best place I have ever played at. It's the history that makes it unique. I know they've rebuilt the stadium now and demolished landmarks like the Twin Towers, but it will always be Wembley, the Venue of Legends. I have watched so many finals from there on television, and attended many games there. For a lad from Huyton, Wembley was like the promised land. To play at Wembley for Liverpool or England, that is huge. Looking around at the stadium and all the fans, I was just in awe as I lined up for the national anthem. Standing shoulder to shoulder with England team-mates for the first time, I felt so proud singing 'God Save the Queen'. But there was serious work to do.

The moment Michel blew the whistle for the first time, I immediately learned that international football was a real step up from the Premiership. I sat in midfield with Macca and Scholesy pushing on in a 3–5–2. God, I was busy. Technically, the Ukrainians were a lot better than us. Their strikers, Andrei Shevchenko and Sergei Rebrov, were different class, at the time one of the most potent partnerships in the world. When we watched the tapes before the game, Keegan picked them out as Ukraine's dangermen. They kept dropping off Southgate, Adams and Campbell so I had to pick them up. Shevchenko and Rebrov were very good, always keeping the ball, particularly Shevchenko. When I got near them, I was dead wary. They had touches and skills that could make a fool of anyone rushing in. But I did all right, and grew in confidence. Applause followed one move I was involved in. Midway through the first half, I dummied a crossfield pass and set off as Southgate picked up possession. I raced past Yuri Dmitrulin and got the ball back from Gareth. Beckham looked for the ball, so I quickly gave it to him, and sprinted back to cover midfield in case Ukraine counter-attacked. It felt fantastic, charging around Wembley, spraying passes to world stars like Beckham and tackling class operators like Shevchenko. My spirits lifted even higher when we took the lead through Robbie, and then Tony added another.

With nine minutes remaining and victory secured, Keegan replaced me with Kieron Dyer. As I walked off, I glanced back and memorized the image of Shevchenko standing there. I had shared a pitch with the great Shevchenko! It was a dream. Mad. Afterwards, a soggy pile of Ukraine shirts were delivered to our dressing-room. I picked out the one belonging to the fella who used to play right-back for Arsenal, Oleg Luzhny. I gave it to my dad. I sent my shirt to the Ukrainians and kept another. I wanted a personal souvenir of my England debut. It's upstairs at home, on display in a special room.

After the game, I was quickly on the phone, ringing friends and family. I just wanted to talk about the incredible scenes in the dressing-room beforehand. So many positive emotions raced through my mind as I walked out of Wembley that May night. Elation at a 2–0 win. Pride that my parents were watching and listening as the England fans clapped me off. A sense of relief as well. For this was by far the hardest game I had ever experienced.

The match flashed by in a blur. Mentally and physically I was shattered. But deeply happy. I knew I had been in a battle where wits and stamina were tested by the very best. And I survived. I knew Keegan was impressed. Euro 2000 beckoned.

7

Love and Hate in Spa

Homesickness ruined Euro 2000 for me. Uncertainty crept into my mind shortly after we left home, and it grew during a stop-over in Malta, where England played a warm-up match on 3 June. Valletta seemed a beautiful place with lovely weather, but I was not in the mood to take in the scenery. An Achilles problem had flared up, ruling me out of the game and casting doubt over my fitness for the start of Euro 2000. At the time I didn't realize my moodiness was actually homesickness; I thought it was frustration over the Achilles. When I was eventually able to resume training, I brightened up a bit.

I checked into the England hotel near Spa in Belgium eager to get stuck into practice. I was excited at arriving for such a big tournament, no question about that, yet still I couldn't shake off this depression. What the hell was wrong with me? I was living every man's dream, competing against the best players in Europe for a fabulous prize. So many huge names were out there: Thierry Henry, Alessandro del Piero, all of the continent's big guns. Euro 2000 seemed the perfect stage for me to perform on, yet I wanted to fly home to 10 Ironside Road, Huyton, where I felt secure. This tournament was the first occasion I had been away from my family for any amount of time. Holidays and football trips had separated me from my family before, but only for a week. Seven days cut off from my family I could handle; Euro 2000 was different. Even before kicking a ball in anger, England had been away from home for ten days. Five weeks away sounded to me like a prison sentence.

My stomach was a mess. I desperately wanted to get back to Mum, Dad and Paul. To familiar surroundings. Friends. Neighbours. Relatives. I longed for all that again. Watching Mum get the tea. Talking to Dad and Paul. I hated being away. At home, I felt safe. Within those four walls, I could trust everyone and open up. Fuck it, I missed home. Badly. I sat in a chair in my room in Spa, stared out of the window at that dark forest and wanted to scream for help.

At first, I couldn't bring myself to tell Mum and Dad when I rang home every evening. Embarrassment stopped me. 'Oh yeah, everything's fine, it's brilliant out here,' I would say. And it should have been. I was a professional footballer earning good money and privileged enough to represent my country. I was surrounded by good guys in the squad, players I could share a laugh and a joke with, friends like Michael Owen whom I had known for more than ten years. Kevin Keegan was always brilliant with me. Kevin had taken a gamble in picking a young, untried midfielder for Euro 2000. I was lucky. Everyone back in England would have jumped at the chance to swap places.

Homesick? Fucking grow up. Get a grip. But I just couldn't shake the feeling.

One night, I confessed all to Mum. 'I don't want to be here,' I told her. 'I just want to be home with you. I get feelings in my stomach. I can't sleep. I want to be home.'

Mum and Dad were obviously concerned. They care so deeply for me and Paul. But they didn't want me to do anything rash and ruin all I had worked for. Dad came on the line. 'Steven, you are missing nothing here,' he said. 'If you come back for a day or two, you would want to go to Spa. Enjoy it.'

'I am enjoying it, Dad. I'm loving it. I want to be here, but I also want to come home. I don't know how long for, but I want to come home.'

'Do you want to mention it to the manager?' Dad asked.

'No,' I replied firmly. How could I? After one cap, I could hardly go knocking at Kevin's door, saying, 'Listen, boss, I'm homesick.' He might bounce me out for good. Euro 2000 had not even officially started, so I was worried Kevin would replace me with a stand-by player. Persevering was the only answer, and focusing on the tournament.

Homesickness is a part of me that will never go away. I still feel homesick at times. I endured a bad couple of days at Euro 2004 in Portugal. I'm prone to the blues when I travel. I am a home person. Fact. If I wasn't a footballer I wouldn't go away from home for two months. I hate being on my own. Hate it. Even to this day, I loathe rooming on my own with England. If my family were there in my hotel room, I could be away for as long as ever. Put me on my own, and I can't. I go mad. It's boredom. Even if I am in the house on my own, after an hour I need to get on the phone. I can't come home, sit around all day on my own and not speak to anyone. I love company. Love it. Especially family.

It's strange, I know. At tournaments, two emotions run through me: happiness and sadness. Even with the shadow of homesickness at Euro 2000, I was still buzzing. Friends called, told me how lucky I was, how made up they were to see me selected for England. For all my gloom, I was still delighted to be in Spa. I was experiencing a world most people aspired to.

Before we left England, the sense of excitement gripping the country was inescapable. Flags fluttered outside houses and in the back of vans. England stickers appeared everywhere. Newspapers were bursting with page after page of build-up coverage. I was desperate to be part of it. When Keegan named his final squad shortly after the Ukraine game on 31 May, I was blown apart to be included. I thought I had missed too many games. No chance, surely? Yet there was Keegan, reading out my name among real stars such as Alan Shearer, David Beckham, Tony Adams and Paul Scholes. After only eighty-one minutes on the pitch for England, I was off to the European Championship in Holland and Belgium!

For all my problems, Spa was good. Kevin and the FA made sure we had plenty to occupy ourselves with back at the hotel: there were pool and table tennis tables, an arcade packed with computer games, pitch and putt, eighteen-hole golf, the works. We lacked for nothing. No expense was spared by the FA. Along with all the entertainment laid on by the FA, the players organized race nights, Macca and Robbie strutting about as if they were at Aintree. A card school also formed, sharpish. Kevin joined in with the players at the back of the bus. One newspaper claimed money was involved, but that was bollocks. Games of three-card brag or hearts for cash took place in certain rooms all over the hotel, but never on the bus. The card schools were always easy to find because of the noise; the banter was top-class. Cards are not my bag, but I loved listening in. Press criticism of Kevin for being involved in the card school was ridiculous. His approachability was good management, not a sign of weakness. He opened up to the players, and they opened up back. I prefer a manager to be sociable rather than stand-offish; a cold, distant coach would have intimidated me. Kevin was straight and honest and always open. He acted like a father figure to me during Euro 2000.

Despite my inhibitions, Kevin's upbeat personality meant everyone mixed around the camp, and I was slowly drawn into the England family. It wasn't cliquey at all. I would be walking down the corridor and Gary Neville would pull me in for a game of pool – Liverpool v. United, but with cues, and smiles. I spoke to all the players during the tournament. Initially, I was wary of Dennis Wise, but during the tournament he too opened up with everyone and was good company. No-one, however famous, was offhand with a newcomer like me.

I was still scared stiff of Shearer. If I came down from my room and England's celebrated captain was at the dinner table, I would avoid sitting by him. I was that intimidated. During my YTS days, all the talk was of 'Shearer, Shearer, Shearer' and 'Fowler, Fowler, Fowler'. Luckily for me, I worked with Robbie at Liverpool so I knew him; I gradually shed my fear in his company. Shearer was different. He was an idol to me when I arrived at Spa. No-one possessed his aura. When he marched into a room, everyone stopped what they were doing and looked. He just has this phenomenal presence. During Euro 2000, I discovered what a terrific bloke he is, as well as a magnificent centre-forward. No airs or graces. No big 'I Am'. A typical Geordie, so welcoming and friendly. He kept telling me to sit down for a chat. Eventually I plucked up enough courage to join the great man. 'Are you all right?' he enquired. 'Are you enjoying the trip? How's Liverpool?' Shearer's public image is of someone hugely competitive on the pitch but quiet off it. On TV, he comes across as a serious person. Meeting him properly surprised me. Shearer was fantastic with me, telling jokes, talking about everything, trying to make me feel at home. Top man.

Hanging out with Shearer, playing pool with Gary Neville, listening to the craic at the card schools – it seemed a perfect way to relax. Spa should have been paradise, but as I said, it felt like hell at times. As well as the homesickness, I just couldn't shake off a feeling of insecurity at being surrounded by superstars. I didn't feel comfortable knocking on the door of a household name who had won titles and cups and saying, 'Do you fancy a game of table tennis?' I waited to be asked.

Thankfully, Aston Villa's Gareth Barry had made the trip too. Each player had his own room, but mine had a shared living-room. None of the other players wanted it so Kevin allocated it to me and Gareth as the new boys. Our bedrooms opened out into this living-room, and it worked out well. Gareth became a really good mate of mine at Euro 2000, and has been ever since. We just clicked. Like me, Gareth was shy and frightened by the big names in the England squad. He too comes across really quiet, but from rooming with him I know his banter is good. I found him excellent company. We played pool and table tennis, and went down to meals together. It was like we were married! Everyone knows what a terrific player Gareth is. I remember him doing some crosses from the left in training and even the senior England players were saying to each other, 'That Gareth Barry is class.' Keegan always checked on the two of us, making sure we were part of the party.

Kevin's assistant, Arthur Cox, was also different class with me. So were three of the other guys Kevin called into the camp, Nigel Spackman, Peter Beardsley and Kenny Swain. These three were good football men who understood how newcomers like me and Gareth could be prey to nerves. Without Nigel, Peter and Kenny, my home-sickness would have been far worse. They weren't really part of the coaching staff, so I could open up to them, almost as if they were friends. When we were in the swimming pool or the Jacuzzi, or playing table tennis, I would confess that I was struggling to settle in. Nigel, Peter and Kenny became my confidants; their support was both immense and genuine. 'Chin up,' Nigel would say. 'How you doing?' Peter would chip in. 'Fancy some pool?' Kenny might add. They were like three brothers protecting me. As well as encouragement, these respected former pros pointed out things in my game I needed to improve. Even in our short time together in Spa, Nigel, Peter and Kenny made me a better person and a better player. I'm forever grateful to them.

Some of Keegan's other staff pissed me off, though – two coaches in particular. To this day, I have no respect for Les Reed or Derek Fazackerley. I was a young lad who had never been away from home to play football before. I felt that Reed and Fazackerley could have shown more care and sympathy. They were always pushing me, always telling me to buck up my ideas. They didn't seem to understand that not everyone can climb on board a plane, settle in a strange hotel far from the family they love, and find it easy. In fact, they made me feel like shit. My homesickness worsened whenever I was forced to be in their company.

Somehow, I pushed the homesickness to the back of my mind. I wanted to give myself a chance of looking forward to the games. I was desperate to force my way into England's starting eleven, so I really got stuck into training at Spa. One moment that set everyone talking came when Gareth Southgate and I challenged for a loose ball. Gareth was right in front of me, looking for the ball. He is one of those honest defenders who never goes in to hurt an opponent, and he went in as fairly as he usually does. As I had been in only one or two squads by then, Gareth probably expected me to pull out. No fucking chance. I wanted that ball badly. For me, a tackle in training is the same as a tackle in a game. No pulling out. No half measures. No prisoners.

Bang. As we crunched into each other, this loud noise

reverberated around the Belgian forest. Everyone looked up. All the media were there, filming and watching. Some even ducked for cover. The noise sounded like a gun going off, not a tackle going in. Keegan exaggerated the incident afterwards. 'That showed the commitment of the lads,' he said. 'I thought the ball was going to be taken off on a stretcher!' To me, it was just a tackle. I got on with it straight away, chasing the ball. Privately, though, I smiled to myself. A point had been made. Keegan and the rest of the lads knew there and then that I was up for the challenge of Euro 2000.

Even though I was making my mark in training, and coming out of my shell a tiny bit more every day, I knew I had no chance of starting England's first game, against Portugal in Eindhoven on Monday, 12 June. Paul Ince was the man of steel in our midfield. He had a calf problem for the game against the Ukraine, but now he was fit, and he was well established in the side. Whenever he pulled on the Three Lions, Incey was brilliant, shifting up a gear from his Liverpool form. He was my hero. Incey had the job I craved with Liverpool and England: tackle, kill, pass. My ambitions were obvious to him, but he was still as good as gold with me around the England camp. Even when he moaned at me, I felt he was helping me. Anyway, Incey knew he was top dog. Keegan might have rated me, but he wasn't stupid. He was never going to put an untested kid in against the likes of Luis Figo, Rui Costa and João Pinto ahead of an experienced international like Incey. No chance.

I was on the pitch before kick-off, warming up with the rest of the England squad. PSV's stadium was packed out, but I caught a glimpse of Dad in the crowd. The FA had set up a scheme whereby friends and families could fly in and out; the cost was deducted from our match fees, and it was worth every penny to have Dad's reassuring presence in Eindhoven. Sneaking a look around to check if Keegan or any of the other coaches was looking, I sprinted over dead quick and shook his hand. 'Good luck,' he said, in case I came on. I knew I wouldn't.

I sat on the bench and watched the game. When Scholesy and Macca put England 2–0 up within twenty minutes, I was buzzing. England were up and running, playing like they owned the tournament. And Portugal were no mugs. Their team was full of class names, but England were taking the piss out of them. I was so excited I was up and out of my seat, geeing Macca, Incey and Michael on. Go on! Go on! Do it! Get the third! Kill them off! I could just imagine the scenes in the dressing-room afterwards, everyone laughing and shaking hands and saying we could win Euro 2000. I thought about the coach journey back to Spa, the singing, the card games, the happy banter of a team after a memorable win. I couldn't wait to learn Dad's view before calling home to hear about the celebrations, the parties, people going crazy over England's glory.

Then it all turned sour, like a runner leading a race suddenly encountering quicksand. England began to sink. Suddenly, we couldn't cope with Portugal's clever passing. Figo was outstanding. What a player! What a leader! The Portuguese refused to give up. They simply would not be led that last step to their execution. So they went for us, turning the tables. I couldn't believe my eyes.

It didn't make sense. We had the game sewn up. We had the players. Shearer, Owen, Beckham. The belief was there, but it just went. The confidence drained away as if someone had pulled the plug. Even the great Tony Adams, the rock on which England teams had been built for so long, made a mistake. England's jugular was exposed, and Portugal went for it. Figo and João Pinto made it 2–2 by the break and we knew the second half promised only more torture. The fire had gone out of Keegan's players. On the hour, Nuno Gomes got the winner, and Portugal's celebrations sounded like a nail being driven into a coffin. Nightmare.

Devastated, the players crept back to the dressing-room. Keegan had a little go. 'You cannot give away the lead, you cannot make defending errors,' he said. 'But the tournament's not over. We can get back into it.' Kevin couldn't say too much. No-one could. Everyone was shell-shocked. Players, staff, subs. No-one could absorb any words. Feelings were too raw, minds too clogged with dis-appointment. I sat in the corner, telling myself how glad I was that I hadn't played. That game was a bit too big for me. When a team like Portugal turn on the power, it's like being run over by a juggernaut. The old doubts came racing back: could I cut it at this level? Good players, stars I had watched and admired week in, week out in the Premiership, were sitting there almost motionless. Just empty. Crushed. Figo and João Pinto had sapped all the life from them. As Keegan finished his brief talk, the only sound I could hear was the laboured breathing of the players – almost sighs of regret. My idols just sat there, heads in hands, occasionally raising them to drink some fluids. This wasn't a dressing-room, this was a morgue.

Slowly, life began to pump through those shattered bodies again. Some began to move towards the showers, as if to wash away the trauma. Keegan's coaches started to go round, Cox and Fazackerley having quiet words with each player individually. It was not a time for lectures or long speeches, just a few words about what the player had done right or wrong. Gary Lewin, the physio, tended to strains and bruises. Nothing, though, could heal the wounds Portugal had just inflicted.

Becoming invisible seemed the most diplomatic move. I shrank into the corner. I hated intruding on private grief, although it was my pain as well: I was desperate for England to do well at Euro 2000. Nerves were so exposed that I didn't talk to anyone. I didn't even offer consoling words to my Liverpool friends, for fear of getting my head bitten off. Witnessing the distress and anger in that Eindhoven dressing-room taught me what football was really all about, how much it meant. Up until then, I had just played a few games. Football, to me, was fun. If I lost, yeah it was bad, but I got on with it. But this England embarrassment was proper serious shit. Defeat is sport's version of death.

It was time to leave. We filed out to the coach, re-sembling a line of captured prisoners as we walked, heads down, to the bus. As we hit the road to Spa, Keegan sat down briefly with me and Gareth Barry. 'I hope you are learning from all this,' he said. 'Watch the opposition. Learn. You will both be involved in this tournament somewhere down the line.' 'Yeah,' I thought, 'as if.' I was convinced I was just there to make the numbers up. Still,

I would have loved just one minute on the pitch to say I had played in a major tournament for England. The next game was against Germany, the enemy. I prayed Keegan would give me a chance.

The feeling about England's game with Germany on 17 June in Charleroi was simple: do or die. Our loss to Portugal meant the lads were up for the match even more. All around the hotel, groups of players met and talked about our date with destiny. 'We need to win this one or we're history' was the gist of the conversations. The pressure was on big-time. Tension checked in to our hotel. Players and staff became edgy. Everyone knew what was riding on this: our place in Euro 2000, our reputations even. The whole country would be thrown into depression if we lost to Germany. God, it scared me just thinking about what the mood would be back home if we slipped up. History weighed heavily on this fixture: two world wars, 1966, 1970, Italia 90 and Euro 96. All the players understood this was a fixture like no other, almost a derby match, spiced by events on and off the pitch. 'We just cannot get beaten by Germany' became our motto. Bitter rivalry with the Germans is ingrained in every English footballer. I was no different. The thought of piling into a German midfielder, testing his shin-pads and his bottle, was as much a part of my professional existence as breathing.

I never thought Keegan would risk me in Charleroi. The stakes were too high, surely? A must-win game against opponents like Germany was no place for a kid. Keegan put me on the bench again. Before kick-off, I bumped into my Liverpool team-mate Didi Hamann, and we had a chat. He was starting for Germany but still had time for a word of encouragement for me.

'Is there a chance you can get on?' he asked me.

'None,' I replied.

I settled back to watch the match. Even while I was doing my warm-ups in the first half and during the break, I never thought I would feature. Eight minutes after the break, Shearer scored. Game on! The Euro 2000 dream was back on. England were back in business. But could we hold on? Germany would not go down without a fight. Keegan whispered something to Fazackerley, who turned and shouted at me: 'Go and get warmed up. Really warmed up.' This was it. None of the other sub mid-fielders had been ordered down the touchline. I had to be coming on. Keegan wanted to kill the game off, and that challenge on Southgate in Spa had shown him I loved a tackle.

As a manager, Keegan was not known for his caution, and there he was, pushing at the boundaries of his technical area, screaming at England's players: 'Let's keep the result!' Kevin could see salvation just thirty minutes away. All the stick he'd received after Eindhoven would be replaced by praise.

I warmed up like a madman, getting every sinew and muscle ready. Then the moment came for Keegan to let me loose. Michael Owen's number went up – a brave move by the manager. Michael can make a goal out of nothing, but Keegan wanted to sit on the 1–0 lead. I stood on the touchline, flicking up a boot behind me to let the linesman check my studs. Butterflies danced in my stomach. I had played for Keegan only once, in a friendly. What the fuck was he putting me on for in a competitive match as crucial as this? 'I don't need this,' I was thinking. Sensing my unease, Kevin put his arm round me and said, 'Just do what you do for Liverpool. Be disciplined. Keep the ball for us. Break up Germany's attacks, because they are starting to come on to us a bit.' Kevin paused then. His next comment will stay with me for ever: 'Steven, enjoy it as well.'

Enjoy it? Fuck me! I was about to step into a storm for my competitive debut against the team England loathed most, and Kevin was telling me to treat it like a stroll in the park! Unbelievable. But that was fantastic man-management by Kevin. To tell a nervous kid to enjoy himself in such a serious situation was inspired.

I crossed the white line, into battle, my head spinning with thoughts. Me in central midfield, Shearer up front on his own. Against Germany. Fight to the death. Bring it on. Full house going mental. England fans singing till they were hoarse. Cannot let them down. Cannot let Germany through. Let them fucking have it.

The Germans had a good team, class from back to front. Oliver Kahn – one of the best keepers in the history of football. Defenders of real quality in Markus Babbel, Jens Nowotny and Christian Ziege. Legends like Lothar Matthaus. Big target-man in Carsten Jancker. Tricky play-makers like Mehmet Scholl. 'Get tight to Scholl,' Kevin had told me. 'Stop Scholl.' I knew all about the Bayern Munich man. I hadn't been expecting to play, but I'd still watched the tapes to learn who Germany's dangermen were. Sitting in the team meeting, I'd day-dreamed about how much I would love to test myself against Scholl. Now was the time to put theory into practice. I immediately put a big tackle in on him. He was class, so I tackled him again. And again. No doubt about it, this was an exceptional German side that would not go quietly.

Certainly not with Didi in their midst. I knew Didi too well to believe Germany would surrender tamely. That's not Didi's way. He gives everything, and then some more, drawing from a well of resilience few other pros have. When Didi arrived at Liverpool, I was ecstatic. He's a great player, and I learned off him day in, day out. I have always watched Didi, picking up little tips to improve me and I was gutted when he left Liverpool in 2006. He is the ultimate holding-role player, a clever sentry who allows other midfielders to bomb forward. His qualities were not restricted to the art of tackling and passing. My admiration for him as a man grew during my twenty-nine minutes in opposition to him in Charleroi. After my first few passes, Didi ran past and said, 'Keep doing what you are doing.' Unbelievable. I was stunned. We were sworn enemies until the referee's final whistle, representing rival countries in a vital game with half the world tuned in. Yet here he was, helping me. Incredible. Germany themselves had so much riding on the game. They had drawn their first match, with Romania, and were trailing here. Yet even in the heat of battle, Didi was prepared to think about me, a young club-mate struggling not to sink in unfamiliar international waters. Didi could see in my face that I was sweating, nervous and panicky. When the ball next went out of play, I turned to him.

'I am shitting myself here, mate,' I said. 'I'm fucking terrified.'

Didi looked at me. 'Relax, Stevie,' he said. 'Just do what you do normally.'

Didi's kindness to an opponent that evening showed he was a real mate. As long as I live, I will never forget our exchange of words in Charleroi.

I still wanted to thrash his team though. No amount of generosity of spirit from Didi could dull my desire to run Germany out of town. A couple of minutes after my chat with Didi, he went past me with the ball. Fucking cheek. That did not even happen in training at Melwood. The Kaiser was stepping it up. Time to raise my game some more. 'I'm going to have him,' I thought. 'Watch out, Didi, I'm after you.' He was making a dangerous break. I had to bring him down. I chased after Didi and hit him with a full-whack tackle. Bang. Take that. Down you go. Don't try to fucking go past me. Didi shouted something in German, and I didn't need to understand his words to realize he was not happy. He was rolling around on the ground, moaning. I lost it. 'Fucking get up, Didi!' I screamed at him, standing over him. 'I didn't fucking touch you. Get up! I'm going to get a yellow unless you fucking get up now. Two yellows and I miss the quarters.'

After the game, I told the press that Didi had 'squealed like a girl'. That was naive of me, and totally unnecessary. It was a stupid comment that I regret deeply. All I can say in my defence is that it was uttered shortly after the final whistle when the only thing going through my mind was adrenalin. England had held on for victory, I had played well, and I wasn't thinking straight. I have so much respect for Didi, particularly after he helped me settle into such a difficult game. I hope he reads this. He has never,

ever once mentioned my comment about him squealing like a girl. Too polite. I've never really had the chance to apologize, until now. I'm sorry, Didi. You are too much of a man to squeal like a girl.

I treasure the shirt he gave me at the final whistle. It's upstairs, and when I look at it all the memories of that night in Charleroi come flooding back. The nerves, the tackle, the three points. 'All the best in your next game,' said Didi, before heading off to the demoralized German dressing-room. Typical Didi. Even then, in what must have been a time of real heartache, he was prepared to think about someone else. My life took a turn for the better the day I met Didi Hamann.

As Didi disappeared, I was engulfed by people. Well done. Brilliant. Congratulations. Well played. Kevin was in tears, hugging me. England's changing-room was buzzing, players and staff happy. Me? I was on cloud nine. Keegan stood in the middle of the room and said, 'We've got a chance of qualifying now, boys!' I shook hands with all the lads and congratulated them. But it hadn't yet sunk in; it was as if I hadn't played. Me, a hero for England? Impossible. Only when I left the room and had had time to gather my thoughts did I start to appreciate that it really had been me out there, flying into tackles, helping to get England back on track at Euro 2000. It really was me playing a part in England's famous victory.

As I walked back to the bus, I wanted to share my joy with my family, so I called Dad. He didn't go over the top in his praise – that's not Dad's way – but I could tell from the tone of his voice that he was really happy for me. It was Father's Day, and Dad said, 'That performance was a tremendous present, Steven.' Just to detect that pride in my dad's voice meant the world.

Back at the hotel, the dining-room felt different. The gloom was gone, dispersed by Shearer's goal. That night, I actually looked forward to coming down from my room. I knew everyone would be happy. After the Portugal loss five days earlier it had been a case of in for your meal sharp, back to your room sharp. Gareth Barry was made up for me. 'Brilliant, Stevie, well done,' he said as we unwound in our sitting-room. Tiredness soon overcame me, and I said goodnight to Gareth.

The moment I shut the door for the night and lay down in bed, I was besieged with all my old nerves. The homesickness kicked in again, bringing me down from my Charleroi high. I almost packed my bags and ran for cover. It was so strange. I should have been on top of the world after the Germany game; instead, I felt like I was staring into a black hole of depression. I just wanted to be at home. God I missed Ironside.

First thing next morning, I rang home. Just hearing my parents' voices calmed me down. I asked them to read out the headlines in the English papers (we never got the papers straight away at Spa; they were often a day late). 'Full Steve Ahead: an England Star is Born' declared one. 'Move Over Ince, Gerrard is the New Guv'nor' said another. That cheered me up! Shit! I guess this was my Michael Moment, when it all goes mental and everyone knows your name. When I finally got hold of the papers myself I almost ripped them to pieces, such was my haste in turning the pages. Some of the things I read, about me being 'England's future', I felt I shouldn't be reading.

'Ignore those,' Dad urged me. 'Don't believe it. Just focus on doing the same again.' Good advice, as always with Dad. But I was drawn to those papers. It was fascinating reading about myself. 'Don't take any notice of the hype,' said Gérard Houllier when I spoke to him later that day. Steve Heighway said the same. Foot on the ball; don't get carried away. Keegan did, though. 'Steven Gerrard gave a cameo of what England's future will be,' said the manager. Didi also spoke well of me in the press. 'Stevie will be England captain one day,' he said. 'I wish Germany had a few players like him.' Top fella.

One grey cloud filled the sky for England: our fans rioted in Charleroi. Even in our Spa cocoon, we learned what had gone on. The television pictures looked bad. When I saw water cannons sending fans flying and soaking that big town square, it was unbelievable, like an image from a medieval war. England fans are passionate, but it shocks me when it spills over into violence and fighting with police. I wasn't embarrassed by their behaviour, because most England fans have been brilliant to us, but it wasn't good to watch. All the players understood that outbreaks of hooliganism meant bad news for the team. We had all heard the rumblings from the big boys at UEFA that England could get kicked out of Euro 2000. 'Christ,' I thought, 'that would be so unjust, a real kick in the teeth.' We had worked so hard over ninety minutes against Germany to turn our group around. Now a few nutters threatened to ruin it.

It became a hot topic of conversation in the hotel. The players kept talking about the trouble, and the threat from UEFA that we would have to pack our bags and go home if the violence erupted again. FA officials called a meeting with the players in Spa. They were shitting themselves. One of the FA officials, David Davies, was desperate to get a message through to the fans to calm down. 'Whenever you do any interviews, warn the fans about the gravity of the situation,' Davies told us. 'Tell them they are letting the team, and the country, down. We really could get booted out.' All the players were praying it wouldn't get to that stage. Luckily, it never did. The trouble subsided.

We want the passion and commitment of the fans, but not the dark side. England supporters are always tremendous in the stadium. They spend all their hard-earned money and give up their time to follow us around the world. It's unbelievable. Truly, England would be knackered without the fans. It means so much to sit in a dressing-room in some cold foreign stadium and be able to hear the England fans outside. "Come on, England! Come on, England!" It's reassuring to come out of the tunnel at some inhospitable venue and see all the St George flags. When we are down, the fans lift us. We owe them big-style. The rioting of a minority cannot dent my admiration for the majority.

Back in Spa, we soon forgot our concerns about the fans. We had three days to prepare for our final Group A game, against Romania, who were fighting for their lives with only a point to their name. Again, we were really up for the match. Training was unbelievable, with a real bite to it. I was flying. All the papers were full of my name. Everyone, it seemed, was talking about me. As I walked out to training, Michael was alongside me. We were chatting about everything and nothing, just joshing around. My old mate then turned serious. 'You played really well against Germany,' he said. 'You have to be pushing for a place against Romania.' Similar encouragement came from Robbie and Macca. 'You must have a chance,' they said.

A situation vacant sign did hang in central midfield. Scholesy was too good to drop, but one position was still up for grabs. Wisey could slot in there, but Kevin tended to use him out wide. Incey's position was the vulnerable one, according to the papers, who said he looked tired in the first two games. But I wasn't plotting on nicking Ince's job, I just wanted to impress as much as possible in training and let Kevin make the decision.

I went to work as if my life depended on it. The day before the Romania game, I couldn't wait to get stuck into my last chance to convince Kevin. Such was my desperate enthusiasm that I charged into a nightmare of my own making. Off the bus, top speed on to the pitch, couldn't hold back, let's get cracking, and then I felt it go. My calf. Pulled. No question. Fuck it. Didn't warm up properly. Shit, shit, shit.

Desperation coloured my subsequent actions. Because of what a few players and papers had said, I thought I had a chance of starting, so I didn't tell anyone about the calf. Not the physios, and definitely not Kevin. I trained on, running hard to disguise the problem. It hurt, but I knew missing Romania would cause me more pain. I didn't realize how bad I had pulled it. I'm no bloody doctor. Might just be a bit tight, I told myself, grabbing any strand of comfort; I'll have a painkiller when I get back to the room and stretch the calf in the bath. I might just get shot of it before kick-off. God, let it just be a bit of tightness, maybe just some slight tension that will disappear overnight. Oh God, don't let me miss Romania! I couldn't bear it.

The high of Germany suddenly seemed a world away. I dropped into a depression, sent tumbling there by a simple failure to warm up. How stupid was that? I cursed myself under my breath as I continued to train. 'Come on, let's get back to the room, see if we can find an escape from this nightmare,' I told myself. My heart pumped fast, my mind working overtime with thoughts. Uncertainty about whether or not I was in Keegan's plans still reigned. He gave no clues in training; we did no shape work that signalled who might start in midfield. Kevin was obviously going to announce the eleven in that night's meeting. I had to get my calf right.

Back in the privacy of my room, I hobbled around. Shit. This felt like something more than a bit of tightness. This was serious. 'I can't play, but I am going to play,' I told myself. Somehow. Christ, I've just got to.

I left my room early as dinner-time loomed so that no-one would see me walk in slightly stiffly. The other lads soon bounded in and sat down, chattering about Romania. Some of them believed Keegan would start me against Romania. They'd been talking to journalists they knew. 'You're playing tomorrow,' Robbie said to me. A weak smile came to my lips.

After dinner, I snuck down to the physio room to see if Gary Lewin could have a look at it, maybe weave some magic. I opened the door and walked straight into Alan

Shearer and Tony Adams, who were enjoying some banter with Gary. Shit. Spinning 180 degrees, I sped back out, terrified at the thought of revealing my injury to Gary in front of England's two senior players.

Back up in my room, I reconsidered my options. In times of trouble, my first instinct is to call home. Dad answered the phone.

'Dad, I can't believe it,' I said. 'I've done my calf. Badly. In training.' I was stuttering. Disappointment prevented me from speaking properly. Tears formed in my eyes. 'Dad, I really think Keegan is going to pick me against Romania. We've got a meeting in an hour and I'm sure I'm in the team. But my calf's a mess. It's really tight. There's no way I can play.'

As I was talking, there was a knock on the door. 'Come back later!' I shouted. Bloody cleaners. They were so busy, in our rooms all the time. You'd hardly put a cup down and they'd come flying through the door like the SAS to tidy up. Another knock. I was on the verge of screaming 'Fuck off!' I am usually polite with people, I almost never swear at them, but my head was gone. Completely gone. My world was in ruins, shattered by a damaged muscle. Knock, knock. Busy cunts! Can't they leave me alone? They had only just left the room ten minutes earlier.

'Hold on, Dad, I have to get rid of the cleaners,' I said.

I went over to the door, opened it, and standing there was the England manager.

'Boss! Come in, come in.' I picked up the phone again. 'Dad, the manager's here, I'll phone you back.' Dad tried to say something, but I buttoned him. My mind was on Keegan, the calf, and the game with Romania.

'How are you, Steven?' Keegan began.

'I'm all right, boss, fine.'

'Sit down, Steven.'

So we sat at this little table, a smiling England manager on one side and a heartbroken kid with a wrecked calf on the other.

Keegan looked directly at me. 'You're starting tomorrow,' he said.

No! No! Don't tell me that! Christ! I felt trapped in a horror story that kept getting worse. It was unreal. Keegan had just knocked on my door to tell me I was starting a European Championship game for my country, and I was seconds away from limping down the corridor, tapping on his door and confessing all. I had to come clean. Keegan had always been so good with me. I couldn't mislead him now; it would be unfair on him and the team.

'Thanks, boss,' I said, 'but I have something to tell you.'

A confused look spread over Keegan's face. 'What is it?'

I paused, searching for the courage to get the words out. Speaking to Keegan was a new experience. I was shy, relieved in the past just to listen.

'Come on, Steven, what is it?'

Finally, I found the strength. 'Boss,' I began, 'listen, I'm sorry. I have something to tell you, something I have been hiding from you. I've done my calf.'

The world stopped spinning for a moment. A silence took hold for what felt like an eternity.

'What?' he said, his voice crackling with disbelief. 'Why haven't you mentioned it?'

'Boss, I just wanted to play so badly. I went down to the

team room before but the physio wasn't there.' Gary had been there, of course. I was lying, hiding behind any excuse so that the England manager wouldn't think so badly of me.

'Have you pulled it or is it just tight?' Keegan asked.

'There is no way I can possibly play tomorrow,' I replied. 'I did it early in training, but played on because I wanted desperately to be involved tomorrow. I didn't mention it to the physios in case they ruled me out or told you. It wasn't until I got back to the room that I realized how bad it was. I'm struggling to walk properly. It's getting worse.'

A big lump formed in my throat. How I'd got the words out I will never know.

Keegan took hold of me and said, 'Thanks for telling me. I appreciate it.' He knew how gutted I was.

'I'm sorry, boss,' I said again.

'Don't you be worrying,' he said. 'Your future is sorted. Get it right for the game after. Forget about it. I will take the blame. I will tell Gary you told me but that we were going to see how it was.'

And Kevin did take the whole blame. If I had been older and more experienced, Kevin would probably have hammered me. He could have hung me out to dry with the physios and in public, but he didn't. Keegan cared for his players, and to me his sympathy meant everything.

He led me, this distraught kid, down to the physio room where Gary Lewin examined my calf. 'No chance,' he announced, and that was it. Officially ruled out.

Word spread fast in the camp. Everyone was brilliant, consoling me, telling me they would go out and beat

Romania so I could play again later in the tournament. Well, not everyone was brilliant. Fazackerley's reaction was, I thought, disgraceful. Still struggling with homesickness, and now with a battered calf, the last thing I needed was someone sidling over to me and saying, 'Are you injured again? Are you not warming up properly?' I felt like going for him. Punching Fazackerley's lights out crossed my mind a few times during Euro 2000. He upset me that much. He was good to me at times, but otherwise he was frosty and hurtful when I needed comforting. He just dealt with me all wrong. I was down. I didn't need some cold-hearted tosser pushing me further down. He simply didn't understand how low I was.

Fortunately, Keegan cared, even when I was of no use to him. He put me on the bench, stripped, as if I were available to come on, covering up my injury from the media so I didn't get stick. He knew the papers would give me all that old shite about being a young crock. Kevin did me a huge favour that day. Although the press were informed that something was wrong with my calf, they thought it was only a twinge, and that Kevin was being wary by starting with me on the bench.

I sat there in despair, wishing I was playing against Romania. What a mad game it was, swinging one way and then the other. England lost 3–2, to a penalty in the final minute after Phil Neville brought down Viorel Moldovan. The dressing-room was bad afterwards, with players going crazy, screaming and shouting as the bitterest of post-mortems was conducted. A look of anger took up residence on the faces of Ince, Adams and Martin Keown. They sat there spitting out venom over an abrupt end to Euro 2000. Nothing got thrown. Players raged at the situation, not at each other. A few people sought to console Phil Neville, but no-one blamed him. Other players just sat there, towels over their heads, unable to speak. Keegan was distraught. Everyone was. As a squad we knew we had failed. People had expected England to have a right good go after promising displays at Euro 96 and France 98. We had let the fans down – a crime, given their fantastic support. Being on the first flight home from Euro 2000 was a disaster.

Grim inquests soon began. Keegan got some unbelievable crap thrown at him. I knew Michael was unhappy with Keegan. Michael loathes being substituted, as he was in all three games. He feels it is an insult, and that's the right reaction. Managers don't want players who race happily to the touchline when the fourth official holds their number up. They should be angry, wanting to stay on. When I'm taken off, I feel almost physically ill. What I didn't know during Euro 2000 was that Michael wasn't enjoying Kevin's training sessions. Michael wanted more pattern-of-play work and fewer small-sided games. He was also critical of Keegan's organization. It got personal between Michael and Kevin, and their relationship broke down.

Keown also laid into Keegan, slamming him as 'tactically naive'. Everyone made a big fuss about Martin's comments, ignoring the fact that players not in the starting eleven always have an axe to grind with the manager. That's normal. Whenever I am not in the line-up, it feels like the end of the world. Nowadays, football is more of a squad game and players are more accepting of rotation.

But during Euro 2000, tension was written all over people's faces as the manager read out the team. Nerves raged around the room. Everyone wanted to be in that eleven. It felt like the worst failure not to be picked. This is England. We are ambitious individuals not used to being overlooked, so feathers are bound to get ruffled. A camp is naturally almost split into two during a tournament – starters and understudies. Nowadays, teams have more of a team spirit, greater togetherness. Managers are better at drilling it into players that it is about the squad, not the team.

Kevin got stick because he was not so good at looking after those like Martin who were not in the team. I felt differently towards the England manager. I flew back from Holland and Belgium thinking that he was different class as a man and a manager. Keegan treated me as if I were Pele. He made me feel like I was the best player in the world. He made me feel so important. He gave me my debut and stood by me in my darkest hour. My respect for Kevin Keegan will never die.

8
Make Mine a Treble

My homesickness was cured the moment I set foot in Merseyside again, but a new problem awaited. Photographers lurked outside the house – a first for me. This was the England effect, the price to be paid for twenty-nine eye-catching minutes against the old enemy Germany. The media seized on me as the one scrap of hope from England's screwed-up stay in Holland and Belgium.

Flavour-of-the-month status didn't appeal. I don't mind being recognized, but this was organized stalking. It was not just me being shadowed. Friends and family were trailed, which is a disgrace. The morning after the Germany game, the intrusions began. Reporters knocked at relatives' doors and shoved microphones in their faces, demanding their take on 'Stevie G – England Hero'. Back in Spa, I was shitting myself. What were these reporters after? Leave my family alone! My relatives reacted differently. 'No comment,' some said. 'We're really pleased for Steven,' replied others. Nothing satisfied these reporters. Like locusts, they spread across Merseyside hunting juicy morsels about me. They invaded Cardinal Heenan and St Mick's. On returning home, I found the papers full of my old teachers coming out left, right and centre and reminiscing about me. The press got hold of all sorts of pictures of me, past and present. Me at school. Me in the local team. The full paparazzi treatment was focused on me. Germany changed my life for ever. I became public property – a prospect that didn't exactly fill me with joy. Sharpish, I disappeared on holiday, got some sun, caught my breath and readied myself for the new season. The pressure was on, big-time. Could I repeat my Germany display? Everyone was watching me. Was I just a flash in the pan, a one-game wonder? I had to produce.

Just before that 2000/01 season kicked off, I learned Bryan Robson was chasing me. Middlesbrough were prepared to offer £5 million – a massive sum for someone as inexperienced as me. Liverpool were having none of it, and sent Robson packing in no uncertain terms. Leaving Liverpool was a million miles from my thoughts, but it was still flattering to hear an icon like Robson rated me. After the Euros, Robson was interviewed in the papers talking me up. When I read those articles, I wanted to cut them out and frame them. Fuck me, Bryan Robson, England legend, praising me! His approval meant the world. I looked at the pieces and thought if I could become a tenth of the player Robson had been, I'd die happy.

As a kid I once wore a Manchester United shirt with 'Robson' and his number 7 on the back. I detested United with a passion and loathed the idea of putting on one of their strips, but this was different. A mate of mine owned this Robson top, the old blue-and-white one with dashes on it. We were kicking about on Ironside and I asked him whether I could be Robson for a while. I slipped out of my Liverpool shirt, and put on the Robson one. It felt fantastic. I wore it for an hour, charging all over, flying into tackles, scoring brave goals, pretending I was Robson. Because the shirt had Robson's name on it, I forgot about the United bit. It didn't seem like treachery to Liverpool, more homage to an England god.

Unfortunately, Dad looked out the window and went ballistic. 'Get inside now!' he screamed. Scarcely through the door, I ran into a right good grilling. 'What the hell are you playing at, wearing a Manchester United shirt?' he asked.

'But Dad, it's Bryan Robson's shirt,' I explained.

Dad couldn't have cared less. 'You should know better,' he said.

It was a United strip, and Dad wasn't having any son of his dragging the Gerrard name through the Huyton gutter. What would the neighbours think? Honest to God, I thought I was going to have to move house! I was only a baby, but I was convinced Dad would kick me out for putting on that United shirt.

Apart from those trial matches when I tested Liverpool's loyalty, I never made the mistake of wearing United's colours again. My admiration for Robson never disappeared, though. I was buzzing that he believed in me. The new season couldn't start soon enough. Robson's interest meant I was steaming even more to get stuck in. This was going to be my year. Still, not even in my wildest dreams could I have envisaged what an extraordinary year it would be. One cup would have been good, two unbelievable, but the Treble? No chance. Surely not? Those who despise Liverpool call it the Mickey Mouse Treble, but it was still a monumental achievement. We needed to rewrite all the odds and predictions to lift that Treble.

Liverpool had a good team that season. I knew that. Gérard Houllier assembled a quality outfit. The odd concern still nagged away at me, though. I wasn't completely convinced by our goalkeeper, Sander Westerveld. The Dutchman's kicking was excellent, and his shot-stopping and communication skills good, but he was prone to mistakes. Not blatant errors like fumbles, but goals he should really have prevented. Analysing videos of our games with Carra and Michael, we noticed certain shots or headers went past Sander a bit too easily. I kept quiet. I was still only twenty, still learning my craft. What right did I have to stand up in team meetings and question Liverpool's keeper?

Sander was fortunate that he was protected by a brilliant defence. Our right-back was Markus Babbel, a smooth German whose name was rarely chanted at Anfield but who was highly regarded in the dressing-room. Markus was an unsung hero in our pursuit of the Treble. He was awesome in training, fit as fuck, a great defender and completely dependable. Gérard pulled a belter out of the bag with Babbel, who arrived from Bayern Munich on a free as a centre-half, but shone at full-back. Liverpool got one magnificent season out of Babbel. Sadly, the following year Markus contracted a weird illness called Guillain-Barre Syndrome that causes havoc with the nervous system. Liverpool's club doctor, Mark Waller, told us Markus wouldn't be around for a while. The doc explained the illness, and how serious it was. 'Markus will be back,' he promised, 'but whether he will be 100 per cent, I don't know.' Us players got nosey. Markus was a mate, and we worried about him. 'How did he get this illness, doc?' I asked. Doc Waller didn't know. Markus's illness started off like flu and then drained nearly all the life from him. Markus was so tough and brave in fighting it. He was away from Melwood for months. 'Where's Markus?' everyone kept saying. 'We need him back.' He eventually returned from Germany in a wheelchair. I was stunned. I couldn't believe this was the same person. Markus had been toned, clean-shaven, a good-looking guy glowing with health. Now, I found myself shaking hands with a ghost. He was grey, and much thinner. His weight dropped from almost thirteen stone to eleven stone. His muscle tone went, too. All I recognized was the familiar Babbel smile. One of the best players of our Treble season was suddenly in a wheelchair.

Markus recovered, but he was never the same all-action defender again, not like he had been during our march to the Treble in 2000/01. Markus was switched to right-back because Sami Hyypia proved a revelation in the middle. Gérard did not bring the tall Finn in as first-choice. Liverpool's management got a really big surprise with Hyypia. We all did. From the moment Sami arrived in 1999, he was brilliant; £2.5 million from Willem II in Holland was a bargain. Sami was just what Liverpool craved: an aerial presence in defence. Liverpool had been slaughtered for years for not having someone commanding in the air. Any cross came in against Liverpool and we were screwed. Whenever we played Man United, David Beckham notched up three or four assists from crosses or corners. Sorting out the defence became one of Gérard's urgent requirements.

I remember seeing Hyypia for the first time at Melwood, and watching this lanky Scandy loping out to training. 'Who the fuck is this?' I whispered to the other guys. No-one had heard of Sami Hyypia. We thought he had been bought in case injury or suspension knackered our main centre-halves. The next thing I knew Sami was clearing balls a hundred yards, making fantastic tackles and passing the ball out well. Left or right foot, no problem. His only weakness was speed. Sami never boasted the pace of centre-halves like Rio Ferdinand or the Italian Alessandro Nesta. But it wasn't an issue. Sami's reading of the game was so good that during his first couple of years at Liverpool nobody got past him. He was truly world class for those two seasons.

Sami struck up an immediate understanding with Stéphane Henchoz, who came in from Blackburn Rovers. Stéphane was solid, never giving anything away, always there to make vital interceptions. He and Sami were like rocks at the back. Opposing attacks just crashed onto them and fell back, bruised physically and mentally. Sami's partnership with Stéphane won us the Treble. No doubt. They were the heartbeat of a magnificent defence, with Babbel on the right and Jamie Carragher on the left.

I love Carra. So do managers. He'll play anywhere across the back, no problem. Carra's best at centre-half, but he never complained when Gérard shoved him in at left-back for the Treble season. A true pro, Carra just knuckled down. In training, he worked overtime developing his left foot. He got YT boys to ping balls at him on the left, time after time. He almost wore a hole in his left boot. Practice, dawn till dusk, turned Carra into a brilliant two-footed defender.

Some people will be surprised to learn Carra is a student of the game. He's not a thick Scouser from Bootle. He's always reading books about football, always talking about it. Conversations with Carra are 90 per cent football. He's not a Statto or a bore, he's just football-mad. Ask Carra any football question and he'll answer before you've finished. Get Carra on past or present players, and he'll rattle off their goal record, club history, strengths, weaknesses, birthplace and probably even their star sign and favourite holiday destination. Any football quiz, Carra is there, bloody Mastermind, cleaning up. Toss him a trick football question, and Carra will never be caught out. Bang. He'll hit back the right answer.

I have always admired Carra as a bloke, a footballer and a leader who has never needed an armband. He always behaved like a captain. In that Treble season, I often turned to Carra for advice. If I had the raging hump about something, and was steaming in to see Gérard, Carra would stop me, calm me down and sort me out. Television interviews don't give the right image of Carra. He's bright, as well as being a top lad.

When another wise head, Gary McAllister, joined Liverpool, I was not alone in the dressing-room in wondering what the hell Gérard was doing. He seemed an odd buy. OK, he was once a terrific midfielder for Leeds

United and Scotland, but McAllister was now thirty-five, his best days surely behind him. His arrival was of particular concern to me. Would he limit my appearances? 'It's a bit of a strange signing,' I remarked to the lads when Gérard wasn't around. 'Isn't McAllister over the hill? I've seen him play for Coventry recently and, yeah, he's good, but why've we signed him?' No-one came up with an answer. The word from above was that McAllister had been brought in as cover. I rang my agent, Struan Marshall, who knew McAllister well. 'Stru, what's all this about?' I asked.

'Don't worry, Stevie,' replied Struan, 'Gary Mac will be brilliant for Liverpool, and for you as well. Listen to him. Learn from him.'

'Fuck off, Stru,' I said. 'McAllister can fucking well learn off me!'

How wrong I was. Meeting this intelligent Scot was an important moment in my career. As a midfielder and a man, Gary Mac was special. He strolled into the dressing-room at Melwood and immediately went around all the players introducing himself. That was class. We knew who Gary bloody McAllister was, but that gesture showed his modesty. We liked that. He also had the medals, the caps and poise that trigger instant respect. It felt like football royalty breezing into Melwood. Should I bow? Gary was never destined for the ressies. No chance. Almost immediately, he was a fixture in the first team, directing operations like a general at a battle, turning the game Liverpool's way with his vision and touch. What a player.

And what a teacher. On away trips, I timed my run to

the bus so I could sit next to McAllister, absorbing advice. It felt like being on the school bus with the best master next to me. Every journey was like a lesson, with me as the awestruck pupil. Gary Mac definitely helped me, particularly with my passing. Sometimes I hit a long ball when I should have chosen the shorter option. Gérard and Thommo often pulled me on it. 'Pick your passes better,' they said. At one point, a bloody debate even broke out in the press about my passing. Jesus! It did gnaw away at me, all this talk about whether I was trying too many Hollywood long passes. So one day I sat next to Gary on the bus, flicking through the papers, reading all this stuff about my passing.

'How are you?' Gary asked.

'Fine, fine,' I replied.

The bus started moving, and soon I opened up.

'Macca, why am I choosing to play a long pass instead of a short one, or vice versa? I can't get my selection right.'

'Don't be worrying,' said Gary. 'You're still young. It'll come. If you give the ball away, keep your next pass short. Only play a long pass if you know it will definitely get there.'

During matches, if I lost possession, Macca would say, 'Keep the next one.' He was such a clever man in possession himself, and his opinion was valued by everyone. Macca was one of those players who could stop a session and suggest something and everyone listened, even the coaches. Just watching Gary in training improved me. He was a master-class on legs.

Experienced and stylish, Macca had been there, done that, and bought the designer shirt. His clothes were always the best, still are. His shoes were always spotless. He was a star at Liverpool and he remains a star in my eyes. Still to this day, I'll phone Macca, even if it's nothing to do with football. He's just one of those likeable, popular guys whom anyone would feel proud to know. I trust Gary like family. If I've had a shocker, Gary will be on, lifting my spirits, offering advice that is invariably right. I owe him so much.

Gary combined the experience of his thirty-five years with the phenomenal engine of a twenty-five-year-old. He was as fit as anything, but then he always looked after himself. Gary Mac made twenty-one Premiership starts that 2000/01 season, starred in the three cup runs and became an instant legend at Liverpool. Gary's brilliance in the middle along with Didi Hamann meant I was often shifted out to right midfield. It pissed me off that if I ever had a bad game alongside Didi I was shifted out towards the flank. Gérard never gave me another game to put it right. Macca came flying in and I was left fighting with Danny Murphy and David Thompson for right midfield. Danny, Thommo and I called it the 'graveyard shift'. 'Who's got the fucking graveyard today?' we'd laugh with each other as Gérard read out the team. The graveyard was well named: anyone playing right midfield for Liverpool that season was guaranteed to have their match killed off early. Whoever was on the Graveyard – me, Danny or Thommo – would start sweating after fifty minutes, knowing the man on the bench was about to signal the end. It became a running joke: 'Fifty minutes and you're dead.' Ha bloody ha.

All three of us were handy players and we did get

annoyed. Thommo was a good midfielder, full of energy, and he loved a tackle, but Danny was different class. Danny was my room-mate, almost my soul-mate. A schoolboy Red, Danny was the king of banter, really funny and sharp. We clicked immediately. For a couple of years we scrapped like dogs for the same place yet such intense rivalry never spoiled our friendship. We'd laugh, muck about, wind each other up. Any problems I had in my private life, Danny gave me spot-on advice. I am still gutted to this day Danny is not at Liverpool. It kills me. Really does. He was a top, top player who was never properly appreciated by the management. Danny is good enough to play in Liverpool's starting XI now. No problem. God, I miss him. I was devastated for Danny when he got shipped out to Charlton Athletic and then Spurs. He didn't want to leave Anfield. People go on about player power, but Danny was powerless to stop Liverpool selling him and breaking his heart. Danny loved Liverpool. I heard the rumours that Liverpool offloaded Danny because he was a bad influence on the younger players. That was total, utter bullshit. Danny never thought about himself. In truth, Danny deserved Liverpool's gratitude for helping the younger players. He was always class with me. He's a lot more clever and mature than people think.

Liverpool were not short of talent in midfield. Patrik Berger suffered with injuries, a few really bad ones, which was tough on him and the team. When I did play with Patrik, he was the best left-footed striker of a ball I have seen. He could place the ball wherever he wanted – a breathtaking skill. As a bloke, Patrik was OK. He was from the Czech Republic, and he kept himself to himself.

He was really cliquey with Vladimir Smicer, another Czech. Vladi was sub a lot, blowing hot and cold. When he flew in from the French club Lens for almost £4 million, he was sensational in training. His brilliant touch made things look so easy. But Melwood was one thing, Anfield another, and Vladi rarely transferred his training-ground form to match-day. The difference between what Vladi had and what he delivered disappointed me. The ability was there, but not the impact, although he was unlucky with injuries and Gérard rarely used him in his proper position.

We also had Nicky Barmby in midfield, who shone when he first signed for us from Everton in the summer of 2000. He had some balls crossing Stanley Park. That was brave. At the time Barmby was Everton's main man, yet he jumped ship. Fair enough. If you play for Everton, and Liverpool come knocking, it is tempting. Anyway, the argument that raged about his move was stupid. Barmby had to leave Goodison for Anfield. He wanted success. End of debate.

Along with Barmby, Gary Mac, Didi and the rest, my job was to shift the ball forward to Michael, Robbie and Emile Heskey. Everyone knew about Michael's class, his deadly eye for goal. Same with Robbie. Emile was different. He had much to prove after leaving a smaller club, Leicester City, in March 2000 for as big a destination as Anfield. Emile was great to play with because he offered midfielders options. His speed meant I could ping the ball over the top for him to chase, but he also dropped short and held the ball up. I then bombed on and had a pop at goal. Perfect. Emile was a truly versatile target-man who enjoyed a great first full season, smashing in twenty-two goals. Unfortunately for Emile, that tally set a benchmark which everyone judged him by. For years afterwards, everyone expected Emile to rattle in twenty goals a season. The stick aimed at Emile is only because he never delivered the goals he should. Confidence is key to Emile. If he felt appreciated, he'd fly. Sadly, he was held back by niggles and tactics. But up front for Liverpool in his first full season, Emile was unstoppable. He loved that role, working alongside Michael. When Gérard shifted Emile out to the right or the left, that was unfair. Poor Emile. He was under so much pressure, so much in the public eye; the last thing he needed was to be pushed out of position. I felt for him.

In January 2001, Liverpool's strike-force was strengthened further. From the moment I saw Jari Litmanen at Melwood, I was bewitched. This skilful Finn was different gravy in training, running the small-sided games with his touch and clever movement. Jari was like a chess grandmaster, always anticipating three or four moves ahead. He was certainly on my wavelength. Every pass I tried, he read. Few footballers worked that space between defence and midfield better. The very first time I drilled a ball in to Jari, I immediately understood this was a forward who'd spent his career alongside top players at Ajax and Barcelona. Jari knew how to receive a ball, how to turn an average pass into a good one. I sensed instinctively that he was a class act in his day. He was still useful, more than useful, but we were getting Jari as the curtain began to fall on a wonderful career. He never really had the legs for the Premiership, but he had the ability, cunning and awareness. In big games, Gérard liked playing compact, which didn't suit Jari. Someone schooled at Ajax and once resident at Camp Nou preferred a much more expansive game.

Litmanen arrived only after our run in the League Cup was well underway. The trophy was then known as the Worthington Cup, and I missed the first two rounds. Injury ruled me out of the extra-time victory over Chelsea, and then Gérard rested me against Stoke City. The boys hardly missed me. They thrashed Stoke 8–0. I watched the tie at home, laughing my head off. Not at Stoke – they ran their hearts out. No, the tears chasing each other down my face were because of Pegguy Arphexad, our keeper standing in for Sander. Pegguy, a top lad who never got many games, tried to control the ball, their fella took it off him, and hit the post. I almost fell off the sofa pissing myself.

I returned for our fifth-round tie against Fulham on 13 December, which we won 3–0 in extra time. There was more London opposition in the semi-finals. Crystal Palace are a decent club, but back then they had a complete prick of a centre-forward. Clinton Morrison fancied himself so much he should have married a mirror. Before the game, he gave it all the big shit in the papers about how good he was. Clinton is one of those players who gets a buzz off seeing himself in the press. If the bookies had offered a bet on Clinton Morrison talking himself up before our games, I would have had my mortgage on it. We arrived at Selhurst Park having heard and read about all these things Clinton was going to do to us. Big scary Clinton. Hoping for an upset, TV showed the first leg live. Liverpool were all over Palace. If this had been a boxing bout, the referee would have stopped it to prevent Palace suffering further. We pulverized them. Their goal led a charmed life. Michael was so unlucky. He could easily have got a hat-trick; 7–2 wouldn't have flattered Liverpool, honestly. Unbelievably, Palace won 2–1.

We were smarting at the injustice, desperate to get Palace back to Anfield to put them and Clinton in their proper place. I wished the second leg had been the next night; waiting a fortnight for revenge felt far too long. Stupidly forgetting there was a second leg, Clinton mouthed off again. How thick was that? I couldn't believe what I was reading in the papers. None of the Liverpool players could. It did our heads in, those Morrison quotes, like, 'I would have scored the chances Owen had.' Michael just laughed. England's hero of St-Etienne was not going to worry about the hollow jibes of some second-string striker. 'Whatever!' shrugged Michael, smiling. Clinton angered me more than he upset Michael. His comments showed a lack of respect. If you want a really sound laugh, compare the respective goalscoring records of Michael Owen and Clinton Morrison. European Footballer of the Year v. Mr Average. Clinton could talk for Ireland, but could he back his words with goals at Anfield? With everyone's eyes on him? With an angry Kop slaughtering him? No fucking way.

When we walked into the Anfield dressing-room, there on the wall were all Morrison's offending articles, like a list of crimes pinned up outside a court-room. '"I'm going to score at Anfield in front of the Kop," says Big Clint.' Oh, yeah? There it was, in black and white, Clinton's boast. Any time anyone dared criticize Liverpool, Phil Thompson would stick it up on the notice-board. Bang. Read that. Sort him out. Personally, I'm not a great fan of that. Cheap talk shouldn't stir big responses. No footballer needs extra motivation. I certainly don't. But seeing all those headlines on the Anfield dressing-room wall, and knowing Cocky Clinton was in the room down the corridor, certainly fired our players up that night.

Poor Palace. We absolutely destroyed them. We were 3–0 up in twenty minutes, smashing them all over Anfield, and eventually won 5–0. Take that, Clinton. He got booed all game by Kopites at their merciless best. Clinton was trapped in a nightmare he'd scripted. At one point, he tried to do an overhead kick and almost broke his back. Liverpool fans pissed themselves laughing. By the final whistle, Clinton was like a little sheep walking off the pitch with his tail between his legs. That's why you don't come out and say stupid things. Learn your lesson, Clinton.

Leaving Clinton by the wayside, Liverpool were through to the final at the Millennium Stadium. Our opponents were Birmingham, then living in the Football League, a rung below us, but still a decent, hard-working side who deserved our respect. Sensing a first trophy in six years, our fans poured excitedly into Cardiff on 25 February. Everyone wanted to be there. So did I, although I lacked sharpness because I'd been carrying an injury. Aware there might be a problem, Gérard pulled me on the eve of the final.

'Are you fit?' he asked.

'Yes,' I lied.

What other reply could I give? It was a cup final, a chance for medals and memories. Professionals dream of these moments: the buzz of expectation as the coach nears the ground, weaving through the throng of fans; then the walk out into the packed arena, and the first crunching tackle to test your opponents' bottle. I love finals. Big stage. Big stakes. I couldn't miss the Millennium. My injury felt OK, I just wasn't match-fit.

'If you are fit, you'll play,' said Gérard.

'I am,' I insisted.

I wasn't. My sharpness wasn't there. I had a good run on goal early on, until their centre-half Michael Johnson clipped my ankles. Gérard took me off after seventy-eight minutes, putting on Gary Mac, with the game seemingly won.

Robbie's great goal in the first half vindicated Gérard's decision to start him ahead of Michael up front with Emile. The sight of Michael being relegated to the bench shocked all of us. 'I can pick only two out of three,' Gérard explained of his dilemma. He did, after all, have three England strikers. Michael took it professionally, with his usual dignity, but inside he was fuming. A man for the big occasion, Michael hated rotting on the sidelines. I never understood why Gérard didn't partner Michael and Robbie. All the pundits claimed they would duplicate each other's movements and strengths, but that wasn't true. Michael is right-footed, Robbie left. Robbie could come short, Michael go long, and vice versa. The presence of both would have guaranteed the team a goal threat. Gérard disagreed. Strange.

At Cardiff, his plan worked until the ninetieth minute,

when Birmingham equalized through Darren Purse's penalty. More spot-kicks decided the day. The shoot-out was dead funny. I saw the penalty-takers getting assembled by Gérard, and the shout came over that Carra was taking the fifth kick. 'Oh no!' I cried. 'Carra's got some front!' A strapping defender taking a pressure penalty in a final? That took bottle. Carragher had only ever scored two goals for Liverpool, and about three own-goals, so the joke was that Carra was on minus one. 'Christ,' I thought, 'our first four takers better be on the mark.'

The kicks were taken down at the Liverpool fans' end, which helped. Martin Grainger missed for Birmingham, Didi failed for us, so up stepped Carra. He put the ball on the spot, turned round and started walking – and walking and walking. Carra's run-up was so long they should have put an athletics track there. It looked about a hundred metres! I didn't want to watch because I was worried a good friend would stick the ball in the stand. But I had to. It was hilarious. 'Carra, what are you doing?' I said out loud. He had me in stitches. I tried desperately to keep a straight face because if Carra screwed up and somebody took a snap of me laughing, I'd be in serious trouble. With his socks down around his ankles like Johan Cruyff, Carra's run-up and kick lacked the grace of a total footballer; it was more giraffe than gazelle. But up he came, like a run-away train, and smacked the ball in the top corner. Brilliant! Players and fans went crazy, particularly when Andy Johnson missed to give us the Cup. Carra, the penalty king! He's impossible now. He'll never let us forget it. When we have pens in training, Carra is unbelievable. 'Let me through,' he says. 'I have a 100 per cent record for Liverpool. I'm the best penalty-taker at the club.'

Carra was unstoppable that day. When the karaoke started at the party back in the hotel, we couldn't get him off. That's Carra. First on the karaoke mike. First on the dance-floor. No shame! He loves it. He actually moves better on the dance-floor than on the pitch! I steered well clear of the karaoke. You'd never catch me on that, making a fool of myself. I can't dance, and I definitely can't sing. Anyway, I was just loving watching all the players and their relatives having fun. Liverpool won together and lost together. We celebrated together and commiserated together. The Liverpool way. Liverpool's family feel is essential to someone like me who works best in a strong, caring environment. No club in the country can rival Anfield's sense of community.

If the Worthington Cup felt good, the FA Cup run was truly special. We started off against Rotherham in the third round at Anfield, Emile getting a couple and Didi another. We then got a pig of a draw, away to Leeds United, a class outfit at the time. Woodgate and Ferdinand at centre-half, Bowyer and Batty in midfield, Viduka and Keane up front. Some team! And Alan Smith came on for them. They ran us ragged. Leeds' fans were going crazy, screaming for a goal. Somehow Barmby and Emile struck in the last three minutes and Leeds were out, desperately unluckily.

I missed the fifth-round win over Manchester City but was back for the quarter-final on 11 March: Tranmere Rovers away. Across the Mersey, but still a derby. We knew Tranmere would be pumped up for our visit. No question. Tranmere live in the long shadow Liverpool cast over the region. Big brother was visiting, and this was a rare chance for Tranmere to give us a bloody nose. Short in miles, the journey still felt like a long trek into enemy territory. We knew what lay in wait at Prenton Park. We'd read the papers. We'd listened to Rovers manager John Aldridge talking about how his team would be right up for the challenge. We didn't expect anything less from Aldo or his players. Aldo is a top man, really honest, a Liverpool legend, and as passionate as they come. He was desperate to put one over on his old club. Aldo's no fool, though. He knew the gulf in class. Tranmere needed to drag us down to their level, and that meant only one thing: a kicking match. 'It's their cup final,' Gérard warned us in the modest away dressing-room at Prenton Park. 'Tranmere will be going for you, hard and fast. Be careful. I've picked an English team because this is going to be a fight. This team will be able to stand up to it. They'll come at you immediately. Weather the storm, win the fight, then play them off the park.'

Tranmere v. Liverpool was a scrap between neighbours, so Gérard threw all his home-grown players into the fight: me, Michael, Carra, Robbie, Danny and Wrighty. An FA Cup quarter-final at an inhospitable ground like Prenton Park against opponents who wanted to carve us up was no place for foreigners like Patrik Berger. Us English lads understood what was at stake, the local pride as well as a ticket to the semis. Me, Michael and Carra had grown up aware of the amazing tradition of the FA Cup, its love of upsets. We were determined not to feel the underdog's bite. The whole country would have pissed itself had we lost. 'No fucking slip-ups,' me, Michael and Carra said to each other. 'Don't give them a chance.'

Wound up by Aldo and their fans, Rovers came flying at us. All that stuff in the papers about them launching everything at us was true. Tranmere didn't disappoint. Looking into the eyes of Aldo's players at kick-off, I saw the fire burning within each of them. Their existence depended on beating Liverpool. Brilliant. This was my kind of game. A good old English scrap on a shite pitch with only the strong-hearted surviving. And Gérard's decision to field English players paid off handsomely. Danny, Michael, me and Robbie all scored in a 4–2 victory. On a better surface, like back at Anfield, we would have creamed Tranmere 6–0. The fire soon went out of Aldo's men, their fans as well. Tranmere supporters lacked the real intensity of Everton's. In the end, the tie lacked edge because we knew we were a lot better than Tranmere.

My direct opponent that day was Jason Koumas, my old mate from the Vernon Sangster Sports Centre. His departure from Liverpool had been strange. Apparently, he wasn't happy with the way Steve Heighway and Hughie McAuley used him in the younger teams. Jason wanted to be pulling the strings in central midfield but they played him out wide so he disappeared to Tranmere. He progressed really quickly there, and it was good to see him again. We always got on well. Not that I showed any mercy. I always enjoyed playing against Jason because I always get the better of him. He doesn't like the physical side. Boot Jason early and he fades.

The semi-final draw smiled on us: we could have pulled out Arsenal or Spurs, but instead got Wycombe Wanderers, a team two divisions below us. Without any press hype, Liverpool would have walked that game. But everyone built the semi up so much that suddenly Wycombe believed they could cause a shock. In Lawrie Sanchez, Wycombe had a manager who'd stunned Liverpool in the Cup before, with that header for Wimbledon in the 1988 final.

Like Aldo in the quarters, Sanchez had his team pumped up. It pissed down at Villa Park, and we certainly made heavy weather of edging past Wycombe. They held us for seventy-eight minutes, but then Emile scored. Five minutes later, we won a free-kick in a terrific position, on the edge of Wycombe's box. Five of us gathered around the ball. Gary Mac took responsibility.

'I'm on it,' he said.

'OK,' I said, and stepped back, out of the way.

'All right, Macca,' said Robbie.

We all respected Macca's ability with a dead-ball, but Robbie had other ideas. He sneaked up and smacked the ball in the top corner. Bang!

'Fucking hell, Robbie!' Macca shouted.

'Get in!' laughed Robbie, and ran off.

Everyone thought Macca was chasing Robbie to congratulate him. Bollocks. He was trying to throttle him! Wycombe pulled one back, but it was too little, too late. Liverpool were in the FA Cup final. Class!

I couldn't wait to celebrate. I got home, went into town, and the atmosphere was quality. All the Liverpool fans were out in force, buzzing we were going back to the

Millennium. Everyone around the world would be watching Liverpool's FA Cup final date with Arsenal – a real glamour pairing. As a kid, the FA Cup final had always mesmerized me. God, I envied the players. Now it was me. Bring it on.

The build-up to the big day, 12 May, passed in a blur. Was I actually going to the final, or just locked in a childhood dream? I had prayed for this moment. The cup final suits, the banter and interviews, the sense of expectation around the club and the city. Everyone flying. All the trivia on the telly, the speculation about line-ups, and cameras around the hotel. Non-stop rolling news, focusing on us, the finalists. The attention was unbelievable. It was like no other game ever mattered as much as this one. To think some cynics were suggesting the FA Cup had lost its magic. What a joke! Try telling that to the tens of thousands of Liverpool fans who charged down the motorway to Cardiff in May 2001, singing all the way, flags and scarves streaming from windows, a Red army on the move. Try telling that to the players, Englishmen like me, who view the famous old trophy as a Holy Grail. Our dads taught us about the Cup, sat us down on that great Saturday in May to watch, and explained that few honours can beat being the man who steps up to lift the FA Cup. Try telling the foreign lads the FA Cup means little. Their cup competitions are sideshows. Not ours. The foreign boys know all about the massive significance of the FA Cup. Didi didn't need a history lesson; he grew up watching it. Didi's first word in English was probably 'cup'.

This huge anticipation meant I never slept a wink on

the Friday night. As I walked out of the Millennium tunnel, into the heat of the day and the fever of our fans, I thought of past finals. I followed the footsteps of so many men who made footballing history. All the clichés of the Cup flashed through my mind. Enjoy the day, seize the moment, and all that. Cup folklore also demands that a team needs a touch of luck to win, and our 2–1 victory over Arsenal certainly proved that. Arsenal smashed us all over Cardiff for eighty-three minutes. They deserved to win. No dispute. They had the ball while we chased mocking shadows. It was a good Arsenal side, with defenders like Tony Adams and Ashley Cole, and attackers like Thierry Henry and Robert Pires. Patrick Vieira was immense in central midfield. We've faced each other many times, but never has Vieira played better than on that day. He was fucking magnificent, winning the ball, running midfield, setting up attacks – head and shoulders above anyone. The final was hardly a classic, it just drifted by like a lazy stream, but Patrick moved to a different, faster rhythm. He took the game by the scruff of the neck and dominated. I wanted his shirt. Badly.

When Freddie Ljungberg scored I thought that was it. Game over. Dream dead. Shake Vieira's hand and go home. Loser. Try again. Arsenal were too good for us. How they were leading only by Ljungberg's goal, I don't know. Well, I do actually. Stéphane Henchoz played like a goalkeeper for us for a while, unofficially sharing the handling duties with Sander. Fortunately for Liverpool, referee Steve Dunn did not notice his hand-balls. Thank God. We'd have been 2–0 down by half-time if Dunn had awarded nailed-on penalties, more if Arsenal had taken the chances they kept creating.

Everyone expected Arsenal to chew us to pieces and spit us out. They outplayed us, no question, but they never broke us. Liverpool had a spirit that wouldn't crack. When Freddie's goal went in, Arsenal got all cocky and thought they had won. But we are Liverpool. We don't throw in the towel. Never. Our fans wouldn't let us. I wouldn't let us. Suddenly, with seven minutes left, a ball fell in the Arsenal box and I thought I had a chance. I swung my foot back and then brought it down and in. No contact. The ball had gone. Michael had pounced in front of me. Half-volley, full impact, past David Seaman, 1–1. Thank God Michael hit the ball before it came to me. I would probably have shovelled it over the bar. I was still going through with my redundant shot when Michael sprinted away, making for Liverpool's fans. He did that celebratory toss-over of his, with me, Robbie and Emile grabbing him, going berserk with happiness. I couldn't believe we were level with Arsenal.

Hold on. Keep it tight. Steady. Arsenal will hit back. Extra time seemed our aim. Then, with the stadium clock showing eighty-eight minutes, Michael did the impossible. He has this fantastic knack of scoring spectacular goals at vital moments. The ball was put between Martin Keown and Lee Dixon, and Michael was in like a flash. Nine times out of ten when Michael runs through with the ball on his right foot it ends with a goal. On his left foot, Michael still had a lot of work to do, but what a finish! Bang. Take that, Arsenal. Lightning had struck twice. Seaman was beaten, and so were Arsenal. The life ebbed from them. What a turnaround. Still to this day the Liverpool lads joke about that 2001 FA Cup final being Arsenal versus Owen. I don't dispute we had luck on our side that day, but we also had Michael.

The final whistle sounded so sweet. I walked across to the Arsenal players, who lay scattered about like victims of a motorway pile-up. Vieira was my target. I found him, and we hugged. Two sportsmen who had hammered away at each other parted, a mutual respect deepened. But some Arsenal people were graceless in defeat. I couldn't believe the reaction of Arsène Wenger and Ljungberg, for instance. They moaned on in the post-match interviews, saying, 'Liverpool didn't deserve it. We did. It should be us with the winner's medals.' No-one likes a sore loser, and no-one loses as sorely as Arsenal. Wenger and Ljungberg kept complaining about the hand-balls. Get real, boys. That's football. Grow up. I've played in loads of games Liverpool dominated and should have won but ended up with nothing, except a nasty feeling of frustration. Unfortunately for Arsenal, their bad luck came in an FA Cup final. So what? I wasn't interested in Arsenal's bitter reaction. I just wanted my Vieira shirt, my winner's medal, and to get back to the hotel to celebrate. I left Arsenal to their sour grapes and went off for some beer.

Typically, Gérard urged moderation, reminding us that the season was not over. Just four days away was the UEFA Cup final. 'Only two beers,' he ordered. We tried briefly to keep to the limit, honestly. Tried and failed. Two beers was insufficient to honour the FA Cup. I had a few more than a couple. All the players had a good drink. We were so happy. We weren't thinking about the UEFA Cup, we were thinking about the FA Cup, which was now heading to Anfield. I looked around at all the other players and sensed the deep satisfaction flowing through them. They had fantasized about this moment all their lives. So we drank, and we toasted Michael. Tomorrow could wait. Tomorrow, we'd get rid of the hangovers and get ready for the UEFA Cup. But that precious night, we sat and drank and joked and revelled in our achievement. For me, that was the highlight of Liverpool's Treble season. Nothing rivals the FA Cup.

Being French, Gérard felt differently. He was more turned on by the UEFA Cup than the FA Cup. Liverpool's dressing-room was split between the English lads excited most by the FA Cup and the foreigners more interested in the UEFA Cup. I smiled at Gérard's pleas after Cardiff. 'Live like monks,' he urged me, Carra and the rest. 'I know you've won the FA Cup, but the UEFA Cup means so much.' Gérard was obsessed with the trophy. He told us how much it weighed, and all about its history, but the UEFA Cup never raided my dreams like the FA Cup.

Europe was still a wonderful experience that season, though. The early rounds of the UEFA Cup saw Liverpool progress past Rapid Bucharest and Slovan Liberec, where Carra had the only nightmare I can ever remember him having. 'Are you all right, son?' Gérard asked Carra at half-time. 'Are you not well?' Carra was that bad. We were all pissing ourselves laughing. He was pulled, but we still got through, booking a third-round tie with Olympiakos. When we turned up in Athens towards the end of November, it was dead hostile: 50,000 loons, flares going off, and flags everywhere. The Greek fans were far away from the pitch, but they have a good arm on them. Their missiles still covered the distance. Great atmospheres like that really get me going, and I scored a glancing header off a Gary Mac corner.

Injury ruled me out of facing Roma in the fourth round, which was frustrating. I fancied playing against Francesco Totti, who's my kind of player – a real gladiator. Fortunately, Totti was also injured so I didn't miss out on a duel I craved. Unbelievably, Roma players slagged off Liverpool, saying they would walk all over us, which gave the lads all the motivation they needed. Beating the likes of Gabriel Batistuta and Cafu 2–0 in the Olympic Stadium gave the boys the confidence to believe the UEFA Cup could be lifted.

Next up were Porto, a really defensive side with a touch of skill in Deco and Capucho. We got the clean sheet we wanted at the Stadio Das Antas in early March, because we knew Portuguese sides don't really travel. They were duly finished off at Anfield a week later. I hit a volley and their keeper, Espinha, pulled off a worldie save.

Not even a rabid Evertonian could accuse Liverpool of taking the easy route to the UEFA Cup – the semi-finals brought mighty Barcelona. For many players, Camp Nou is the greatest stage on earth. I was buzzing to play there. Training there on the eve of the first leg, I couldn't concentrate. No chance. I was a tourist, looking round in admiration at this magnificent building. Carra and I kept smiling at each other. 'Some fucking stadium,' I said to him. Having a kick-about at Camp Nou felt a long way from playing bare-arse on Ironside. The next night, I wasn't really bothered about the result. Just let me on the Camp Nou pitch, let me hear those 90,000 mad fans. I just wanted to enjoy the occasion, and not think about winning or losing.

Barcelona were brilliant. Pepe Reina kept goal with the assurance he now shows for Liverpool. In attack, Rivaldo and Patrick Kluivert toyed with us. Barcelona never really had a front-man; those two just moved wide and deep, letting midfielders like Luis Enrique and Marc Overmars through. My job was in the middle, and rarely have I been so exhausted mentally and physically by opponents' un-believable movement. Barcelona fielded Pep Guardiola and Philip Cocu behind the midfield, and whichever one I tried to screen, the other came in to receive the ball. I went dizzy trying to follow them. Barcelona gave us a lesson in pass and move, qualities supposed to be Liverpool's hall-mark. The possession stats must have been seventy-thirty in Barcelona's favour. When Robbie came on in the second half, he asked Frank de Boer for a loan of their ball! On the few occasions we managed to get out of our half, I heard the shout from our bench: 'Great!' Nicking a 0–0 was a fabulous achievement. I immediately ran to Kluivert to swap shirts. I occasionally look at that shirt and remember that footballing lesson in Catalonia.

Tactically, we delivered a smart performance at Camp Nou and came away with a goalless draw, so I couldn't understand the criticism assailing us. 'Cautious Liverpool' was one of the kinder headlines. So fucking what? Going gung-ho against Barcelona would have been suicide. The press, particularly in Spain, labelled Liverpool as 'boring'. That got under a lot of people's skin at Anfield. It never worried me because I was building a medal collection in that 2000/01 season. One, two – count them. If Gérard had made us more adventurous that season, my haul would have been smaller. We were strong defensively and then hit teams on the counter-attack – bang, bang, you're dead. It suited the players we had. At Anfield in the second leg we reached our first European final in sixteen years with a Gary Mac pen and then another unbelievable defensive display in the second half. Job done.

Boredom was certainly not a word used to describe the final in Dortmund on 16 May. The atmosphere was special, because we were FA Cup winners. We didn't have the cigars out, but we certainly landed in Germany with our chests out. No matter what happened against our opponents, Alaves, Liverpool's season was a success. I was so relaxed, I slept like a baby every night in the run-up to Dortmund. I awoke on the morning of the final to discover our wonderful fans were everywhere in Dortmund, painting the town red. The journey from the hotel to the stadium was bedlam. Massive numbers of Liverpool supporters lined the streets, cheering us on, causing traffic chaos. Just parking the bus took half an hour. The fans wouldn't let us in. They had not seen us since Cardiff, and were determined to salute that victory. As security tried to force a way through, I looked out of the bus window and saw all the T-shirts: 'FA Cup winners 01' and 'Treble 2001'. Everyone believed the Treble was now inevitable, but no-one anticipated such an extraordinary match against Alaves, the surprise Spanish package. Finals don't come much more entertaining.

Because we had won the Worthington Cup and the FA

Cup, there was no pressure on us, and we just went out and enjoyed ourselves; if we had lost to Arsenal, we would have been a lot more cautious, sitting deep, stifling Alaves and playing on the counter-attack. Within four minutes, Gary Mac lifted over a ball and Markus Babbel put us ahead – a brave header, because he received an elbow for his troubles. Gary Mac's set-pieces were vital for Liverpool that season, and they were no flukes. Small details determine big games, and Gary Mac's constant practice, day in day out, meant he had corners, free-kicks and penalties off to a T. He was in such good form that Gérard gave me the right flank against Alaves. Thanks a lot. Gérard took the easy option. Rather than take on a respected old pro like Gary Mac, he sent a youngster out on the graveyard shift. Complaining was pointless. Gérard wouldn't listen, and moaning is not my style. Besides, I soon scored. I owe Michael a lot because his ball through was spot-on, inviting me to try my luck. Head down, smash it, 2–0. Alaves were no fools. They fought all the way. Ivan Alonso came on, pulled one back, but then Gary Mac slotted in a penalty: 3–1.

Coming into the dressing-room at half-time, we thought we'd won. Liverpool's fans were shouting about the Treble. Some players whispered it. The staff even mentioned that if we kept doing what we were doing, the Treble was ours. I was not alone in that Liverpool dressing-room in thinking that the Treble was done. Alaves never showed anything in the first half to worry us. That's why we returned to the fray far too casual. Alaves punished us, Javi Moreno netting twice. Unbelievable. Gérard sent Robbie on, and within seven minutes he had put Liverpool back in front with a fantastic shot. That seemed to be it. Alaves' resilience finally appeared broken. But we had one weakness. Sander suffered some dodgy moments during the season, and he screwed up again here, missing a cross which Jordi Cruyff dumped into our net. It was 4–4, and extra-time. It had to be Jordi, ex-Manchester United.

Gérard switched me to right-back for the additional period, where I immediately began worrying about penalties. 'If Gérard asks, I'll take one,' I told myself. To refuse would be to let the team down. I'd never let Liverpool down. I was still thinking about penalties when Macca put that free-kick in and Delfi Geli headed an own-goal. Gérard had spoken about golden goals, but I'm not a good listener in meetings. I didn't realize the game was over and we'd won. I was waiting for the re-start. 'Fuck me, that's it!' I eventually shouted, and I started leaping about in celebration. What a weird way to decide a final, and how harsh that it was an own-goal. At least it finished in open play and not with penalties.

So that was it. The Treble was completed, and the singing began. All the fans were chanting 'Houllier, Houllier'. Liverpool supporters will always respect Gérard, because when he arrived at Anfield he promised trophies, and he delivered. He never got the main one, the Premiership, but to collect three cups in one season was phenomenal. But, once again, he would not let us celebrate properly. Shit. I was dying for a session. But we couldn't. We had a match at Charlton Athletic three days later laden with significance. The Treble was good, but to beat Charlton to qualify for the Champions

League was more important financially for Liverpool.

Throughout the season, we had worked hard to stay in contention for third place and had even won at Old Trafford for the first time in ten years. The memory of this match on 17 December 2000 will never leave me. The press built up the game as a clash between me and Roy Keane. 'Are you scared?' people asked me. No fucking chance. I couldn't wait. I felt I might lose a fight with Keane, but I wouldn't lose many tackles. At the time, Keane possessed all the qualities that make a top midfielder. Obviously, I hated watching Manchester United, but I loved watching Keane. I wanted his aura, his ability to be everywhere on the pitch, tackling hard and passing well. Keane was impressive on television but simply awesome in the flesh. On telly, you don't see the runs he makes, the covering positions he takes up and the orders he gives. I lay in bed the night before the game, unable to get the image of Keane the leader out of my mind. 'Everyone is talking about Keane, so stand up to him, don't be bullied,' I told myself. 'And if Keane wants to mix it, fucking well mix it.'

Over breakfast, I flicked through the papers which all had page after page on the game. Ferguson even spoke about me. The biggest, and probably only, compliment someone from Manchester United ever paid me came from the United manager in the papers that day. I couldn't believe my eyes as I read his view of me. 'Gerrard's physically and technically precocious, a good engine, remarkable energy, reads the game and passes quickly,' said Fergie. 'I would hate to think Liverpool have someone as good as Roy Keane.' Fuck me. I knew how much

Keane meant to the United fans, and to Ferguson. For Ferguson to compare me with his captain was some accolade. Still, his admiration was no secret to me. The United lads told me at an England get-together. After reading Ferguson's comments, I just wanted to go and prove him right, to let him know Liverpool did have a Roy Keane of their own.

Visiting Old Trafford is like negotiating an assault course as it rains vitriol. That 2000 trip was no different. Driving behind enemy lines triggered the usual stick. Liverpool's coach was belted, the United fans jumping up at the windows, their faces contorted by sheer hatred. We got the full welcome: V signs, wanker signs, knife signs. 'Fuck off, scum!' they'd shout. 'We'll fucking kill you!' 'In your Liverpool slum . . .' they sang. The poison dripping from the United fans never ceases to shock me. Shit, they really loathe us. Bang. A window splintered and a brick nearly bounced off my head. Jesus Christ. Here we go again. I ran for the gate leading to the dressing-rooms.

Of course I knew what Liverpool–Manchester United games were all about from my YTS days. I had some right kicking matches then with Wes Brown and Richie Wellens, who plays for Oldham now. Two men and a dog watched those YTS meetings, but we approached them the same way, do or die. And during ninety minutes of football, I want United to die. I have never known hatred like United's. Everton fans have grown to despise me because I score against them so regularly, and because I keep saying I love beating Everton. They loathe me when I play against them, but I think they respect me as a player. At Old Trafford, it's different. Everyone there just hates me because I'm Liverpool. That winter's day in 2000 was no different. I almost couldn't hear the first whistle because of the booing. 'Fuck me,' I thought, 'this is show time. Get on my game or get fucked.'

For ten minutes, United gave an exhibition of possession. All of Fergie's players, not just Keane, kept the ball well. I had played against decent sides and players before, but United were on a different level. I didn't get a kick for ages. I had been warned. In the dressing-room, Gérard and Thommo said, 'Press them, choke them, stick together, be compact. And whatever you do, don't lose the ball.' Why? Because Keane will kill you. Because United's fans will piss themselves. Giving away possession at Old Trafford is close to suicide. I lost a few passes, Keane got the better of me a few times, and I had 60,000 Mancs laughing at me. Shit. No-one is welcome at Old Trafford, particularly not neighbours from along the East Lancs Road, and that is why United have been so successful. They have a great team housed in a stadium that scares the shit out of visitors.

We held firm, and when Danny scored the free-kick to settle the game it was just an amazing moment. We had only a few thousand fans there at Old Trafford, but it was like winning a cup final. Playing against Keane felt like a ninety-minute lesson which improved me. He shook hands, said 'well done', and that was it. I was too intimidated to ask for his shirt. I would like one of Keane's Ireland shirts, but I would never take a Man United top home. United shirts are banned in my house.

That victory kept us on course for the Champions League, but the real push was accelerated by an astonishing 3–2 win at Goodison on 16 April, when Macca won it for us with a forty-yard free-kick. Qualification rested on that final game at Charlton, and we won it 4–0. We won all our final games that amazing Treble season.

On the back of my contribution to the Treble, Liverpool sought me out over a contract extension. Struan rang to say that Rick Parry, Liverpool's chief executive, had been constantly on the phone. Liverpool sounded desperate. 'Stru, they are steaming for me to re-sign,' I said. I scored ten goals that season, played well and was doing all right for England. 'We are offering Stevie a six-year deal,' Rick told Struan. 'I think that's too long,' Struan said to me. 'Six years is a massive commitment. Four years would be better. That gives some freedom for movement later on.' I agreed. Struan was always brilliant with my finances. The deal was done and dusted sharpish. Maybe Liverpool were worried that someone would come in for me. Rick agreed to the four years and put me on really, really good money – £50,000 a week. Players who rise through the ranks rarely get top wages, but Liverpool were different class with me. It was a massive jump up financially, and Liverpool certainly made sure I knew that.

After I signed, Rick, Gérard and Thommo talked to me about the future.

'We are giving you a big contract because we rate you so highly,' said Gérard. 'We don't want you to change. Carry on training and playing the way you have been. We're really happy with your behaviour. Don't change.'

I was buzzing. The money was great, but my life had been comfortable before the new deal. For someone like me, a kid from Huyton, I was doing well. I had my own apartment. I sorted out Mum and Dad for a few quid. But money wasn't an issue. What really delighted me was the fact that Liverpool were anxious for me to stay. Brilliant. My love affair with Liverpool was continuing.

9
Tackling a Problem

Playing abroad doesn't appeal to me for one dead simple reason: I love the blood and thunder of English football too much. Our league and cup competitions have an intensity and honesty that cannot be found anywhere else in the world. The physical nature of the Premiership suits my style. Tackle and be tackled. Get up and get on with it, mate. Don't roll around pretending you're hurt. This is England. Piss off to Spain or Italy, where they niggle, dive, and pull shirts. I can't stand that. Switching from the Premiership to the Champions League is like speaking a different language. Over time, I've learned to adapt in Europe. Whenever I step onto a continental pitch, I'm very careful because opponents exaggerate the force of even harmless challenges. I hate that. Take the physical out of football and the game will be destroyed as a spectacle. For me, nothing beats a wet pitch, sliding into tackles, and going for the ball – brilliant. Nothing stirs me more than hearing passionate fans screaming 'Get stuck in!' That's me. I was put on this earth to steam into tackles. When I finally bow out of the game I love so much, I want to be remembered as hard but fair.

For most professionals, tackling is a technique. For me, it's an adrenalin rush. It's a chance to beat an opponent one-on-one, win the ball and then launch an attack. The sight of the other team with the ball makes me sick. If it's Everton, Man United, Arsenal, Chelsea, or whoever, I have to claim it back. It's my ball, and I'm going for it. Tackling is a collision which sorts out the cowards from the brave. I never hold back in a tackle. I can't. I put my heart and soul into it, as well as my body.

Down the years, that approach has sometimes got me into trouble. Even back in my YTS and reserve days at Liverpool, I was desperate to make my mark and occasionally did so literally. I'd see someone with the ball and that was it. Bang. I flew in, got the ball and left him in a heap. My boots were not guided by malice as they crashed in. He had the ball; I wanted it – end of story. Liverpool's coaches always warned me against it. Sod that. Restraint was not a word I understood. In one training session, Steve Heighway ran down the wing, taking the piss really, so I belted him against the wall. Straight through, crash, smashed against the wall. 'What are you playing at?' Steve shouted when he got up. He was livid. 'You've got to cut out those sort of tackles.' All the staff had a go at me.

Liverpool actually like a bit of devil in their players. They were always trying to toughen us up. Our five-a-side YTS games were often invaded by two pros, Steve Harkness and Eddie Turkington. Some of the tackles going in were ridiculous. Harkness booted all the YTS boys, even elbowed us. My blood boiled. 'He's not doing that to me, no fucking chance,' I told myself once as I saw him line up on the other side. 'You're not coming over here, kicking me.' I was ready for him. Steve was a decent player who could look after himself, but I went right through him. Bang. More than once. Bang bang. Don't mess with me. Turkington as well. He was meant to be this big hard-case in the ressies, I reminded myself. Let's find out. Right into Turkington, hit him, belt him. Eventually, Heighway called Dad in. 'What's up with Steven?' Heighway asked. 'Has he got a problem at home? He comes in so angry. He wants to kill people in training.' Steve looked at Dad, waiting to make sure the seriousness of the situation was sinking in. 'We don't want to take away Steven's aggression, because that's one of his strengths,' Steve continued, 'but he's going through tackles wanting to really do damage. Please have a word with him. He'll either break someone's leg or injure himself.' Dad pulled me at home. 'You must calm down,' he said. Even Ronnie Moran paused from working with the first team to give me some advice about the big tackles. 'Stop them,' he told me. I couldn't.

At sixteen, I saw a sports psychologist about the tackling. Bill Beswick is well respected in the game and worked a lot with Steve McClaren at Middlesbrough and also with the Man United boys. Howard Wilkinson introduced me to Bill when I represented England U-18s. 'This guy is brilliant,' Howard said. 'Listen to him.' Bill talked to me about my tackling. 'Imagine a set of traffic lights,' Bill said. The idea was to know when to go for the ball, and when to stop. Bill advised me on how to approach games. 'Fire in your belly but ice in your head' was one of his favourite sayings. 'It will work perfectly with you, Steven, because we don't want to take aggression out of your game but we do want you on the pitch. That's where everyone wants you.' Bill even came to Melwood to chat to the Liverpool lads. My confidence was boosted by Bill. I would never consult him personally now, but at the time he helped me. But even with all this good guidance, from Bill, Steve, Ronnie and my dad, I still crunched into tackles as a youth-team player. Even when I made Liverpool's first XI I was a liability at times. Growing up as a player sometimes proved painful. A feeling of shame fills me when I recall the moments that scarred the early stages of my career.

The first came on 27 September 1999 at Anfield. We were up against the enemy, Everton. I was aching to play. In the team meeting, Gérard Houllier read out the eleven starters: 'Sander; Veggard, Sami, Carra, Stan; Vladi, Didi, Jamie, Patrik; Michael and Robbie.' Not me. Gutted. Big lump in the throat. I deserved to start but got bombed. Why? My head was a mess. I sat on the bench in a huge sulk, seething at the injustice.

On the pitch, it was all soon kicking off. Franny Jeffers and Sander Westerveld tangled and got sent off. I wanted to be in there, sorting Everton out, showing everyone I should have started. 'If you get on,' I said to myself, 'just belt one of them. Fucking belt a Bluenose. Let Gérard know he is not dropping me for another derby. Ever.' I was a red card waiting to happen the moment Gérard sent me on. My fuse was short and burning fast. Bang. I went in high and late on Kevin Campbell. No mercy, no excuses: straight red. I escaped the pitch as quickly as possible. I sprinted down the tunnel and bumped into Franny, who was laughing his big-eared head off. 'Ha, ha, ha,' went Franny. 'Thanks, Stevie! You took the pressure off me!'

As the red mist cleared, I realized how much I'd screwed up. 'Little selfish bastard,' I told myself as I stood in the showers. Liverpool's players would be fuming. We were only 1–0 down, still with a chance of getting back into the derby. But then I nailed Campbell, and the lads faced mission impossible. Shit. I'd let them down badly. I expected stick off the players, off everyone.

When I switched my phone on, the first text was from Dad. He got straight to the point: 'What are you doing, you knob-head?' I knew exactly what he meant. A crazy tackle and a three-game ban was not the best way to convince people I could be trusted with a place in Liverpool's starting XI.

When I arrived at Melwood the next day, I was ordered to Gérard's office. The boss laid into me. 'Your head wasn't right from the moment I told you that you weren't playing,' he said. 'We could see you were sulking. You have got to sulk for ten seconds and then forget about it.' Gérard banged on and on. 'Think about the team, not yourself, Steven. Stop doing tackles like that because we need you on the pitch. We brought you on to change the game and you let us down.'

I'd heard enough. My natural defiant streak kicked in. 'I was expecting to play,' I answered back. 'You just dropped me in the derby. I was desperate to play.'

As I was about to add that Liverpool wouldn't have

been 1–0 down if he had started me, I saw the look on Phil Thompson's face. Thommo was standing behind Gérard, glaring like a madman and ready to pounce if I dared have a pop back. That was Thommo to a T. 'Take it,' I thought. Arguing the toss was pointless. I knew I was out of order.

When I drove out of Melwood that day, I stopped to sign some autographs for a few fans and they were buzzing for me. 'Dead right, well done, at least you cared,' they said. They were wrong. I shouldn't have done it.

A few weeks later, I had a meal at Est Est Est in Albert Dock and somebody told me Sami Hyypia was next door in the Blue Bar. I nipped in to see him. We had a drink and soon I needed a piss. I went through the door of the toilets and, bloody hell, who was there at the urinal? Kevin Campbell. We stood there, side by side, having a piss. The last time I saw him he was lying on the ground at Anfield with the Everton physio sticking him back together.

'All right?' Campbell said.

Christ, I felt embarrassed. 'Listen, Kev, sorry about that tackle, my head had gone.'

Campbell laughed. 'Forget about it, Stevie. But I did have some stud-marks on my thigh!'

He was very forgiving, but I wasn't taking any chances. Kevin's a bit of a unit, built like a heavyweight. I feared he might take his revenge right there and then in the Blue Bar toilets. I got out sharpish.

Fast forward a year, to 1 October 2000, and Liverpool were getting soundly whipped by Chelsea at Stamford Bridge. I'd just had enough. I hate losing. Frustration squeezed all sense out of my mind and I went for Dennis Wise, belting him. Dennis grabbed me by the neck, and we were pushing and shoving, scuffling away. As fights go it was handbag stuff, and I thought people would quickly forget about it. Fat chance. A couple of days later, England met up at Burnham Beeches to prepare for a vital World Cup qualifier against Germany, the last international at Wembley before the bulldozers rolled in. Wisey was in the squad. So was I. Robbie Fowler and Steve McManaman dropped by my new place in Whiston to pick me up. The three of us all drove down to Burnham together and they were merciless all the way. Macca and Robbie had me by the balls.

'Wisey won't be happy with you,' laughed Macca, winding me up.

'Tough bugger, him,' Robbie chipped in. 'Crazy Gang and all that.'

'Fuck him,' I replied. 'If he wants some, I'll give it to him.'

Would Wisey really pull me for a one-on-one? What would the other England players think if Wisey and me started battering each other again? I wasn't scared of Wisey; I was just thinking I was a little shitty-arsed kid and Wisey was an established international.

'Be on your toes, Stevie,' Robbie warned me as we drove into Burnham. 'Wisey's waiting for you.'

My heart pumped madly as I walked into the hotel, braced for an ambush by the little Chelsea man. I kept expecting Wisey to jump out and shout, 'Oi, Gerrard, what's your fucking game?' I was ready. If he wanted another war, I wouldn't disappoint. He could have another scrap, big-style. But Wisey wasn't in reception. 'Maybe he's waiting for you in the meal-room,' Robbie said helpfully. Slightly nervously, I entered the meal-room. Wisey was there, big grin on his face. He walked across. 'This is it,' I thought. 'Action stations.' My fists clenched. Wisey's right hand came out sharpish, stretching towards me. But he only wanted to shake my hand. ''Ow are yer?' he said, and rubbed my head. And that was it. No war, nothing. Top man.

Liverpool against Leeds United is another lively old fixture. And on 13 April 2001, at Anfield, it was a top-of-the-table clash. I was up for it and was soon piling into tackles. I picked up a caution early on, for clipping Alan Smith. Nothing nasty. Hardly a yellow. Just doing my job, chasing the ball. Soon I was closing down David Batty, going in cleanly to win the ball. Batty stitched me up bigtime. He dived. I never touched him. My heart fell as the referee reached for his notebook again. That was me off, for two nothing tackles. Ridiculous. 'Don't send him off, ref,' said Batty, trying to plead my case. Clever lad, Batty. I was already on my way. The ref was never going to change his mind. But there was Batty coming over all innocent, even pretending to be my mate. Bollocks. Batty wanted me out of the game. That was why he went down so easily. I have met Batty since and he seems a decent enough guy, but that sending-off stank. It was a stitch-up.

The next time I remember my blood really heating up was on 8 September 2001 during a match with Aston Villa, again at Anfield. We were struggling. I equalized just after half-time, but the match was turning into a nightmare. George Boateng was running midfield, out-muscling me time and again. Frustration took over. Suddenly there was Boateng in front of me, in my sights, and I just launched myself. It was a coward's tackle. I admit that now. I lunged with both feet and caught him with one, my studs thudding in high up on his leg. He went down and just lay there. No wonder. It was a filthy challenge, one I deeply regret to this day. Television occasionally replays the tackle, and I always wince. How could I inflict such a vicious challenge on a fellow pro? It was unforgivable, and I knew it. The ref knew it too, because he waved the red card. And my team-mates certainly knew it. 'Out of order,' Gary McAllister told me. Other lads slated me as well. 'Sorry,' I replied. What else could I say? Gérard marched in and harangued me, which was fair enough. I felt terrible, miserable. My head was close to exploding. Dad called, and his words echoed Gary Mac's: 'You were out of order.' Then my agent, Struan Marshall, phoned. 'Go home, and get your head together,' he said. 'I want to speak to you tomorrow.'

Home should have offered some sanctuary, but sleep was impossible. I lay in bed, thinking, 'I could have broken Boateng's leg.' Fortunately, George was a strong, tough type. In the morning, the papers were brutal towards me – understandably so. The picture of me diving in was shocking. Struan called. 'You must change your tackling or you are going to be remembered for it,' he said. 'Rather than being remembered as a good player, you will be tarnished as a dog. Still be aggressive, but just time your tackles better. Don't get frustrated.' Struan's words hit home hard. He was right. I loathed the thought of being remembered for hurting other players.

'Can you get me Boateng's number?' I asked Struan.

'Give me a couple of minutes,' Struan replied, and rang off.

I was just about to give Gareth Barry, the one Villa player I knew well, a call when Struan rang back with Boateng's mobile number. As I punched in the digits, I thought, 'I never, ever want to be in this situation again.'

Boateng answered.

'George, it's Steven Gerrard. I'm phoning to apologize. It was a bad tackle.'

I paused, expecting him to have a rant back.

'Listen,' he said. 'You are a fucking good player. Just get that out of your game and you'll be all right. I'm OK. But you're lucky you never hurt me. I accept your apology.'

Relieved, I said goodbye and pressed the end-call button. Thank God that was over.

I was banned for three games. No complaints. The banishment should really have been longer. Gary Mac was so concerned about my tackling that he spoke to Struan, and then confronted me. 'Calm yourself down,' Gary said. 'You are going into tackles wanting to kill people. You are going to end up doing yourself in. Take it from me, I've had some bad injuries. Tackling is not just about throwing everything into it, there's an art to it. Learn when to tackle, how to tackle, how hard.' Ever since breaking into the Liverpool team, I have always listened to the older players I respected, like Fowler, Redknapp, Staunton, McAllister, Carragher, even Michael. Gary Mac's advice on tackling made sense, but altering something so ingrained would take time. 'I'm not changing my tackling for anyone,' I told myself when the lectures were over. 'Tackling is part of my game.'

The Community Shield is supposedly an exhibition match to kick the season off, and it certainly did kick off in August the following year. Meetings between Liverpool and Arsenal are always hugely competitive. Patrick Vieira and I have had some bruising run-ins, and this was definitely one of them. Patrick, remember, bossed me in the 2001 FA Cup final in Cardiff. Wanting to stamp my authority on the game early on, I deliberately hit him with a hard tackle after five minutes. Vieira made the most of it, writhing around and whingeing. 'Shut up, and be a man,' I thought. I got booked. So what? Liverpool needed to show they were not scared of Arsenal and all their big names.

Arsenal's post-match reaction pissed me off. Arsène Wenger slaughtered me in the press. He said I was a hatchet-man and my challenge was a leg-breaker; he said I was reckless and should have been red-carded. Rubbish. When Vieira stopped rolling around, he got up and carried on for the rest of the game. A young kid tackles Wenger's captain, as I did, and Wenger protests. If Patrick had gone through me, I'd have got on with it. Hypocrisy rules with Arsenal. Whenever I come up against one of Wenger's teams, I know I am in for a physical test. Fair enough. Martin Keown and Tony Adams have come through the back of me. Vieira has done me. Dennis Bergkamp could give you an elbow or stamp on you. Unlike Arsenal, I don't complain.

There was more mayhem on 22 December 2002 in the derby at Anfield. Avoiding controversy against Everton has never been easy for me. Being nice to the neighbours is not in my nature. Derbies agitate something in my blood. In this game, I challenged for a loose ball with Everton's full-back, Gary Naysmith. I thought he was going to do me, so I got my retaliation in first. I'm not proud of my reaction as Naysmith came in. I left the ground with both feet and lunged for the ball. In mid-air, I knew it would hurt Naysmith, but there was no stopping. I had to land somewhere. I hurtled into his legs, opening a gash and splashing blood on his white shorts.

Pandemonium erupted. Out of the corner of my eye, I saw this rampaging ox charging at me. It was Wayne Rooney – a real headache that day. At full tilt, he shoved me and then grabbed me round the neck. He almost took my head off. So this is the famous Wayne Rooney. Everton's wonder-kid needed little introduction. I watched him in the FA Youth Cup and knew all about his talent. He was brilliant against us that day in 2002, a whirlwind in blue. As well as bundling into me, Rooney smashed into our keeper, Chris Kirkland, and then hit the bar. What a class act! Even in the warm-up, Everton's fans sang 'Rooney's going to get you'. How right they were! Me and Wazza laugh now over our scuffle. Whenever I see the picture of him piling into me, I just crack up. It's hilarious. 'I'd have done the same to you, Wazza,' I tell him. Sorting out whoever topped my team-mate is the way I am. Wayne too. We share an aggressive streak. It's part of life in Huyton and Croxteth. And Rooney had every right to wade in. The kid was just defending Naysmith. Fair dos.

What incensed me was the reaction of Everton's senior players, David Weir and Alan Stubbs. They hurried across, like busybodies on a mission, and tried to get me sent off. Weir and Stubbs are always at it. Always trying to get players dismissed. They tried to get Michael Owen booked and sent off once. I watch Weir all the time. Any little incident and Weir is over to the ref sharpish, badgering him to wave a red. When Stubbs moved briefly to Sunderland he took his bad habits with him. When Liverpool played Sunderland in the 2005/06 season, Stubbs tried to get me sent off again. Fortunately, the efforts of Stubbs and Weir to persuade Graham Poll to give me my marching orders failed at Anfield. Poll was looking the other way when I went into Naysmith. The ref knew something bad had gone on, but he couldn't punish me for something he hadn't seen. Straight away, I tried to explain to Poll: 'Listen, I caught him, but I didn't mean to hurt him.'

Things calmed down a bit, the game finished 0–0, and I immediately went to apologize to Naysmith. In the corridor near the dressing-rooms, I spotted David Moyes, Everton's manager, being interviewed by Sky. After he finished, I approached him.

'I'm sorry,' I said. 'I know the tackle looks bad, but I didn't mean to do him. Is Gary about for me to apologize?'

David said, 'I will send your apologies on to him.'

I don't think Moyes wanted me going in Everton's dressing-room. I might not have got out again.

Poll saw the tackle again on television and highlighted the incident in his report. The FA summoned me to a disciplinary hearing at the Reebok, Bolton Wanderers' stadium. I felt fairly confident. Naysmith was going to nail me, so I'd had to tackle that way. It was defensive. During the hearing, the suits from the FA said they understood. 'In mid-air, you wanted to pull out but couldn't.' Exactly. 'But we have to think of the other player and your previous tackles.' Shit. That was me done for. The FA took past challenges into account so I had no chance of a fair trial. They recalled my tackle on Boateng, and gave me a three-game ban for the Naysmith incident. Talk about being harshly treated. The FA should have judged me just on one incident, not raked up past offences.

At the end of the season, I booked a flight to Portugal, where I own a house. I was late heading for the gate, so late that the airline put out a message on the Tannoy: 'Will passenger Gerrard please report to gate six as the flight to Faro is ready to depart.' Shit. I rushed to the gate, made it in time, got on the plane and looked down the aisle. It was one of those low-budget jobs where you sit anywhere. All these punters were pulling faces, going, 'Cheeky bugger – you've had us waiting here.' My eyes searched out a spare seat. The plane was completely packed, but there had to be one seat left. I finally saw it. I moved down the aisle, and as I neared the seat, a feeling of horror rushed through my body. The empty seat was next to, of all people, Gary Naysmith and his missus! Escape was not an option.

'All right, Gary?' I ventured as I took my seat, trying not to blush.

'Yeah, Steven, I'm fine,' Naysmith replied. 'You all right?'

'Yes.'

I sneaked a look out of the corner of my eye, and Gary's missus was giving him the hard elbow. Amazingly, he never mentioned the tackle. He was quiet on the flight. We hardly talked. I was scared to fall asleep in case I got an elbow!

Graeme Le Saux was the next player to feel the full force of my frustration. On 11 May 2003 we were battling Chelsea at Stamford Bridge for the final Champions League position. So much was at stake. People bang on about the dosh for the club, but it's more than money. For players, the Champions League is the only place to be. It's where the big teams and big players live. So everyone was flying into tackles that afternoon. Chelsea were too good for us. My pre-match fears were coming true. Our record at the Bridge was never the best, and Chelsea had some class players: Frank Lampard and Eidur Gudjohnsen started, and Gianfranco Zola came on. Sami Hyypia scored with a header early on, but Marcel Desailly equalized, and then Jesper Gronkjaer bent one in. Half an hour gone and we trailed 2–1. The Chelsea fans were crowing about them heading for the Champions League while we were destined for the UEFA Cup. Liverpool had spent all season slaving to get in the Champions League. Now the dream was dying.

With a minute remaining, I couldn't stand it any more. Anger swept through my brain, breaking all the restraint mechanisms. Chelsea's full-back was nearest to me, and he received a good old-fashioned clattering. Some people thought it was something personal against Le Saux. It wasn't. Graeme's a likeable bloke who was always fine with me when we crossed paths with England. He was just the closest when I flipped. Bang. Second yellow, straight off, season over.

I sat in the dressing-room, livid about the way the season ended. Gérard was outside, talking me up. 'If we had ten more like Steven Gerrard, we would be in the

Champions League,' the gaffer said. Nice sentiments, but nothing could console me. Missing out on the Champions League was a disaster. The atmosphere, quality, excitement and interest levels of the UEFA Cup are far below those of the Champions League, which is closer to playing for England. No wonder I lost my cool at the Bridge.

Come 3 August, we found ourselves playing Galatasaray at the Amsterdam ArenA. There was no chance of this being a gentle pre-season work-out. Tensions between England and Turkey were running high at club and international level. A few months earlier, in a Euro 2004 qualifier, England had beaten Turkey at Sunderland's Stadium of Light, and it was a real battle. In two months' time, England were heading to Istanbul, so everything was being built up, every little fire stoked into an inferno. In Amsterdam, Galatasaray targeted Liverpool's English players. No question. Fucking blatant. I was on the bench, watching the Turks laying into Michael and Emile. I was steaming to get on, because there was so much going off out there. 'Put me on, put me on!' I kept telling Gérard.

With half an hour left, the boss relented. Harry Kewell got hooked, and I stormed on, looking for trouble. It was like a scene from a Wild West film. A fight raged between the two sides, and I needed to make up for lost time. Galatasaray's players were putting in nasty little tackles, pulling shirts and spitting at us. Hakan Sukur was right in the middle of it. All the Galatasaray players were. Hakan Unsal, Umit, the lot. What sly bastards. Suddenly an elbow jabbed into my face. My eye watered up, my lip thickened, my anger intensified. I went looking for Sukur and Unsal. I hit Unsal with a tackle, and the Dutch ref, Rene Temmink, booked me. Now the Turks were really after me. Another elbow. Bang. I was taking so many blows to the head, I felt like a bloody boxer. Chaos reigned. Neil Mellor, our young striker, was goaded badly. He tackled Gabriel Tamas, a nothing challenge, but Temmink sent him off. Shocker. Now I was really on the warpath, chasing around, hunting Turks, kicking anything that moved. Temmink gave a silly free-kick against me, for a foul on Unsal, and all the Turks immediately surrounded us. Their spit ran down my face. I wiped it off, and tried to walk away. Sukur pinched me. It was the old Turkish game of provocation, and I fell for a classic stitch-up. Wound up by the Turks, I was maddened by Temmink's decision, convinced he had been conned by them.

'You fat cheating cunt,' I told him.

'What?' he said. 'Come here.'

Bang, second yellow, red, off. Bollocks. The Turks were all smug, knowing their cheating had paid off and they were cruising to a 2–1 win.

I couldn't believe Temmink would understand. He was foreign. I knew that because he was speaking foreign in the tunnel on the way out. But he knew English, or certainly the words I directed at him. 'You know that counts for the season?' said Gérard. It suddenly dawned on me: this red card could affect me in the UEFA Cup. Shit. Joe Corrigan, Liverpool's goalkeeping coach, also had a go at me. So did Thommo. I was fuming with myself, and with Temmink. Gérard went to see the ref and had a quiet word – a plea, really. The gaffer then returned with a quiet smile on his face. 'I talked to the ref, and Temmink said, "I am not putting it in my report. Gerrard was aggressive, but he didn't use foul and abusive language." ' Result! Fair play to Temmink – I'd turned the air blue!

Temmink's mercy still didn't erase the bad memory of being dismissed. Red cards are humiliating. No indignity matches the despair of sitting in an empty dressing-room, listening to the shouts of the crowd outside and knowing your team-mates are struggling without you. Letting the lads down is a cardinal sin in football. I've played in teams when somebody has been sent off and it's pure graft, extra running, with little chance of getting anything from the match. I had to change, because I was becoming a liability to Liverpool. It was around this time that I really started responding to the advice of people like Struan and Gary Mac. I altered my tackling technique, going in with one foot, not two. The red mist still lingers, especially in derbies. After a silly booking for kicking the ball away against Everton in the 2005–06 season, I got another yellow for a late tackle on Kevin Kilbane and was sent off, so I've not eradicated the problem yet. I still love the thud of a good tackle. That's why I enjoy watching England play rugby. Big hits and bloody battles are my idea of sport!

I have been on the receiving end of a few painful hacks myself, of course. One of the worst was Viorel Ganea's coward's tackle on me when Liverpool played Wolves at Molineux on 21 January 2004. I'd just returned from three games out and the last thing I needed was some mad Romanian ploughing into me. He did me. Blatant. My sock was ripped from knee to ankle, my leg badly gashed. What angered me most was that Ganea did not even get booked. Nothing. Fucking scandal. He bloody nearly broke my leg. I suppose it was hard for the ref, because he was following the ball. The ball had gone, but Ganea kept coming and he did me good.

After the match, I limped past Wolves' manager, Dave Jones. 'That was a fucking coward's tackle by Ganea,' I told him.

Dave agreed. 'It was out of order,' he said. 'How he hasn't been sent off I don't know.'

I respected Dave Jones for saying that. Everyone knew Ganea had gone in to hurt me. Phil Thompson went bananas.

My old Liverpool team-mate Paul Ince patrolled midfield for Wolves that day. Incey and I have enjoyed plenty of argy-bargy down the years, mainly during his time at Middlesbrough. I find it really strange with Incey. We can be laying into each other all game, hammer and tongs, no respite, yet moments later, in the players' lounge over a drink, Incey is my good mate. He can switch the aggression on and off. One minute Incey's screaming 'I'm going to fucking have you!' The next, showered and changed, suited and booted, it's 'How's your family?' Bizarre. 'Top man, Stevie!' Incey will say, giving me high fives moments after we have been kicking the shit out of each other. I admire him for that.

I'm different. When I have a run-in with someone, I worry how they will react when I see them next. Most are brilliant, like Incey. And that's the great thing about the Premiership. What happens on the pitch stays on the pitch. Dust-ups get forgotten the moment the final whistle blows. All resentment stays within those four white lines. I love all that walking off the pitch, shaking hands, apologizing for ninety minutes of aggro with a 'Hey, let's go have a drink.' That, for me, is real sportsmanship. That is why English football is the best in the world.

It's not perfect, of course. Gamesmanship goes on – diving, shirt-tugging. I'm not an angel, I'll admit that. Just ask Aston Villa fans. The Holte End hate me. Ever since the Boateng foul, I get serenaded with 'Steven Gerrard is a wanker' whenever I play at Villa Park. And I enraged Villa supporters on another occasion. Back in 2001, I was through down the right, played in by Jari Litmanen, speeding into the Villa area. One of their defenders committed himself, slightly touching me, but nothing heavy, nothing I couldn't ride. I could easily have stayed on my feet, but I went down. Penalty! It didn't appear a dive. It looked a blatant pen. But it wasn't. I stitched up Villa's defenders. After the match, I thought long and hard over whether I'd done the right thing. I'm not a diver, but I did exaggerate the force of the challenge that day.

Captaincy has matured me. Since the bad days of the Boateng and Naysmith tackles, my disciplinary record has improved radically. It is my responsibility to look after the younger players, to represent Liverpool the right way. Showing respect to referees is vital. Incey loved abusing refs, but they are far stricter now. Any lip shown to officials brings instant yellows. As Becks and Wazza have discovered, even clapping your hands at the ref in Europe means the end of you. Slaughtering refs is dangerous.

When I first broke into the Liverpool team, refs were routinely abused. I slated them over shite decisions. It helped get frustration out of my system. Even as captain, I'll still have a go at refs if they screw up, but I have great relationships with them now. The good ones, like Mark Clattenburg and Graham Poll, understand the importance of communicating with captains. They enjoy the banter and keep the dialogue open. Poll can't stop chatting and joking; he bloody loves a chat! Mark Halsey relishes a bit of banter as well. That's good. Clattenburg and Poll are the best refs around; confident in themselves, they treat players as equals. So we respect them back. There's none of this 'I'm in charge and you're a little boy, so behave yourself' crap from Clattenburg or Poll. Firm but fair, those two don't care in which famous ground they are refereeing, which difficult managers are in the dug-outs or how much pressure players try to put them under. I watch Clattenburg and Poll a lot on the TV and they are never influenced by the occasion. I can tell a good ref in ten minutes, and I knew immediately Poll and Clattenburg were top-drawer. They have an aura about them but no arrogance. Paul Durkin was the same. He was brilliant, top-class. All the players liked and respected Durkin. I never felt like testing Paul's patience because he just wanted to get on with the show. His retirement disappointed me, yet even with that setback, the standard of refereeing in the Premiership has improved.

As captain, I view refs in a different light. It's handy to build a decent relationship with a ref, to get him on Liverpool's side. I'm quite cynical about that. It's gamesmanship. A tight decision in the ninetieth minute may go my way if I've spent all game being friendly to the ref. He's only human. An official like Poll or Clattenburg is likely to be more sympathetic if I work with them than if I am in their face like a cheeky Scouser, as I was years ago. I used to think refs were steaming to book me, but since getting the Liverpool armband I've realized they have a tough job. So I try to help. Players should help them more. Sometimes, when Liverpool are doing badly, I blame it all privately on the refs. They are shite, useless, hell-bent on destroying our season, in league with the oppo. Then I think clearly and realize that, given what is at stake in modern matches, English refs do a good job.

Sadly, there are a few referees around who I simply don't rate, like Uriah Rennie and Neale Barry. News of Jeff Winter's retirement did not upset me. Winter was a moaner. The worst refs are the arrogant ones who don't talk; they just look away, have a chip on their shoulder, and actually think they are celebrities. Jeff Winter is on Sky more than me. No matter how blatantly wrong the ref has got it, Winter will go all the way around the world to stick up for the ref. Jeff, come on, just say, 'That's a bad mistake.' But no, Winter goes, 'If I was in that situation I would have done this.' He refereed me loads of times and, in my opinion, fucked up big-time. He wasn't one of my favourites. He never listened. I haven't got much time for Mike Riley either. He's actually a decent ref, but he went down in my estimation when he refused to punish Tiago for trying to take the lace out of the ball when Chelsea played at Anfield in 2005. Tiago's was one of the most obvious hand-balls ever in the history of football. Diego Maradona's Hand of God looked sound in comparison.

Liverpool were blatantly done by Tiago and Riley that day. We were convinced Riley was going to blow for it. He began, but then stopped. 'You put your whistle in your mouth!' Carra shouted at Riley. It was a disgrace. When Wazza got that penalty out of Sol Campbell at Old Trafford, I was in the Sky studio. I knew Riley had been tricked. It was the type of decision given by a referee to Man United in front of the Stretford End at Old Trafford. Would Wazza have got the penalty yards from the North Bank at Highbury? No chance. Riley has made a couple of howlers.

The best ref was Pierluigi Collina. Bar none. Foreign refs are far fussier than their cousins in the Premiership – apart from Collina. The Italian was pure class, demanding and getting instant respect. Jesus, he scared me. 'Gerrard!' he'd shout if I crossed the line into what he considered unacceptable, and he'd wave that long, bony finger at me in admonishment. Shit, I'll be good. Collina's bulging eyes were terrifying. Answering back was one step from suicide. I did once, and Collina gave me a glare that screamed, 'Don't fuck with me!' I miss him. It's a shame for all football that Collina has retired. He would have been a star in the Premiership, because he does let a good tackle go. And I love a good tackle.

10
Three Lions, Two Beers and One Swede

My world turned upside down on Saturday, 7 October 2000, and I wasn't even playing. Kevin Keegan quit after England's 1–0 World Cup qualifying defeat to Germany at Wembley, a decision that really distressed me. I felt terrible for Kevin. He's a proud man who loves England intensely, the country and the team, and no-one hurt more at losing to bloody Germany. I let him down, I suppose. I ached to face Germany until an old enemy of mine, the hated groin injury, hacked me down.

If I can walk, I always report for England duty, whatever the state of my injury. So I showed up.

'How's the groin?' Kevin asked as I arrived at the hotel.

'Not too bad, boss,' I replied, although it wasn't the best.

Little mentions were made in the media that I might start. Incey was out, so I had a chance of the holding role. Me against Didi again – bring it on. Please, God, let the groin get better.

On the Friday, I stepped gingerly out for training and headed off for some work with the physio, Gary Lewin.

Kevin jogged over. 'Steven, you're in the team tomorrow. How is it?'

'Not brilliant,' I finally admitted.

'Try it a bit more, and if it's no good, then fair enough,' said Kevin, and nipped back to work with the team.

With Gary watching, I tried twisting and turning, but the groin wouldn't respond. No chance. I was out.

Wembley's stands were a depressing place to be that afternoon. Gareth Southgate stood in for me, a centre-half in midfield, a decision Kevin copped a lot of flak for. I sat there, helpless and frustrated, watching a shit game in shit weather. Of course, Didi went and scored the bloody winner, the last goal at the old Wembley.

As Germany celebrated and England fans howled their anger, I shot down to the dressing-room to see the boys. Consoling words were useless; I just wanted to show solidarity. As I reached the dressing-room area, there was a buzz along the corridor. Groups of people, some telly and some FA, were whispering to each other. 'He's walked out,' I heard someone say. Who's walked out? Must be one of the players, pissed off with the result. I hurried on, and entered the dressing-room. All around sat shell-shocked players, my friends. They were all down, silent, devastated. Normally Kevin would be going around, lifting spirits.

'Where's Kevin?' I asked.

'He's speaking to the press,' someone mumbled.

Then Keegan walked back in, his eyes dulled with pain. He didn't hang about. 'My time's up,' he said. 'It's time for somebody else to have a go.'

Keegan had resigned! Shit. How to react? I looked

around, embarrassed, not knowing what to say. Tony Adams tried to talk Kevin round, pleading hard with him. 'Don't do it now. Wait. Kevin, slow down, don't do it.' Too late, Tony. Kevin's mind was made up. 'Thanks for everything you have done, lads,' he said. 'You are a great set of players. I'm proud to have worked with you. But that's it, lads. I'm off.' Kevin had told the FA, informed the press, and he was now off out the door. Amazingly, he stopped on the way and looked at me.

'How are you, Steven?' he asked.

Jesus, what could I say? Kevin had just quit as manager of England but he was still concerned for me. 'I'm all right, boss,' I muttered.

'What did you think of the game, Steven?' he added.

Fucking hell. What a time for chit-chat! I was gob-smacked. Words failed me. Kevin smiled and disappeared, out of Wembley and out of my life. I kicked myself. Say something. Shout after him. He capped you. He believed in you. Too late – he'd gone. I regret never getting the chance to thank Kevin – until now. I hope when Kevin reads this he will understand how much I admired him as a bloke and a manager.

Selfishly, I was hacked off. England lost a manager and I lost a mentor. Keegan rated me. The moment I was fit I was straight into Keegan's England, first choice in the middle, no question. Now I must start again. Impress the new man. Best behaviour. Every day I flicked through the papers to see who was being linked with the job. News that the FA were considering going foreign alarmed me. I prayed the FA would choose an Englishman. They would know me, appreciate my strengths. I wasn't against foreigners, of course. If they have a top CV they are good enough to manage England. But I had reservations. Would an overseas coach like me? Would he even know me? Would he prefer the experienced players to fresh names? If only Kevin had stayed. English, familiar, and trusted. Many people in the press, pundits and ex-players, were screaming that England shouldn't have a foreign coach. 'Maybe they are right,' I thought, 'especially if the foreigner doesn't believe in me.'

My nerves tightened when the FA appointed a Swede. But all my fears disappeared the moment Sven-Goran Eriksson picked me in his first squad for the friendly against Spain at Villa Park on 28 February 2001. In interviews, Eriksson spoke well of me, so maybe he'd be all right. On reporting for England, I was quite looking forward to meeting the man. Injury again ruled me out, but I drove down to the Midlands to have the problem checked over by Gary Lewin.

As I climbed back in the car to head north, I got a call from Michelle, the team administrator. 'Steven, don't go home yet,' she said. 'The manager and Tord Grip want to see you over at training.'

Christ. Here goes. Important moment. Good impression. I drove over to training and found Sven and Tord, his number two.

'I have seen quite a bit of you,' Sven said, after shaking my hand. 'I rate you. Tord has been coming to Liverpool's games and watching you. We are desperate to get you fit. If you need any help, we can advise you. We are going to keep close contact with Liverpool's medical people. I've spoken to Gérard Houllier and Kevin Keegan and they rave about you. Get yourself fit, Steven, and you are in the team.'

Jesus! Eriksson hadn't even seen me train with England yet! I certainly didn't know Tord was scouting me. After all the disappointment of Keegan's departure, my world began to come good again. Although gutted about my injury, I left the camp with a smile on my face. 'Get yourself fit, Steven, and you are in the team.' Sven's last words made welcome companions on the M6 home. I had got off to the right start with my new England boss. Eriksson's warmth surprised me. He was really friendly. His English was pretty decent as well. When I'm speaking to foreigners, I always wonder how well they understand me. Many of them have difficulties making sense of English, let alone Scouse! With Eriksson, I talked dead slow, to make sure he took it all in. I didn't know much about him, apart from his winning Serie A with Lazio, which was a tidy achievement. But Eriksson valued me, and that was all that counted. As I headed back to Liverpool, I thought to myself that Eriksson would improve me. Gérard was making me a better player. Why couldn't another foreigner?

Eriksson's impact was immediate. He restored confidence, got England's shape right and had us playing to our strengths: shifting the ball forward quickly to exploit Michael's pace. When we arrived in Munich for the return with Germany on 1 September 2001, we were ready. Revenge was in the air. England must batter Germany, get back on track for the World Cup, and pay them back for the misery of Wembley. Privately, some of us wanted to win it for Kevin, too. I certainly did. The game was massive, like a cup final and a big Champions League tie rolled into one.

To our surprise, Eriksson booked us into a city-centre hotel, which showed how relaxed he was. No hiding away in the country. No fear. A message was sent to the Germans: we are here, in the middle of your city, and we are going to take you apart. I loved being in my room, hearing the German and English fans outside our hotel singing their songs. Every shout from below reminded me how much was riding on this game. I lay in bed, unable to sleep because of the unbelievable racket. It didn't matter. Tiredness wasn't an issue. Listening to the England supporters just made me more determined. I couldn't let them down. No way. They travelled to Munich in their thousands, hoping to see England perform after the embarrassment of Wembley. We had to deliver.

There was no escaping the huge interest in the game. Whenever I switched on the TV, all the channels, German and English, seemed full of pictures from training or pundits discussing what might happen. The two nations talked of nothing else. All the interviews with Germany's players detailed what they were going to do to us. We'll see about that. Germany's keeper, Oliver Kahn, whipped up a storm with critical comments about England's qualities. Typical. Experienced players on either side always stir up a blizzard of headlines before major matches. It's a deliberate trick, to make the opponents tense. The media spun Kahn's comments into a controversy, stoking the fire raging about the game. The long, often bitter rivalry between England and Germany added more fuel. Good. Pressure suits me. All our players were up for this. The Liverpool boys – me, Michael and Emile – had just sorted out old man Kahn in the Super Cup. The whirlwind that hit Bayern Munich in Monaco was now heading Germany's way.

The atmosphere in England's final team meeting was fantastic. I looked around at Becks, Scholesy, Michael and the rest and knew they were all as pumped up as me. Let's fucking get at the Germans. Come on! We wanted to win. We had to win. Simple. Everybody was focused. Eriksson was so calm that we felt completely in control. On the bus to the Olympic Stadium, all the lads talked about how much the match meant, the volume rising higher and higher. In the dressing-room, most of the players were really vocal. Eriksson said a little bit, but the real noise came from the players. The language was dead lively. Fucking come on! No club dressing-room could ever compare with this decibel level. Unbelievable. Deafening. At Liverpool, one or two of the lads shout and get everyone going; with England in Munich that night, the whole room went mental. Shouts everywhere. Big Dave was right up for it. Come on, lads, this is it! Gary Neville screaming. Let's do it! Rio, Sol, both psyched up. Germany didn't know what was going to hit them. Ashley Cole talked away, not loud words, but constructive, giving off a quiet determination. Everyone knew he meant business out there. This was England v. Germany, a derby with pride and vital points at stake.

In the tunnel, the Germans were yelling stuff. They, too, desperately wanted to beat us. I saw Didi, a friend for life but an enemy tonight. We nodded at each other, but this was no time for pleasantries. Anyway, Didi knew how much I respected him. He also knew how ready England were for Germany.

Not that anyone could tell from the first ten minutes. Germany were all over us. It was a miracle they led only through Carsten Jancker's goal. Sebastian Deisler had a great chance. Germany were good, full of belief. Jancker dominated the air. Ballack ran the game on the deck. Must get close to them. Can't. Shit. Doubts filled me. Away from home, the odds looked stacked against us. The German crowd began crowing: 'Olé, olé!' Fuck them. Come on! Big Dave made a magnificent save. Thank God – 2–0 and it would all have been over. Just believe. Long way to go. Trust in your team-mates. Trust Michael to give us hope. Michael always does.

When he equalized, the whole mood spun round. Now let's go and win this. Suddenly, Eriksson's tactics looked spot on. We played 4–4–2, deep and compact, hitting on the break because we had burning pace up front in Michael and Emile. In all our team meetings, Eriksson instructed us to smack diagonal passes behind Germany's wing-backs. Hit Emile. Get Michael behind them. Now deliver. We had the passers to release them. In midfield, Becks was on the right and Nicky Barmby on the left, both working overtime. In the middle, Scholesy played more defensive than normal. My job was to break everything up, smash the Germans before they got going. Thanks! I'd prefer to be more attack-minded, but this was still good, banging into Germans.

England were now playing it around, getting on top. Just before half-time we got a corner. A goal now would go through Germany's nerves like a wrecking ball through an old wall. Their walk to the dressing-room at half-time would be a funeral march. Here goes. Beckham, eager as ever to keep things moving, sprinted over to the flag, placed the ball and swept it over. Panic filled German eyes. All speed and flight, Becks's corners are a nightmare to deal with for defenders. I wasn't in the box. In our set-piece practice the day before, Eriksson had me lurking on the edge of the area, looking to pick up the pieces and any nod-downs. I never got a touch in training. No clearances came my way. Nothing. I was a spectator. Match-day proved different. As 63,000 fans watched, Beckham's corner flew across, German heads straining to reach it. Rio was magnificent, timing his leap well. 'Set!' I screamed at Rio. 'Set!' I was perfectly placed. If Rio set me up, I knew I'd score. Nailed-on goal. Would Rio hear and see me? Most defenders are daft as brushes. They don't listen. They get frightened and head the ball anywhere. Not Rio, the king of composure. His awareness was brilliant. Jumping with other players, Rio somehow managed to see me. He met the ball superbly, heading it down to me. Great flick, perfect set. All yours, Stevie. Don't screw up.

As the ball came down, I knew there was no margin for error. People think it's a dead good position, hanging around on the edge of the box, waiting for a loose ball to ram back in. The risks are huge, though. If England got hit on the counter, it was so dangerous. Beware their pressure. Shoot quickly. Don't let the Germans nick it. Good touch and hit the target. Luckily enough, I caught an absolute worldie. The ball flew into the bottom left-hand corner. Take that, Kahn.

He was nowhere. That's for all your comments about us.

The German keeper was well beaten. Afterwards, everyone banged on about my accuracy, but I never intended to place it there. I just meant to hit the target with power. Bang. Get in! Not a bad time to score my first England goal! I couldn't believe it. I took off in celebration. Seeing the England fans in the corner, I sprinted towards them. Get close to them. Share the moment with them. I began to run out of pitch, so I dived full length, screaming with joy as I slid on the Munich turf. Dad was among the fans going crazy. I pointed towards them. 'That's for you, Dad,' I thought. 'You backed me all the way. You made this possible.' Emotion overcame me. All the hard work, the years of training and dreaming, had paid off.

Racing down the Munich tunnel at the break, 2–1 up, I knew what our dressing-room would be like. Buzzing. We can kill Germany off now. The lads were flying so much they even wound me up big-time. Each player walked over to Barmbs and patted him on the head. 'Well done, Barmbs, great goal. Fantastic reaction to Stevie's pass!' Robbie, typically, came across and pretended to console me.

'I bet you're gutted, aren't you?' he said.

'Why, Robbie?'

'Well, Barmbs just told Sky the goal was his.'

My head went. 'Fuck off, all of youse. It's my fucking goal.' I was steaming.

Fowler then burst out laughing. So did the others. I'd been done. Nicky was smiling. Fair play to him, Barmbs did well to get out of the way of my shot. He actually helped, because Kahn was unsighted. And I put some bend on it!

Eriksson was his usual self at half-time. Calm. Composed. His message was simple. 'You played really well for the last twenty-five minutes of the half,' he told us. 'Keep doing what you are doing. The next goal is important. If we get the next goal, we have won the game.' This was it. Let's finish the Germans off. No mercy. Kill them.

Amazingly, the Germans had nothing left. Their hearts and legs had gone, drained like a boxer who had taken one too many punches. They were on the ropes, and we spent the second half battering them. With their wing-backs high and centre-halves slow, Michael's runs down the channels into all that lovely space on such a big pitch destroyed Germany. Becks and Scholesy kept picking him out, and his pace, touch and eye for goal did the rest. Michael was Michael in Munich: quiet, then bang, bang, bang. Three goals, thank you, and auf wiedersehen, pet. Michael and England were unstoppable. At one point, we put together a twenty-pass move, including a drag-back from me around Didi. People thought I was taking the piss. Bollocks. Didi closed me down dead quick, so I flicked the ball around him. My aim was to keep the ball from Didi, not humiliate him. The press made a meal of that moment, and even suggested I gestured to Rudi Völler, Germany's coach, to hook Didi. Rubbish. I signalled to our bench that I was cramping up. Eriksson sent on Owen Hargreaves, and I spent the last twelve minutes sitting on the bench, just smiling at the carnage Michael caused.

The atmosphere in the dressing-room afterwards was

different gravy. Everyone was shouting, punching the air, shaking hands and laughing. Eriksson said little; he just sat there smiling. Go on, you old Swede, let yourself go! Scream and shout and get into the party! No chance. Eriksson was too restrained, but he must have been bursting with pride inside. We all were. England sent out a message to the world that night. We are fearless. We don't give up. We have players like Michael Owen who can demolish any defence. After that victory and performance in Munich, we genuinely believed we could go anywhere, however inhospitable, and succeed.

England still faced a huge obstacle before qualifying for Korea and Japan. Greece came to Old Trafford a month later and we had to match Germany's result against Finland to keep top spot. A massive game, no doubt. The build-up to the match on Saturday, 6 October, was very intense, particularly for me. The Sunday before, I was knocking about my apartment in Southport when some mates called, asking if I fancied a night out.

'Yeah, good shout, but I've got to make sure I'm in my bed quite handy,' I said.

'OK,' they promised.

There seemed no problem in going out. Eriksson told us to report to the Worsley Marriott outside Manchester on Monday. A couple of beers wouldn't hurt. Greece was six days away, so I felt I could unwind. I'd earned it.

I was enjoying myself in the bar in Southport, relaxing nicely, when this Everton fan walked over.

'Flash cunt,' he shouted at me.

'What?' I replied.

'You've only played a few games, so what are you doing fucking driving around in a flash car?'

'If that's what you think, that's what you think,' I said to him. I had a nice Merc, but nothing fancy. 'Anyway, what's wrong with having a nice car?'

'You shouldn't fucking have one,' he said. 'Who the fuck do you think you are?'

Dickhead. I decided to keep the peace. 'Fine, fair enough,' I said to him, and turned back to my friends.

The lad disappeared, so I thought that was the end of it. The following day, I headed off to the Worsley, having forgotten what went on. Then Struan phoned. 'Stevie, there's a piece going in the *Daily Mail* tomorrow about you,' he said.

'What the hell about?'

'Some kid tipped the paper off that you were drinking in a bar with a big England game coming up.'

Shit. It was that cocky Everton lad.

With a heavy heart, I checked into the England hotel, went training, and then had to do a press conference. Nothing sinister in that; it was just my turn. I still shat myself in case any of the reporters mentioned it, but only the *Mail* knew. The next day, I got down early to look at the papers. There it was: news pages and back page. 'England Star Out Drinking'. So fucking what? I was twenty-one and entitled to a bit of fun now and then. This was ridiculous. I was harshly done by. If I had been out on the town in Southport, rotten stinking drunk until five in the morning, I could understand the problem. But I wasn't. The truth was that I went out, had two beers and a couple of glasses of Coke, and was back in my flat at

12.30. I was out trying to pull a few birds, not trying to get drunk. I lived on my own, a single lad, and I had a right to relax occasionally. The next day, I had a lie-in before driving over to Worsley for 12.30. No hangover, no nothing. I had four days' serious training ahead of me before the game with Greece. What the hell was the fuss about?

The situation got totally out of hand. In the press, people slaughtered me left, right and centre. Debating player behaviour was all the rage at the time. Eriksson had just left Frank Lampard out of the squad after an incident involving some Americans after 9/11. Footballers were in the public eye like never before. Me? I was being used for target practice. Struan phoned again, and we talked through the mess. 'I'll go and speak to the manager and tell him exactly what I did,' I told Struan. Eriksson was superb. 'Just learn from it,' he said. 'You're young. People want you to sit in the house and live like a monk. Don't worry about it, concentrate on the game. Just be more careful when it's coming up to a game.' I was relieved. I really appreciated Eriksson's stance. Sven showed a real human side. No bollocking, just advice. 'Thanks, boss, and I'm sorry for what happened,' I said.

The FA released details that I had apologized. I said I had done wrong, but I hadn't. My only real crime was the time I went to sleep. Yet half-midnight is not a hanging offence. I was gutted by the press reaction. Why me? Like Sven, the other players were dead sympathetic. Robbie said, 'I was out with Macca!' 'Yeah,' said Macca. 'We had a couple of beers, but no-one knew!' I appreciated Macca and Robbie trying to lift my spirits, but I couldn't stop thinking about the furore. My head was bursting. 'Forget about it,' Macca said. 'You haven't done any harm.' I wished I could be as laid-back as them about these things. I hated being caned in the press. Becks sought me out as well. 'Don't worry about it,' he said. Becks behaved like a captain and a friend. 'If you need to talk, I'm there for you,' he added. 'What the papers are doing is out of order. You've done nothing wrong. It happens to all of us. You get good press and then bad.' Dad was devastated. 'Next time, Steven, just stay in,' he said. 'The main thing now is to get it out of your mind. You've got a massive match on Saturday. Concentrate on that.'

All the people who really cared for me rallied around. Gérard called, and I told him the truth. Gérard was first class. 'Don't worry,' he said. 'It's normal behaviour for someone your age. Just be careful because you are high profile now. Limit the times you go out. If you socialize, go to the right places. Your career is so short, Steven. You have so much ability. Make the most of it.' A father figure to many of the young lads at Liverpool, Gérard was always full of good advice. One of his favourite sayings was, 'Why go to a nightclub now when you can own one at the end of your career?' Fair point. Like Sven, Gérard drilled into me that I needed to be on my toes. 'Because you are well known, everything you do and say, whoever you speak to, you are in the spotlight,' said Gérard. Yet the gaffer also understood that pros are humans.

I was twenty-one. I wanted to go out with my mates, have some fun, nick a bird. Usual lad stuff. The problem then was that those friends didn't realize I had to be in bed at a sensible time. Living on my own, young, free and single, buzzing because I was in Liverpool's first team, I fancied nights out. And yeah, perhaps I was out on the town too regularly. I just wanted to celebrate a Liverpool win with mates who had been at the match. The alternative was sitting in my flat, watching the telly, screwing up a pasta recipe, and doing my head in. Sometimes when the phone rang, I said, 'No, guys, I'm stopping in.' This image of me being a party animal is bollocks. After my Liverpool debut, I never touched alcohol for six months. I have never been out twice in a week in my life. Even back then, when most twenty-one-year-olds are on the lash all the time, I hit a bar two or three times a month, maximum. I drink even less now. I'm practically a monk! My mates now appreciate the strict demands of my profession. They come round, drink tea, coffee or water, and we just chat. I'll still have the occasional night out, of course, and why not? I'm twenty-six. If I want a night out, I will go wherever I want. The majority of footballers go out after a game if they don't have a match until the following weekend. Timing is the key. Back then with the Southport bar incident, I just picked the wrong place at the wrong time and suddenly newspapers questioned my lifestyle. Oh, here's another mad, piss-head footballer, they said. Bollocks. The people who wrote the story didn't know me. They heard about one incident and blew it out of all proportion. It proved a useful, if painful, lesson. Maybe if that hadn't happened, something worse would have hit me. I might have got involved in a fight. All that negative press, the apology and feelings of anger made me determined to avoid bad publicity again. After that, when

I went out I kept a low profile. Once bitten, twice shy.

Michael is spot on when he describes Liverpool as a 'rumour city'. One quiet beer gets exaggerated into a wild session. I'm idolized by many people around here, but the interest is not always positive. Liverpool is strange like that. Many people want to see me fail, and would love to tell a bad story about me, or sell a rubbish story about me to the press. That sort of jealousy and greed disgusts me. Before I started doing well at football and making good money, I admired those who did well and wished them luck. When Fowler scored, I jumped all over the Kop. When Michael was shooting towards stardom, I was so made up for him. I don't understand envy. When young English players like Wayne Rooney break through, I'm happy for them. The negative mentality of that little tit in Southport sickens me.

One night out in Southport never affected my perform-ance for England against Greece. The hysterical reaction did. Every time I got on the ball at Old Trafford, I knew the papers were watching, waiting to leap on any mistake as confirmation I left my form and fitness in a bar. Jesus, I was so nervous. The ball felt like a hand-grenade coming at me. Normally, adrenalin flows through my veins. Here, it was pure fear. I was scared stiff. Couldn't focus, couldn't get rid of dark thoughts. I played shite. Going into the last minute, England were 2–1 down and auto-matic qualification for the World Cup was going up in smoke. The play-off lottery beckoned. I knew where the blame would be laid. Against me. As the seconds drained away, I imagined the vicious headlines coming my way like runaway trains. All that 'Stevie Blunder' shite. Pens were being sharpened to stick into me. I was going to get it big-time. No question. No escape, surely?

I was shaken from my nightmare by a roar sweeping around Old Trafford. Becks and Teddy Sheringham were lining up a free-kick outside Greece's penalty area. Teddy wanted it. He's terrific at dead-ball situations, and Becks had already missed with six. It was a key decision. The twenty-five yards between them and the net could mean England travelling halfway around the world. Who would take it? Becks was captain, and he was confident of his ability with his free-kicks. 'It's mine,' he told Teddy. Becks's courage has never been in doubt, but this was a real pressure moment. I wanted him to take it. After six attempts, he was getting his range and technique right. It made sense for him to carry on. I watch David in training, and when he takes ten free-kicks, he usually scores two or three, top corners, often more. Go on, David. Put this one in.

Old Trafford went quiet. I could feel my heart beating loudly. Becks didn't let us down. The ball flew in and Old Trafford went crazy. What a worldie goal from Captain Marvel! In fact, Becks was brilliant all afternoon. England didn't play well, but Becks was everywhere, dragging us to the World Cup almost single-handedly. When England desperately needed someone to take the game by the scruff of the neck, he stood up to be counted. He was man of the match by a million miles. Top man.

Becks's dynamic performance amazed everyone, but not me. His energy levels down the right for United were always frightening. Up and back, up and back, non-stop. Moving to Real Madrid hasn't altered his all-action style.

He's the same with England, always shuttling up and down the right. Becks is great to play with, defensively and going forward. Obsessed with football, he contributes so much. In a way, that's his downfall. People have such high expectations of Becks because of displays like Greece. But it's madness thinking he can perform like that every time. He'd have to be Superman. Opponents are so good, they just won't let Becks run the show each week. I can't deliver every match either. Opposing managers analyse my contributions, and Becks's, and set their players up to stop us. Yet if I'm not an eight out of ten, I get coated. If David isn't a nine out of ten for England, he gets slaughtered. Fortunately, Becks put in an eleven out of ten performance against Greece.

When the Dutch ref, Dick Jol, blew the final whistle moments after Becks's wonder-strike, a sense of un-believable relief rushed through me. Selfishness ruled. I thought only of myself, of the backlash if we hadn't qualified, and how much more the press would have blown up the Southport incident. Thanks to Becks, the heat was off me and we were off to the World Cup. As I dreamed of what lay in store in Korea and Japan, I thought of all the great players who have graced World Cups. I thought of England in 1966, and how special it would be to bring the trophy home. I couldn't wait. Exciting images of the Far East replaced bad memories of a Southport bar.

But just when the sun seemed to be shining on me, another dark cloud swept across the sky. Injury. The curse of my growing years. My personal stalker. I hated it. Why me? Why would I be charging around, limbs pumping away like pistons, and then seize up? All that season my groin was troublesome, a persistent pain and worry. Getting on the pitch was still possible, but I needed to break the bad cycle of three matches on, one match off crocked. Liverpool's players sensed my frustration. 'Come on, Stevie,' said Didi. 'You need to see my guy, a surgeon in Germany. He's the best. He'll sort you out.' Typical Didi, fretting over my welfare. Trust Didi to know Dr Hans-Muller Wohlfahrt. Robbie would have recommended Edward Scissorhands! I talked the situation through with Gérard. He knew all about the famous Dr Wohlfahrt, who treated Michael's hamstrings. 'Go over, hear what he says, come back and then we'll decide,' the boss said.

Accompanied by the Liverpool physio Dave Galley and club doctor Mark Waller, I flew out to Munich. Fears and doubts kicked in. I'm a footballer. It's what I do. If my body keeps breaking down, I'm no use to anyone. Just a lump of meat with no future. As I sat on the plane, I closed my eyes, and suddenly I was back on that stretcher in Accident and Emergency at Alder Hey, a rusty fork sticking into my toe, with Steve Heighway arguing passionately with the doctors to save my career. All my dreams were on hold. Life seemed so fragile, oblivion a moment away.

I was brought back to the present with a jolt as we landed. Be strong. Meet the challenge. Beat the challenge. Remember the last visit to Munich. Good memories. A stadium is a second home to me, though; hospitals scare me. Before long I was in a cold clinic being examined by Dr Wohlfahrt from head to toe.

'To sort your body out you need four operations,' he told me.

'Four?' I couldn't believe it. 'Are you sure?'

'Yes. One knee operation, one on the ankle, and probably two hernias.'

Christ! The doc had only seen me for a short time and he wanted to rebuild my whole body. *Four* operations? Shit. This trip to Munich was fast turning into a nightmare.

'But I need to confirm the hernias,' Dr Wohlfahrt added.

So he packed me off to see a groin specialist. She checked the scans, nodded her head, and confirmed Dr Wohlfahrt's suspicions. 'You need operations on both groins,' she said. Forget the scalpel to the knee, groin and ankle, this was a knife to the heart. I looked anxiously at Doc Waller. He clearly wasn't convinced. 'We'll call you,' Doc Waller said to the Germans, before we beat it sharpish back to the airport.

I flew back to Liverpool with my head all over the place. I felt a write-off. My body was giving up as my career was really starting.

Back at Melwood, Liverpool held a crisis meeting. Me, Gérard, the physios and Doc Waller searched for the right solution. 'There's no way you need four operations,' Doc Waller kept repeating. I trust Doc Waller with my life, but these German guys were specialists. The walls of Dr Wohlfahrt's clinic were covered with diplomas and degrees from the best medical schools. He came recommended by Didi. Michael swore by him. Jurgen Klinsmann and Boris Becker used him. Dr Wohlfahrt was the business. But Doc Waller stood his ground. 'A lot of people have been to see Dr Wohlfahrt, been told to have ops, but didn't and carried on playing,' he insisted. True, but I also knew how many people in football Dr Wohlfahrt had sorted out. His name was respected throughout the game. I had a choice: go with a foreign specialist's advice or trust in a Liverpool doctor's instincts. As usual, I stuck with Liverpool. I have worked with Doc Waller so long. He lives around the corner and tends my family. He has always had my interests at heart. Doc Waller would never put me through surgery unless it was the last resort. My faith in him is unshakeable. 'OK, let's do it your way,' I told him. He sent me to see other specialists. I got four more verdicts with different solutions. None of the four said I needed four operations; a couple said I needed at least two.

Gérard was still worried. Even if it was only two ops, Gerard didn't want me cut open unless it was absolutely vital. An op meant missing a long stretch of the season, and it's always risky. But was there any alternative? Gérard thought so. 'Go and see Philippe Boixel in Paris,' he said. 'He will make you more supple through stretching. That may help.'

So off I went again, passport in my hand, fear in my heart. I flew to Paris where I met Boixel, an impressive man who works with the French national team. 'If he's good enough for Patrick Vieira,' I thought, 'he'll do for me.' Boixel examined me and made me do all these complicated stretches. 'You don't need any operations,' he said at last. 'Your groins just need strengthening work. My mentality is don't fix it, work on it, and avoid surgery.

You can have an op on any part of your body, but it can mess you up.' Thank God. Doc Waller was happy, Gérard too. I placed my future in the strong hands of Boixel. 'Come and see me once a week at first, and then once a fortnight,' he said. He went to work first on my back, the root cause of all my troubles. 'Because of the shape of your back, it puts pressure on all your muscles,' said Boixel. 'Not just your groin, but ankles, knees and calves. That's why you're getting niggles.'

I felt reprieved. Maybe I didn't need surgery after all. An op would have been a nightmare, timing-wise. Sacrificing Liverpool in the short term to guarantee my fitness for England in the summer of 2002 was something I just couldn't do. Just imagine me announcing to Kopites: 'Sorry, lads, I'm taking three months off now so I'll be fine for the World Cup. Sorry about screwing up Liverpool's season. Don't worry, the UEFA Cup will be fun.' No chance. That would have caused a riot. Liverpool needed me, and I would never let the club, the fans, the players or the management down. So between matches I kept nipping over to Paris, where Boixel sorted me out a lot by changing the shape of my back. My groins improved. Injuries were less frequent. Two games a week became manageable. Liverpool were pushing hard for the second automatic Champions League place, and I was right in the thick of it. We had to get that spot. Liverpool needed the money, and the Champions League was the only stage for me. I strained and sweated hard to get the points.

Little did I realize that my body still wasn't right. The healing hands of Philippe Boixel could only help so far. The pressure built up. On the last day of the 2001/02 season, 11 May, we tore into Ipswich Town at Anfield, knowing victory would book our ticket to Europe's best arenas. I was right up for it. I sprinted on to the pitch, determined to smash down the last barrier to the Champions League. No holding back. Get stuck in. After thirty-three minutes, I stretched for a ball. Bang. My groin ripped. No, no! Not again! Not now! Shit. Back to square one. Back to the treatment table. Back home while the boys are at the World Cup.

Gérard called a meeting for the following morning at Melwood. When I arrived, everyone around the place was made up because Liverpool's 5–0 win had guaranteed us Champions League qualification. Next season would be good. Get the map out. Brilliant. But I was having none of this celebration shit. I couldn't think or talk I was so devastated. I wandered around Melwood like a zombie. Up the stairs to Gérard's room, sit down, listen to the gaffer and the doc. 'Steven, even if we patched you up and sent you off to Japan, your groin could go again in the first game,' Gérard said. 'You probably wouldn't even be ready until the semis. I know it's not what you want to hear, but it's really best that you stay home and we get you ready for next season.'

His words felt like a punch in the face. No. Don't say it. Stop. I don't want to hear it. Sven didn't want to hear it either. When Gérard called my injury against Ipswich 'a blessing for England', I could understand why Sven went through the roof. England were livid at Gérard's comments. I could just imagine Sven, sitting in his office at Soho Square, telling Tord Grip, 'Yeah, it's a real blessing we've lost Steven Gerrard.' To me, the injury felt like a curse not a blessing. Of course, I don't blame Gérard. How was he to know my groin would break down in that particular game? It was a freak injury. Liverpool didn't overuse me, as some people claimed. If Gérard had left me out for the Ipswich game, I would have set fire to his office. I hate being rested. Hate it. Even if I know it's for my own good, I'm a nightmare, kicking up a stink, turning the air blue. Play me! Being deprived of football is like being starved of air. I live and breathe the game. Missing one minute of one match feels like death.

The club-versus-country balance is always delicate. Liverpool respect England and understand how much the players love pulling on the Three Lions shirt. Representing England is such a boost to a player's career. But clubs are selfish. They pay our wages. I understand their fears. Gérard's priorities were straightforward: winning games for Liverpool, and qualifying for the Champions League. England was not Gérard's problem; getting me ready for next season was.

'I'm sending you to see another specialist on Monday,' the boss continued, 'and I'll call Sven and tell him you can't go to Japan. I'm sorry, Steven.'

Another trip to another groin surgeon. 'You do need two operations,' this specialist said, 'but not hernia ops as you've been told. You need a simple operation on both sides to release a muscle. You have a muscle either side that keeps getting tighter and tighter because of the position of your back. I can release them because you don't need them.'

And so my dreams of the 2002 World Cup ended up on

an operating table. The closest I got to Japan was Dubai. I was going mad hanging about at home, so I took my girlfriend Alex off on holiday. 'I've got to get away, Alex,' I told her. 'I can't be here with the whole country going crazy over England.' I was steaming to leave, to get on a beach and bury my frustration in the sand. I checked with Gérard. 'Steven, we'd rather you had the op now and got going with the rehab,' he said. I checked with the surgeon, who was spot on. He sensed how desperate I was for a break. 'You'll need a holiday this summer, so take one now and I'll operate on you when you get back,' he said.

As the players boarded their plane for Japan, Alex and I climbed on a flight to Dubai. Swimming in the sea felt good, but nothing could wash away my anger. I missed the World Cup so badly that I even walked up and down the beach in a pair of England shorts. Inevitably, I was drawn to watching the matches on television. Michael, Becks, Scholesy – they are my friends. I was desperate for them to do well, so I found a bar with a massive screen for the Argentina game.

A punter walked across. 'I wish you were out there, Stevie.'

'Thanks, mate, so do I.'

A few other fans came over, asking for autographs. They were good as gold. They knew how bad I was feeling. They gave me some space and left me to my thoughts. Phil Thompson came in – Dubai is always packed with football people – so we shared a drink and a chat. Thommo's great in situations like that, dead positive. He consoled me briefly and then we sat back to watch the pictures from Sapporo.

The moment I saw the lads lining up in the tunnel, that was it, my head went again. It rammed home everything I was missing. This was England v. Argentina, what World Cups are made of. Hand of God. St-Etienne. Decades of history, hurt and glory. Jealousy seeped through every fibre of my body as I watched the boys making their last-minute preparations. Christ, I envied them the feeling of anticipation as they flicked their leg muscles, rolled their necks to loosen up, and stared at the enemy. Even from thousands of miles away, I smelt the tension. This was my sort of battle – tough, intense. Fucking get stuck in, lads! The man who had taken my midfield place, Nicky Butt, was standing there, his concentration total. Go on, Butty. I know you can do it. Hammer the Argies. I was praying for him to have a good game.

From the first whistle, I kicked every ball with Butty, Becks and Scholesy. In my head, I steamed into tackles on Diego Simeone and Juan Sebastian Verón. Fucking take that! Come on, just win. We have to win. Penalty for England! Bar goes mental. Becks steps up. That arsehole Simeone tries to put him off. Fucking ignore him, Becks, just bury it. He does. Bar goes completely crazy. Suddenly, I'm not a frustrated injured player any more, I'm an England fan, shouting the place down, singing the songs, fist in the air. Here we go!

The next day, I scoured Dubai for the papers. Look at the pictures, read the match reports. Every word. One paper carried an interview with Pele where he said I was the best player not at the World Cup finals. Pele implied that England really missed me in midfield. Thanks, mate, but what about Butty? He had a stormer against the Argies.

My holiday over, I returned to reality. The surgeon's knife awaited. The operation complete, I limped around my apartment in Southport, catching the rest of the World Cup. A few friends called and asked me round to watch the Brazil quarter-final. I couldn't. England v. Brazil was too personal for me to share the experience with other people. All my mates would be sitting around, buzzing, when I would just be sunk in a depression over missing such a colossal occasion. World Cup quarter-finals against Ronaldinho and Ronaldo don't come along too often. I had to watch the game on my own. Doors locked. Phone off. Just me and my misery.

It dawned on me that the lads were just three games away from becoming champions of the world. If they beat Brazil, they'd be favourites. Semi-final, then final. God, how the hell would I deal with that? I'd be made up for Michael, Becks and the boys, but missing out on a World Cup winner's medal would haunt me the rest of my life. Stop it. Be positive. Quick, send a text to Michael – 'All the best'. I meant it.

The game passed in a blur. Michael scoring. Brazil hitting back. Ronaldinho's goal. Seamo's tears. Heartache. Brazil looked fresher, better suited to the hot climate. At the final whistle, England's players slumped to the ground, drained and defeated. I sat there in silence, my heart breaking for them. They are not just England players to me, star names people see in papers and on the telly. They are good friends, and I was devastated for them. For all my frustration and jealousy, I would much rather have seen Michael and Becks with World Cup winner's medals around their necks than Ronaldinho and

Ronaldo. I am selfish, I want to fill my upstairs room with medals, but there was no sense of private relief at watching England return home from Japan empty-handed. I was as distressed as them. Like Becks and Michael, my determination doubled to bring the World Cup home in 2006.

11
Good Guys and Bad Buys

For all my frustration over missing the World Cup, my admiration for Gérard remained immense. He cared passionately about Liverpool. People forget he almost lost his life working for the club. I will never forget when he was almost taken from us.

The boss seemed fine and healthy as he gave us some last-minute advice on 13 October 2001, talking us through what we should expect from Leeds United, the visitors to Anfield that Saturday afternoon. We returned to the dressing-room at half-time 1–0 down, expecting Gérard to be waiting to have a go at us. Instead it was Thommo, who's a bit noisier. 'Gérard's not well,' Thommo explained as we looked around for the boss. 'He's gone to hospital for a check-up.' The staff were outwardly very calm. Thommo didn't want to distract us from the task of turning the game around. Points were at stake. But we couldn't help but worry about our manager. We knew it must be serious for Gérard to be rushed off to hospital. We managed to focus enough on the game to equalize, through Danny Murphy, but everyone was down afterwards. Being without Gérard hit us hard. Imagine Manchester United coping without Sir Alex Ferguson. I drove home feeling worried. When I got in, I sent the boss a text: 'Hope you are all right'. No reply. My concern deepened. Gérard is usually sharp back on the text, or he calls. But nothing. Not a word.

At Melwood the next day, Doc Waller gathered all the players in the meeting room. 'Gérard has undergone emergency heart surgery,' he told us. 'It took eleven hours and it was a dissection of the aorta.' Such medical terms meant little to me, but the serious look on Doc Waller's face told me everything I needed to know about the manager's plight. 'He will be away for some time,' Doc Waller continued. 'He sends his regards and asks you to focus on the next games, not on him.'

Typical Gérard. Always thinking of Liverpool, never himself. I feared his 24/7 commitment to leading Liverpool had damaged his health. Constant pressure takes a toll. Gérard would never have listened to any signs from his body to slow down. Now he had been at death's door, saved only by a surgeon's skill.

'Gérard will be back,' insisted Thommo, 'and until he does, I'll be taking over. We must stick together to make sure we are in a good position for when the boss gets back. He has all your interests at heart. He fights for you. We must show that fight for him.'

We flew out to Kiev later that day for a Champions League game, and the long trip was desperately gloomy. When we got to Dinamo's stadium, Thommo put a sign up on the dressing-room wall: 'Do It For The Boss'. We did. I poured all my concern for our missing manager into that tie, even scoring the winner in a 2–1 victory.

Gérard Houllier was a well-liked manager, a player's manager, and very human. He is one of life's good guys. So is Thommo. Like Gérard, everything Thommo did was for the good of Liverpool Football Club. He was a Scouser like me, and I respected him because he lifted the European Cup for Liverpool. He was always honest with me, always told me when I was not training or playing well enough. I liked him. Still do. The perception of Thommo as not the cleverest is wrong. He knows his football and he did a good job as caretaker.

Of course, we fell out at times. Thommo's a fiery character, and I'll not hold back. On one occasion, before Thommo became caretaker, we flew back from a European tie into Manchester airport. Gary Mac asked Thommo if he could leave the group at Manchester and make his own way home, rather than catch the bus back to Melwood. 'No problem, Macca,' said Thommo. I overheard this. My nan was in hospital at the time, so I was keen to get to her sharpish. 'Can I make my way home from the airport?' I asked Thommo. I never mentioned nan was ill, because I didn't want to make a fuss. Besides, Thommo told Gary Mac he could go, so why not me? 'Yeah, yeah, Steven,' said Thommo. He was taking the piss, but I didn't realize.

I left the team at Manchester airport, got picked up by my mate Bavo and raced to the hospital. I jumped out and ran in, leaving my phone and other stuff with Ian. While I was inside, it rang. Bavo answered.

'Hello?'

'Who the fuck's that?' came the reply. It was Thommo, raging. 'Hey, put Steven on the phone. I know he's there, next to you.'

'He's not, Thommo, honest,' said Bavo, scared shitless.

'Liar,' screamed Thommo.

'I'm not lying. Stevie's not here.'

'Tell him he'd better call me dead quick. No-one gave him permission to leave us at the airport. He's in deep shit.'

Poor Bavo! When I reached the car, he was still shaking, all red and shocked.

'What's up?' I asked.

'Phil Thompson just caned me for nothing,' Ian said. 'You weren't allowed to go home from the airport. He said you were out of order.'

I wasn't having this, bollocking my friend when neither of us had done anything wrong. I grabbed the phone and punched in Thommo's number. Before I could explain, he just roared at me. Cheek. I ripped into Thommo, calling him every name under the sun. Swore blind at him. 'Don't fucking lay into my mate!' I shouted at him. 'It's nothing to do with him. You told me I could go home from the airport.'

'No I didn't.'

'Yes you bloody did.'

'You're taking the piss, Steven. Why are you different from everyone else?'

'Fuck off, Thommo.'

It was a right old slanging match.

'That's it, Steven, see me tomorrow,' shouted Thommo.

I rang off. A minute or two later, Gérard was on. 'Steven, you're getting a fine.'

'All right, I'll pay the fine, but let me explain the situation.'

'No, you listen, Steven. Phil says you put the phone down on him. We're fining you five grand. We'll talk tomorrow when you have calmed down.'

Calmed down? Me? I'd had enough. I switched the phone off on the boss. Bang. Enough. Bloody Thommo. He'd obviously just been straight on to Gérard. I was steaming. I rang Struan. 'You won't believe this, Stru. I've just been to see my nan in hospital and it's cost me five grand. I've had Thommo and Gérard on, fining me, caning me. What a joke.'

Struan was full of good sense, as usual. 'Relax, Stevie. Just see them in the morning and explain everything. They'll understand.'

I wasn't sure Thommo would.

On arriving at Melwood the next day, I found Gérard all smiles. Struan had been on and told him the real story. Thommo was there, standing just behind Gérard. I was still seething about him having a go at Ian.

'Don't call my mate a liar,' I said to Thommo. 'And I genuinely thought you said I could go. If you didn't, I apologize.'

'I'm sorry as well,' said Thommo.

Peace broke out. But they still fined me.

I can live with the club dipping into my pocket for five grand. Big sums like that go to charity. Everyday fines for being a couple of minutes late, or using your mobile, are thrown into a players' pool; at the end of the season, the staff and players go out for a meal with the wives and girl-friends. My fine meant nothing; it was more the principle

Helping Hand Gérard Houllier was my manager, mentor and father figure at Liverpool.

Opposite page, clockwise from top left:

Team-mates And Soul-mates Jamie Carragher and I share a passion for lifting Liverpool to great heights; **Looking At What Could Have Been** Jose Mourinho is a brilliant manager but I decided to resist Chelsea's lure; **Arms And The Manager** Rafa Benitez continues to inspire and challenge me; **The Treble, Step One** Beating Birmingham City's Stan Lazaridis to win the Worthington Cup in 2001; **The Guv'nor And The Gladiator** Paul Ince and me get told to cool it; **Demolition Derby** I pile into the Blues' Gary Naysmith and see red.

This page, from top: **The Treble, Step Two** Me, Danny Murphy and Robbie Fowler celebrate the FA Cup final win over Arsenal.

The Treble, Step Three Shooting to thrill, I batter Alaves' defence in the UEFA Cup final.

Silver Service Me, Robbie Fowler and Sami Hyypia bring home the Treble.

No Focus In Basle
Off-field distractions
brought misery in
Europe.

Above, **Shooting Star** I needed all my strength to break down Olympiakos's defence at Anfield and keep Liverpool on the road to Istanbul.

Right, **Mission Impossible?** The half-time score-line in Istanbul made bleak reading in the 2005 European Cup final.

Below, right, **Heading For A Comeback** I climb high to make it 3–1 and give us hope against AC Milan in Istanbul.

Below, **PENALTY!** The real fall-guy is Milan's Gennaro Gattuso as he brings me down. Xabi Alonso scored to make it 3–3.

Mission Impossible Accomplished After an unbelievable
final, I get my hands on the European Cup.

Above, **Back Where It Belongs**
Me and Rafa Benitez land
with the European Cup. That's
Liverpool's fantastic chairman,
David Moores, on the right.

Left, **Wave Of Euphoria**
So many people came on to the
streets of Liverpool to see the
European Cup that our bus could
hardly move.

Below, **Letting Fly** I had just
enough energy left to make it 3–3
in that amazing 2006 FA Cup final
against West Ham in Cardiff.

Romance Of The Cup
I have always loved the FA Cup and lifting it as captain was a schoolboy dream come true.

at stake. Trust is so important to me. After Phil and I apologized to each other, it actually brought us closer together. Whenever we've had little run-ins since, we've always been man enough to patch things up afterwards. We both want what is best for Liverpool. I didn't always say sorry, though.

If Thommo and I rucked in training, we just forgot about it, but some players couldn't bring themselves to apologize to Thommo. Robbie once had an unbelievable spat with Thommo at Melwood. The pair never got on, but this was mad, absolute mayhem. It kicked off because Gérard always drilled into us not to muck about with balls in the middle of sessions. 'You should be focusing on what we are doing,' Gérard warned. 'Do some stretching, have some water, but don't mess about.' I agree, but footballers are going to kick balls, aren't they? If I see a loose ball in training, I'll hammer it at goal. I love kicking balls as far as I can. Hard not to. It's what my body is programmed to do. It sends the staff crazy, because I should be concentrating on whatever pattern-of-play stuff they are going through. And some poor sod has to go round collecting the balls.

Anyway, Thommo was lifting the net one day, kicking the balls out as we got ready for the next session, and Robbie pings this penalty into the top corner, nearly knocking the stanchion off. Right by Thommo! He shat himself. We pissed ourselves laughing. Thommo went ballistic. 'Robbie!' he screamed, convinced it was deliberate. They went head to head, tearing into each other. I sprinted across to pull them apart. 'What the fuck are you getting involved for?' shouted Thommo.

'Fuck off!' I left them to finish their argument.

'You fucking meant that, Robbie!' yelled Thommo.

'Fuck off!' replied Robbie.

Both were out of order. Robbie didn't kick the ball meaning to hit Phil, and Phil shouldn't have overreacted. Eventually they stopped, but the tension remained for a couple of weeks.

When Thommo was named caretaker during Gérard's illness, it felt strange, but no-one could question how much effort he put in. But we missed our leader. When Gérard eventually reappeared at Melwood five months later, in March 2002, while Thommo was preparing us for a big European game against Roma, we were all overjoyed, but I was shocked how pale he looked. He'd lost a lot of weight, and wasn't sharp at all. But he still knew how every game had gone, how each of us had done. Typical Gérard. Even while recuperating, he was obsessed with Liverpool. 'I want to be on the bench tomorrow – if the doctor lets me!' he told us. Well, that just made training even sharper. Everyone was flying to know the boss would be back watching us. The atmosphere at Anfield is always special on European nights, but that evening was unbelievable. Word spread fast that Gérard was in the ground. The Kop went crazy, chanting his name. The whole place was buzzing. We needed to win 2–0, and we knew we would. Our manager was back. All was well in the world.

Gérard's return kept us rolling on, riding high in the Premiership and in Europe. Just before our Champions League quarter-final at Bayer Leverkusen on 9 April, Gérard declared, 'Liverpool are ten games from greatness.' Everyone seized on the boss's comment, debating whether this Liverpool side really could win the Premiership and the Champions League. Personally, I didn't take any notice. I was too busy focusing on Leverkusen, a decent side with a brilliant player in Michael Ballack, a German with a massive point to prove after the 5–1 England game in Munich. Still, having won 1–0 at Anfield the week before, we were confident heading to Germany.

Leverkusen went 1–0 up when I stupidly jumped in on Ballack, who turned me and scored from the edge of the box. Gérard caned me for that, quite rightly. Ballack played well, scoring another with a header in the top corner. Before long the score was 3–2 to Leverkusen and we were going through on away goals. The German side kept pressurizing us, and we needed all our experienced players to keep them at bay. Gérard took off Didi – a decision he probably now regrets. Didi was doing a brilliant job for us in the middle, holding things together, reminding the Germans of his capabilities. We lost control when Didi went off. Gérard got a lot of stick for that. Lucio, the Brazilian defender, snuck in for the winner. Liverpool were on their way out. Nightmare. Leverkusen's fans were all triumphant, singing 'Football's Coming Home'. Revenge for Munich, I suppose. I was gutted. If we had gone to Leverkusen, played crap and been battered, then fair enough. But we were in such a great position to go into the last four of the European Cup. We screwed up.

In sight of both finishing lines, we faltered: last eight in Europe, runners-up in the Premiership. Arsenal deserved to win the league. They were a great team, better than Liverpool, but we got eighty points. Such a total would have won the Premiership in another season. After the Treble, and then coming second, I felt the title was only just around the corner. If Liverpool strengthened in the right areas for the 2002/03 season, the Premiership dream could become real.

Before the start of every season, Gérard handed around pieces of paper and told us to write down our ambitions for the year. When Gérard's back was turned, most of the lads complained, saying, 'What are we doing this for? It's bollocks.' Usual footballer cynicism. After coming second in 2002, one of the boys wrote, 'Finish in the top six.' What a piss-take! Gérard was unimpressed. He just wanted to know how confident we were. I usually scribbled, 'Improve league position and try and win a cup.' In August 2002, I wrote, 'We'll win the title.' But then Gérard signed El-Hadji Diouf, Salif Diao and Bruno Cheyrou for nearly £18 million. Those three were meant to be the signings that took Liverpool to the next level, to the Premiership title and Champions League glory. That was the plan. But after a promising start, Liverpool slid downhill fast.

I respect Gérard immensely for what he did at Liverpool. He brought me six trophies, and I still keep in touch with him, but managers are judged on signings. The players Gérard bought in the summer of 2002 let him down. They were bad buys. You don't have to be a rocket scientist to work that out. With Salif, I knew after a week in training that he wasn't going to be good enough. Everyone goes under the microscope at Melwood. All flaws are exposed. I read in the papers that Diao was the 'new Patrick Vieira', and I saw him do quite well at the World Cup for Senegal. Diao's a good player, but not Liverpool class. That was £4 million not well spent. Cheyrou, who cost slightly less, was a great French lad with loads of ability, but he lacked pace and suffered with injuries. When he was fit, he also found it difficult to get into his preferred position, central midfield. Didi and I were already there. I wasn't moving. No chance. I was on fire after my operation and Didi was one of the first names on the team-sheet. We weren't shifting for Cheyrou.

Diouf arrived with the most potential, and he ended up causing the most aggravation. As soon as Gérard started playing him on the right, I knew he was a poor signing. Everyone banged on about the Senegal centre-forward being the man to bring more goals to Liverpool. So what was Gérard doing sticking him out on the wing? It was strange, particularly as Diouf had been brought in to replace Nicolas Anelka, a real centre-forward. 'We've decided not to keep Anelka,' Gérard said in a pre-season meeting with Liverpool's experienced pros – me, Carra, Michael, Didi and Sami. 'We've decided to bring El-Hadji Diouf in. We feel he's a better player, got a better attitude, and will be a better signing for the club. Nicolas is a good player, but we are not sure how he will react if we make his loan deal permanent.' I was gobsmacked. I wanted us to keep Anelka. All the players did. I didn't say any-thing to Gerard, but I came out of the meeting gutted. Who was this Diouf anyway? Anelka had done well for Liverpool and seemed an all right guy. Anelka actually surprised me. He had a reputation for being trouble, for being moody, but I liked him. He was dead quiet, and he just got on with things. He was a star at the time, a far bigger star than me. I was buzzing to have him at Anfield. When Paul Joyce from the *Express* sent me a text saying 'You've got Anelka', I was made up. Michael had all the pressure on him to score, so Anelka's arrival midway through the season really helped. We had one game, against Newcastle United, when he was just awesome, running the Geordies ragged. Everyone expected Liverpool to keep Anelka, but not the man who mattered, Gérard Houllier. We finished second in 2002 with Anelka and fifth in 2003 with Diouf. Draw your own conclusions.

I wasn't El-Hadji Diouf's number one fan. Being around Melwood and Anfield, I knew which players were hungry, which players had Liverpool at heart. To my mind, Diouf was just interested in himself. His attitude was all wrong. I felt he wasn't really arsed about putting his body on the line to get Liverpool back to the top. He was out on the town a lot, wasting his energies. Diouf wasn't desperate for success like the rest of us. Some of the crazy clothes he wore and the way he behaved seemed designed to make the following statement: 'I am the best player in the world'. He wasn't, by a million miles. For him to do so well at a World Cup, there must have been a half-decent player in Diouf somewhere, but Liverpool rarely saw him. He was nicknamed 'Serial Killer' in Senegal for his goals, but he only got three for us in the league that season. Maybe Gérard rushed through the deal because of how well Diouf did at the World Cup. Danger always lies that way. Clubs should spend £10 million on a player only when they have watched him for years, on and off the field. They need to check if he is a party animal. Patrice Bergues, Gérard's old assistant at Liverpool, was Diouf's coach at Lens and he obviously talked to Gérard. He trusted Patrice's advice 100 per cent, so he signed Diouf. Gérard didn't let Liverpool down by signing Diouf; Diouf let Gérard down by not caring. He even spat at a Celtic fan in a UEFA Cup tie at Parkhead. He hit the kid in the face with not just a bit of phlegm, but a real hoik. All the Liverpool lads were livid with him. Spitting is disgusting. English players are drilled not to spit. Most players would rather be butted than to have to wipe someone's saliva from their eyes.

Before Liverpool got shut of Diouf to Bolton, he did give us a belter of a game, the Worthington Cup final win over Manchester United on 2 March 2003. Diouf always played well against United. Maybe he raised his game because it was a big occasion against famous opposition. In the Millennium Stadium, Diouf gave Mikael Silvestre nightmares, and always showed for the ball. He was a constant threat. He could be a good outlet on the right, holding the ball up and allowing others to get into space, but that season he never really delivered. At least that trip to Cardiff gave us some silverware for 2002/03. My shot hit Becks and deflected in over Fabien Barthez, United's keeper. No matter how lucky the goal was, it felt brilliant to score against the old enemy. Michael, as usual, also found the mark as Liverpool ran out 2–0 winners. The League Cup is not the most respected trophy in the world, but United were definitely up for it, and so were we. Fergie put Keane and Juan Sebastian Verón up against me, and Didi and me had a right old scrap with them. What was especially good was that Jerzy Dudek played a blinder. He had been slaughtered for a mistake that allowed Diego Forlan to score when we met United earlier in the season. Football always gives you a chance to make amends. Down in Cardiff, Jerzy paid us back for his Forlan howler.

That was the high point of a season that descended into disappointment. Fifth was nowhere. No Champions League for 2003/04 was a killer. Liverpool were in decline, and Gérard came under mounting pressure. Snipers in the press and on the phone-ins targeted him. Liverpool were trapped down a cul-de-sac with no obvious means of getting out. I began thinking about my future. 'I'm worried, Stru,' I told my agent. 'Playing in the Champions League helps get me in the England squad. Sven always watches Champions League games. People look down on the UEFA Cup.' I knew I could survive one season out of the Champions League, but two would harm my career. Struan took a few phone calls from agents representing clubs in Europe, enquiring about the situation with my contract. Barcelona, Roma and Inter Milan were apparently interested. I was flattered to read pieces saying Real Madrid were chasing me, but I wasn't tempted. Liverpool's season had been shite, but I didn't want to leave the club I love.

12
Darkness in Basle

The most depressing point in my relationship with Gérard Houllier came in the pretty Swiss town of Basle on 12 November 2002. Everyone in Liverpool's colours needed all their energy and focus for this massive Champions League tie, the most important game of the season, but my head wasn't right. For some time, I'd been a moody bastard. Tension between me and Gérard built and built. When the boss took me off against Spurs at Anfield on 26 October, I snapped. Straight down the tunnel, no acknowledgement. Straight into the dressing-room, door slamming, boots flying, absolutely steaming. I hate being hooked, however rubbish I'm playing. For Christ's sake, not in front of the Kop, where my mates are watching. When the fourth official holds up my number it feels like a judge passing a sentence. Game over. I have no control; I have to leave the pitch, and everyone stares. Not good enough today, Stevie lad. The humiliation kills me.

Storming past Gérard at Anfield pissed him off big-time. The boss immediately sent Doc Waller to come and get me. 'No chance,' I told the doc. 'I'm staying here.' Doc Waller caught the fury in my eyes and knew he would need an army to budge me. I was selfish, I knew that, but I just want to do my best for Liverpool and I can't if the manager subs me. I stayed in the dressing-room, alone with my anger. Gérard went mental and fined me. Even an apology couldn't repair the damage. He put me on the bench against West Ham, and then subbed me at Middlesbrough. What a mess. As we flew out to Basle, Gérard wasn't in my good books, and I wasn't in his.

It was my fault. My form wasn't right. Bad problems off the pitch distracted me. I couldn't tell anyone at Liverpool because it was too personal. Mum and Dad were splitting up. There was trouble in the house, arguing, fighting. I love my parents so much it was desperate to watch them tearing each other apart. Shit. It was supposed to be perfect. I had bought a house in Whiston and the three of us lived there, with Paul, my brother, keeping Ironside. I was gutted Paul didn't come with us. Family means everything to me, all together, sitting around and laughing, under one roof. I wanted the magic of my Ironside childhood to last for ever. However crazy my life became with Liverpool and England, I wanted that protective wall of my family around me. But Paul decided to stay at Ironside. Still, there was Mum, Dad and me living together. Together. That's what mattered.

Family life at Whiston seemed great to start with. The better I did on the pitch, surely the better life should be at home? That's how I thought it would work. We had money, a nice house, each other. Mum and Dad weren't working, so it wasn't as if they were spending time apart. They were always close. What could go wrong?

Everything. People fall out of love with each other, I suppose. At first, I didn't know my parents were quarrelling. They kept it from me, didn't want to upset me, didn't want to disrupt my career. But they couldn't hide the tension for ever. I found myself getting dragged into their nightmare. When I came back in from Melwood or a match, I heard the arguments which they quickly tried to stop when they realized I was home. I tried to speak to them about it, tried to help, but they were too far down the road to breaking up. Even now, looking back, it still rips my heart apart. I just wanted everything to be perfect, for everyone to be together. No fights. No rift.

The turmoil at home destroyed my game. My form hit a brick wall. As I pulled my boots on and did up my laces, my thoughts were miles away. In training and matches, all I could think about was that two people I adored were going their separate ways. The split happened over a couple of months, and I couldn't handle it. It felt like a bereavement. Only one word can describe my life as winter approached: carnage.

Before we flew out to Basle, Gérard hauled me into his office at Melwood. He'd had enough. He wanted to find out what was bugging me. I walked in to be confronted by Thommo, Sammy Lee, the goalkeeping coach Joe Corrigan and head scout Alex Miller, as well as Gérard. Christ, they looked like a bloody firing squad standing there. Gérard opened up first: 'What's eating you, Steven? Is your family all right?'

I stared at the floor. I should have talked, but I didn't feel comfortable. Not in front of them all. My silence goaded them. One by one, they each got stuck into me. They hit me with so many questions it was like being punched in the face time after time. 'You are not training good enough,' said Thommo. 'You are sulking around the place,' Corrigan chipped in. 'You are down, not yourself, always snarling, not happy,' added Miller. 'Has it all gone to your head?' Gérard asked. 'Do you want to talk?' said Sammy. 'Have you got problems at home?' The questions and criticisms kept coming, wave after wave. I was hanging around with the wrong people; I'd got too big for my boots. Question after question. What the fuck was going on? A goalie coach was having a go at me. A chief scout was laying into me. Fair enough if it were Sammy, Gérard or Phil. I could accept that. But this mass interrogation was all wrong. I can take criticism, but this was five grown men, pointing their fingers at me, slaughtering me.

Incensed, I struggled to control my fists. I was that close to attacking them. 'Have you lot finished?' I finally said, and walked out the room. Steaming. How could I possibly stand there and tell five men that my mum and dad were fighting? Every time I thought about it a lump came into my throat. I didn't want anyone to hear about our family problems. I trusted Gérard with my life, but I didn't want to tell him about Mum and Dad and then add, 'Don't say anything to anyone.' It would have looked like I didn't believe he could keep quiet. So I kept my problems to myself and just took all the shite off the management staff.

I revealed my anguish to one person. In Basle, I shared a room with Danny Murphy, and I told him everything about Mum and Dad and Gérard's firing squad. Danny endured the same grief with his parents. He understood the pain I was going through, how it affected my football. Danny was superb. I would not have survived that Basle trip without him. 'Don't worry,' said Danny. 'You'll get through. Be strong. Just forget what's happening for a moment and go out and play.'

Amazingly, I started against Basle. After the ruck with Gérard and his staff, I assumed I would be on the bench again. The boss played me in my favourite position, too, central midfield, but I was shocking. Not focused. Not involved. Not at the races. Every pass I made went to a Basle player or into the crowd. I wasn't running enough. I felt so detached, as if I was watching someone in a horror film. Gérard might just as well have put me in with the fans. Liverpool needed a big performance from me. We had to beat Basle to reach the knockout stages of the Champions League. But my mind was elsewhere. I looked around St Jakobs Park and just wanted to be back in Whiston, trying to keep Mum and Dad together. With me off the pace, Basle grabbed a three-goal lead by half-time. And my night was about to get even worse.

In the dressing-room, I was scarcely through the door when Gérard shouted, 'Steven, shower.' That was it. Me off. Fuck's sake. All the lads felt embarrassed because I looked stupid. If a player has a nightmare, a manager can react in two ways at half-time: either give the player another five minutes so the subbing doesn't appear that bad, or humiliate the player by not allowing him out for the second half. Gérard should have allowed me five more minutes, just to give me a chance to make some impact. I deserved better treatment than being shown up in front of the team. Gérard had embarrassed me like that before, bringing me on and taking me off in the same game against Newcastle. That pissed me off no end. This was worse, far worse.

Corrigan walked into the showers. 'Keep your chin up,' he said.

'Fuck off,' I told him. I was in no mood to talk.

I stood there in the shower, listening to Gérard giving instructions for the second half. It was mission impossible. 'Salif, I want you in central midfield where Steven was,' Gérard said. Salif Diao? That made my subbing even more shaming. Even if I was playing on a four out of ten I could do what Diao did. In fairness to Salif, he did help turn the game round. Liverpool pulled three goals back, through Danny, Vladi and Michael, which made me look even worse. Afterwards, when the staff came into the dressing-room, I just walked into the toilets and stayed there while they talked to the boys.

We stopped the night in Basle. The next morning I got word Gérard had had a pop at me. The boss told journalists, 'Once a player starts to believe everything that is written about him and thinks "I am king of the world", there is difficulty and danger.' Basically, Gérard questioned my commitment, suggesting I was a Big-Time Charlie who enjoyed the reflection of his own image. Bollocks. At the airport, I sought out Joycey, who I knew would have been at the press conference with Gérard. Joycey would give it to me straight, no bullshit.

'You're not going to like the papers in the morning, Stevie,' he said.

Christ.

'Did Gérard really say all that shite about me thinking I was king of the world?' I asked.

'Yes.'

I was steaming. All the journalists had their heads together, working on what was a massive story. The headlines were going to kill me. I sat on my own on the plane. Not in the mood for company. A few players came up and said, 'Fucking hell, Gérard didn't need to do that.' Everyone knew, and the papers weren't even out yet.

The next morning, the stories were as brutal as I feared. Gérard accused me of reading too many headlines. I certainly read these ones he whipped up. I talked to two people I trust, Chris Bascombe of the *Echo* and Liverpool's press officer, Ian Cotton.

'Did Gérard say it the way it has been printed?' I asked them.

'Yes,' Basco and Cotton both replied.

I needed to know for sure. Sometimes a manager's words get twisted on the way from a press conference to a headline. Not in this case.

When he called me, Gérard claimed it was typical press overreaction. 'I had a go at you in the press, but they blew it out of proportion,' he said. Bollocks. Gérard meant every word. It wasn't malice. The boss just wanted to shake me out of my poor form. In Gérard's mind, he'd tried every angle, from one-on-one talks with me to the full firing squad, and nothing lifted my depression. Basle was the last resort, the shock tactics, and it hurt like hell.

Liverpool managers have always kept criticism in-house, saying things privately to players rather than slagging them off in public. What Gérard did in Basle broke the code. At the very least he should have warned me what he was planning to tell the media, not throw an unexpected bomb at me in a crowded press conference. Managers must be careful what they say to the media. What happened in Basle showed a lack of respect on Gérard's part. I felt badly let down. My phone was red-hot with calls from the team. Everyone was saying or texting how shocked they were by Gérard's action.

'Go and see him, he's out of order,' said Robbie.

'It's not normal what the gaffer's done,' agreed Jamie Redknapp. 'What are you going to do?'

'I fancy going to Melwood and slaughtering Gérard to his face,' I replied.

'Be sensible,' said Jamie. 'Be careful what you say. Don't go in there and be too harsh.'

Gary Mac gave me good support as well. So did Struan. My dad hit the roof when he picked up the papers.

'What the fuck is going on?' he asked me. 'I know why you're not playing well. It's not because you are a bad player, or have the wrong people around you. It's because of what is happening in our house between me and your mother. Doesn't Gérard understand that?'

I couldn't reply. It was too painful.

'Doesn't Gérard know?' Dad said again.

I shrugged my shoulders. 'I've not told him,' I replied eventually.

'It's our fault, and *I* am going to tell Gérard,' Dad said.

'No! Leave it!'

'Come on, Steven, either you tell him or I will.'

'I'm not.' I was really upset by this time. I felt trapped. Dad was livid. 'Give me Gérard's number.'

'No.'

'Right, that's fucking it. I'm going down the training ground to have it out with him.'

I couldn't stop Dad. He was out the house before I could react. I hoped he would calm down and have second thoughts as he drove there. No chance. Straight down to Melwood, straight up to Gérard's office, knock on the door, and in. Nothing was going to stop Dad saying his piece. He was raging. He explained everything to Gérard and Thommo. 'It's mine and Julie's fault that Steven's off his game,' he told them.

While Dad was in there, I got a call off Boggo. 'Stevie, your dad's in with Gérard.' I was gutted people knew my old fella was in the boss's office. My mobile went again. It was Gérard, asking me to come in for a meeting. I rushed over.

Dad was just sticking up for me, I know. When I got back to Whiston, I thanked him. He knew how unhappy I was. Dad knows me better than anyone. 'I haven't seen you smile for ages, Steven,' he said. 'You are not the happiest of people anyway! But I can tell.' Dad got everything out in the open, and from then on my form came back sharpish. I felt as if a huge stone weight had been lifted off my chest. I was grateful to everyone at Liverpool for keeping news of my parents' split quiet. No-one outside the club or house knew. Mum and Dad broke up, but it was not an aggressive fall-out in the end. They just sat down, talked, and went their separate ways.

Merseyside buzzed with gossip about me, all of it bullshit. It was the usual 'rumour city' stuff. People claimed Gérard worried about me hanging around with lads who took drugs. Throughout my career, I have heard all sorts of sneaky stories linking me with drugs. Struan calls and says, 'I have had another journalist on, saying he's got a story about you and drugs.' Lies, all lies, a million miles from the truth. This drugs slur needs nailing once and for good. I have never taken drugs. Never. Coming from Huyton, I know people who do drugs. Drugs are rife, a sad fact of life, a curse for many, but I have never succumbed. After Basle, I got really pissed off about being linked with drugs on the Merseyside grapevine. I spoke to Robbie, a mate who suffered similar smears. 'Don't worry about it,' said Robbie. 'I've had it all the way through my career.' Robbie is good at giving advice. I took all the rumours about me with a pinch of salt because I knew they were all rubbish. Sad people dug around for stories, but there was no dirt on me.

A lot of people actually sympathized with me over Basle. When I next went down to England, the journalists I knew there said they couldn't believe the way Gérard behaved. I remember a few pieces saying Gérard was out of order. Fortunately, Basle didn't harm my relationship with Gérard in the long run. Before we travelled up to Sunderland in December, the boss called me into his office. 'Sami is out for the game and I want you to be captain,' he said.

Captain of Liverpool!

Basle seemed a distant memory as I led Liverpool out at the Stadium of Light. We lost, but the feeling of having the armband on was special. 'One day, you will captain the club permanently,' said Gérard. 'Keep learning.' He mentioned the captaincy a couple of times that season, but

I never really thought anything of it. During training one afternoon the following season, 2003/04, Gérard said, 'Come and see me afterwards.' I showered, changed, and ran upstairs to the boss's office. Thommo was sitting there next to Gérard.

'We've had meetings with the staff,' Gérard began, 'and have spoken to a few players. We feel as if we need to change the captaincy of the club. Sami has been a good captain, but we feel you are ready to take the captaincy on. We feel it would help the team.'

I was stunned. Everyone respected Sami. A big, vocal centre-half, Sami was a natural leader.

'How is it going to be with Sami?' I asked.

'Don't worry,' replied Gérard. 'I've spoken to Sami.'

When I left the office, I looked around for Sami, but he had gone home. Pity. I wanted to address the issue as quickly as possible.

I didn't sleep much that night. Feelings of pride mixed with concern over how Sami would react. Sami hadn't been playing that well, so maybe taking away the arm-band would allow him to focus on his own game, rather than the team. Still, it can't be nice to have such an honour taken away. I'd be devastated.

As I arrived at Melwood the next day, Sami pulled me.

'Stevie, can I have a word?'

'Yeah, of course, Sami.'

'Listen, I spoke to the manager and Phil yesterday and I want you to know there are no hard feelings. You deserve the captaincy. It was only a matter of time. Good luck. If you need any advice, I'm there for you.'

Some man, is Sami. That can't have been easy for him,

but he handled it with real dignity. My admiration for him rose even higher. I wanted to be a captain like Sami, a good ambassador. Becks was my other role model. Until he stepped down after the World Cup in Germany, Becks proved an outstanding captain for England. Becks always led by example, always gave everything on the pitch, always gave sound advice off it. Becks was brilliant with the young lads, especially those new to the set-up and slightly in awe. When I became Liverpool captain, I watched Becks even more closely with England. Saw how he dealt with issues, how easily he handled the responsibility.

Sometimes I stop on the drive home from Melwood and just sit in the car and tell myself, 'I'm captain of Liverpool Football Club.' For a kid who grew up in Huyton, who stood on the Kop, being Liverpool captain is an unbelievable honour. I think of all the greats who have led out Liverpool, real leaders like Ron Yeats, Emlyn Hughes, Thommo, Graeme Souness, Alan Hansen. And now me. I can never thank Gérard Houllier enough. I owe Gérard so much. I'll always remember what Gérard did for my career.

13
Stars and Strikes

I even captained England. It was only a friendly, a trip to Sweden on 31 March 2004, but it felt like the World Cup final as I led my country out in Gothenburg. This was a moment I had dreamed of since I wore the Bryan Robson shirt while kicking about on Ironside. We lost, to a goal from Sweden's clever striker Zlatan Ibrahimovic, but the armband and the memory will stay with me for ever.

Just before then, the press questioned how much we players love representing England – a disgraceful claim. The controversy stemmed from the build-up to our final Euro 2004 qualifier in Istanbul on 11 October 2003. Six days before this massive tie, I drove to Manchester airport with Emile and Carra for the flight down to London. We met the United lads at the gate and had a chat. Usual stuff, until Carra noticed Rio Ferdinand was missing. 'Where's Rio?' Carra asked. 'Is he not in the squad?' Scholesy, Butty and Gary Neville explained Rio had been left out on Football Association orders, because he missed a drugs test. Well, he hadn't deliberately missed it. He'd forgotten, left the training ground, and when he remembered, the testers had gone. Rio took a test later and passed. But the FA were livid and stopped Sven picking him. Carra, Emile and me were shocked.

The saga was only just beginning. When we arrived at Sopwell House, our base near St Albans, the place was in uproar. Quite a few of the England lads were steaming over the FA's treatment of Rio. We should have been focusing on training with Sven and getting prepared for Turkey, but all the boys could talk about was Rio. Carnage lay around the corner.

On the Tuesday we managed to train in the morning, and then Becks called a meeting. He spoke, and so did Gary Neville, very forcefully. 'We need to stick up for Rio' was the gist of Gary's argument. The majority of the squad sat and listened to the players driving the argument, those with links to United like Gary and Becks. Gary talked tough towards the FA because Rio's a United lad. I admire Gary. He was sticking up for a team-mate. We all wanted Rio, a good friend and a great player, back with us, but I didn't want to get into any trouble. The FA's chief executive, Mark Palios, was allowed into the room to explain his reasons for kicking Rio out. He wasn't very convincing. I looked around the room and realized support was strengthening even more behind Rio. Palios was in an awkward position. He had banned Rio from joining up, but he didn't want it to affect his relationship with all the other players. 'I had to do it,' Palios kept saying. After ten minutes, Palios left and Becks stood up. 'The team stay behind,' said England's captain.

More speeches. More debate. Then Becks and Gary

organized a ballot over whether to support Rio, with the understanding that could mean not going to Istanbul. A strike! Just mention of the word makes me shudder. It would be a hugely controversial call, a decision that would live with us for the rest of our lives. Abandon England? Christ. What were we getting ourselves into? I wanted Rio back in the squad, and I wanted to show my support, but the thought of striking scared me. Could I really follow Gary Neville and turn my back on England when it counted? My team. My dream. Istanbul was not just any old match; if we got a point we reached Euro 2004. I'd missed the 2002 World Cup and was desperate to play. I felt Gary was too strong in calling for a strike. He possibly should have taken more time to consider the consequences, not just for him but for all the players, particularly the young ones. They sat around as senior pros argued for a strike which would blacken everyone's names in the eyes of the public and press. I didn't want to be slaughtered for not playing for my country. England fans would be outraged. But I couldn't bring myself to voice my concerns. I took a back seat and listened. It was a horrible meeting to be in. We're footballers, not politicians. I wanted to be out there training, not sitting around taking a vote.

Fortunately, David James spoke out, calling for clear heads before we considered striking. 'We've got to think about the fans,' said Jamo. 'With all due respect to Rio, and I want him back in the squad as much as anyone, there are going to be more problems than we all think if we go on strike.' People say goalkeepers are mad, but Jamo always talked sense. I really admired him for what he did and said at Sopwell. Jamo made everyone realize the dangers of a strike, that it wasn't going to benefit any of us. Gary put forward one argument, and Jamo just looked at the situation from the point of view of a few others at the meeting, the ones like me who never said anything. After Jamo spoke, I felt better. The consequences of not going to Turkey were obvious. 'If we support Rio 100 per cent and don't go to Istanbul, we'll all have to take the flak,' said Jamo. Fucking hell, I thought, this is so serious. My heart beat fast.

We can't go on strike, but we must stick together. Send out a message to the FA: don't mess with us. The best sides are those where the players stand shoulder to shoulder, like soldiers in a war. We were all in it together, even those with reservations. Eventually, I decided to follow the experienced players like Becks and Gary. So did the rest of the squad. We all agreed the FA had to bring Rio back or face the consequences. Whatever the reservations of players like myself, we were united. One out, all out. Though I prayed we wouldn't have to go through with the strike. Gary and Becks knocked up a statement from the England squad which read: 'It is our opinion that the organization we represent has not only let down one of our team-mates but the whole of the England squad and its manager. We feel they have failed us badly. They have made the team weaker.' We gave the statement to the FA and sat back to see their reaction.

Becks quickly told Sven. He wanted the dispute settled sharpish, but he backed us all the way. On the Wednesday, as the controversy intensified, Sven told all the cameras at Sopwell that he was behind us. God knows what Palios thought of that! Every England player really respected Sven for that. He could have ducked the issue, or sided with the FA because they pay his wages. Sven didn't. When the team needed the support of the manager most, Sven stuck up for us. It was a horrible day, though. Whenever I flicked Sky on in my room, people were criticizing us for talking about striking. We were getting unbelievable stick. I felt we'd made our point by publicly backing Rio and it was time to move on, to get back to football. I was not enjoying the caning. None of the players were. A sombre mood fell over Sopwell.

That evening, the players held another meeting. 'Right, we've made our point,' said Becks. 'We've shown the FA that they cannot mess about one of our players.' We all agreed we should now go to Istanbul.

Just as well. As Jamo predicted, and I privately suspected, the newspapers slaughtered us for even thinking of striking. The story had spread from the back pages to the front. It became a huge national issue. At breakfast on the Thursday, I picked up the *Daily Mirror*, which had the story of the proposed strike on the front and the back. Photographs of every player were printed on the front underneath the words 'Who the hell do they think they are?' Jesus, if that was a warning of the coverage we would receive if we went on strike, thank God we pulled out. Chaos was just a ballot away. No-one wants to be battered from pillar to post in the press. It's a brutal experience. All my friends and family called, wondering what the hell was going on. Thank heaven it was sorted and the media wave of criticism could subside. Rio sent us a message saying how much he appreciated our support, stressing that he didn't want us to go on strike. We'd done the right thing to stand by Rio and then fly out to Istanbul.

As the plane hurtled across Europe, my mind finally turned to what sort of reception the Turks would lay on for us. Our home game, at Sunderland on 2 April 2003, had been quick, intense and nasty. The Turks were up to all their old tricks at the Stadium of Light, leaving the foot in, pulling shirts, the usual sly stunts, anything to break up our flow. Even players who have spent time in the Premiership, like Tugay, an opponent I respect, tried to provoke us. That's the Turkish mentality. Bulent scratched my face, drawing blood. Turks don't care how they win, as long as they do. Turks will try to con their way to victory. But cheats never prosper. When Tugay and his mates arrived at Sunderland, they ran into Wayne Rooney. Turkey didn't know what hit them. Rooney was brilliant in that 2–0 victory, all muscle and touch.

In those few days up in the north-east of England, I realized exactly how special Rooney was. One day, in training at Slaley Hall, Rooney announced to the whole England squad the massive size of his talent. We were playing a practice match towards the end of training when Rooney picked up the ball, dribbled past a few players and chipped Jamo. Astonishing. Silence reigned for a split-second, as if everyone was trying to take in exactly what we had just seen. Then we all burst into applause, every-one, even established stars like Becks and Owen. We all glanced at each other, as if to say, 'This boy can play.' Only seventeen, and already heading for greatness. I knew Wazza was talented because I had seen the goals he scored for Everton, I'd watched him on the telly, and I'd read all the press coverage. But that day at Slaley Hall made me realize quite how brilliant he was. I needed to train alongside him, watch him close up, to appreciate the quality of his first touch. His self-belief too. Most players would be cautious during the build-up to their first start. Not Wazza. He charged into Slaley Hall, trying all sorts of skills. Nothing fazes Wazza. It's a Scouse trait. No wonder we hit it off immediately.

By the time we landed in Istanbul, Wazza and I were good mates. What I love about Rooney is, however big the occasion, he's relaxed. England's journey to Fenerbahce's home ground would have unsettled even the toughest customer. Not Rooney. Wazza just smiled out the window at all these Turks throwing bottles at us, giving us the finger, screaming abuse. When Rooney was ready, he just ran out of the tunnel into this wall of noise and laughed. Is that your best? Try harder, shout louder, because I ain't bothered. That's Wazza. He went towards one goal and started banging balls around. Scholesy was the same. Out the tunnel, pinging balls around, no warm-up. I don't know how Scholesy and Rooney get away with it. If I had not done some stretching first, working on my hamstrings and calf, I'd have pulled every muscle in my legs. Not Rooney. Rooney's talent was shaped on the streets of Croxteth, and he has not lost that street-player's streak. Out the front door, bang, into a game. No warm-up, no tension, let's get cracking, lads. No worries. In Istanbul, he almost looked bored as he warmed up. Chewing gum and smiling – just a kid belting balls around. He kept wellying the ball high up in the air while the rest of us were working on our stretches. How his hamstrings survived I don't know.

Before kick-off, Becks gathered us together and reminded us what would happen if we screwed up. The fuss over the threatened strike would return with a vengeance. Doubled. Imagine the headlines, lads. We had to get that point. Qualify for the Euros, and we'd go from zeros to heroes in the fans' eyes again. All teams visiting Turkey need strong bonds between players, and the Rio controversy bolted all the players even closer. All that off-the-pitch unity now needed to be shown in the teeth of a Turkish hurricane.

The atmosphere in Istanbul was crazy. There were 42,000 Turks screaming blue murder at us. Love it. All that hostility turns me on. When I went near the crowd, to pick up the ball for a throw-in, Turkish fans drew fingers across their necks, making as if they wanted to slash our throats. Bring it on. At half-time, it all kicked off between the players in the tunnel. I was one of the last to arrive, because I was on the other side of the pitch when the whistle went. It was typical Turks, ambushing opponents. There was shouting, spitting, pushing and kicking. Alpay, the Aston Villa centre-half, was right in the thick of it. Someone spat at Ashley Cole. By the time I got there, Rooney was sorting out a few Turks. Fortunately, Pierluigi Collina was there to calm tempers. The sight of Rooney, Ashley, Emile and the rest all standing up for each other showed England's togetherness. Even when Becks missed a penalty, which was given after Tugay tripped me, no-one blamed him. He slipped. Penalty-taking is a lottery anyway, so no-one was going to dig Becks out. How many times has he got England out of trouble? Countless. We are a family at England, and we look after each other like brothers.

The goalless draw was enough to give us what we'd gone to Turkey for: a place at Euro 2004 in Portugal the following summer. I fancied England's chances. Good squad, great spirit, and everyone up for it.

14
Pleasure and Pain in Portugal

We landed in Lisbon among the favourites. Our team was settled, with Wayne now established alongside Michael, and the midfield situation sorted following two warm-up games at the City of Manchester Stadium. In the first, against Japan on 1 June, Sven shifted me out to the left of a diamond – a decision that disappointed me. I'll play anywhere for England, of course. No-one doubts my commitment to my country, but my strengths lie in central midfield. No question. Confronting the enemy head on, getting the ball, bombing on, finishing moves off – that's me. I envied Scholesy his position at the tip of the diamond against Japan, a real attacking role. I'd have caused chaos there.

Before kick-off, I was presented with a trophy for England Player of the Year – a fantastic gesture from the supporters. I've had awards from journalists and players, but this honour was different: it came from England fans who spend their life, and their hard-earned cash, travelling around watching us. My heart swelled with pride. England Player of the Year! Sounded good. Time to show it was deserved.

Cutting in from the flank, I helped set up Michael's goal against Japan, but I hated life on the left. I love the centre-stage, not playing out on the fringe. Being moved around was wrong. Sven often used me in different positions, sometimes telling me only hours before a game or changing my role during a match. As a footballer and as a human being, I must feel settled before I can be happy and deliver. I crave the nod days before, so I can work on the role, eradicate mistakes in training, and talk the assignment through with Sven, the coaches and other players. Even good footballers find it difficult to adapt if told their role only twenty-four hours before a massive game. But whinging is not my style. I never raised my unease in public after the Japan game. I just read with interest the debate raging on the sports pages over where I should play for England. No debate, guys. I'm best in the middle. End of story. I do have the legs to play out there, but I'm not John Barnes, beating three and getting crosses in.

Fortunately, diamonds are not for ever. Four days later, Sven restored me to England's heart against Iceland. We thrashed them 6–1, and I was there to stay. Thank God. By then, Frank Lampard had edged out Butty, so England flew into Portugal with a midfield of me and Lamps in the centre, Scholesy on the left and Becks right. It looked good. 'This is my midfield for Portugal,' Sven told us. My sigh of relief was long and loud, although I felt sorry for Scholesy, who got the graveyard shift. I wanted Scholesy to shine on the left at Euro 2004 so Sven wouldn't banish me out there.

As we checked into our Lisbon base, the Solplay, every-thing appeared perfect. The hotel boasted all the five-star trimmings. The weather was magnificent, so in our spare time we gathered round the pool to relax, or nipped out for a knock of golf. Every camp needs a joker and we had Jamo, a bubbly character, brilliant at getting the spirit going. In the hours after training or between matches, Jamo always lightened the mood with his dry humour. Spending weeks abroad can trouble players. Boredom and homesickness gets to people. Not at Euro 2004. Anyone feeling down would immediately be lifted by Jamo's banter. I like Jamo being around. From the outside he can come across as a strange character, but with England he's like an experienced father-figure, good for advice and a laugh.

Gary Neville is more serious than Jamo, but is just as important to the squad. Always focused, always pro-fessional, Gary is the ideal team-mate with England. People think of Gary being Red Nev, a union leader on a mission, but he just stands up for the rights of the England squad. Gary is fiercely protective of the young players, always helping them. He fights for the team, on and off the pitch. At Liverpool, Steve Finnan reaches towards Gary's level, but in terms of consistency over the years, Gary is the best right-back I've played with. Captain of Manchester United, Gary's a leader, a winner. Sitting around the Solplay, some had doubts whether we would do well at Euro 2004. Not Gary. 'We can win this,' he kept saying.

But, inside, we all knew it would be difficult. We weren't firing on all cylinders. Euro 2004 was do-able, but we needed to raise our game, individually and collectively. People had high expectations of me, particularly now I was back where I belonged, in central midfield. I was in the holding role, but at least I was central. Having a nation's eyes on me was not a problem. My club form had been good. But England faced a stiff start, against France, the champions, the team of Thierry Henry, Zinedine Zidane and Patrick Vieira – a familiar opponent from Premiership war zones.

Everyone made England underdogs for this opening Group B game at the Stadium of Light on 13 June. Everyone tipped France to thrash us. France's team-sheet was pinned up in our dressing-room. Michael and I looked at the names. 'Fucking hell,' I said. 'These are top players. I'll have to be right on my game.' I sat down, put my kit on, and as I tied my laces tight I reminded myself of an old saying in football: 'Respect them, but don't fear them.' Spot on. Zidane was class, but we had top players as well. 'I'm not fucking having this,' I said out loud. 'Let's show everyone what we can do.' We had Michael. We had Wayne. Wayne! I looked across at him. Not a care in the world. Relaxed, confident, ready for any opposition, however good. He just banged a ball against the wall, first time, bang. Back it came. Bang. Back it went. Back and forth, almost hypnotically. Wayne was just messing about with the ball, as if he were going out for a Sunday League match. He stopped as Sven gave us some last-minute orders. When Sven finished, Wayne also had some instructions. 'Just give me the ball,' he told everyone. 'Give me the ball. I will do it. I want it.' Wayne wasn't being bigheaded. He knows what he can do. Everything! We had a chance against France. Wayne would breeze through them.

The atmosphere in the dressing-room ripped into life. Jamo, standing tall in the middle of the room, screamed encouragement. Becks, Gary Nev, Sol – all shouting. Sol is amazing. A great player for Spurs and Arsenal, he really comes to life at tournaments. The moment he stepped into the dressing-room before the French game, he became a different person. A leader, a warrior. So serene around the hotel, England's Colossus was fired up to face the French. His voice and presence filled the dressing-room. Shouts were now coming from all corners of the room. No-one was quiet. No-one was scared. This was it. France. Vieira. Fucking come on! Door open, into the tunnel, out into the stadium.

Nothing prepared me for the sights and sounds that greeted me. The Stadium of Light held 62,487 that night, and they all seemed to be English. White flags waved everywhere. Even in the French corner, I saw hundreds of England supporters, faces painted with the Cross of St George, singing 'Three Lions', not giving a monkey's they were in the French section. Our supporters are truly fanatical. They launched into the national anthem so loudly the hairs stood to attention on the back of my neck. Controlling my emotions was a struggle. Focus, focus. But the adrenalin was pumping, racing even quicker as I poured my heart into the anthem. Amazing moments. The singing and formalities completed, I sprinted into the middle. This was it. Into battle. Come on, Vieira.

England settled the quicker. All the predictions were

being turned on their head. We passed the ball around well, even taking the lead. One of Lamps' main strengths is raiding into the box, getting goals. At Euro 2004 he got off to a flier with a fantastic header past Fabien Barthez. Pick that out. That goal was the making of Lamps, filling him with confidence. His first game at his first tournament, and he'd just scored against France. Not bad. I was delighted for him as a midfield colleague, and as one of the nicest blokes I've ever met. Good company, good banter. I spent some very enjoyable hours at the Solplay chatting away with Frank, about the tournament and about what was happening at Chelsea and at Liverpool.

France were caught out, sent reeling by the intensity of England's football. I got stuck into Vieira and Zidane. Frank raced forward. Rooney stretched France, pulling Lilian Thuram and Mikael Silvestre all over the Stadium of Light. France were totally unprepared for this one-man tornado from Croxteth called Wayne Rooney. He battered them. Wayne never looks scared in matches, never hides from the ball. He could be back on the street in Merseyside. We all knew how special he was; that night at the Stadium of Light was the moment the whole world realized England boasted an extraordinarily gifted teenager. A star was born in Lisbon. Since then, Wayne has become the key man for England. He's such a character and joker around the hotel. He is always up to something. I didn't know Gazza too well, but I heard all the stories about Gazza's antics lifting team spirit. Wazza is the same – always smiling, always happy. He'll wind anyone up. At the Solplay, all the players marvelled at his confidence for someone so young. Rooney knows he is the main man. When he passed twenty caps, I mentioned to Michael, 'It's like he's got eighty, he's so settled and relaxed in the squad.' Tactically, people wondered whether Michael and Wayne could play together. Neither is a natural target-man centre-forward in the old Alan Shearer mould, I know that. But Wayne and Michael are the perfect partnership, a model for the modern era. They actually complement each other superbly. Michael runs in behind defenders, poaching goals – an option if I want to launch it long. Wayne is brilliant between the opposition defence and midfield, always there, always looking for the quick ball to feet, a joy to link with. Wayne can run at players, beat them and set goals up. One of his many runs against France panicked Silvestre into giving away a penalty. Becks missed, but we still felt in control.

Sensibly, Sven sent Emile on for Wayne to see the match out and keep our new strike threat fresh for England's next game. Our fans were singing, celebrating, generally going wild. We were up and running at Euro 2004, three points surely in the bag. Surely? It still sickens me to record what then occurred at the Stadium of Light. Emile fouled Claude Makelele, Zidane bent in the free-kick, and the life went out of us. Having led for so long, Zidane's goal was a crushing blow. Heads down. Play for time. Cling to the draw. Keep the point. No more mistakes. Almost there. In injury time, I received possession quite deep in our half and I knew instinctively what to do. Run the clock down, waste time, play it safe. Pass back to Jamo. Shit. Thierry Henry. The great French striker was lurking behind one of our central defenders, and if you are going to hide behind anyone, hide behind big Sol. Once I

played the ball back and realized there was a Frenchman
there, I prayed to God it was anyone but Thierry. He's
lethal. I have passed accidentally to Henry since, at
Highbury, and when he picks the ball up it can lead only
to a goal. Jamo sprinted out, fouled Henry, and Zidane
swept in the penalty. From 1–0 up to 2–1 down in the
space of two minutes. Nightmare.

A feeling of utter desolation closed in around me. My
mistake made me feel so wretched I thought I would be
physically sick. I could hardly look at the other England
players, or our supporters, as I raced back to the dressing-
room. Some of the French players intercepted me, offering
consolations. I shook hands and disappeared as quick as I
could. I never even swapped a shirt. I couldn't. I felt
ashamed, devastated. I let everyone down. Trying to be
clever, trying to hold on to a point, I'd thrown it away.
Shit. In the dressing-room, I sat there with my head in my
hands. Michael, Becks and the lads tried to comfort me.
'Don't worry about it. It's gone now. Forget about it,' they
kept saying. Kind words. Appreciated. But just leave me
to my misery.

From down the corridor came the sound of French
celebrations. Their players were singing, trumpeting their
victory. Sven made sure the door stayed open so we could
hear them. 'Listen to them,' someone said. 'We'll prove
them wrong.' French crowing spurred the squad on,
making us doubly determined to recover from this
setback.

As the other players got dressed, I stood in the shower,
trying to wash away the frustration, the guilt. Why
didn't I look? England had played so well. My own

performance, apart from the back-pass, was satisfying, but the back-pass made the headlines. 'Be strong,' I told myself. 'Adversity will not kill you. Fight back.' I phoned Struan, and Dad. 'Keep your head up,' they said. I didn't switch my phone off, or hide from the fact that I screwed up.

The next day's papers did not make pleasant reading. There was nothing for it but to make amends in England's next game, against Switzerland in Coimbra on 17 June.

The night before the match, Steve McClaren called a meeting with the midfielders. 'Get the French result out of your system, because we have another important game tomorrow,' Steve told me, Lamps, Becks and Scholesy. We had tried two formations out in training, the diamond and the flat four, and Steve asked us which we preferred. There had been talk of England using a diamond against Switzerland because Hakan Yakin could cause problems in the hole. If we had a diamond, the sitting midfielder would look after Yakin. 'I prefer the flat four,' I told Steve. Lamps and Becks agreed. Understandably – that was the way they played with their clubs. Scholesy would rather have had the diamond, because he was getting frustrated out on the left, but he went with the flow. The meeting was cordial, and Steve promised to raise our concerns with Sven. In the papers the next morning, it said we had summoned McClaren to a meeting and told him which system we wanted. The normal accusations of 'player power' were levelled at the team. Nonsense. Steve listened to us and, in the end, we went with the flat four that suited us best. That was good management by Sven and Steve.

Sven kept faith with the same players, apart from John Terry returning from injury in place of Ledley King. Spurs' strong centre-half had done well against France, but JT is a formidable competitor. He had to start. No-one knew it, but I was a doubt for the game. Against France, I had put the wrong padding on a blister. Sweat loosened the padding, rubbed the blister raw and opened up a hole on the ball of my foot. The doc gave me an injection to numb the pain for a couple of hours, simply to get me through the game. Needles don't worry me. I'll do any-thing to get on the pitch. I couldn't let the team down, especially after my cock-up against France.

Sven was good before the match. 'Just play like you did for eighty-nine minutes against France,' he said. 'Build on that.' Wayne certainly did. He was unstoppable, his confidence boosted by positive headlines about him after the French game. He charged out and destroyed the Swiss, scoring after twenty-three minutes. I was amazed how he kept sprinting about in the heat. I have never endured hotter conditions. At 48°C in the shade, breathing became difficult, let alone sprinting. After ten minutes I wondered whether I would survive. My head was pounding, heart racing and legs slowing. 'Keep the ball,' I shouted to the other players. We couldn't afford to give away cheap possession, or go chasing shadows. Every break in play, the staff threw us water-bottles. At half-time, there were ice-baths in the dressing-room. 'It will cool your muscles down,' said Gary Lewin, the physio. I stripped off and leapt in. I almost froze my balls off!

Refreshed, we tore into the Swiss after the break, Wayne adding another. Inevitably, tiredness began taking its toll, so Sven sent Owen Hargreaves on for Scholesy, and moved me to the left. With eight minutes left, we broke down the right, and I had enough legs to get into the box and finish the move off. Three goals, three points and a big win, particularly for me. I sweated my French mistake out of my system against Switzerland.

Victory was made the sweeter by the disgraceful behaviour of the Swiss striker, Alexander Frei. After colliding at a corner, we exchanged a few short, sharp words of disagreement, and as Frei turned away he spat at me. He missed, but I knew. I saw his neck muscles clench, his lips open and this stream of phlegm coming past my face. I never reacted; I concentrated more on the corner. After that, I got on with the game. Unluckily for Frei, his gobbing was spotted by television.

As I changed after the match, an FA official said, 'Frei has been caught on camera spitting at you. What do you want to say about it?'

'I don't want to say anything about it,' I replied. 'I'd rather forget about it.'

The next day, I was asked again. UEFA, the tournament organizers, were in touch and were adamant I commented on the incident. 'Did Frei spit at you?' they asked.

'Yes,' I replied.

I prefer things to remain on the pitch, but I could hardly lie. Frei deserved his ban. Anyway, I was furious. Spitting's degrading. I would rather be butted than spat at. Tosser.

We were really firing by now, and Croatia stood no chance at the Stadium of Light on 21 June. Wazza, England's new super-hero, struck twice as we took them apart 4–2. Our French mess forgotten, we kept piling forward, committing too many bodies to attack at times. Sometimes it was just the four defenders and me left behind to deal with the Croatian counters. It was crazy, pell-mell football, end to end, probably fantastic to watch, yet back in the dressing-room the coaching staff were concerned about the goals we conceded. 'We were overrun at times,' said McClaren. It was worrying. Against better finishers than Croatia, we would get caught out. Concern tempered our celebrations at qualifying for the quarter-finals. Three days to recover. Barely enough time to feel the life seep back into my legs. Exhaustion stalked me.

Portugal blocked the road to the semis. Some road-block: the hosts, the only team with bigger support than England, the team of Cristiano Ronaldo and Luis Figo. Ronaldo was all slick skill at speed, the king of step-overs, really loving his time in the limelight. He overdoes the tricks at times, but he's a nightmare to deal with because of the way he races through the gears. Figo was a different animal, slower, stealthier, but similarly capable of opening up any defence. I thought I knew everything about the great Figo – technique, pure class on the ball – but I didn't realize how strong he was. My impression of him was formed largely by the telly: I felt he was a top-of-the-range showboater who got fouled a lot and wasn't that tough. When I tried to hound him around the Stadium of Light, I quickly learned he is physically strong, a hard man to dispossess. Whack Figo, he comes back for more. Whack him again, he gets up and runs back at you. Figo possesses the quality I call moral courage. Even when he's battered and bruised, he has the heart to keep going. What a legend. We knew we had to nail Figo and Ronaldo. If England stopped Portugal's creative forces, we had enough attacking threat of our own to hurt them. We had Rooney. We had Owen.

By the end of the Croatia match, me and a few others were trying to set up Michael, because he still hadn't scored, which was surprising. When Michael notched one, I knew he would net a dozen. When Michael is off and running with goals, his confidence soars; he would give us the goals to win the tournament. What impressed all the lads about Michael is that he was never down. Not Michael. Never. Even if he's suffering a bit of a drought, Michael always believes a goal is a second away, a corner away, a loose ball away. Less than three minutes after kick-off in the Portugal match, Michael scored. Brilliant. Great for him, and for us. That, surely, was the catalyst for England to go on and win the game. The last four beckoned. This was it, I felt; nothing could stop us now. A winner's medal glinted on the horizon.

Suddenly, bang, the wind was ripped from our sails. Chasing the ball with typical hunger, Wayne ended up with a broken metatarsal. As he limped away, I swore out loud. 'Shit!' Losing Wayne was a massive blow. And when I saw Sven sending on Darius Vassell to take Wayne's place, I was surprised, bordering on shocked. There is no question that Darius is a good striker, but he is far too similar to Michael. Nippy ball-chasers, Michael and Darius both like to sprint in behind defenders. 'They'll make identical runs,' I thought to myself. 'We are seriously up against it here.' Sven should have gone for big Emile, who blends well with Michael, giving us more of a balanced front-line. Portugal were always going to be lifted by the sight of Wazza going off, so they were bound to come strong and pressurize us. We desperately needed an out ball. Emile could have done that. He is a great target-man for us. The ball can be pumped long to Emile, who can hold it up and give us time to get out. I don't know whether Emile's costly challenge against France was held against him by Sven. One thing I do know is that England would have been stronger had Emile come on rather than Darius. No offence to Darius, it is just that this was a job screaming out for Emile.

Portugal gained in confidence and possession. Ronaldo kept getting the ball. Ashley Cole kept tackling him or sending him down blind alleys. Manchester United versus Arsenal – a game within a game, a top battle. Lightning-quick wingers like Ronaldo can destroy full-backs. Not Ashley. I have never got to know Ashley too well because he sticks with his own group of people around the England hotel, but I can see he has every quality a world-class full-back needs. His touch is good, he's brilliant going forward, and he's really aggressive for his size. Because he naturally plays as a left-winger, Ashley is perfect for England. He allows the left midfielder to move inside, which was a relief for Scholesy. It was no surprise Ashley did so well at Euro 2004. He didn't give Ronaldo a yard. Maybe he was stirred up because Ronaldo plays for United, and Arsenal and United loathe each other. For me, this was the night when Ashley became the best left-back in the world.

Portugal tried other attacking avenues. I was tiring fast, chasing Figo and Deco around, putting out fires, sweat pouring from me. Cramp ram-raided my body. My muscles just locked, seized up. No more. No movement. Three games in quick succession caught up with me. My fitness wasn't tip-top, I'll admit now. Those blisters prevented me training fully. With nine minutes remaining of normal time, I hobbled off, replaced by Owen Hargreaves. Two minutes later, Helder Postiga headed an equalizer. Yet England still could have won it in normal time. Sol rose for a corner, and headed the ball in. 'Goal!' we all screamed on the bench, leaping up in celebration. Then Urs Meier, the Swiss ref, blew for a foul, apparently for JT on Portugal's keeper Ricardo.

Bollocks. I shouted at the TV boys who were nearby, 'Was it a goal?'

'Yes,' they replied. 'Nothing wrong with that.'

The ITV and BBC lads had the monitor. They could see JT hadn't impeded Ricardo. What the hell was Meier thinking? I felt cheated. All the England players felt cheated. Meier screwed up big-time. A proper ref like Collina would have given it. He understands that contact is inevitable in a crowded goalmouth. Meier didn't. Poor Sol, who was also denied a similar goal at France 98. Poor England, too. Extra time beckoned. Rui Costa and Frank exchanged goals and it was off to penalties.

Watching from the bench, I felt confident. I looked at the two keepers, Jamo and Ricardo, and felt we had the edge. First up for us was Becks. Dead cert, I thought. This will fly in. No problem. In training, Becks is frighteningly accurate. He stepped up. Disaster. Becks slipped as he went in, the turf coming away as he planted down his left foot before he hit the ball with his right. Off-balance, he never made the right connection and missed. It is a risk Becks takes with his penalties. He goes in at an angle with his left foot so he can get full power and whip with his right. No blame could be attached to Becks. He just lost his footing. The Stadium of Light pitch was really greasy, and if the turf moves you are in serious trouble. No wonder they relaid the penalty spot after the game.

But we were still in it. Michael, Frank, JT and Hargreaves stuck their pens away, and Rui Costa obligingly missed his. When JT came back, he said, 'Lucky! I mishit it!' The tension intensified.

Sudden death arrived. Volunteers were needed. Sven already had the names of his remaining takers, some of them, I suspect, unwilling candidates. Ashley took responsibility, and stepped up to score. Postiga made it 5–5. The pressure was unbearable. Sven had asked Darius, 'Do you want a penalty?' Darius had declined. Fair enough. I could see he had no confidence in himself to take a penalty. Sven was looking round for anyone to take a kick. Anyone? Sol, Gary Neville and Phil Neville were available, but it needed a striker, someone who knew where the net was. It had to be Darius.

Poor kid. He was a bag of nerves, clearly dreading the thought of walking up with the eyes of the world on him. He missed, and no wonder. Psychologically, he was a mess. Advantage Portugal. They, too, were running out of players, but no-one expected them to send Ricardo into action. A keeper! 'What the fuck are they doing?' I said. We couldn't believe it. I didn't fancy his chances. A keeper, taking a penalty, against Jamo? 'Cocky twats,' I said. Ricardo, carrying the expectations of all Portugal, turned, calmly ran in, and swept the ball past Jamo. Great pen.

My heart immediately went out to Darius. Shoot-outs always produce scapegoats, but we couldn't blame Darius for England going out of Euro 2004. 'It wasn't your fault, Darius,' I told him. 'We just didn't do enough in the ninety minutes or extra time.' None of the players pointed the finger at Darius. If Meier had been a decent ref and not bottled a big decision in front of the hosts' fans, England would have been through to the semis. Our defeat was Meier's fault more than Darius's or Becks's. The press snipers had a pop at Becks. Typical. But Becks cannot rescue England every time. Sven got some stick too, with the usual hail of criticism of 'Why don't England practise penalties?' None of us expected the match to go the distance. Sven's decision not to order practice sessions didn't surprise me. A player can convert ten out of ten pens in an empty training ground and then fall to pieces walking towards the spot in a packed stadium. The goal goes smaller, the keeper grows bigger.

England failed. We let the fans down. I let the fans down. They spent shed-loads travelling to Portugal, forking out fortunes to acquire match tickets, and they expected England to go further than the last eight. I'm sorry. We should have done better. The truth was that England were knackered at Euro 2004. 'If only we had got through,' I told Michael, 'we would have had a good rest before the semis.' Everyone was tired. A long, hard season took a terrible toll.

Some players had had enough. It didn't surprise me at all on the plane back when Scholesy announced he was retiring. Deep down, he knew he wouldn't get many more games in the middle because Frank did so well at Euro 2004. Scholesy is not a holding-role midfielder, so he couldn't compete with me. I sensed his rising frustration with England at Euro 2004. Scholesy wanted to be in the middle, getting on the ball, creating stuff, grabbing a game by the scruff of the neck. Criticism hurtled his way for his contributions on the left. 'Sod it,' Scholesy must have thought, 'time to concentrate on United.' He was touching thirty, and wanted more time with his family. I knew that. Whenever I saw Scholesy with his family, it was obvious how much he adored his wife and kids. He knew he could be spending international weeks with his kids rather than sitting on the bench. He'd done his England tours of duty and earned everyone's respect. Paul Scholes is one of the best players I have ever played with, blessed with a natural ability in abundance. His shooting was accurate and ferocious, and he created magic with delicate touches. He was also a really quiet person, but a silent assassin on the pitch. Christ, you should have seen, heard and felt some of his tackles – real crunching, no-prisoner specials. I miss him.

And he wasn't the only one considering his future.

15
Feeling Blue

The good times would roll with England again, but my career stalled at Liverpool. No question. I was running across quicksand. Striving to move forward, I found myself sinking deeper and deeper into mediocrity. A sense of depression blew into my life like a dark cloud that would not go away. Frustration bit deep. I hated constantly worrying over whether Liverpool would qualify for the Champions League, the playground of Barcelona and Real Madrid, AC Milan and Juventus. Names that inspire. Names Liverpool's history demand we mix with. Michael and I shared one fear: playing for a club that wasn't among Europe's elite. 'We have to be in the Champions League,' I told Michael. 'We have to. I can't stand watching it on television.' Michael agreed. He and I both knew that Liverpool, the club we loved, was falling away from the top three of Arsenal, Manchester United and Chelsea. Everybody kept mentioning it. Pick up the paper and read, 'Liverpool are thirty points behind the leaders.' Turn on the radio and hear, 'Liverpool are going nowhere.' Flick on the telly and listen to some pundit calling Liverpool also-rans.

Thirty points. The number kept turning over and over in my mind. It chilled my blood. I hated all the verdicts, but I couldn't fight the truth: the final Premiership table for the 2003/04 season showed Liverpool thirty points behind the champions, Arsenal. A massive margin. Doubts filled my waking hours. Did Liverpool have my ambition? Did we have the players to compete seriously for the Premiership and Champions League? Questions, questions. I certainly questioned my future at Anfield. Should I leave? Could I tear myself away from the club and city I love so passionately? Chelsea had ambition, resources, a bright new manager in Jose Mourinho, and they obviously wanted me. In the summer of 2004, temptation entered my life.

Another kick in the teeth was getting knocked out of the UEFA Cup by Marseille in the quarters on 25 March 2004. Christ, that pissed me off big-time. The UEFA Cup is nothing special, an ugly kid brother compared to the handsome Champions League, but it is still a trophy, still a winner's medal. Emile scored early on against the French, we controlled the game, but then Igor Biscan made a stupid mistake and got sent off. Marseille took over and we were out, thanks to Biscan. Liverpool would have won the UEFA Cup that year but for that tit's shirt-pulling. We would have played Newcastle in the semis, Valencia in the final, and beaten them both. I was livid.

Liverpool were stagnating under Gérard. Everyone could see it, inside and outside Anfield. Shortly after the end of the season, Gérard was dismissed. I was devastated for him, but not surprised. Liverpool went backwards after the Treble. Fact. Gérard leaving was for everyone's benefit. After six years, he needed a different challenge, and Liverpool needed a new manager to freshen things up. I needed to play for a new manager. Rumours were rife in the press that I had been on to Rick Parry, Liverpool's chief executive, and told him it was time for Gérard to go. Bullshit. Those stories insulted me, and Rick. Captaining the team was my responsibility, choosing the manager was the board's.

The parting of the ways between Liverpool and Gérard made sense, but it was still painful to watch. I hurt bad. Gérard was a father figure to me, and that bond was now severed. A little part of me died when he left. He cared for me. Typical Gérard, when I called him to commiserate, he was more worried about me. 'Steven, you are at a fantastic club,' he said. 'You are going to be one of the best players in the world. Trust me. Just keep going, keep learning. And do not worry about me. I will be all right.' Gérard is a good, honest man, and I am so made up we have stayed in touch. He did so much for my career. My respect for him will always remain strong. Before big England and Liverpool games, he always calls, telling me to be relaxed, wishing me all the best. 'How's the family?' he asks. A great man. I also still speak to Gérard's old assistant, Patrice Bergues. His sessions were really good, keeping everyone involved, no standing still. When he told me I was doing something wrong, I knew he was right. Patrice knew his football. Patrice had already left for Lens. Now Gérard had gone as well.

A couple of days after Gérard's departure, Rick called.

'Steven, can I have a chat with some of the senior players?'

'Yes, Rick, not a problem.'

'Get some of the lads over, and I'll be round.'

By then, I had moved to Blundellsands, so Rick came there. Most of the lads were busy, but I rustled up Carra, and we sat there and talked football with Rick. Usual stuff: ambitions, players we rated, teams on the rise. Suddenly Rick said, 'What are the players' feelings on another foreign manager coming in? Are there any problems with it?'

'No,' I replied. 'The majority of the players had a great relationship with Gérard. We won a Treble under him. If another foreign manager came in, took the club forward and brought success, then fine.'

Rick nodded. Liverpool's board were clearly thinking of appointing another overseas manager. One fear nagged away at me, a concern I had to voice. 'Rick,' I said, 'I'm English, and I will always edge towards an Englishman coming in. They know who I am.' And after six years with a Frenchman in charge, many Liverpool fans wanted an English manager. The *Post* and *Echo* were crammed with supporters' letters pleading for an Englishman.

Rick paused, looked at me, and said, 'What do you think of Rafa Benitez at Valencia?'

My eyes lit up. Foreign, yes, as Spanish as tapas, but what a coach! I smiled at Rick. 'I'd go for Benitez.'

Rafa bloody Benitez! Me and Carra were excited by the possibility of Benitez coming to Anfield. Rick was clearly delighted.

'Why do you rate him?' he asked.

'Simple,' Carra replied. 'We've played Valencia three or

four times and been murdered every time. Benitez is a top coach. Valencia play good football and win things.' I agreed. I watch a lot of Spanish football on the telly, and Valencia broke the stranglehold that Barcelona and Real Madrid had on Spain. With little time and money, Benitez transformed Valencia. 'Tactically, Valencia are the most difficult side I have ever played against,' I added. 'They give you no space to play. Great organization. We just couldn't get the ball off them. We knew we couldn't beat them the moment we kicked off. Valencia were fitter than us, physically stronger, and very strong mentally.'

Could Benitez do that with Liverpool? Why not? No-one expected him to overturn Barca and Real in La Liga, but he did. So what was to say Benitez couldn't give Man U, Chelsea and Arsenal a run for their money? Uncertainty still nagged away at me, though. Could one man really revive Liverpool? Would I remain stuck in a cycle of struggling to make the Champions League?

I flew into Portugal for the European Championship with a bag full of troubles. Anything to declare? Yeah, mate, a ton of doubts. If I was homesick in Euro 2000, I was distracted at Euro 2004. Head screwed up. Concentration difficult. My mind kept flicking back to events at Anfield. If I learned one thing in Portugal, it was to go into future tournaments focused solely on the job in hand. I admire players who carry on performing no matter the distractions in their life. I can't. My head must be clear. I never set Euro 2004 alight because I was thinking about Liverpool. After training or matches, I'd be on the phone home, wondering what was going to happen to Liverpool and me. Friends and family kept calling and telling me about the latest club I had been linked with in the papers. Chelsea, Real Madrid; Chelsea, Inter Milan; Chelsea, Barcelona; Chelsea, AC Milan; Chelsea again. It did my head in. 'Are you staying?' Dad asked. 'Are you going?' asked Paul. God knows.

A fire of speculation raged, and I ended up burnt. My football went to pieces. No-one was to blame for my crap performances at Euro 2004 except me. My fault. Mine alone. I let England down. Shit, I'm sorry. I screwed up big-time. I was naive, inexperienced, incapable of handling all the rumours about my future while busting my lungs for England. I let down the players, the fans and Sven. On and off the field in Portugal, I was edgy. In the England hotel in the middle of a massive tournament was the worst time and place to learn top clubs were chasing me. Real Madrid definitely sniffed around. Arsenal, too. Both Milan clubs, and Barcelona. Fact. Everybody mentioned Chelsea because their owner, Roman Abramovich, is loaded. Many clubs were in the hunt, and all of them made their interest known through the papers, dropping little hints here and there. I couldn't pick up a paper without reading how much Real or Chelsea wanted me. When I should have been getting ready for kick-off, my thoughts drifted away into imagining what it would be like playing for Chelsea or Barcelona. Arsène Wenger, Jose Mourinho and Sir Alex Ferguson talked me up before the tournament, so I knew they fancied signing me. Fergie even did an amazing piece in the *Sunday Times* in which he called me the 'most influential player in England, bar none'. Bloody hell!

If that comment wasn't enough to make me realize

United were after me, an incident during Euro 2004 confirmed it. I was hanging around my room at England's Solplay Hotel in Lisbon, catching some football programme, when there was a knock at the door. I opened it, and one of Fergie's players stood there. He came in and said straight out, 'We'd love you to come to United.' That's how clubs' interest was expressed to me. The Arsenal, Man U and Chelsea players in the England squad kept coming up and saying, 'Are you coming to us?' I had no problem with that. It wasn't unfair of them to approach me. The boys respected me as a player and wanted me in their team. I've done it myself. I've approached players. I've said to Wayne Rooney, 'I'd love you to come and play for Liverpool every week.' That's not me tapping Wayne up, that's me showing my huge respect for Wayne. Come on, Wayne, come and play in my team. I love Wazza as a player. He'd be fantastic up front for Liverpool. Me on the ball in midfield, finding Wazza. Me running forward, Wazza finding me. Goal! I still dream of Wayne pulling on a proper red shirt. I'm not sure the Kop would be so keen, though!

That knock at the door made me realize all the top managers thought there was a race on for me. And that race couldn't wait until after Euro 2004 in those managers' minds. I was target number one, and it got messy. All the other players in the England squad thought I was leaving Liverpool; it was just a case of clarifying my destination. Of course, I was flattered. Big-time. It felt like I was back in the playground picking sides. But it shattered my focus on Euro 2004. Struan, as usual, tried to help. 'Right, Stevie, we are not going to talk about your future,' he said early in the tournament. 'Leave it for now. Anything in the papers, anything that anyone says, any approaches from the England lads, leave it until the tournament finishes.' Good plan, impossible to achieve. I could hardly tell close family to shut up whenever they mentioned a story in the papers to me. 'Barcelona are after you.' 'Chelsea definitely fancy you.' 'Hey, Stevie, Wenger's interested.' And always, 'What the fuck is going on?' My family love me, and they were concerned about me, about my happiness and my future.

It pissed me off that my family had to read bollocks in one paper during Euro 2004 that Carra battered me. The story said Carra and I fell out over all the uncertainty between me and Liverpool. We had a fight, the paper claimed. Carra came to my room with the paper and said, 'Have you seen this shite?' At first, we both laughed about the idea of us having a fight. 'Who won?' I asked Carra. We read the piece. Carra had, according to the paper. Well, that's another lie! I'd quite fancy my chances against Carra in a one-on-one! Really, though, it was no laughing matter. Carra and I did our best to squash the rumour straight away. We put something in the *Liverpool Echo*, stressing what good friends we were, and even joked about getting in the ring for charity. Coming in the middle of Euro 2004, this story of a divide between me and Carra definitely wasn't helpful. It set my family and friends on edge, and some of the other England players read it and thought it could be true. So this 100 per cent complete nonsense was damaging. When I first came through at Liverpool, Carra was really close to Michael, but we immediately hit it off. When Michael and Danny Murphy left Liverpool, Carra and I lost our two best mates in the team so we bonded a lot more. Our relationship has got stronger and stronger over the years. Yet this story about Carra and me fighting cropped up every so often. We even got Liverpool's press guy, Ian Cotton, to look into it. It just seemed the papers were hell-bent on stirring up trouble between me and Carra because of the tension between me and Liverpool. No wonder I was distracted at Euro 2004.

Sven was concerned as well. 'Are you OK, Steven?' the boss asked one day. 'You seem a bit quiet. You seem to have a few things on your mind.' Sven knew. Having Sammy Lee in the England camp, where he helped out with coaching, probably alerted the boss to my problems. 'Try to focus on the tournament,' said Sven. 'Whatever you decide, just make sure you make the best decision for yourself, not for anyone else.' This was hardly eye-opening advice, but I appreciated Sven's guidance. He didn't suggest where I should move to, he just encouraged me to think clearly. 'Steven, the demand for top players like you is unbelievable,' he added. 'You are already at a fantastic club in Liverpool. But I'm not surprised all the top clubs are after you. The most important thing is to keep playing well. If you let all the speculation distract you, the top clubs won't want you.'

No-one at Anfield called. I didn't really expect them to. Rick Parry's position was clear from what he was telling the papers: Liverpool wanted to keep their captain. Anyway, Rick was busy appointing Rafa Benitez as Gérard's successor. Rafa was unveiled on Tuesday, 16 June, and Liverpool's new manager flew out to Portugal on the Friday. He clearly wanted to talk to me, Michael and Carra. On the flight, Rafa sat next to Gérard, who introduced him to my mum. She was flying out for England's game against Croatia on the Sunday. Rafa shook Mum's hand and said, 'Does Steven like money?' First question! Unsurprisingly, Mum was taken aback. She wasn't expecting a question like that from someone she had just met. It annoyed me, actually. It was unfair of Rafa to ask Mum a question about my money. It's got nothing to do with her. But that is what Benitez is like. He is mad on learning a player's mentality. Rafa was just trying to find out from Mum whether or not I was motivated by money. Behind the scenes, he was busy doing his homework on me.

Mum and me are really close. Before Rafa's cab even pulled up outside the Solplay I knew the questions he had asked her. Swallowing my irritation, I was still fascinated to meet Liverpool's new leader. Me, Michael and Carra found a quiet room at the Solplay and sat down to chat with Rafa. Sven was OK about Rafa's visit. He understood that Rafa needed to talk to his new Liverpool players. The meeting included Sammy Lee for twenty minutes, and then Rafa said, 'Sammy, can you leave me alone with the players?' Sammy left, and Rafa took over.

It was a strange meeting. Rafa kept asking for our opinions, but I sensed that whatever we said, it didn't matter. Rafa was his own man, not the type of manager to be swayed by others' views. He had his own methods, which worked wonders at Valencia, so why did he need advice? He was just judging us. At that time, Rafa's English wasn't too clever, so it was never going to be an in-depth chat. He had only just started learning the language, so the meeting was difficult for him. But he did make us understand his plans. 'I have been doing a lot of homework on Liverpool,' he said. 'I know a lot about the club. I am confident I can bring success to Liverpool. I will bring in my own training ideas, my own players. I never really had the power at Valencia. I wanted to be a manager rather than a coach. For Liverpool to go forward, I need all my best players. I want to keep all the good players. Anyone who doesn't want to play for Liverpool, or who I don't want, will leave.'

Rafa immediately impressed me. It cannot have been easy walking into England territory and meeting the three most important players at his new club. Rafa was bold, and firm. I liked that. He didn't try to suck up to me, Michael or Carra. A weaker manager would have come in and tried to win us over by talking a load of bullshit. Rafa never did that. He didn't promise the world, just steady development. Rafa was different to Gérard, who believed we were always ten games from greatness. A sense of realism characterized Rafa. I liked that, too. Me, Carra and Michael were excited.

Rafa left the Solplay, and I returned to my room to think over my first meeting with my new boss. I was glad to meet him but my future remained unclear. The more I thought about it, the more I felt the meeting should not have taken place until after Euro 2004. Our Lisbon get-together was really a bad idea. Having met Rafa, I kept wondering what life would be like back at Melwood. More complications invaded my life, and I became even more distracted. One comment of Rafa's really chewed me up. 'Liverpool have not got loads of money,' he told me. 'There is money there for me to strengthen, but not massive amounts.' What the hell did that mean? Were Liverpool skint? Do they want to cash in on me? Are they going to bite on these offers? My head was battered.

Chelsea's pursuit quickened. The vibes I got off all the Chelsea lads at the Solplay was that Mourinho wanted me big-time. 'Jose really likes you,' they kept saying with a smile whenever I saw them. John Terry also told me, 'Claudio Ranieri wanted you before.' Now Mourinho had replaced Ranieri and their interest seemed even stronger. Chelsea definitely excited me. I cannot deny that. Mourinho is special, a top manager. Chelsea also boasted class players like Lamps and JT. They were going places. No question. The massive wages they were supposedly offering wasn't the issue for me. Silverware, not cash, sets my adrenalin going. Dazzled by the idea of trophies, I looked long and jealously at Chelsea. I envied Lamps going for the Premiership. I wanted a bit of that.

I rang Struan. 'How serious are Chelsea?' I asked him.

Struan checked out and reported back. 'You were top of a short-list under Ranieri, and you are top of it under Mourinho,' he said.

The papers claimed I talked to Mourinho and Chelsea's chief executive, Peter Kenyon, but that was bullshit. What was true was that things were moving fast. Kenyon faxed Parry a bid for £20 million, adding that it was in everyone's interest to get the deal over with quickly. Mourinho said, 'I will wait for Stevie with open arms.' I didn't have a clue what was happening. Chelsea made their offer because they suspected Liverpool were short of cash. A new manager would need funds to bring in his players, so Chelsea hoped Liverpool would be tempted to sell me and give the money to Rafa. Chelsea knew I had not been happy at Liverpool. I had gone public a few times about the fact that Liverpool must challenge for major honours, and we weren't. A club of Liverpool's standing and history should not be scrabbling around nicking points in the last week of the season to scrape into the Champions League. The situation was far from satisfactory. Chelsea wanted to test Liverpool. Would Rick crack? Did Rafa want the money? Throughout Euro 2004, I was waiting for my phone to ring and to hear Struan say, 'Liverpool have accepted a bid for you.'

The speculation worsened. One paper claimed I sent a text to Mourinho after we lost to Portugal in the quarters, saying I was looking forward to joining Chelsea. Bullshit. Another paper said my family received death threats from Liverpool fans incensed I was even thinking of moving to Chelsea. Bullshit, again. No texts, no death threats, just a lot of soul-searching and talks with my family. My dad, a passionate Liverpool fan, said, 'Steven, you are not going anywhere. I don't want you to go.' Paul agreed. 'Stay,' said my brother. 'Benitez will sort it out.' Both Dad and Paul understood my frustration at finishing thirty points off the Premiership leaders, and off the pace in Europe, but I listened to them and to my heart and came to one conclusion: I couldn't leave Liverpool. My roots went too deep.

On 28 June, I rang Rick. 'I'm definitely staying,' I told him, 'but I need signs we are strengthening and improving.'

'We will be,' Rick promised.

16
The Long and Winding Road to Istanbul

Rick was true to his word. Liverpool chased Xabi Alonso, who I knew was a decent player. Real Madrid were also pursuing Real Sociedad's playmaking midfielder, but he wanted to work with Benitez. Within twenty minutes of Xabi's first training session at Melwood, I thought to myself, 'Top signing. Pure class. Touch, vision, the creative works.' I looked forward to playing alongside him.

Another arrival was Djibril Cissé, from Auxerre, a signing put in motion by Gérard Houllier. I was still on my break, recovering after the Euros, when my phone shook to a text from Danny Murphy: 'You should have seen Cissé in training today. Unbelievable. Never seen anything like it. Frightening. He scored this spectacular overhead kick.' When I raced back into Melwood, the players were still banging on about the goal. Excitement was in the air, and I breathed it in deeply, big lungfuls of optimism. 'I'm up for this season,' I thought. Then I watched Cissé in training. Problem.

Cissé is a decent finisher, but more of a powerful striker than a poacher. He is nowhere near as prolific as Michael. He's different in many ways to Michael. Cissé looks a bit weird because he changes his appearance every two minutes, but inside he's a really nice bloke. Liverpool gave him the number 9 shirt, so as I was number 8 we sat next to each other in the dressing-room. I got to know him. The main thing about Cissé is that to do well, he needs encouragement. Now and then, a captain like me has to put his arm around players like Cissé to pick their confidence up, particularly when they are left out of the team. Cissé gets down a lot.

Our new Frenchman must have known he could never replace Michael. Before our Champions League qualifier at Graz in Austria on 10 August 2004, I noticed Michael was quiet, distracted. 'That's unlike Michael,' I thought to myself. 'He's usually buzzing with banter.' What the hell was up with my mate? All the papers carried stories about Michael's future, but it was surely just the routine, page-filling speculation. No way would Liverpool sell Michael, one of our top players. No chance would they let him go. Michael was as much a part of Liverpool as the Kop and the Shankly Gates. This Is Anfield; this is where Michael Owen works. For ever. Something was definitely up, though. Michael seemed lost in his own thoughts, so I never pried. The alarm bells really began ringing when I noticed Benitez dragging Michael into a corner before the Graz game. They spoke, and the next thing I know Michael is on the bloody bench. That's it. He's definitely off. If Michael played, he would be ineligible for any other side in Europe that season. Benitez protected Michael's market value. The next moment, Real Madrid called and Michael was off to the Bernabeu. Bang, bang – just like that.

I was heartbroken. For me, Michael was the best striker in the history of Liverpool Football Club. Goals, work-rate, stamina, speed, intelligent movement and toughness – Michael possessed all the qualities that define the world's leading forwards. Now he was gone. Shit. My career had been so intertwined with Michael's. I'd lost a fantastic team-mate, a striker whose runs I could pick out in my sleep. When Michael left Anfield, a part of me left with him. Michael is a friend, a man who always gives me honest advice, and I still miss him badly.

For all my frustration, though, I understood the situation. If Michael had been unwilling to go, I would have felt let down by Liverpool. Michael went because he was offered a fabulous opportunity. Real Madrid! The all-white strip. The Galacticos. Ninety thousand fans. The history. The challenge of another league. Some tempt-ation! We'd talked in the past, and he'd often told me, 'Stevie, I dream of playing abroad.' When Real announced Michael was joining them, I sent him a text: 'I'm really happy you got the move you wanted. All the best.' I hid how gutted I was. But I was dying to add a couple of lines at the bottom of the text, saying, 'You prick! What are you going off for?' When I then flicked on the TV and saw Michael run out all in white, playing for another team, racing on to another midfielder's passes, I felt slightly betrayed. But I wished him luck.

Another top team-mate and friend soon disappeared: Danny Murphy. A new manager had come in to Anfield and I was losing all my mates! I never blamed Liverpool nor Benitez for Michael going. Real Madrid were too big a lure for Michael. But I was surprised they let Danny go. Why? On our pre-season tour in America, Liverpool's press officer Ian Cotton showed me some cuttings of the British papers and Benitez was talking up Danny, saying how well he had played and what an intelligent player he was to have in the squad. No hint of a sale there. The next minute Danny was gone, sold to Charlton Athletic. Another blow to me. Danny and I shared a room on trips, so I took his departure really personally. I enjoyed chatting to Danny. He was one of the many reasons why life at Liverpool was so special. Now he was out the building. My good mate Michael was gone; my best mate Danny was gone. What the fuck was happening?

I rang Struan. 'I seriously wonder how we are going to cope without Michael and Danny, Stru,' I said. 'Danny scored eight goals last season, Michael got nineteen. Where are our goals going to come from?'

As usual, Struan calmed me down, telling me to be patient. 'Benitez is building,' he explained. 'Give him time.'

Liverpool made a lot of money from selling Michael and Danny, so that would help Benitez bring in some talent. And my belief in Benitez was strong. 'Come on,' I told myself, 'quit fretting and get on with the season.'

I still had Carra, Didi and John Arne Riise in my group. Didi is a German Scouser, spot-on, a top friend. Riise is another I get on really well with. Yet soon after arriving, Benitez set about breaking up the cliques. Our new Spanish leader called us together at Melwood and said,

'From now on, you must change your table every time you eat. Get to know people you don't know or you will be out. And when we travel, your room-mate will change every trip.' I saw where Benitez was coming from: having everyone eating at the same table and rotating rooms was good for team spirit. But life was difficult under Benitez at first. Back then, his English wasn't great. As his grip on our language improved, so did my relationship with him. For a while, though, communication between staff and players at Liverpool was poor. The atmosphere changed, hardened in a way from Gérard's days.

Benitez was very different to Gérard – chalk and cheese. Gérard was really close to his players; at times, it felt like having a father overseeing training. He was a kind character, more of a man-manager than Benitez. Our new boss just focused on training, preparing us for games. Benitez is friendly, but I am not sure he is that interested in players as people. He rarely communicates with us on a personal basis. We are cogs in a machine for Benitez. Fair enough, I've no problem with that. We're all professionals. Benitez's task is to win games, not popularity contests. Someone once asked me, 'Is Benitez a warm person?' 'No,' I replied. 'Definitely not.' All that matters to Benitez is football. To Benitez, I am Steven Gerrard, footballer and LFC employee, not Steven Gerrard, flesh and blood, thoughts and emotions. The boss is obsessed with football. Any conversation with Benitez is football, football, football. Matches, tactics, players. He rarely passes me in the corridor at Melwood and enquires, 'How's the family? How's the new house?' For Benitez, my life revolves around only Anfield and

Melwood. Not home. Not my family. This is not a criticism of him. However much I may prefer the human touch, I cannot question the success of Benitez's methods.

At Graz, after Benitez finished talking to Michael, he called me across to explain a few things. Here we go, he's going to fill me in on what's up with Michael. But nothing. Just tactics. Was it not my business that Michael could be off? Apparently not. The gaffer just wanted to talk about my role against Graz. 'Steven, I want you to get into the box all the time,' said Benitez. 'That's how I want you to play all season. Box, box, box. We have Didi in who is really defensive. I'm bringing Xabi in, who likes to get on the ball and play. I want you to get up and link with the forwards.'

In all the uncertainty, Liverpool needed me to deliver. After my flirtation with Chelsea in the summer, I knew when I ran out against Graz that Liverpool's fans would be watching me like hawks, checking my body language closely. Is Stevie G committed? Is he still distracted by all the speculation that ruined his Euro 2004? Many questions needed answering in the Schwarzenegger Stadium that night. So I launched into an all-action performance to stress how much I wanted to wear that Liverpool shirt. I ripped into Graz, scoring midway through the first half. Rafa's plan was working: I bombed on, linked up with Cissé and caused real damage. With twenty-five minutes to go, Rafa signalled for me to push further up, playing just off Cissé. Never before had I done a striking job for Liverpool. Loved it. Brilliant. I netted another. I actually scored three goals, but one was disallowed – ridiculously in my eyes. I was absolutely devastated. Cissé tried an overhead kick just as I completed my hat-trick, and the referee gave a foul. What a joke. I wasn't happy. Denied my first hat-trick!

Liverpool lost the second leg 1–0 at Anfield, but so what? We were up and running, qualified for the Champions League group stage, back with the big boys again. Istanbul, the venue for the final, seemed a million miles away, though. The Turkish city was never in our thoughts in the autumn of 2004. Nor in our dreams. No-one thought it could be Liverpool's year. Pundits and bookmakers ignored us. 'Let's just get in the groups and see what happens,' I told Carra. 'Let's get up against some great sides. That's when the serious stuff starts.' And the smiles. I watched the draw with a massive grin on my face. The Champions League is like an exclusive club, and Liverpool were members again. Bring it on. Group A pitted Liverpool against three decent sides, teams I respected. Monaco boasted attackers like Javier Saviola and Emanuel Adebayor. Olympiakos had Rivaldo and Giovanni. Juan Valerón and Diego Tristán still lurked at Deportivo La Coruña. Liverpool stumbled through the group, managing only victories over Monaco at home and La Coruña away, with a point against the Spanish at Anfield. No fluency. No real finishing edge. People continued to write us off.

Our final Group A tie against Olympiakos on 8 December was effectively a play-off. We needed to win 1–0, or by two clear goals. Inevitably, Anfield crackled with atmosphere at kick-off. Kopites were in good voice, and good heart. Even when other supporters give up, Liverpool fans always believe. Like those of us preparing for battle in the dressing-room, the Kop knew we couldn't afford any mistakes. 'We cannot give away a goal,' I said to Carra before we went out. 'If we slip up once, we'll have a mountain to climb.' The quality of the Champions League is so good, it's difficult to score one, let alone three. Logic suggests such comebacks don't happen. For Liverpool, though, this was the year of mocking logic, of classic comebacks.

Sure enough, Rivaldo scored, setting us a daunting mission. The Brazilian had not seemed a massive threat. He was in the twilight of a glittering career, going through the motions. This was not the Rivaldo whom I'd tried to mark when Barcelona beat us 3–1 at Anfield three years earlier. Rivaldo was frightening that night. Now, playing for Olympiakos, he wasn't on the ball so much. His body language spoke of a man scratching around for motivation, his famous creative strengths clearly fading. The Brazilian certainly should never have scored. His free-kick went over our wall and sailed into the middle of our goal. Our keeper, Chris Kirkland, came sprinting out and blamed the wall. Bollocks. I was in that wall, and if a ball goes in the middle of the goal, it's the bloody keeper's fault. Fact. Frustration got the better of me and I was cautioned for kicking out after the ball had gone. Fuck. I'm out of the next game, I realized. Stupid yellow. Stupid goal. I get on really well with Kirky, but it was time for a bollocking. 'Your mistake,' I pointed out to him at the break. Then I cooled down. 'We must stick together if we are going to turn this mess around,' I told myself. There was no point in shredding the confidence of a young keeper. 'Forget about it, Kirky,' I said. 'We'll get the goals back.'

That season in Europe, Liverpool encountered a few crisis points, and Olympiakos was certainly one of them. The fact that our problems came in the first half at least gave us the opportunity to regroup at the break, clear the air, fill our lungs, and let the boss organize the great escape. After I had my say with Kirky, Benitez took control. He was calm. Straight away, the tactics board came out. He stood there, detailing the changes, making us more attacking. His half-time messages are always simple, always easily understood. 'No mistakes at the back,' Benitez stressed on this occasion. 'Let's have a go. We have forty-five minutes to stay in Europe. Go and show me how much you want to stay in Europe. Go and show the fans. Olympiakos are not the best side. Chances will come. If we don't make another mistake at the back, we can win.'

Benitez's substitutions changed the game. One of the gaffer's many strengths is that he genuinely has a magic touch with subs. 'Djimi off, Florent on,' he said. Three at the back – brave! Pongolle's impact was immediate. Released by Kewell, Pongolle poached a close-ranger after two minutes and spent the rest of the match terrorizing the Greeks, stretching them and opening space for the rest of us. Pongolle's a super-sub. When this French kid started, he never produced the goods, but unleash him from the bench and he is transformed into a far more effective weapon. His energy and pace hurt teams, particularly when he runs in behind them.

Pongolle's goal changed the atmosphere. After Rivaldo scored, the mood went flat. Certain parts of Anfield had presumed that was that – game over. Pongolle's goal brought hope. The fans were right behind us, screaming as we chased every ball, every chance. People who have been around Anfield for many years described it as the best atmosphere since Liverpool beat St-Etienne in 1977. With the Kop at fever pitch, we laid siege to Olympiakos. Still we couldn't break through. With twelve minutes left, Benitez waved his wand again. He hooked Milan Baros, sent on Neil Mellor, and told us to bombard the Greeks. Like Pongolle, Mellor made his mark sharpish. He was buzzing around, full of confidence, determined to batter Olympiakos's defence. Within three minutes, he made it 2–1 with a typical goal, a loose ball lashed in from close range. No finesse, just raw power in the finish. Mellor doesn't do much in and around the box, but he scores goals. He's done it for the reserves for years. Two goals from two subs! When I look back on that amazing season in Europe, I never forget the contribution of Pongolle and Mellor that night against the Greeks. They grafted hard, making us play with a higher tempo. Olympiakos couldn't control us.

If Liverpool qualified, I knew I'd miss the first leg, but I had to get the team there. Can't let the team down. Push on, tackle, fight. Don't give up. Big players don't hide. They don't sulk. Michael Ballack in the semi-finals of the 2002 World Cup. Roy Keane in the semi-finals of the 1999 European Cup. Booked, but defiant. Don't fade like Gazza at Italia 90. Fight for the team. Get them through.

Anfield was going crazy. After Mellor's strike, we had nine minutes left to find the goal to keep us in Europe. Just one goal. One chance. One shot. As we raced towards the Kop, I kept glancing at the electronic clock. Time was running out. We tried everything – long, short, wide and set-piece – but Olympiakos stood firm. The remaining minutes soon became seconds. Come on! Now or never. Liverpool's strongest characters came to the fore. Xabi slid into tackles, keeping the ball in play. Carra was immense, charging into midfield, doing Cruyff turns out wide, and, suddenly, chipping a cross in to Mellor. 'Set it, set it!' I screamed. Could he hear? Did he know I was perfectly placed? Please! Mellor heard, and he delivered, nodding down brilliantly towards me.

Twenty-two yards lay between me and glory. Everything stopped around me, melting into a background blur. All that mattered was me and that ball. All my vision, all my concentration was focused on it as it dropped towards me. In my mind, I heard the words of Steve Heighway and the boys at the Academy. Keep the head still. Weight over the ball. Make good contact. Make the keeper work. Here goes. Bang! The ball flew away from my right foot and accelerated towards the goal. The Kop held its breath. A split-second of silence reigned, save for the sound of the net pulling at the stanchions. Bullseye! Goal! Everyone screamed it. Goal! We're through!

Pure joy swept through my body, sending me hurtling towards the Kop. 'Fuck the ref,' I thought, 'I'm going in.' I saw the fans, saw the expression of pure passion and love of Liverpool on their faces, and thought, 'Yeah, I'm with you, I'm one of you, I'm coming in.' I felt my team-mates breathing down my neck to catch me. I pushed Mellor away as I headed for the fans, launching myself into the arms of my people. My wild celebrations could easily have brought me a second yellow. We all know the rules about not leaving the pitch. To hell with that. Those laws are written in cold ink by an administrator; hot blood pumps through a goalscorer's veins in moments of ecstasy like this. Fair play to the ref, a bloke called Manuel Enrique Mejuto Gonzalez. This Spaniard realized it was a big goal and ignored my celebrations. Anyway, I couldn't have cared less if he sent me off. I was missing the first leg of the next round anyway.

People always remind me of that goal. Millions saw it on TV. It was a good strike, one I am incredibly proud of for its execution and significance, but it is Andy Gray's commentary on Sky that really makes the goal. I've heard it since, and he goes crazy. 'Yes! You beauty!' Andy made the goal even more special. If you want a commentator on a really sharp goal, it has to be Andy Gray and Martin Tyler on Sky or Clive Tyldesley on ITV. Andy certainly got carried away over my volley. A Bluenose, Andy got some stick afterwards for raving about a Liverpool goal. I've listened to his commentary on loads of Liverpool games, and sometimes he doesn't give us credit because he's a Blue. Fair enough. But he summed up the emotion of the Olympiakos game brilliantly. And Liverpool deserved it. With Benitez's subs changing the match, we were awesome in the second half. Anything felt possible after that turnaround.

I looked around the dressing-room afterwards and saw the fire of ambition in my team-mates' eyes. It was a fantastic place to be. Smiles, handshakes, singing. With Benitez around, the dressing-room was never going to go completely mad, but we did celebrate. Carra and I looked at each other, at the ice bath, and then at Doc Waller. Trouble.

'Do it,' I said.

'OK,' replied Carra.

Quick as a flash, we grabbed Doc Waller and threw him in the ice bath.

Dried off, and buoyed up, Liverpool were now in the knockout stage, with no margin for error. UEFA's draw-makers threw us in against Bayer Leverkusen, the Germans good enough to have finished ahead of Real Madrid in Group B. Everybody outside Anfield considered Leverkusen slight favourites. Suspended and frustrated, I watched the first leg, on 22 February 2005, sitting alongside Struan at Anfield. Liverpool survived a couple of scares early on. Buzzing everywhere up front was Dimitar Berbatov, a Bulgarian striker who had been linked with us and who is now at Spurs. Berbatov was class, but gradually Liverpool took control. We were cruising to a 3–0 win when Jerzy made a mistake. He fumbled, Franca pounced, and suddenly Leverkusen grasped an away goal. 'I hope that doesn't come back to haunt us,' I remarked to Struan as we left our seats.

Leverkusen had thrashed Real 3–0 at their BayArena home. I knew the same thing could happen to us. We just had to be professional over in Germany. Keep calm, and take our chances. From the first whistle, we destroyed them. I played off Baros, Luis Garcia was unstoppable, and we ran out comfortable 3–1 winners.

For the quarter-final draw, I nipped over to Mum's apartment with Gratty, a very good mate of mine. Gratty's real name is Paul McGrattan, who's a budding actor with dreams of being Al Pacino! As we settled down on the sofa, my text rattled into life. Carra. 'Who do you want?' he asked. I showed Gratty the text. 'I can't text him,' I said. 'Whoever I say, we won't get.' I couldn't risk it, so I ignored Carra's text. I couldn't ignore the draw, though. First out of UEFA's glass bowl was us and Juventus. 'Shit,' I said, glancing at Gratty. We both knew the Italians were a class outfit, certainly not one of the teams we wanted to face in the last eight. Juventus's reputation was for being really defensive. Gianluigi Buffon in goal, with Fabio Cannavaro and Lilian Thuram the eagle-eyed sentries in front of him. Christ, they would be a tough nut to crack. Juventus were packed with world-class attacking players too, like Pavel Nedved, Alessandro del Piero and Zlatan Ibrahimovic. They were flying in Serie A, while Liverpool struggled in the Premiership.

UEFA could not have sent Liverpool down a more emotional route to the final, either. The Heysel disaster loomed large over the two legs. Inevitably. Liverpool had not met Juventus since thirty-nine supporters died at the 1985 European Cup final in Brussels. All the Heysel stuff started straight away on Sky Sports News. Everybody, it seemed, was talking about it. Liverpool never mentioned to the players how sensitive the match was. They didn't need to. Me and Carra knew all about Heysel. We also knew Liverpool fans would give the right reaction when Juventus visited on 5 April. On the night, the Kop held up a mosaic saying 'Memoria e Amicia' – 'In Memory and Friendship'. That was a nice touch. Michel Platini and Ian Rush paid a tribute towards the Juventus fans in the

Anfield Road end. The behaviour of Liverpool's supporters really warmed my heart that night.

So much of the build-up was about Heysel, but the players concentrated on the here and now. Benitez made us watch tapes of Juventus for hours. 'Juventus like to control the tempo, slowing it down like a chess match,' the boss told us in our final team meeting. 'All Juventus's players like to have time on the ball. So we are not going to give them any. They want to slow the game down. We are going to speed it up. So go for them. Chase them. Press them. Don't let them settle. Play at a high tempo. Juventus will hate that.'

We had to set the tone early, so I launched into Emerson, their hard-man midfielder. Take that. Juventus did not know what hit them. We were all over them, seizing a 2–0 lead through Sami and Luis Garcia within twenty-five minutes. Garcia's strike was made by Anthony Le Tallec, a surprise starter. Le Tallec's a good player, an attacker we believed in, but Benitez hadn't used him much before. It proved an inspired decision, as Le Tallec gave Juventus all manner of problems. Scotty Carson pulled off a world-class save to keep out Del Piero. As we went in at the break, I looked at the Juventus faces. They were in shock. They'd expected a gentle breeze blowing through Anfield, but instead found themselves in the thick of a hurricane. Our mood in the dressing-room was of quiet confidence mixed with respect for the Italians. Benitez warned us to be on our toes. 'Juventus will come back at you,' he said. Cannavaro pulled one back in the second half, and we knew it would be tough the following week over in Turin.

Except I wasn't going. Ruled out by a thigh strain, I got my mates round to the house in Crosby to have a few beers and watch the game on TV. But I couldn't stay in the room. Every time Juventus got in our half, I walked out and waited in the kitchen until the danger cleared. 'OK, Stevie, it's safe now,' would come the message from the TV room, and I'd return for a while. My nerves were being put through a shredder. I was so desperate for Liverpool to get through. When the shout of 'That's it, game over' came through, I dashed back in to see all the lads in Turin celebrating the goalless draw on the pitch. 'Fuck this,' I thought. 'I'm not staying in.' Jeans on. Shirt ironed. Out to Southport. A few beers would be no problem; my damaged thigh was going to keep me out of next weekend's match anyway. As we sped into Southport, my thumbs were working like pistons over my phone, sending congratulation texts to Carra and the boys in Turin. They were awesome.

I couldn't wait to get in to work to see the lads. I shot into Melwood the next day, and they were all there, covered in smiles. Benitez, as usual, played the achievement down, but the boys were all proud of outsmarting the Italians. Bloody right.

Talk immediately turned to Chelsea. Everyone in England had a view on this all-English semi-final. UEFA had set the pairings for the semis during the quarter-final draw, so the Chelsea semi was built up for weeks in advance. Papers, phone-ins and television shows focused on little else. We lost interest in the Premiership. Our days and night-time dreams became filled with the thought of beating Frank Lampard, John Terry and Jose Mourinho and reaching the Champions League final. Liverpool had so much unfinished business with Chelsea. So many scores to settle. Chelsea had beaten us twice in the league and in the Carling Cup final back in February, when I scored an own-goal. A desire for revenge flowed through me, Carra and the boys. This was the big one.

The team were buzzing as we travelled down to London for the first leg at the end of April. 'It's good we're away first,' I told Carra. 'Let's go there, be compact, keep it tight, nick a draw, and do them at Anfield.' That season, Liverpool had a knack of getting the right away result. Worryingly, though, I arrived in London with a problem: an abscess in my mouth. Murder. The swelling intensified the night before the match. I could feel the pussy liquid inside waiting to erupt. Food was impossible. Just the thought of anything near the abscess made me almost faint.

'Doc, it's fucking agony,' I told Doc Waller.

'Get through the game and then we'll take you to a dentist,' he replied, tossing me some pills.

I returned to my room and spent the rest of the evening pouring Paracetamol, painkillers and antibiotics down my throat. Sleep was impossible. I kept expecting the abscess to rupture. A fear of drowning, of choking on pus, kept me awake. The pain grew and grew. A monster lived beneath my skin and I had to kill it. I sought out the doc.

'I don't think I can get through this, doc,' I said.

He gave me stronger painkillers. 'Go and have your couple of hours' rest and see how you feel,' he said.

As usual, I followed the doc's advice, but it was no good. I was now in complete agony, my mouth ready to explode. The doc and I went to see Benitez, and he said, 'Find a dentist quick. Get it taken out.' Within the hour, I was lying back in a dentist's chair, my mouth full of tools and tubes. I looked up at the dentist and wanted to ask him, 'Are you a Chelsea fan?' He could have done anything to the captain of Liverpool! Made me groggy for twenty-four hours. Gone to work with a pneumatic drill. I couldn't speak, my mouth was so packed with utensils. 'Please don't be a Chelsea fan!' That's all I thought. Fortunately, he was a first-class dentist who did brilliantly for me. He drained the abscess, tidied up the mess, and sent me off to Stamford Bridge. I knocked back so many painkillers before kick-off I almost rattled every time I kicked the ball.

That first leg was cagey, but we felt the happier with a 0–0 draw. The only disappointment came when the referee, Alain Sars, booked Xabi for a challenge on Eidur Gudjohnsen, which ruled Xabi out of the Anfield return. What really angered us was that Gudjohnsen clearly conned Sars. He dived. No question about it.

'I never touched him,' Xabi said in the dressing-room afterwards.

'Don't worry, Xabi,' I replied. 'We'll get through. We'll beat Chelsea. We'll sort Gudjohnsen out for you. Join us in the final.'

But Xabi was inconsolable, close to tears. He loves playing and felt bitter resentment towards Gudjohnsen. We all did. Xabi is a huge player for Liverpool, and a really popular guy, and a big match like Chelsea at home was made for a midfielder of Xabi's class. We read all the allegations in the papers that Gudjohnsen told Xabi he knew he was on a booking. True or not, that fired us up more. Chelsea were going to fucking well get it at Anfield.

The temperature was stoked further by the papers – surprise, surprise. Any tiny comment was used to spark an inferno. In the papers, Benitez singled me out as the 'key' for Liverpool. Liverpool's manager heaped pressure on his captain. Fucking hell, boss, thanks very much. I don't need more pressure. The boss thought he was helping me, giving me a boost by saying I was the 'key'. But I wished he had never mentioned me. Leave me alone. I don't need motivating, especially not for a Champions League semi-final against Chelsea, of all teams. Anyone whose pulse isn't racing before such a meeting should retire. Benitez knew how ready I was. He told the world, 'I looked into Steven's eyes and saw the determination.' What else would he see? I craved the chance to lift the European Cup, to put Liverpool back where we belong – at the top. The thought of getting knocked out within touching distance of Istanbul and Chelsea going on to win made me almost physically sick. Christ, there was more than determination in my eyes. Staring back at Benitez was a burning will to win. Nobody was going to stand between me and the final. Not Lamps. Not JT. Not Makelele. And certainly not that cheat Gudjohnsen. I couldn't wait to launch my hungering body into Chelsea.

A touch of arrogance accompanied Chelsea into Anfield on 3 May, and Benitez brilliantly played on it. 'Chelsea's players think they are in the final,' he told us. 'Chelsea think they have beaten you. Now go out and show them how wrong they are. And remember Xabi.' We also heard Chelsea booked a room, at a place called the

Mosquito, for an after-match party. Chelsea's confidence was mentioned more than a few times before kick-off.

Chelsea did not just run into eleven stirred-up Liverpool players that night. The Londoners were hit by a whole wave of emotion rolling out from 40,000 fanatical Scousers, who could not have had a voice between them the following morning. They screamed themselves hoarse that night. Kopites knew the team had a really good chance of going to the final. It was nail-biting – they wanted victory so badly it hurt. Kopites had waited twenty-one years, and endured the humiliation of the Heysel ban and of watching Manchester United lift the trophy. Liverpool fans are obsessed with Europe. Anyone can win a title, but only Liverpool had dominated Europe. Whenever I look at the Kop, I see all the banners reminding everyone of past successes in Europe. The European Cup glides through the dreams of every Red. I saw it in the faces of the Liverpool fans that night. 'Make Us Dream' ordered one banner. I heard it in their songs. Get us to the final, Stevie. Lead us back where we belong.

Kopites also wanted us to remind Roman Abramovich that money isn't everything. They saw the match as a collision of new money and history, Billionaire's Club v. Community Club. As usual, Mourinho made a few inflammatory comments beforehand. Mateja Kezman angered Liverpool supporters even more by saying of the Anfield Roar, 'I played at Anfield on New Year's Day and I don't know what this big fuss is all about.' Just wait, mate. When Kezman came on later in the game, he had a shocker. Don't be disrespectful. Kopites gave it to Kezman and Chelsea big-style.

I have never, ever experienced an atmosphere like it. Celtic Park was massive when we visited, but this was bigger. Running out to warm up forty-five minutes before kick-off, I couldn't believe my eyes or ears. Anfield was three-quarters full. Usually when we warm up, Anfield's empty. Not that night. The fans were so impatient to slaughter Chelsea and praise us that they poured out of the pubs early and streamed into Anfield. The stadium was bouncing. As I stretched my muscles, I was mesmerized by the Kop. The fans sang all the Liverpool players' names individually and then vilified Chelsea's players. 'Fuck off Lampard, fuck off Lampard' could be heard. Straight away, Liverpool fans were right on Chelsea's back; straight away, they built us up. 'We can't let them down,' I remarked to Carra, 'and we fucking well won't.'

We headed back down the tunnel for Benitez's final instructions, and to get our match shirts on. Back in the dressing-room, everybody talked about our amazing fans. 'I can't wait to get back out,' I said. It makes a hell of a difference, at home, knowing all the fans are completely, passionately with you.

Looking along the Chelsea line in the tunnel, I realized they had some strong characters, men like Lampard and Terry, who would not be intimidated by the hostility directed at them. Big international players, tough guys who can handle the heat. Then I wondered how their weaker team-mates might react. Would they wilt? Would they hide? Abuse chased every Chelsea player around Anfield that night. Whenever Gudjohnsen received the ball, he got the bird big-time. Every time a Chelsea player lost possession, he was assaulted with insults. When me or Carra steamed into a Chelsea player, a roar went up. The Kop cheered every pass, every tackle. The fans' noise worked on my body like an endless injection of adrenalin. I was so pumped up. So was everyone wearing Liverpool red that night. We flew out of the traps, tearing into Chelsea, hammering at everything they stood for, turning them inside out.

That's why we scored so early. Four minutes! When Riise megged Lamps out wide, me and Milan ran into positions. Instinct, shaped by training, took over. I was backing away to create space as Riise's cross came in. Out of the corner of my eye, I saw Milan making a run in. If I got the ball to Milan, he was through on goal. With Terry in the way, I had to keep the ball off the floor, so I put some sting into it, slightly over-hitting it to make sure it got past JT. Baros was really brave and got a touch, taking it away from Petr Cech, who brought Milan down. 'Pen!' I shouted. Cech had to be off. Cast-iron penalty.

Everything happened in a split-second. As Milan fell, Garcia appeared from nowhere, got this contact and put the ball in the net. William Gallas hooked the ball out. Was it in? Where's the ref? There he is. What's he doing, saying? Lubos Michel blew and pointed towards the halfway line. Goal! My arms went up. Celebration time. I ran towards the Centenary Stand. All Anfield shook. Liverpool fans went mental. Chelsea fans and players went into meltdown. 'It wasn't across the line!' they screamed at Michel. I couldn't tell. Even now, I still don't know. The Slovak ref gave it because of the noise behind the goal. The reaction of the Liverpool fans, all of them leaping up and celebrating, persuaded Michel that Garcia had scored. Chelsea moaned about it. Mourinho still does. I laugh. Chelsea's complaints are ridiculous. If it wasn't a goal, Cech would have been red-carded for bringing down Milan. What would Chelsea have made of that? We all know how important Cech is to Chelsea. Down to ten men, facing a penalty, probably down 1–0. Is that what Chelsea wanted? Liverpool could have gone on to win 4–0. Chelsea got off lightly. They should keep quiet. All this bollocks about it not being a penalty, a sending-off or a goal. Who cares? The ref gave it. End of story.

I raced back to the halfway line, shouting instructions at the lads. 'Keep it tight. Give nothing away. Make every tackle count. Every pass.' I knew Chelsea would hit back. JT and Lamps wave a blue flag, never a white one. Mourinho was off the bench, yelling at his players. Chelsea were livid over the goal. Their blood boiled and they sought revenge. Time to stand firm. Anfield staged a re-run of the Alamo. We were under siege, under attack from every angle. Chelsea had players everywhere, like it was thirteen against eleven. Fuck me, I could hardly breathe I was so busy chasing around. Arjen Robben came flying on. Christ. Another fire raging. Big Robert Huth went up front. A towering inferno to put out. Chelsea, the wealthiest team in the world, a side with so much skill, were going Route One. Desperation stuff. Long balls rained down on us.

We survived because of one man – Jamie Carragher. I looked at Carra and saw a man hell-bent on not letting the lead slip. He was prepared to offer the last drop of sweat and blood in his body to get us to Istanbul. Carra knows his history and knew what it meant for Liverpool to reach the final. He did everything to prevent Chelsea ruining Liverpool's dream. He tackled, blocked, headed. Good at the Bridge, Carra was a Colossus at Anfield. 'If I get a booking,' he kept saying, 'I will miss the game.' But he didn't. In fact, Carra was awesome all the way through the tournament. No wonder Inter Milan were interested in him. He kept stifling some of the best centre-forwards in the world. He saw off Zlatan Ibrahimovic when we played Juventus. Didier Drogba didn't get a sniff, either. And when Huth, the mobile mountain, came up front at Anfield, Carra handled him brilliantly, too.

I began looking around for the fourth official. How much injury time would he give. Three? Four, tops. The electronic board went up. Six minutes? Six fucking minutes! What the hell was going on? I couldn't believe it. Honest to God, I wanted to strangle the fourth official. How can we survive? We are in trouble here. Running on empty. Shattered. I glanced at Carra. Shit. His face was stained with sweat and worry. Even heroic Carra had nothing left to give. He had dug deep so often. Liverpool were like heavyweights who had taken so many punches and now clung to the ropes. Keep going. Head the ball away. Tackle. Just find that extra drop of energy to make the run. Keep fighting. Jesus, those six minutes felt like sixty. Chelsea's pressure was like an electric drill, hammering away at the rocks of our defence. At some point an opening would surely appear.

With seconds left, the ball fell to Gudjohnsen close in. Not Gudjohnsen. Of all Chelsea people. That was it.

Goal. He can't miss. Dream over. I couldn't bear to watch as he made contact. Then a roar swept around Anfield. He'd missed! And it's a goal-kick! Fuck. I smiled at Carra. 'His shot touched my legs!' laughed Carra. 'It was going in. I was waiting for a corner!'

Then Michel blew for full-time. Bliss. Safety. We had hung on by the skin of our teeth. 'We're going to the final,' I said to Carra as we partied on the pitch, 'and we're going to win it!' Liverpool deserved to be in Istanbul. For all Chelsea's whinging, we were the better side over the 180 minutes. Sorry, 186 minutes. I still don't know where those extra six minutes came from.

I shook hands with Chelsea's England lads. JT was really good. 'Good luck in Istanbul,' he said. At first, I wasn't sure he meant it. But the more I thought about JT's comment, the more I believed he probably did. John's genuine. Still, I could see how devastated he was. All the life had drained from his face; he was gone, emotionally a wreck. Poor guy. I knew how much Europe meant to him. Chelsea wanted it badly. I heard the Chelsea lads out on the England tour in America couldn't bring themselves to watch the final. Some people criticized them for that, for being small-minded. I didn't. I understood Chelsea's re-action. If they had gone through, I would have wished the England lads all the best, but I'm not sure I could have stomached seeing JT lifting the European Cup.

Back in the dressing-room, it was going mad. Everyone was dancing, hugging, punching the air and shouting. Istanbul! Final! Fucking brilliant! 'Right,' I shouted. 'Into town now. Everyone.' So off we went, the boys in their trackies, wives and girlfriends in their smart clothes, all piling down to the Living Room, a great bar. Everyone congregated there. Carra, as usual, led the dancing and singing. People were bouncing off the walls. Adrenalin made up for the tired legs. We'd won nothing, just the right to compete for the European Cup, but the lads partied like we had won it.

Only in the cold light of day the following morning, when I leafed through the papers, did it fully sink in what we had achieved. Liverpool were back in the European Cup final. Carra came over and we sat and talked, and then watched the highlights on Sky, even the extra six minutes conjured by a fourth official out of thin air. 'Definite corner!' laughed Carra as Gudjohnsen's shot brushed him.

That night, I met up with John Arne Riise at the St Thomas's Hotel in town to watch the second leg of PSV Eindhoven against Milan. 'I hope PSV go through,' I said to John Arne. 'We'd have a better chance of beating PSV than Milan.' The Italians had so many good players, like Andrei Shevchenko, Kaka and Andrea Pirlo. 'Don't fancy playing them.' Over the two legs, PSV deserved to make it, but Milan pipped them at the death. As I climbed back into my car, I knew one thing: Istanbul was going to be hellishly tough.

17
The Miracle

Istanbul was madness, pure, utter, wonderful madness. Scousers everywhere. In the airport, in the hotel. In bars, up trees. Everywhere. We couldn't move. Even on the journey from Istanbul airport to our hotel, I kept looking out the window and seeing people I knew. Amazing. Kick-off was still forty-eight hours away! Whenever I stepped out of my hotel room, Liverpool fans were walking down the corridor, giving me the thumbs-up, slaps on the back. 'All right, Stevie lad? All the best.' Time after time. Fans booked rooms in Liverpool's hotel, others just blagged their way in. 'There can't be anyone left back in Liverpool,' I said to Carra. 'They must all be here.' Every time we came down to eat, we weaved through masses of Liverpool supporters. Every time we went out to train, we got stopped for photographs, autographs. I love Liverpool fans, but their invasion of our hotel became a serious dis-traction. Every time I tried to catch some sleep, the fans' singing shook my room. I closed the window, pulled the curtains tight, and put the pillow over my head. Still it came. Song after song. 'You'll Never Walk Alone'. 'The Fields of Anfield Road'. It was like trying to sleep on the Kop. Old anthems mixed with new favourites, like 'In Istanbul, We'll Win It Five Times' and that endless 'Ring of Fire' chant. Johnny Cash's famous song played through my head every night like machine-gun fire. Dud, dud, dud, dud, dud, da, da, da. I find myself singing it now. It's so catchy and takes me back to the madness and the miracle of Istanbul.

Even when I managed to find some quiet in my room, my mobile went crazy. Mates and family kept calling to wish me luck and to check on tickets. Tickets were bloody gold-dust; it was like a scene from *Charlie and the Chocolate Factory*. The whole world, and certainly half of Merseyside, hunted one of those precious, reddy pieces of paper with the Champions League logo and 'Ataturk Olympic Stadium' on it. Sorting out tickets proved a mental job, far more difficult and time-consuming than actually preparing for the final. 'You will each be allocated twenty-five tickets,' Liverpool told us. Brilliant. 'My list of names already runs to fifty,' I told Carra. He laughed. Carra was the same. He had a whole army coming out to Istanbul. With a bit of sweet-talking here and calling in favours there, I somehow scrounged the fifty. Family got sorted first, Paul and my dad. Mum wouldn't come, and nor would Alex. 'You've got to come to Istanbul,' I pleaded with Alex. 'It's the final. Special. You can't miss it.' Her reply was a firm no. I understood. Alex doesn't like flying. I called up Boggo, who also hates plane journeys.

'Come on, Boggo, you don't know what you're missing out on here,' I said.

'I can't fly for four hours on a shit flight,' Boggo replied. I begged him. 'Struan'll sort you a good flight. Don't worry.'

Christ, Struan was busy. Agent, travel agent, friend. His phone was red-hot. Players kept calling him to pass on good luck messages. John Terry phoned. 'Give Stevie all the best from me,' JT told Struan. When Stru passed on JT's message, I was genuinely moved. JT already had massive respect from me, but he went up even higher in my estimation. We'd beaten Chelsea, but JT didn't think of his own disappointment. Just of me. If Chelsea ever get to a Champions League final, I'll call JT to make him aware that I'm behind him all the way. Another top man, Thierry Henry, also got a message through. Thierry and JT were my rivals, opponents I had torn into all season; now they showed their class as blokes. I'll never forget their calls of support before Istanbul. Never. If John Terry or Thierry Henry ever find themselves in a corner off the pitch, I'll be in there, fighting for them. I promise. When Arsenal reached the 2006 final, I was straight on to Thierry, wishing him all the best. I was gutted Arsenal never held on against Barcelona in Paris.

A year before that, Istanbul felt like a giant, over-crowded waiting-room for me and the rest of the Liverpool squad. We trained, we ate, we tried to sleep, but all we did was run down the clock until D-Day. Training was good, although we were all amazed at the Ataturk Stadium. We drove along roads into the middle of nowhere, and eventually the stadium loomed up in the distance, like a spaceship abandoned in the desert.

'Where the hell are we playing?' Carra said.

'Fucking strange place to play a European Cup final,' I agreed.

At least the journey helped kill some time.

I had to attend a press conference at the stadium with Milan's famous captain, Paolo Maldini. As I left the lads to make my way there, Carra shouted after me, 'If you see the European Cup, don't touch it.' All the boys yelled similar warnings. Footballers are a superstitious bunch. Sure enough, I walked into the press conference room and there it was, the silver trophy with the big-ear handles, standing in pride of place on a pedestal. I had to walk past it to reach my seat. 'Don't touch it.' Carra's words boomed in my head. Don't tempt fate. Maybe tomorrow I'll touch it, hold it and lift it to the heavens. Only then.

Christ, it was tough. As I inched past the cup that fills the dreams of everyone at Liverpool, my palms flooded with sweat. I felt it call out to me. Touch me. Feel me. I was mesmerized by it. One glinting trophy, a million memories. I thought of all those great players who'd touched it before. Kenny Dalglish, Graeme Souness, Alan Hansen. Liverpool legends. European Cup winners. I wanted it so badly. I just wanted to take it home, back where the European Cup belongs. Anfield. Somehow, I reached my seat without touching it. Carra would never have forgiven me.

I sat down and turned to Maldini, all suave and Italian. Jesus, Maldini looked relaxed. Been there, done that, got the T-shirt – a high-fashion one. I was a kid next to Maldini, an apprentice next to an experienced master. Maldini's all right, a decent guy, but he had been in this situation so many times. It was another season, another final for this Milan great. He smiled at me. I saw his perfect teeth, caught that look of confidence in his eyes. 'Fuck me,' I thought, 'Milan think they have fucking won this.' We shook hands for the cameras. I stared at him, and then at the cup. Which of us would hold it tomorrow? Which of us would take that cup home?

Maldini cut into my dreaming. 'Good luck tomorrow,' he said.

Milan were the favourites. History, the bookmakers and the pundits sided with them. Everyone expected Maldini to be the captain who touched the European Cup in Istanbul. I was desperate to say to him, 'Listen, Paolo, you've lifted this fucking cup four times. Just let me lift it once.'

Lost in thought, I climbed back into a UEFA car to head back to the hotel. Tomorrow would be the toughest night of my life. Fears crowded in. Meeting Maldini reminded me of the quality of opponent barring our way to the European Cup. Images flashed up in my mind like pen-pix plucked from the match programme: Andrei Shevchenko, Cafu, Kaka, Hernan Crespo. My stomach twisted in knots.

Bollocks. My natural competitive streak quickly kicked in. Respect, but no fear. We're Liverpool. We're not here to make up the numbers. Carra, me and the boys have been through too many scrapes, passed too many tests. Olympiakos. Juventus. Chelsea. We'd taken the hard road to Istanbul. We have nothing to lose. Nothing. I looked out the car window and saw the thousands of Liverpool fans sitting in Istanbul's bars and cafés, singing and chatting away without a care in the world. So, Stevie lad, where's the pressure? No matter what happens tomorrow, we will return to Liverpool as heroes. Our fans love us. We got them to a final. They are having a party. At the start of the season, Milan expected to be in Istanbul on 25 May; Liverpool expected to be on holiday. The pressure was all on Milan, not Liverpool. Let's have a right good go and then go home.

After dinner, Carra, Didi and Sami came to my room and we talked and talked about our hopes and fears for the next day. 'We have come this far,' I said. 'Let's not fuck up now.'

The day of the game passed in a blur of nerves, snatched moments of sleep, and deep thought. Each player knew he approached the crunch-point of his career, when he could write his name in the history books. Time to go. Time for the bus. The adrenalin really flowed as we worked our way through the crowds outside our hotel. On the bus, sit back in the seat, breathe deeply.

The journey to the Ataturk was weird. Usually on the way to European away games, the sights and sounds are pretty familiar. Sirens, people hanging out of windows, giving us abuse, wanker signs, sometimes a volley of spit, a bottle or stone against the window. But this was bizarre. Because the Turks had built this new ground in the middle of nowhere there was just silence, until we started seeing our fans near the stadium. Playing a final miles from any-where did not stop them. If Liverpool reached a final on the moon, our amazing fans would get there. The memory of all those supporters flocking to the Ataturk, walking across fields, on the hard shoulder, in the middle of the road, will never leave me. The scene resembled a pilgrimage, with 40,000 worshippers trekking miles to a steel cathedral. Liverpool fans waved at us, banged on the side of the bus. 'This means everything to the fans,' I shouted down the bus. 'We can't let them down.'

Passing Liverpool's support congregated on one side of the Ataturk, we drove around to the Milan side, to the main entrance. It was dead quiet there, no-one around – really weird. A few Milan fans were about, but they ignored the Liverpool coach. They were cool. Obviously, Milan fans thought they were going to walk it. I stole a last listen to my phone, read the final good luck texts from Michael and family, and switched it off. Time to focus. Time to exclude all other thoughts from my mind except beating Milan.

Rafa had not told us the team, so our dressing-room was racked with tension. About an hour before kick-off, he finally called for quiet and read out the starting eleven: 'Jerzy in goal; Finnan, Carra, Sami, Djimi at the back; Luis on the right, Xabi and Stevie in the middle, Riise on the left; Harry and Milan up front.' No Didi. That was my immediate reaction. I glanced across at him. Typical German, he showed no emotion. God, I felt for him. He must have been devastated not to start. Instead, Rafa picked Harry Kewell, who had been injured. I was surprised by the decision. Didi had performed really well in Europe. I assumed I would be playing off Baros with Didi and Xabi in midfield. So, yes, it was a shock that Didi was excluded. Baros starting ahead of Cissé wasn't so much of a surprise. He played against Chelsea, and we knew Rafa preferred him. Harry was different. Rafa wanted to attack AC Milan, using Harry's pace. If he had put in a young lad like Le Tallec, that would have been a gamble, but Harry had experience. But was he fit? No, not 100 per cent. All the Liverpool players knew that, but we also all had confidence that Harry could deliver.

Rafa was dead relaxed. The boss never came out with any great rallying cry, just some calm, last-minute instructions. 'Keep it tight,' he said. 'Make no mistakes. Let's settle and try to play our own game.'

It was time. I led the players into the tunnel, lined up, and nodded to Maldini. Shevchenko strolled over and shook hands as if I were his oldest friend. Fuck me, how laid-back were Milan? Rafa's number two, Pako Ayestarán, pulled me for a quick word. 'When you get out there,' he said, 'get the players in a huddle before kick-off.'

I stepped out into the Ataturk Stadium, striding towards my destiny. This was it. I gripped the hand of the mascot. The Champions League anthem sent my heart racing even more. More handshakes, more formalities. I glanced towards the fans, looking for friendly faces, for reassurance before battle commenced with Milan. And then the huddle. Everyone gathered around, arms around each other, bonded together for death or glory. The noise from Liverpool fans was deafening, so I drew the players even tighter into the huddle so they could hear me. People like Carra understood how much this final meant to everyone at Liverpool. The years of waiting. The frustration at seeing other clubs dominating. I had to get this message across to the foreign lads. I'd been thinking about this speech all week, just getting the right words, and they all came flying out.

'We are Liverpool,' I told them, 'and Liverpool belong

in the European Cup final. Just look at our fans. Listen to them. Look at how much this means to them. It means the world. Don't fucking well let them down. You don't realize the reaction you will get from these fans if you win. You will be a hero for the rest of your life. This is our chance, our moment. Don't let it slip. We have come this far, let's not fucking give it up tonight. Let's start well, get into them, show them we're Liverpool. Lads, no regrets. Make every challenge count, every run count, every shot count, otherwise you will fucking regret it for the rest of your life. No regrets. Let's win it.'

Enough words. Time for action. We broke away and sprinted to our starting positions.

So much for my gee-up. Milan were ready and waiting. We ran into a blizzard of white movement. Within a few seconds, Djimi Traore challenged Kaka. Djimi's a bit leggy, he made a bad mistake, and down went Kaka. 'Don't give any stupid free-kicks away,' Rafa had warned us, 'because Milan are very good on set-pieces.' We'd watched tapes, of course, and knew Andrea Pirlo's delivery was second to none. Djimi's error gave Milan the chance they needed: Pirlo to Maldini, slack marking, good volley, 1–0. Christ, what a shite start. I could have bollocked Djimi, but he realized his cock-up. 'Get on with it,' I shouted at Djimi. 'We can deal with this.'

Gifted a goal, Milan then dominated. We were penned in, terrorized by Kaka's breaks. This unbelievable Brazilian ran the show, finding spaces everywhere, firing in these killer balls. 'Stay compact!' I screamed. 'Don't let another in!' This was the half from hell. Harry snapped his groin and hobbled off to the fans' jeers, replaced by

Vladi. Poor Harry. I've got to stand up for him. Liverpool fans didn't realize he was injured. He was down, in pain, no chance of continuing. The fans genuinely believed Harry bailed out, so he got booed. That abuse wasn't just for what happened in Istanbul; the anger had welled up over time. When Liverpool signed Harry, the fans were so happy, but he hadn't produced very much. In the season after Istanbul, the fans started to appreciate how good Harry was. But at the Ataturk Stadium, their frustration with him spilled over. He got dog's abuse, which was bang out of order.

One down, Harry gone, Liverpool were in the grip of a worsening nightmare. Nothing went right. Alessandro Nesta blatantly handled a shot from Garcia. 'Handball!' screamed Luis. 'Handball!' screamed the crowd. Penalties don't come more obvious, but Manuel Enrique Mejuto Gonzalez, our refereeing friend from the Olympiakos game, ignored it. He waved play on. We were distracted, we struggled to get back, and Crespo tucked one away down the other end. 'Keep calm!' I yelled at the team. 'Keep our shape!'

I looked at my team-mates. Stunned and dazed, we couldn't get near Milan. Five minutes later, Kaka conjured up more magic and Crespo poached another. Three fucking nil. It's over. Surely. That's us dead. Never had I faced such a good side. Kaka was a great player, I knew that. Anyone who starts for Brazil must be special. But not until I spent that half running around after him, chasing his shadow, did I appreciate how quick he was in possession. Never in my career had I encountered anyone as fast with the ball at their feet. Kaka was lightning. I'm quite

Capped Crusader I will always be grateful to Kevin Keegan for giving me my England debut in 2000.

Right, **National Service** Sven-Goran Eriksson did me a great honour by making me England captain against Sweden in 2004.

Below, **Friends Re-united** Give me the ball with England and I will find Michael Owen, my old Liverpool team-mate.

Power And The Glory Not a bad way to open my England scoring – against Germany in the 5–1 win in Munich.

All Smiles Me and Wayne Rooney hit it off immediately with England, on and off the pitch.

French With Tears My pass-back against France at Euro 2004 gifted the ball to Thierry Henry, who inevitably scored.

Up For The Challenge I was determined to get England off to a winning start at the 2006 World Cup, which we did by beating Paraguay 1–0 in Frankfurt.

Left In No Doubt Not my strongest, but my left foot found the target in the 2–0 win over Trinidad & Tobago in Nuremberg.

Happy Days I've scored in Nuremberg, Wayne Rooney is back in the team after injury, and all appears right with England in Germany.

Left, **Mersey Dash** Frustrated at being on the bench, I finally sprint on to replace Wayne Rooney against Sweden in Cologne.

Head Master Shortly after coming on in Cologne, I net my second goal in the 2006 World Cup from Joe Cole's cross.

Below, **In With A Shout** After making it 2–1 to England with five minutes left in Cologne, I was convinced we'd beaten Sweden but Henrik Larsson equalized.

Big Appeal My passion for England to do well in the World Cup was immense.

Spread The Word I join in the celebrations of David Beckham's second-round winner against Ecuador in Stuttgart, helped by Ashley Cole, Michael Carrick, Rio Ferdinand and Wayne Rooney.

On The Move Here I lead the charge against Ecuador in Stuttgart.

Right, **All For The Cause** I slide in to stop one of Cristiano Ronaldo's long runs in Gelsenkirchen.

Below, **Down And Out** I can't hide my despair after England's penalty shoot-out defeat to Portugal as Rio Ferdinand, Gary Neville and Frank Lampard try to take in our bitter exit.

Bottom, **All Played Out** I couldn't move from the centre-circle after the shoot-out in Gelsenkirchen, just sitting there shell-shocked.

quick for a midfielder, and usually I reel in most players if they have the ball. Not Kaka. He was awesome, easily Milan's best midfielder. I wasn't worried about Gennaro Gattuso before the game, during the game or after. People rate the Italian for some reason. To me, he's all mouth. He looks aggressive, but in fact he's as scary as a kitten. I swear I wouldn't mind playing against Gattuso every week. He doesn't hurt you. I have never seen Gattuso play a killer ball. He won't nick a goal, either. The type of mid-fielder I worry about is Juan Roman Riquelme, Kaka, or Ronaldinho. They go: through-pass – bang – goal. Gattuso just plays for the fans. Theatrical. Emotional. The Italian was also the one Milan player who had a smirk on his face leaving the pitch at half-time. I saw it. Fuck you. A couple of other Milan players waved at their fans and family. That disgusted me. So did Pirlo's nutmeg just before half-time. Disrespectful. OK, Milan were battering us, but you never behave like that to opponents. Never.

I was steaming as I arrived in the dressing-room. 'These cunts think it's over,' I said. 'It's not.' All words then left me. I was speechless, enraged by our display, my own per-formance and that smirk of Gattuso's. The dressing-room fell quiet for a couple of minutes. We sat there lifeless, our dreams seemingly shredded. Misery clung to everyone in that room. Harry sat there with an ice-pack on his groin. Christ, he was a mess – a lump the size of a tennis ball. Across the dressing-room, there was a controversy going on over Steve Finnan, whether he was injured or coming back on. 'I want to stay on,' Steve kept saying. The physio worked overtime on him.

Gradually, players began to speak. No recriminations.

No blame. Just general laments. 'Fucking hell, lads, what's going on?' I said. 'Rafa told us to be compact, to not make mistakes. There is only one side in this. We haven't even started.' Some of the guys were in pieces. Surely there was no way we could score three goals against Milan, not after the way they played first half? 'Let's just stop this being 5–0,' said Carra. 'Let's not have a massacre here.'

We needed someone to shake us into life, to make us believe. Rafa stepped forward. The boss was brilliant, truly brilliant, at half-time. 'Silence,' he said. All the murmurings and the moanings ceased. We looked up at our manager, wondering how he was going to change tactics to perform a miracle. 'Finnan off, Didi on,' Rafa said, rattling out orders. 'Three at the back. Didi alongside Xabi, but more defensive. The two of you sort out Kaka. Vladi, play like a wing-back rather than right midfield. Steven, play a bit more forward. You and Luis link up with Baros. Pirlo's not very mobile; get either side of him, and stop him playing. Get either side of Seedorf – he's not very mobile. Get at their players. Close them down earlier. And keep the ball.' Just listening to the boss's escape plan lifted our spirits. Rafa was our leader, the man who could help us out of this mess.

Having sorted out the tactics, he went to work on our minds. 'Don't let your heads drop,' he said. 'You are playing for Liverpool. Don't forget that. You have to hold your heads high for the supporters. You cannot call yourself a Liverpool player if you have your heads bowed. The supporters have come a long way. Don't let them down. Believe you can do it and we will. Give yourselves a chance to be heroes.'

Rafa helped change our mood from defeat to defiance. Let's go out fighting, not with a whimper. Rafa kept mentioning the fans. Outside, that huge electronic scoreboard that read 'Maldini 1, Crespo 39, 44' stared at our fans. Proof of Liverpool's terrible performance was written large up there. Looking at that scoreboard, most Liverpool fans must have felt the race was run and lost. Deep down, the fans were simply buzzing we got to the final. They could see the quality of opposition we struggled against. Yet against all the odds, against all the evidence of Milan's superiority, our fans were singing loud and proud. 'Listen,' I said to the players. 'Listen to that.' The singing of 40,000 Liverpool supporters floated down the tunnel, into the dressing-room and into our hearts.

Unbelievable. Liverpool were 3–0 down, being thrashed by Kaka and Crespo, and our fans were singing 'You'll Never Walk Alone'. All the players looked at each other in amazement, and pride. 'They bloody well haven't given up on us,' I shouted, 'so we can't give up either.' By singing 'You'll Never Walk Alone', the fans sent a message to eleven shattered men in the dressing-room: the fans will be with you, through the wind and the rain, through times of adversity like this. No matter how much the players hurt, we'd never walk alone. Our fans were with us. Together. Their message was to play for some respect, play for pride in the shirt. 'The fans are with us,' I said. 'Let's give them something to shout about. They've spent loads of money. They're singing our name and we are getting stuffed 3–0. If we get one, they'll get behind us even more. That will help put another one in for us. Come on, let's fucking well have a go!'

As captain, the responsibility was on me to lead the fight-back. I came charging up the tunnel, staring at the Milan players as I raced past. I was determined to set a new tone: let's get on with the game, we don't believe it's over. Milan's players looked confused. They walked back out into a stadium where the only noise came from Liverpool fans. Even I was almost knocked over by the roar from our support. Milan's fans were overawed. If the 2005 European Cup final had been a boxing match between the fans, the referee would have stepped in at half-time to prevent Milan's followers suffering any further punishment. Confidence seeped back into me. My natural instinct is to fight back anyway. Battered about by my brothers' mates on Ironside, rejected by Lilleshall, pained by injuries, I was used to hard knocks. I'd recovered before. Why couldn't I recover now? Liverpool had forty-five minutes to get three goals. 'Come on!' I shouted at the team as the game restarted.

Immediately, we were reminded of the scale of the mountain we had to climb. Milan were pure class. Within a couple of seconds, Shevchenko bent in a free-kick that Jerzy fisted away – what I call a 'camera save', one for the telly. It was not a great free-kick, and if it had gone in we would have blamed Dudek. Any keeper would have saved that. He just made it look good for the cameras.

When the dust settled from that Milan chance, I took a look at their players. They seemed different. Complacency crept into their game. Milan felt the job was already done. Even if they lost one goal, Maldini and his mates clearly fancied themselves to see it through 3–1. Well, let's just test that. I was getting forward more, released from my anchoring duties by Didi. His arrival was key. If Benitez had the chance to pick his Istanbul eleven again he would start Didi, who was brilliant second half. Milan caused us that many problems without a holding midfielder that Rafa now regrets not starting Hamann. I know how much he rated Didi back then. He gave him a new contract, and played him in big games. Didi has never let Rafa or Liverpool down, and he certainly didn't when called on in Istanbul.

With Didi patrolling behind me, I ripped into Milan. It was time to sort the smirk out, time to take some risks. I bombed on, racing towards Milan's area in the fifty-fourth minute as Riise got the ball on the left. 'If he crosses now,' I thought, 'I'm in on goal. Come on, Ginger, fucking stick the ball in the box!' Shit. Riise's cross got blocked by Cafu. I checked, then went again. Just a gamble – the ball could come in again. Ginger delivered big-time, smacking the ball across before Cafu could close him down again. I was twelve yards out with a yard of space as Jaap Stam failed to react. Riise's ball was travelling in fast. 'Use its power,' I told myself. 'Direct it over Dida.' Milan's keeper put his arms out, but the ball was over him and in. Get in! Some header! A collector's item as well: that was the only header I scored that season and the only header Liverpool scored in Europe that season. And all thanks to Didi and Ginger. I would never have been that far forward if Didi had still been among the onlookers. Credit to Rafa, too, for changing the tactics. The mood changed. I sprinted over to Liverpool's fans and gave them a geeing-up sign. Come on! We have a chance! More noise. Fucking drown out Milan, lads.

Liverpool fans lifted the players, and I wanted to lift the fans. They reacted as I knew they would. The volume rose.

Milan would surely react. Their team was packed with winners, stars like Kaka and Maldini. Before they caught their breath, we had to go for their jugular. Keep pushing. Two minutes on, Didi got the ball and slipped it to Vladi, who was twenty-five yards out and not looking threatening. Milan clearly did not consider him a danger: Seedorf hardly bothered to stretch out a leg to close Smicer down. When he first hit the shot, I thought Dida had to save this. It wasn't that hard. But he flapped at Vladi's strike, and the ball wandered on into the net.

'Fuck me, we can do this!' I thought. 'Come on, let's get the third!' I yelled at the players once we'd finished congratulating Vladi. I was utterly convinced from that moment that Liverpool would not lose this European Cup final. No way. Milan had gone, their heads were down. No talking. No reaction. Milan were dead men walking. Let's bury them.

Carra, unbeatable Carra, my mate and Liverpool's magnificent servant, led another charge three minutes on, feeding the ball to Baros near the box. I was running in behind. I hoped to God Baros saw me. If he did, I was in on goal. 'Milly!' I shouted. 'Milly, Milly, Milly!' Baros heard me, heard my prayers, and found me with a spot-on touch. During his time at Liverpool, Baros was slated for being selfish, for being head down, for creating things for himself, but he showed unbelievable awareness that night in Istanbul. Anyway, my run was so special, how could Baros not see it! His pass came, I pulled my left leg back to shoot, and then bang, Gattuso caught my back leg. I went down. If I could have stayed on my feet, I would have stumbled on because I knew I would have netted. It was me versus Dida, and there would have been only one winner. I was desperate for a brace in the final. But Gattuso took my leg. 'Penalty!' everyone cried. I looked up to see Mejuto Gonzalez's reaction. He was surrounded by complaining players: Milan players claiming I dived, which was bollocks, and Carra telling the ref that the foul was a sending-off offence.

My mind raced. Who did Rafa tell to take any pens? Think, think. It wasn't me, I knew that. Luis tried to get the ball off Carra. Carra remembered Benitez picks a penalty-taker for each game; if that penalty-taker misses, Rafa takes the blame. That's clever management. Xabi was the appointed one. Cool as you like, Xabi took control, collected the ball from Carra and placed it on the spot. Talk about pressure. 'Put that ball in the net, please, Xabi,' I prayed. Xabi hit it hard and low. I started leaping into the air to celebrate. Shit! Dida saved it. Well, that's us fucked. Yet the ball was loose. Xabi reacted quickest. Always the top pro, the Spaniard followed up, and his finish was exquisite. He smashed it in, left foot. Get in! Take that, Dida! Take that, Milan! Where's the smirk now?

God, I was relieved for Xabi. If Liverpool had returned home having lost 3–2 and having missed a penalty, that could have been a massive turning point in Xabi's life. How would Liverpool's fans have reacted? As a character, Xabi is strong, and he could have got over it, but I'm glad a good man and a great player didn't need to find out. I wouldn't want a missed penalty in a European Cup final on my CV.

Relief, joy, every emotion was there as we chased after Xabi. It was a piley-on, Xabi disappearing under shouting, laughing, uncontrollable team-mates. What a turnaround! Six minutes that shook the world. Six minutes that broke Milan's hearts. Six minutes that wiped away the smirk. The suddenness of our comeback killed the Italian side. If the goals had been spread out, Milan might have got their heads together, regrouped and composed themselves. It was the sudden impact of the goals that devastated them. Me, then Vladi, then Xabi. Bang, bang, bang. Milan's players looked like they had been in a car-crash. Staggering around. No direction.

Carlo Ancelotti tried to shake the corpse of his Milan side back into life. Seedorf was knackered, so on darted Serginho, who began flying down Milan's left. Rafa reacted immediately. 'Steven,' he shouted. 'Go right-back, Steven. You've got the legs to mark Serginho.' Vladi had been right wing-back, but Benitez didn't think he was good enough defensively to handle Serginho. So I got the right-back shout. Thanks, Rafa! Serginho was lively and I was close to cramping up.

As Mejuto Gonzalez blew for the end of normal time, my body was a mess. 'Fucking hell, ref,' I thought, 'give a decision on points, because I'm gone.' Cramp invaded my calves. 'Got nothing left,' I gasped to one of Liverpool's masseurs, who went to work on my legs. The Ataturk pitch was massive and the air really humid. I was drained. The thirty extra minutes stretched out in front of me like a life sentence. Moments like this are when a footballer discovers most about himself. I've dug deep once. Can I dig deep again? Have I anything left to give? Doubts briefly besieged me. I lay on my back, my socks rolled down, my shin-pads sticking out as the masseurs pummelled some life back into my legs. The cramp remained, eating away, but I could move and could definitely block the pain out. Thirty minutes remained. Give it all. And again. And again.

Extra time started and Serginho was coming at me again, all murderous intent and burning pace. What was he on? A bloody motorbike? I played from memory, somehow throwing myself into tackles on this bloody Brazilian. From Ironside to Istanbul, I have launched myself into tackles all my life. My body is programmed to do it. So when I was at my most exhausted, my energy gone, my brain closing down, my body followed its natural instinct and kept challenging. My long legs stretched out to get some big tackles in on Serginho. Everyone in red pushed themselves to the limits and beyond. Don't let Milan score! Our so-called lightweight players, the flashy ones like Garcia and Vladi, battled like lions. Backs to the wall. Everyone fought. Bonds of friendship kept us together. Inevitably, Carra was a commanding presence, putting his body in the line of fire, getting blocks in, even with cramp gripping him too. An incredible desire to win consumes every fibre of Carra's body. He's a big leader for Liverpool, helping people, giving advice, often brilliant advice on football because he knows so much about it. Carra's like having another captain behind me. We needed him in Istanbul big-time. He gave everything. At one point, I saw him pushing against the post, stretching his calves to take the sting out of the cramp. Carra remarked afterwards that playing with cramp was worse than playing with a broken leg. I sympathized. We were running on empty, just relying on guts and a refusal to be beaten.

I wished I'd been near a post to ease the pain in my calves. I was out wide fighting a Brazilian fire-storm called Serginho. As I chased him, I remembered the agony of past defeats like the Carling Cup final to Chelsea. I wasn't letting this final get away. That medal was mine. Dead inside, I had to show strength to keep the team believing. Be strong. Be the captain. I kept urging everyone on. Amid all the turmoil, I also wanted to show my respect to Milan, particularly to Shevchenko, a king among strikers and a prince among men. When I tackled the Ukrainian, I helped him up. When we swapped ends after the first period of extra time, I passed him and said, 'Good luck.' I am not a pal of Shevchenko's, but he captained me in that tsunami benefit game, and we got talking. Shevchenko's sound.

He is also among the top forwards in the world, and when the ball fell to him two yards out with two minutes remaining, I thought, 'That's it. It really is over now. Shevchenko will never miss.' I couldn't believe what happened. No-one present in the Ataturk Stadium that extraordinary evening will ever understand. Shevchenko thought he had scored with a header. Jerzy blocked. Shevchenko then thought he had netted the follow-up, but Jerzy blocked again. These were freak saves, not technical ones worked on in training. Some extra force protected Liverpool in those moments. I really believe that. When

Jerzy made that incredible double save, I felt someone upstairs was on our side. Milan felt that God and Lady Luck deserted them. Psychologically, the Italians were shot to pieces, and that is the worst frame of mind going into a penalty shoot-out.

When the final whistle went I was pulled all over the place by different emotions. There was relief and pride that we had fought back to draw, and then held on when Serginho and Shevchenko came calling. But I felt desperately nervous because pens awaited. Rafa marched across and looked at us, establishing who was confident enough to take one. 'No,' said Djimi. 'Yeah,' said Carra, typically. Carra always fancies himself at pens. Rafa also got a yes from Didi, Xabi, me, Vladi, Djibril, Riise and Garcia. From those eight, Rafa chose his starting five. I looked at the order on his list: Didi, Djibril, Riise, Vladi and me. Fifth! Thanks. The pressure is always on the fifth penalty-taker as any mistake usually means oblivion. As I thought about the additional pressure on my kick, Luis badgered Rafa. 'I want a pen,' he said. I was proud that so many of our players wanted the responsibility. Inside, they may have been screaming 'No, no!', but they didn't hide when Liverpool Football Club needed them most.

As Mejuto Gonzalez called the teams together, the reality of pens began to sink in. Can't get out of it now. I began preparing myself, imagining where I was going to put it. When I missed against Spurs, I said publicly, 'I will never take a penalty again.' I lied. Penalties are a great opportunity to score. And as captain, I must take responsibility. I must step up. 'Fair enough,' I'd said to Rafa, 'I'll take the fifth penalty.' I'll go and score it.

First up, I had to go across to Mejuto Gonzalez with Maldini to toss. 'If you win the toss, go first to put the extra pressure on them,' Carra told me as I walked to the ref. Maldini won again. What the fuck was going on? I lost three tosses that night. Did he have a double-headed coin? 'We'll kick first,' said Maldini. They also had the end, which seemed a real advantage. Milan's fans would do everything to put us off. Flares, screaming abuse, everything.

But we had our own secret weapon: Carra. Just before Jerzy set off for the goal, Carra pulled him. 'Do the spaghetti legs,' he told him. Jerzy looked blank. Carra got right in Jerzy's face and began shaking his arms in the air. He explained how Bruce Grobbelaar had done a wobbly legs routine in the shootout of the 1984 European Cup final to put off Roma. I'm not sure Jerzy was up for a history lesson at that particular moment, but he understood Carra's impersonation of Grobbelaar. My advice to Jerzy was simpler: 'Good luck.' Carra's words, though, clearly impressed Jerzy, who jumped around on the line like a scalded cat. We all watched from the halfway line, arms around each other's shoulders – a statement that we won or lost together.

Serginho was first up. Unnerved by Jerzy's dancing, the poor Brazilian shovelled his kick into the crowd. Standing in the centre-circle, I felt the line of Liverpool bodies rise up and the hands of Garcia and Riise grip my shoulders. 'Yes!' I shouted. 'Go on, Didi.' Didi untangled himself from our line, and stepped forward. Some penalty-takers look like condemned men as they walk from the centre-circle to the spot. Not Didi. He's German, and we all know Germans don't miss penalties. I laughed afterwards when Didi casually remarked he had played with a broken foot. 'Didi, you could play with two bust feet you move so little!' I joked. But no, Didi is class, and I knew he would score. He never panics. He's so experienced. He's taken pens for Germany. And he nailed this one past Dida, deceiving the Milan keeper with a stutter during his run-up. Again I felt the ripple of joy course through the Liverpool line. Didi strolled back, towards his footballing family, to a row of smiling faces: Carra, Sami, Djibril, Djimi, Garcia, me, Riise, Xabi and Vladi. All in it together.

We watched transfixed as the shoot-out continued. Jerzy saved Pirlo's penalty. Yes! Cissé scored. Yes! Jon-Dahl Tomasson then made it 2–1 to us, and it was Riise's turn. 'Yeah,' I thought as he walked up, 'I would definitely have him in a five.' Riise's got one of the best left foots in the game, like a bloody hammer. He ran in to hit the ball. Smash it. Bury it. Do like you normally do with the ball, Ginger. Belt it. Surprisingly, Riise placed it, and Dida pulled off a worldie save. Shit. My heart went out to John Arne. If he had the chance to take that penalty again, he would rip the net off, sending it flying backwards over the Milan fans. In training, if Riise ever takes a penalty or a shot from outside the box, he takes the net off. In Istanbul, he changed his mind during his run-up. When he returned to the line, looking shattered, I tried to console him. But there is nothing anyone can say in situations like that. Riise wouldn't have heard anyway. He was lost in his own grief. Ever since Istanbul, nobody has mentioned that penalty to him. No-one would display such disrespect to a team-mate we value so highly. Anyone who has ever missed a penalty knows the pain is intense, and would rightly be livid if someone tried to banter about it. Gary Mac still does not appreciate people coming up and talking about his penalty miss for Scotland against England at Euro 96. Stuart Pearce and Paul Ince don't either. Bloody right too. They showed the bottle to take a penalty in a brutal situation. So did Riise. No-one blames him.

When Kaka beat Jerzy to make it 2–2, it was Smicer's turn to leave the security of the Liverpool line and make that unforgiving walk. Go on, Vladi. Surprise still coloured my thoughts as I watched Vladi go. Why did Rafa pick Smicer among the five? Vladi was leaving Liverpool after the final. Would he be right mentally? Again, Rafa got it right. My doubts disappeared into the back of Dida's net, along with Vladi's fantastic penalty. He strolled back kissing the Liverpool badge. Vladi told me afterwards he was cramping up. No-one noticed! Some pen, Vladi! How calm was that, sending Dida the wrong way? Top man. Wherever Vladi goes in the world, whoever he plays for, whatever he does for the rest of his life, I want him to know that I will think of him and thank him for that penalty in Istanbul, for what he did for Liverpool with his last kick for the club. It couldn't have happened to a nicer person. Things hadn't gone perfectly for Vladi at Liverpool. Sadly, he was always injured, or he underperformed. He did have some good games, but not enough. At least his performance in the final was a perfect send-off.

Vladi's pen meant Shevchenko had to score. 'He will,' I thought as I watched him place the ball down. Usually,

Shevchenko passes the ball hard into the net. Time after time. His finishing is up there with the best in the world. But his mind must have been a mess, especially after that double-miss moments before in extra time. Shevchenko looked to have the world on his shoulders as he took the ball from Jerzy, our new master of the mind games, who added to the great Ukrainian's sense of unease by staring him down, bouncing around on his line and then moving a yard off it. Shevchenko's kick was weak, placed down the middle, and Jerzy saved it.

Yeeeessss! All the nerves in my body disappeared in one long scream of delight. All my anxiety at having to take the next pen went. I don't have to take one! It's done! It's over! Go and party!

Looking back on the moments after Jerzy's save is like trying to recall pieces of a dream. I was so caught up in the emotion. But every day since 25 May 2005, little memories of that night have come back to me and I am now able to paint the picture of those precious minutes. Seeing a photograph around the house or at Melwood or Anfield triggers a memory. Did I really dance like that? Did I really sing like that? Whenever I hear 'Ring of Fire' I'm swept back to those delirious scenes of celebration. As the picture of that night becomes clearer in my mind, my pride swells even more about winning the European Cup.

When Jerzy made that save off Shevchenko, the sprint was on to reach our amazing keeper. Carra was supposed to have cramp, but it didn't look like it! He was first out of the blocks, followed by Finnan, Luis, Riise, Xabi, Didi, then me and the rest. I then took off to the fans. This special moment was for them. Kopites had put up with so much, spent so much. We'd repaid them. I danced around on the running track, surrounded by photographers, screaming 'Yeeeessss!' I looked at the Liverpool fans and saw all the banners and joyful faces. I saw some of Carra's family, and celebrated with them. I saw Joe the Red Man, a massive Liverpool fan who I get tickets for. I saluted him and his wife. I couldn't find my family anywhere, but I knew Dad and Paul and my mates were all in that happy throng. I read the banners, the fans' tributes to 'Rafa's Red Army' and 'Stevie G and Carra: The Italian Job'; there was even a picture of me dressed as a gladiator. I saw grown men crying, breaking down with the emotion of seeing Liverpool back on top of Europe again. I saw fathers hugging sons who should have been at school. I saw the best supporters in the world revelling in a moment that meant the world. Never again would they hear the abuse of Manchester United fans about not winning anything important. 'In Istanbul, we won it five times.' Five! United had two European Cups; we had five. Our fifth trophy meant we kept the cup for good. The European Cup was coming home, and it would never leave Anfield again.

When that thought hit me, it briefly knocked all the pain out of my battered body. I'm Liverpool captain, and I have just won the European Cup. Won it back permanently for the club I love. Tears rose within me, threatening to break out. I choked them back.

Liverpool supporters tried to haul me into the crowd. 'Stop pulling or I'll faint,' I screamed. No energy left to drag myself back. Finally, I escaped the fans' embrace. But my legs had gone. I had the wobbles. Sky's Geoff Shreeves collared me for an interview but I was lost for words, white as a sheet, swaying uncontrollably. My body had given so much over two hours that it was now giving up. Geoff asked me questions, but it was a blur. I wanted to fall to the ground, exhausted. I almost fainted. 'I find it hard to talk at the moment,' I told him. Too emotional to continue, I had to break off.

Slowly, I regained my senses. As people came back into focus, I noticed Shevchenko was still there on the pitch, stunned, as if turned to a statue by his penalty miss. One bad kick cannot destroy a forward of Shevchenko's qualities in my eyes. For me, he will always be a true champion. I hobbled over and embraced him. I looked into his eyes and saw the deep distress. Poor guy. He wore a hollow, haunted look. I heard afterwards that he and the rest of the Milan players threw their medals away. I understood. I wouldn't have a runners-up medal out on display. As I looked at Shevchenko, pictures of my own past disappointments came to mind: my own-goal in the Carling Cup final, the back-pass against France at Euro 2004 – moments when I died a sporting death. My dad and Steve Heighway always taught me to take it on the chin and be gracious in defeat, and some of the Milan players, like Shevchenko, were brilliant to us. 'Well done,' Andrei said as we agreed to swap shirts later. Amazing. He'd endured the worst night of his life, yet there he was congratulating the man who had just beaten him. He rose even higher in my admiration. Maldini was magnificent as well, shaking my hand and congratulating me. Maldini's class, on and off the pitch. 'Enjoy it,' he told me as we got ready for the presentations.

As Maldini applauded, we went up to receive our medals. As captain, I was last. When it was my turn, I collected my medal from the main men at UEFA, Lars Christer Olsson and Lennart Johansson. I kissed the medal and thought of Dad. His pride. His smiling face. 'Thanks, Dad,' I thought, 'this is for you, for all the encouragement and the good advice.' I stood there on the podium, waiting while Rafa and the other coaches were presented with their medals. The UEFA officials hung about, saying things, pointing me this way and that, as officials do. I ignored them. I had eyes only for the cup. There it was. On the pedestal. Closer and closer. Now I could touch it. No inhibitions now. No superstitions. I leant forward and kissed it gently. The silver should have felt cold, but it didn't.

This may sound mad, but I genuinely felt the cup wanted to be with Liverpool again, going back to Anfield. Liverpool people never stopped loving the European Cup, even when it was far away. Even when it was not in our trophy room, the European Cup was always in Liverpool hearts. It's a love affair, and that's why I kissed the cup. I must have kissed it about ten times that night. Alex watched on telly, and when I got home she said, 'You gave that cup more kisses in a night than you give me in a year!' She understood, though. I kissed the cup because I wanted to show the world how much it means to Liverpool Football Club.

'You must be happy,' said Johansson as he prepared to hand me the cup.

'It's for them,' I replied, pointing to our fantastic supporters.

Johansson seemed reluctant to part with it. Carra went ballistic. 'Give him it!' he screamed at the most powerful man in European football. I dug Johansson in the ribs. Hand it over, mate. It's ours. Carra and I had seen it before at presentations, when the person handing over the trophy tries to lift it or help the winning captain raise it. No chance here. The cup was Liverpool's. I wrestled it off Johansson and looked around, loving being in control, knowing all our players, our staff and 40,000 fans and millions more watching on TV were waiting to go through the roof. At my command, unleash heaven! I lifted the cup to the stars and the whole place went crazy. Players leaping up and down, red fireworks and streamers going off, the fans dancing madly. Magical. I held it in the air and felt at that moment everyone in the world stopping what they were doing and watching me.

I carried on kissing. Xabi got a smacker full on the lips. So did some of the coaching staff. Rafa got a massive hug. He's not an emotional man, but if you can't hug your manager when you've just won the European Cup, when can you? I blew a kiss into a television camera for Alex. Carra and I went mental in front of the photographers, dancing around and chanting 'Ring of Fire'. Badly out of tune, but who cares? We'd just come back from 3–0 down to lift the European Cup.

Back in the dressing-room, everyone embraced, sang and carried on partying. Liverpool's chairman, David Moores, was in tears, unable to hold back the wave of emotion, his pride getting to him big-style. I looked at him and thought, 'Yes, this cup is for you, chairman, for all the shite you suffered at AGMs, for all the pressure people put you under. Enjoy the moment, chairman, you deserve it. Always a smile, always a good word. As a chairman, and a friend, you have always been there for me.' On a night of special sights, here was one of the best: seeing the chairman in the dressing-room, cradling the trophy.

Liverpool's dressing-room was mobbed. Gérard Houllier squeezed in, which surprised a few. Some people at the club muttered darkly about whether a former manager should join our moment of triumph. Not me. I was pleased. Gérard wasn't gate-crashing. He came down to congratulate the lads and the chairman. He had earned the right. He genuinely loves Liverpool. He was so happy we had won it, he wanted to congratulate us. Why not? Given his disappointment at leaving, it takes a real man to return and say 'well done'. That impressed me. Other managers with different characters might have got their jealous heads on and not wanted us to win. Not Gérard. He was buzzing for us.

When I got back to the hotel, I was shattered, and slumped into a seat. Some of the lads, like Baros, shot off down to Tacsim Square to party with the fans. Our hotel was crammed with fans. My bed called to me, but thousands of people wanted a word, an autograph, a picture. Fighting back the utter exhaustion, I went to the do Liverpool laid on at the hotel. Nothing wild. A lot of the players had their girlfriends and wives around, and we just sat about talking about the game, the emotions, still trying to take it all in. We had been crap in the Premiership in 2004/05 yet here we were, crowned kings of Europe. Crazy. Why? Some of our players were more suited to European football, a less physical world than the

Premiership. Our technical players got time on the ball in Europe. We never had enough aggressive players to win the Premiership, nor a target-man to give us the outlet away from home.

I couldn't think any more. By now, bed screamed out to me. But my mates came into the hotel, so we had a few more beers, a few more laughs. Everyone raved about Kaka, who'd been sensational for Milan. 'He was the one Milan player I couldn't get near,' I said. Struan came in and we talked some more. 'I really wanted you to take the last pen, for the drama of winning the cup,' Struan said. I was confident I would have scored, but it was good not to have to find out. Struan ran through all the messages he had received, including one from John Terry. 'I'm buzzing,' said JT. 'Hairs out on the back of my neck. Tell Stevie, brilliant. I'm buzzing for him.' JT had seen me lift the European Cup knowing it could so easily have been him, and he still wanted to congratulate me. Top man.

Everyone was so happy and smiling, even Rafa, who is 24/7 serious and dedicated to football. He even stopped picking holes in that first-half display and had a couple of glasses of wine. Amazing! The room was packed. It seemed every Liverpool supporter had blagged their way past security. I didn't want to talk to people because I was that drained, but I did. I stayed on and talked and drank beer until it was light outside. I was one of the last out of the party. As I stumbled out towards my room, I looked back and saw my new best mate, the European Cup, just standing there on a table. There were people in the room I didn't know, and even in my pissed state I thought,

'That's not going missing.' I grabbed the cup and we headed off upstairs together.

Two hours later, I awoke with a start. Where the hell am I? My eyes struggled to deal with the daylight streaming in through the window. Gradually, the outline of something large came into focus at the end of the bed. Fuck me, it's the European Cup! It was just me and the European Cup. My room-mate, Xabi, had his missus staying over so he had gone off to catch up with her. Me and the European Cup were alone together. I never slept with the European Cup. I never had my legs wrapped round it or anything. It never got into bed with me. It just stood there, on one of those tables with a mirror where the missus does her make-up. The European Cup was reflected in the mirror. I was seeing double. 'Morning,' I said to the cup. I could not remember bringing it back to the room, but then I couldn't remember getting myself back to the room. As soon as I hit the pillow I was bang asleep.

I gazed at the cup, and memories of the previous night came flooding back. For twenty minutes I lay there, just staring at the European Cup. Just the two of us. Then, shit! No-one will know where this cup is! Liverpool had waited twenty-one years to get their hands back on the cup and now it had gone. I'd better get down to breakfast.

I staggered into the meal-room.

'Where's the cup?' Carra shouted.

Everyone was there, looking concerned, as if they were about to scramble a search party.

'Don't panic,' I laughed. 'It's in my room. Come and have a look if you want!'

So all the boys piled upstairs and saw the cup again. Then we brought it down, had a team picture taken with it and the hotel staff, and said goodbye to Istanbul.

I hate flying, but the whole trip was heaven. The second we landed at John Lennon International, it all went crazy again. Press and fans, questions and autographs. More pictures. Back at Melwood, we boarded an open-top bus and headed back into town. We had to do the parade that Thursday because all the foreign lads were flying off for internationals. On the bus, champagne open, good drink, good laugh. Brilliant. All the players took it in turns to lift the trophy, showing it to the fans, milking the moment, and deservedly so. The foreign lads were gobsmacked. They hadn't realized we had so many supporters. Only as the bus snaked slowly through the streets did they appreciate how big a club Liverpool is. I'd experienced it before with the Treble, all the passionate support lining the side of the road, but the European Cup tour was even better.

Carra and I were at the back of the bus, sorting out the night's entertainment, enjoying the look of amazement on the foreign lads' faces and waving at the hundreds of thousands of fans. It was a scrum on the pavement, people often spilling off into the road. 'Someone could get seriously hurt,' I said to Carra. And the crush was worrying at certain points on the route. Police horses kept crashing into the side of the bus; fans were getting thrown back. People were a hundred feet up in the air, hanging off lamp-posts, out of trees and buildings. Merseyside Police did a super job controlling all those people because really it was mission impossible. When we got into town, the bus didn't move for forty-five minutes. I kept catching sight of friends, waving, smiling, punching the air. The European Cup was home. Everyone on Merseyside seemed to have come out to watch, even a few Evertonians, who weren't really too happy. I could tell them a mile off!

'These are the best two days of my life,' I told Carra. He smiled back. A great night in Istanbul followed by this unbelievable reception back home.

The tour lasted so much longer than anticipated that Carra and I had to reschedule our evening plans! I caught up, though. The week that followed was a blur of parties, bars and nightclubs. The miracle of Istanbul deserved to be celebrated in style.

In the months to come, everyone wondered why I never got an MBE off the Queen for bringing home the European Cup, particularly when all the cricketers got them for the Ashes. That never bothered me. I know it would be a Big-Hat day for Alex at the Palace, but it's not something I'm preoccupied with. Honestly. The only honours I want are handed out in football grounds – like in Istanbul.

18
Feeling Blue Again

In climbing to the peak of my club career in 2004/05, I endured moments of doubt. The thought of joining Chelsea still ate away at me. Liverpool may have won the Champions League, but the Premiership belonged to Chelsea.

Because honesty is a quality I prize so highly, I was always straight with Liverpool. In a press conference before the Champions League tie with Olympiakos, I was asked, 'What are you going to do if Liverpool don't get Champions League football next season?' I didn't flinch. 'I am going to have to consider my future,' I replied. No choice. So the crazy whirl of rumours intensified because I didn't come out and say, 'I'm not going to Chelsea or Real Madrid.' I didn't want to lie, or claim everything was all sweetness and light at Liverpool. I wanted to wait and see how the season panned out. Ideally, Liverpool would finish first or second, and I could announce, 'I don't have to move.' Sadly, we were soon fighting it out for fourth or fifth again. The fear of the UEFA Cup loomed large.

On 10 December 2004, Rick Parry tried to calm the speculation by insisting Liverpool had 'no intention' of letting me go. 'If we can deliver top honours, I am convinced Steven will remain at Liverpool,' he said. More stories about me appeared during the winter transfer window. 'Is Gerrard Staying?' 'Is Stevie G-oing?' Headline after headline, more fuel on the fire. Again Rick emphasized how highly the club rated me. 'Steven is above money,' Rick told the press. 'He is the future of Liverpool. Even if it's thirty, forty or fifty million, we won't accept offers.' Privately, Rick also came to me twice during the season and said, 'We want you to extend your contract. We want you to stay.'

But I was confused. If they wanted me so bad, why didn't they put a contract on the table? Show me the deal. Show me you really want me. Rafa was also on at me to commit myself. But how could I without seeing what Liverpool proposed? They never contacted Struan, who sorts out all my deals. I didn't understand Liverpool's game-plan. Did they want to keep me? If they did, Rick and Rafa were certainly going about it in a strange way. 'I want to keep you,' Rafa told me one day at Melwood. 'We want to keep you,' Rick told me. But it seemed to me that Liverpool wanted to keep me on their terms. Liverpool's approach was, 'Sign when we say, and if you agree, we'll tell you how much the deal is worth.' As captain of Liverpool Football Club and someone who had run myself into the ground for the team, I deserved to be treated with more respect. Contract negotiations with top players do not work the way Liverpool were operating. I was not some spotty kid just up from the Academy.

The impasse led to further speculation in the press. Chelsea, Chelsea, Real, Real. Non-stop. It was becoming a soap opera. Before our League Cup semi-final with Watford in January 2005, Benitez pulled me and said, 'Listen, you can put a stop to all this stuff in the papers by signing a new deal.' But there was no deal there! Frustration at the situation did my head in.

'You know where my agent is,' I told Rafa. 'Talk to him. He represents me with deals.'

The first time Rafa and Rick cornered me, I said, 'Look, how can I seriously sign a four- or five-year contract now when we are fighting for fourth or fifth place in the Premiership?' I was dead serious, too. I needed to know what Liverpool were offering me financially, but most importantly I wanted Rafa and Rick to guarantee progress. No more pissing about in fifth place. I looked Benitez in the eye and said, 'If I sign and I am playing UEFA Cup football next year, what do I do then? What happens if I fall out of the England fold?'

Rafa stared back and said, 'You are just going to have to trust me.'

I like and trust the Boss. Always have done, always will. But there was too much uncertainty around Liverpool at that time.

'Can't we just wait until the end of the season and find out if we are in the Champions League?' I asked. 'Let's see how we do from now until the summer, and then I will sign a deal. If this club goes forward and you bring success, I'll stay. You will have to trust me.'

My comments about 'trust' did not satisfy Rafa and Rick. Three times in nine weeks during the middle of the

season, they came to me. Soon after that first exchange,
they were back again. I was amazed. I sat there, listening
to two men I respect going on about signing a deal, and
thinking to myself, 'Why are you coming a second time?
You know you'll get the same answer.' I told them, 'I'm
not going to commit myself to Liverpool until I know
whether there is going to be Champions League football
at the end of the season.' I felt like a stuck record, repeating myself again and again. Crazy. I resented Liverpool
trying to pressurize me into signing. Rafa and Rick should
have respected my decision about not being able to
give an answer until the end of the season. Maybe they
were nervous about Liverpool not qualifying for the
Champions League, because we were hardly setting
the Premiership alight. Maybe they felt I would leave if
they didn't tie me down to a longer contract. Maybe they
didn't want me. Maybe they wanted to sell me and use the
money to rebuild the team. Liverpool kept talking about
a new deal, but I never saw any paperwork or figures. I
constantly felt like screaming at them, 'If you want me,
show me a proper contract. If you want to talk in the
summer, fine.'

My feelings towards Liverpool, and particularly some
of the fans, darkened because of events during the Carling
Cup final against Chelsea on Sunday, 27 February 2005.
A day that began so full of hope ended in a mess. It was
only the League Cup, but it felt special because it was the
first time I had led Liverpool out in a cup final. The night
before, I dreamed of lifting the trophy. Me. First with my
hands on the cup. Holding it up. Liverpool fans going
crazy. The reality, however, brought only misery. We were

so close to winning, leading through Riise's early goal. But then I scored an own-goal, Chelsea won it in extra time, and the nightmare kicked in. I was torn apart emotionally. I'd let everyone down – the club, the fans, the players. Gifting a goal to Chelsea made it even more of a disaster because of all the speculation. People made a big deal of Jose Mourinho coming over to console me, but he had a quiet word with all the Liverpool lads. Mourinho was very gracious in victory. I admired that, because I was a wreck. Devastated. Down. Lifeless. Even now, when I see pictures of that final, the hurt comes flooding back. The image of the Chelsea boys collecting their winner's medals is always there in my mind, a reminder of my failure that day in Cardiff.

After dragging my shattered body onto the team bus, I switched on my phone and went through texts from mates, trying to lift my spirits. Dad called. 'Keep your chin up,' he said. 'Forget about it.' The phone rang again. It was Ian Dunbavin, who had travelled down to Cardiff with my mum. 'Stevie, your mum's really upset. Don't phone her yet, she's too upset. Give her a couple of hours.' I texted Mum: 'Give me a call when you want to talk.' I settled back for the journey, and eventually Mum rang. She was distraught. After my own-goal, Liverpool fans sitting near where she was in the family area screamed abuse about me, and about Alex. 'That prick done it on purpose. He wants to play for Chelsea. He's going for the money. Him and his fucking missus want to be down there where all the shops are. They are going for the money. Gerrard's a traitor.' On and on it went, sickening comment after sickening comment. 'Your missus is a slut,

Gerrard! She's a slag!' Coming from Mum, I knew there were no lies or exaggeration. She told it how it was. Poor Mum. She couldn't live with it. None of those Liverpool fans knew she was my mother. She kept quiet. No choice. How do you reason with nutters? Until now, no-one knew that Liverpool fans slaughtered me and Alex at the Carling Cup final. Unfortunately there is a minority of Liverpool fans who let themselves down from time to time. I don't know who these people were, but they wore red shirts, red scarves and red badges, sang 'You'll Never Walk Alone' and abused me in front of my mum. For me, they are not real Liverpool fans. Mum went to the Millennium to watch her lad. She was sitting there all proud, and then she had to listen to that poison. They are cowards. They would never repeat their jibes to my face.

I can take criticism on the chin if it's constructive. I made an honest mistake in a cup final when I was sweating blood for Liverpool, so I didn't deserve that abuse. Being labelled a traitor and having my mum on the phone in buckets of tears I also didn't deserve. Some people might have quit the club there and then, disgusted at the sick behaviour of some fans. Why should my mum put up with that? Why should I? I can't put every Liverpool fan in the bracket of this minority, of course. Liverpool supporters are the best in the world, and the majority have been brilliant to me from day one, but a spiteful few turned against me during all the Chelsea speculation. They believed certain rumours and vented their anger. They should have thought before abusing me. These idiots should just have imagined how their mothers would have felt. I won't forgive them, and I won't forget them. I'm a big boy and I can take the heat for mistakes, but I couldn't sleep at night because of the abuse my mum suffered.

Mum has been back to football since. She loves me, and wants to watch me. But I wouldn't let her go to a game while speculation continued over me and Chelsea. No chance. Why should she sit through more abuse? Alex goes to the big matches, but I always warn her over things she might hear. 'Not everyone is going to be shouting that Steven Gerrard is a hero,' I tell her. She does hear derogatory shouts about me. If I make a mistake, a fan who's paid good money to come and watch me is going to have a go. But that abuse in Cardiff went way over the top. Missing the 2002 World Cup was a low, but hearing Mum crying down the phone because her lad scored an own-goal and his fans were slaughtering him made me feel even lower.

I was fed up with the whole messy saga. I love Liverpool, and it hurt having my powerful bonds to the club strained by the speculation. When we beat Chelsea in the Champions League semis to reach the final in Istanbul, I couldn't hold back. 'All I wanted was to see the club going in the right direction, and this victory shows we are,' I said. That proved my heart lay at Anfield. And once we won that glorious final, I let rip again, pouring out emotions that had been building for a long time. 'How can I leave after a night like this, and all the nights I've experienced?' I said at the press conference in Istanbul, gazing at the European Cup and listening to our brilliant fans partying outside. Surely that showed my love for Liverpool Football Club? 'I'm signing for Liverpool

Football Club for four or five years,' I told the world. Christ, if that wasn't a gesture of deep commitment, what was? I'd been dying to get to this point, to blow away all the clouds of speculation and reveal my passion for Liverpool Football Club. I was with Rick, and I said, 'Come on, let's get it done. There has been that much shit, that much speculation. Come on, Rick, let's get it done.' I would have signed a new deal there and then, with sweat still pouring off my forehead, with a hand that had just lifted the European Cup for Liverpool Football Club. Now. Stop wasting time. Too much talk. Give me the pen. Let's sign. Adrenalin rushed through me in Istanbul, but my mind was completely clear, totally cold in its analysis. I can't walk away. I want to stay. Let me sign. Please.

Silence. I was stunned. There was a contract offer on the table which I didn't consider good enough; I felt I was being taken for granted. Now, I thought Liverpool would be sprinting to me with a proper contract and a pen while the cheers of Istanbul still rang in our ears. Talk about perfect timing. The European Cup was coming back to Anfield, a fifth one that we got for keeps. Stevie G was coming back for keeps as well. The moment was there. Let's seize the opportunity like I seized the European Cup – with both hands. Let's walk on together. But there was only silence. Why didn't Liverpool act quickly? After Istanbul, he thought that because we'd won the Champions League it didn't matter when my deal got signed. No hurry, no fuss. But it bloody mattered to me. It was such a contrast with what happened with Thierry Henry and Arsenal after the 2006 European Cup final: he signed a new deal thirty-six hours later. Arsenal moved quickly. Liverpool never truly realized how desperate I was to get it signed. I admire Rick Parry, who has been a fantastic chief executive for Liverpool Football Club, always acting with the club's best interests at heart. But he didn't seem to understand how battered my head had been over my future ever since Euro 2004.

A wave of doubt rolled through me again. All season, Rick had been saying that Liverpool wanted to keep me. Three times they approached me. I was a symbol of Liverpool Football Club, a hungry lad from Huyton, raised at Melwood and Anfield. Surely they wanted their homegrown captain to stick around? Didi signed a contract the day after Istanbul. Not me. Rafa asked for meetings with three or four players to sort out their futures. Not me. 'Steven, I'll see you when you come back after the summer,' Rafa said after Istanbul. Christ, what the hell was going on?

I spoke to my family and to Struan, just to see if they could throw up a clue over why Liverpool were going cold after months of being warm to me. No-one could understand it. Was it just part of their negotiating tactics? Liverpool sounded positive in public. On 19 June, Rafa was all over the papers, announcing, 'I am not in favour of selling Steven Gerrard.' Five days later, I picked up the papers to read Rick saying, 'We want Steven to stay. There is no delay on his contract.'

The speculation revved up again. Real Madrid were heavily tipped to buy me. Swap deals were mentioned – me for Guti, plus money. Guti is a Real midfielder admired by Rafa, understandably so because he's good. I read the piece. No smoke without fire. By chance, I'd met

Guti on a beach in Spain that summer. I was on holiday, saw him and strolled over to say hello out of respect. A picture was taken, it ended up in the papers, and people speculated I was off to Real. Crap. That photograph meant nothing to any intelligent football watcher. It was just two footballers saying 'hi'.

The Real stories persisted. I considered the Boss's links with Real Madrid, where he had been youth coach, and I began wondering. Spanish papers were crammed with stories about Real's interest. Bernabeu's president at the time, Florentino Perez, talked about me being Real's new 'galactico'. Flattering. What angered me was one story in Madrid claiming I had already told Rafa I fancied a move to the Bernabeu. Bullshit. Complete bullshit. Truth was the first casualty in the feeding frenzy among newspapers in Spain and England.

My mind went into complete meltdown when Rafa was quoted in the Spanish papers saying, 'I don't want star names. I want to sell.' I snapped. I fronted up the Boss on what was being said in the Spanish press. Man to man, face to face. Come on, talk.

'Listen, do you want to sell me?' I asked him.

'No,' Rafa replied. 'Do you want to go?'

I looked at Rafa in astonishment. How could the Boss say that after what we'd been through in Istanbul?

I walked out and called Struan. 'Jesus, Struan, is Rafa waiting for me to push off? Does he want me to say I want to go? What the fuck are Liverpool playing at?'

Paranoia kicked in. Liverpool were broke, they needed the dosh, they wanted me out to fund Rafa's rebuilding. I couldn't think straight. More stories from Madrid. 'Real ready to swoop.' Once again, I challenged the Boss over all the noises in the Spanish media. 'It's your agent leaking things,' Rafa claimed. He blamed Struan for the pieces in the English press, but all the stories in the English media came from Spain. Someone in Liverpool was helping the Spanish papers, whose headlines were then re-run over here. Too many bloody games were going on over my future. I was livid.

Amid all the chaos, on Monday, 27 June, just over one month after Istanbul, Struan and Rick arranged to meet. At last. Surely now we'd come to an agreement. Surely now all the speculation would end. Struan walked into the meeting expecting an improved offer. After all, Liverpool had had enough time to draw up a deal. I waited at home, full of relief that the wheels were finally in motion. I gripped my mobile in my hand, poised to answer at any moment a call from a delighted Struan. I could already hear him talking me through how committed Liverpool were to me and how an agreement had been reached. Just a signature, and on we go. Bliss.

I waited and waited. When Struan finally phoned, his voice was studded with frustration. 'There's no deal on the table,' Struan said. 'Liverpool first want to know what we are after.'

Bollocks. It was up to Liverpool to make the first move.

The following day, Tuesday, Rafa called me into his office at Melwood and put a blank piece of A4 paper in front of me. 'There you are, Steven,' he said. 'Write down on there what you want.'

I was shocked. A quickfire exchange took place.

'No,' I replied.

'Why not?'

'You want me to say what I want? That's why I have an agent.'

Rafa looked at me coldly. 'I don't like agents.'

'But you have an agent, Boss. Did you do your own contract with Rick, or did your agent do it?'

'My agent.'

'With all due respect, Boss, that's what I have got an agent for, too. I just want to concentrate on my football. I have never talked to a manager about my contract before. That's my agent's job.' I felt it was unprofessional of the Boss. I was pretty steamed up. 'You are putting me on the spot, Boss. My agent knows exactly what we are after. We thought you would have an improved offer for us.'

Rafa didn't reply immediately. After leaving a long pause hanging heavily between us, he finally said, 'We'll have to wait and see.'

That week, the tension between me and Liverpool doubled by the day. Throughout the week I read more headlines like 'Benitez Might Want to Cash In on Gerrard', and more speculation about what Chelsea would pay me – £110,000 a week, £120,000. I just wanted to sign a decent deal at Liverpool and stay. Sensing my darkening mood, Struan was keen to break the deadlock. On 29 June, he contacted Liverpool again and indicated what we were looking for in terms of wages. 'It's very reasonable,' Struan pointed out to Rick. 'There are only twenty top players in the world and they get somewhere between these two figures.' The figures usually spoken about are between £90,000 and £120,000 a week. 'Stevie and I are asking towards the bottom figure,' Struan continued. 'If we went somewhere else, we'd ask for the higher figure.' It seemed fair. I was not holding the club I love to ransom. In fact, staying at Liverpool wouldn't have meant a massive difference to the wages I was already on. As all the papers reported, I was already making between £70,000 and £80,000 a week, depending on appearances, and now I was looking for £100,000. I had helped Liverpool win the European Cup, which gave us a chance of playing in the competition the following season, and that was worth a fortune to Liverpool. Anyway, other clubs were apparently going to offer me a stack more.

Rick acknowledged that our parameters for a top player's wages were fair. He also agreed that what I was looking for was towards the bottom end of the top players' scale. 'Give me a couple of days,' he replied. 'I will go and speak to the chairman and the board.'

'Good,' I told Struan. 'Surely Liverpool will sort it out now? Surely they will offer close to that figure and I can sign and the mess will end?'

Any minute I expected a call from Struan to tell me that Rick had been on, everything was sorted, deal done, and all it required was my signature. Sadly, silence reigned again. Each day I went into Melwood and told Rafa, 'You can put a stop to all this shit. I am not enjoying it. I will stay if you give me the contract.' I wasn't confrontational. I admit my relationship with Benitez for that week was strained, but it never got out of hand or aggressive. Stories of a fall-out were bollocks. No slanging matches stained our relationship. A few discussions between me and the boss got heated, but not bitter. For all our differences over this contract, I respected the Boss immensely. He was frustrated as well.

'Steven, I am not enjoying picking up the papers and reading all this speculation,' he told me. 'It's Real Madrid. They are trying to stir it. They want you.'

'To be honest, Boss, if Liverpool want me, tell Rick to call Struan sharpish. I'm not interested in what gets said in the Spanish papers. What interests me is getting my future sorted out, one way or the other.'

'If this delay by Liverpool goes on any longer,' I thought, 'I may have to leave.' The prospect hit me like a hammer-blow. Leave Liverpool? Yes, it was possible. The door out of Anfield was opened by Liverpool's hesitation: I inched towards the door. On 1 July, Struan called Rick. 'Stevie wants to go,' Struan said. 'I need a few more days,' Rick replied.

Carra's wedding was later that Friday. I went, and was dead pleased to see how happy Carra looked. A good party, all his mates, and not a care in the world. I felt like I had the cares of the world on my shoulders. All the lads came up and asked me what was going on with Liverpool. 'It's all in the board's hands now,' I replied.

We still didn't have an answer from Liverpool by the weekend. Nothing. I was at breaking point. On the Saturday, I went into Melwood to see Rafa. As positive meetings go, this was a two out of ten.

'I'm not greedy, Boss,' I told Benitez when he queried my wage demands. 'I just want to be paid what other top midfielders are across Europe. It's the going rate, Boss.'

'Steven, I want to keep you,' he said. 'You can be one of

the top players in the world. But you have got bad people advising you. Your friends, family, whoever is advising you is wrong.'

I resented that because I trust Struan with my life, let alone my finances. 'Come on, Boss, you can phone Rick now and ask, "Are we giving Steven Gerrard a new contract or not?"'

No response.

I'd had enough. As the weekend wore on with no word from Liverpool, Struan and I decided to break off contract negotiations. We were getting nowhere. Struan took a call from an agent asking if I had re-signed. 'The answer is no,' he replied. Chelsea took that as enough of a signal for them to have a go. On the Monday, with all the papers full of me heading out of Anfield, Chelsea made their move, faxing Liverpool an offer for me.

My head was in turmoil. On television, I listened to Benitez talking at a press conference to announce the signing of Bolo Zenden. All the questions were about me. 'I'd like Steven to keep playing for us for the next eight years, and there could be a role for him beyond that,' Rafa told the cameras. 'He could perhaps become manager after I leave.' I didn't believe that bit about me becoming boss, but I was impressed with Rafa's sincerity when he said he wanted me to stay. 'Maybe the boss does want to keep me after all,' I thought. But really, I just didn't know what to think. I was in that bad a state – worried, stressed, head all over the place.

A ray of light then appeared. Liverpool's brilliant chairman, David Moores, called a meeting at Melwood on that Monday afternoon. I know how much the chairman cares for me as a person, and as a footballer. Mr Moores had become concerned by the stand-off between Liverpool's captain and the club. So he decided to intervene. The chairman, me, Struan, Rafa and Rick sat around the table and talked through the situation. Nothing was agreed, but I came out feeling better. As I got into the car, I said to Struan: 'Maybe they do want to keep me'. I began blaming myself about the way I had been thinking. I felt guilty. I thought Liverpool wanted me out, but this meeting in Melwood gave me a different impression of the club's intentions. I still wasn't sure.

A momentum had built up, though. It became madder. The papers went crazy over Chelsea's interest. '£32 million!' screamed Tuesday's headlines. When it all kicked off, Rick hurriedly called Struan and said, 'That offer is still there. Sorry it took so long. It's there.'

Were they for real? I just didn't know any more with Liverpool. Were Liverpool talking about a new contract just to keep the fans onside while they flogged me to Chelsea? I had to know, so I decided to force their hand. I rang Struan. 'Struan, I'm going to find out whether they want to sell me. Put in a transfer request.' Struan phoned Liverpool. 'Take this call as a transfer request,' Struan told them. 'We will back it up in writing if you need us to. But this is it.' Bang. In went the transfer request, a hand-grenade rolled into the Liverpool boardroom.

That Tuesday, 5 July, was mental, the longest, hardest, most emotional day of my life. Action was required. I was sick of all the speculation in the papers, sick of getting pulled into Benitez's office, sick of waiting on Liverpool for an answer on the new contract. I was annoyed with

Liverpool for waiting so long after I told them in Istanbul I wanted to stay. I remembered all the confusion at Euro 2004. Not going through any more of that. A transfer request will shake Liverpool into life.

It was supposed to sort things out, but Liverpool immediately made my request public. Rick had to. He had to be fair to the fans. Madness broke out. I sat at home, my phone in one hand and the TV remote control in the other, staring transfixed as the drama played itself out on Sky. I was the main actor, yet there I was, sitting dazed at home, watching all these people and pundits debating me and my future. When I saw fans burning an old GERRARD number 17 shirt by the Shankly Gates, it did my head in. Fuck off. Show some respect. Don't you know how this is tearing me apart? My phone melted under the calls. 'Don't worry,' someone said. 'They're only doing it because the Sky cameras are there.' That was the rumour. Anything was possible now. The world was going mad.

I called Dad and Paul. 'Can you get over here, please?' I pleaded. They raced round. We went into my bedroom and talked for twenty minutes.

'Steven, don't go,' Dad begged.

'But Dad, look at the TV. Fans are burning my shirt at Anfield. The club aren't stopping them. Liverpool don't want me any more.'

Dad and Paul couldn't believe that.

'Don't walk away,' said Dad. 'Don't leave the club you love.'

After Dad and Paul left, I talked to Alex. She isn't a footballing person, she doesn't understand the game, but she was brilliant. 'Stevie, you have to decide,' she said, 'but whatever you choose, I'll support you. I will come to Chelsea, Madrid, wherever. I'll be by your side. Don't worry. If you leave, I'm with you. If you stay, I'm with you.' Alex was just worried about me. She knew I hadn't been the same person for almost a month. It was reassuring to feel her love was unwavering, wherever I chose to go. As we talked, our beautiful daughter, Lilly-Ella, ran around without a care in the world. If only my life was that simple.

Struan came flying through the door, trying to calm me. He saw I was standing on the precipice, a step away from oblivion. I stared at the rolling news through flowing tears. I was suffocated by stress. My energy had gone, lost during all those frustrating trips in and out of Benitez's office. My head was banging. I was eating Paracetamol like Smarties. Why had it got so bad? I looked at Struan. 'A month ago, I'm lifting the European Cup in front of the whole fucking world, Stru,' I said. 'Then I'm touring the city in front of half a million people. I'm celebrating the biggest cup with fans of a club where I have been since I was eight. Now I'm watching my fucking shirt being burned live on television. How the hell has it come to this?' It was the lowest point of my career.

I broke down. Panic breakdown, complete mess. Some force raced around my body turning off the lights, closing me down, plunging me into darkness. I was burning up, pulse racing off the scale. I poured Paracetamol down my throat but nothing could fight the headache. I managed to call Doc Waller. A friend, a doctor, a man I trusted with my life. 'Doc, I'm a mess,' I told him. He was straight round, and he calmed me down. Doc Waller has always done so much for me. I rely on him greatly. All the players do.

The sight of Liverpool's doctor looking after me made me realize that people at Anfield do care about me. 'Stevie, lad,' I told myself, 'remember Mr Moores calling that meeting at Melwood to show the club's love for you?' I began to think about what I was in danger of throwing away. All that love, all that history between us, the years dreaming of wearing the Liverpool shirt. Could I hand in that Liverpool armband? Could I turn my back on Liverpool, the club and the city that raised and shaped me? Could I let down my dad and my brother? They were mad Liverpool fans; leaving would seem like betrayal in their eyes. Could I look the dad I adore in the eye again? Could I look myself in the mirror again? Christ, so many fucking questions. Could I let the Kop down? Forget that little shite who burned my shirt for the cameras at the Shankly Gates. Liverpool fans always looked after their own. Could I really put on a Chelsea shirt and face Liverpool in front of the Kop? Just think, Stevie. Think hard. I had to get this decision right. Could I really leave? Could I really take that step over the edge, leap into the unknown and leave?

No. No. No. I couldn't jump over the edge of the cliff. I could see the great possibilities of Chelsea, but my heart wouldn't let me leave Liverpool. My beautiful little daughter wouldn't let me leave. Did I want to build another life in Madrid or London with a brand-new family? Lilly-Ella was happy here, with her cousins, her friends in playschool, buzzing around the house she loved. Was it fair on Alex to drag her away from her friends and family, from the environment where she was happiest? I couldn't do it. I was scared to leave what I had at Liverpool. I couldn't cut my roots. The clouds of doubts and questions began clearing. Chelsea had ambition, but I had ambitions for Liverpool. I was the club captain. We'd just won the European Cup. Rafa could take us forward, make us even more successful, as he's the best coach I have ever worked with.

Finally, my mind was made up. I'd walked through the storm. At eleven p.m., I called Struan. 'Tell Rick I want to sign,' I told him. 'I want to stay.'

Struan contacted Rick. 'Is that offer still available?'

'Yes.'

'Stevie will sign it.'

Thank God it was over. My heart stopped racing, and I relaxed. I put the Paracetamol away. I awoke on the morning of Wednesday, 6 July, with a smile on my face for the first time in weeks. On my way to Melwood to see Rafa, I stopped at the chairman's house, in Halsall. My respect for Mr Moores runs deep. The chairman is a man who loves Liverpool with the same passion as me, and he was gutted by the whole saga. 'I can't believe it got this far,' he said. He was devastated the club had delayed the contract. 'Why didn't you phone me much earlier?' he asked. 'I hate seeing you down, Steven.' Just talking to Mr Moores reminded me how right I was to stay at Anfield.

I got back in my car and sped into Melwood.

'Look, I'm made up I'm staying, but I'll hand over the captaincy if you think it's best,' I told Rafa.

'Keep the armband,' he said.

Thank God. Giving up the captaincy would have

broken my heart, but I had to make the offer. I apologized to Liverpool, to Rick and to Rafa, for all the mess, and they said sorry as well. But as I stepped back from the precipice I still felt really pissed off with how Liverpool pushed me to the brink. The blame lay fifty-fifty, I know that, and I hold my hands up to contributing to the mess, but Liverpool could have handled it better. They so nearly drove me out of Anfield. I still received a couple of nasty letters from Liverpool fans, but overall they were good to me. Most of those on the Kop knew how torn I was. Liverpool fans understand how emotionally I feel about the club. When I got round to signing the contract on Friday, 8 July, I said to Rick: 'Take out the escape clause. I never, ever want to leave Liverpool.' My previous contract had contained a clause so that if Liverpool were not doing so well, I could move on. I didn't need an escape clause in my new contract. When I put pen to paper that Friday, it was like signing a love letter. I was so glad my brief flirtation with Chelsea was over.

19
Three Lionesses: Alex, Lilly-Ella and Lexie

The Chelsea saga reminded me just how deeply I was in love with Alex Curran. An amazing girl, Alex has been spot-on with me from day one. I've always opened up to her. Alex is never nosey, although she always knows when something's on my mind. She gives me space, and time, and waits for me to speak. She never, ever gets involved in football. That's my world. The only time I ever talked to Alex about football was over Chelsea. I had to. When I was on my own, it would have been my decision. But in the summer of 2005 I had been with Alex for four years, we were engaged, and we had a beautiful little girl, Lilly-Ella. I couldn't be selfish. I had responsibilities, family commitments.

Alex fills my life and shapes my future. I see situations through her eyes, as well as mine. Of course, Alex is interested in how well I'm doing with Liverpool and England, but her knowledge of the sport is not good enough for her to get involved in a football conversation.

Alex is actually scared to mention football, in case I say something to her. But that's part of Alex's attractiveness. I don't one-on-one with a girl who says, 'You're giving four balls away out of six. You're not hitting the target enough.' I don't want to take shit like that; it does my head in. Before Alex, I went out on a few dates with busy birds who were Liverpool fans. They were always fishing for titbits about players. 'What's Michael like?' 'What's Carra like?' Piss off. None of your business. I erased them. Not for me, thank you. Delete number. Back to the drawing board. Alex isn't arsed about football. She's watched me for four years and still doesn't know what the rules are. She comes to Anfield to enjoy the atmosphere, and to see the other girls. When I get home, she never mentions the match. Alex understands that football is my domain, although I know she is not happy with me having the football on 24/7 at home.

The moment I first saw Alex out in Liverpool, my heart quickened and my life changed. It was one of those sledge-hammer moments. Bang, knocked back on my heels, stunned. I couldn't breathe, couldn't talk. We were out with different sets of mates, but never talked. Just eye contact. I was spellbound. I had to see this woman again. Properly. For a date. I couldn't think of anything else apart from meeting her, and finding out everything about her. Just me and Alex. One-on-one. 'She's fantastic,' I told Danny Murphy. 'I really like her.'

The wheels were put in motion. A mate phoned Alex. 'Steven Gerrard wants your number. He wants to take you out on a date.'

'Well,' said Alex, 'if Steven Gerrard wants to speak to

me, he can phone me. I'm not going out on a date with someone through someone else. Goodbye.'

So I sat down at home, calmed my nerves, drew a deep breath and dialled her number.

'Hello, Alex, it's Steven Gerrard. I saw you the other day.'

'Oh, hi.'

I was so nervous. My throat was dry, my stomach invaded by butterflies. Do it! Here goes.

'Do you fancy going out for a date?' I asked.

'No,' Alex replied. 'I don't know you and I don't go out with people I don't know.'

Bang. Phone down. Silence. That was it. But I wouldn't give up. No chance. Maybe she was just shy, just embarrassed talking on the phone. I'll give her a couple of days to think about it and then have another crack.

When the dust settled, I phoned Alex again. Take two.

'Alex, it's Stevie. I know you don't know me, but if you come for a drink you'll get to know me. Come on.'

Alex sounded a bit more friendly this time, so I did a few moves, got a bit of banter going and tried to win her over.

'I'll think about it,' she said.

I called her again the next day and we got on brilliantly, the ice really broken. 'OK, I'll go on a date with you,' she finally agreed. Happy days. I saved her number in my mobile. Stevie, lad, you are going to need this number now! I had to be careful, though. If any of the Liverpool lads went through my phone, as they often do when I'm in the shower, they would send Alex a naughty text. Guaranteed. I couldn't store the number under 'Alex

Curran'. I thought about putting it under 'Alan Cork', but it ended up under 'AC'.

I texted Danny. 'Got AC's number! Taking her out on a date! I'm fucking buzzing!' I pressed send, and sat back to wait for Danny's reply. Danny would be made up for me. But as I pulled my thumb back from the send button, I had this horrible feeling that in my excitement I might have sent the text to Alex, not Danny. Cancel it quick. Hit the red button. Again, again, again. Too late. It's gone. History.

I sat there, sweating. Danny, text me back. Please. Tell me you received it, not Alex. No text from Danny. Nothing. I couldn't bear it. So I rang Danny.

'Did I just text you?' I asked.

'No.'

'Five minutes ago, you must have got a text off me?'

'Stevie, I haven't had a text off you since yesterday.'

Oh no, you bastard. I phoned Alex.

'Have you just had a text off me?' I asked, praying she hadn't.

'Yes!' she laughed. 'You knobhead!'

Oh no! Nightmare. Actually, it helped. When Alex and I went out for our first date, she was dead shy, and so was I. But the moment she mentioned the text, we both opened up and laughed about it for five hours. It was a brilliant evening: good meal, few glasses of wine, and non-stop laughter. That was me hooked completely on Alex Curran. Of course, Danny went and told all the lads about the text, and I got caned mercilessly. But I didn't care. I was smitten.

Girls have always fascinated me. I would have liked to

have had a sister. Until I met Alex, my life revolved around hanging about places where nice girls went and trying to get them back to my place. Through school and up until the age of twenty-one I had loads of dates, but nothing really serious. I was waiting for the right girl. I was twenty-one when I met Alex and ready to calm down. I also wanted kids. I so admire Alex for what she has been through for me. She was twenty-two, really young herself, when I told her I wanted to get on with having a family. We'd been together a couple of years, and I was desperate to be a dad. It was my decision. I felt becoming a father would be good for my career, to get me even more settled. And I wanted to be a young dad, rather than wait to the end of my career to start having kids. Alex was brilliant. She agreed we should start a family, even though she was so young.

Before Lilly-Ella was born, I was really scared. I arrived at the Liverpool Women's Hospital not knowing what to expect. People tell you this and that, but nothing prepares you for the emotion of watching the girl you love go through all that agony. Everyone told Alex how painful it would be, so she was worried. I held her hand during the birth, but made sure I was down the Kop end. Someone advised me to stay at the Kop end because it gets terribly messy down the Anfield Road end! When Lilly-Ella appeared, I'd never felt such pride, elation and relief. My career has brought me many highs, but nothing has matched the sight of those tiny hands and feet, that sweet face, that little body entering the world.

Before England left for the World Cup in Germany, I experienced the same wonderful sensation when Lexie was born. Again I was choked up, a huge lump in my throat. A lot of men cry when they see their children born. I certainly could have, I was that emotional. I counted all the fingers and toes, and checked the babies were healthy. Always nagging away in the back of my mind was that something might go wrong. But Lilly-Ella and Lexie were perfect. Each time, though, there was work to do. Alex held my hand so tight during delivery that when she finally let go I had to get some feeling back into it. I rubbed it hard to get the circulation going again. I was so proud of Alex. Women in labour are so brave. They go through so much. My love for Alex deepened when she brought Lilly-Ella and Lexie into our lives.

People often ask Alex and me how we chose the names. Simple. I liked Lilly for a girl and Alex liked Ella, so we put them together. If Lilly-Ella had been a boy we would have named him Georgie. My middle name is George and it's my granddad's name. Second time round, we looked for something linked to Alex's name. We thought about Alexa and Alexandra, and settled on Lexie. With Lexie, Alex was suffering so much pain I didn't know what sex the baby was until a minute or two after she was born. I never looked. I was busy down the Kop end, making sure Alex was OK. Then the midwife said, 'Look at that gorgeous little thing. Isn't she beautiful?' She! I knew then I had another girl, which was great because I wanted a girl for Lilly to play with.

Before Alex gave birth to Lexie, I kept bumping into Robbie Fowler at the hospital. His wife, Kerry, was having Jacob just down the corridor. Robbie and I texted each other as we waited for our women to give birth. I got one text from Robbie which read: 'Wish she'd hurry up and stop messing around!' I'd text him back and get him out in the corridor for a chat about football. 'Can I borrow your camera?' I texted Robbie just before Lexie popped out. 'I've left mine at home.' We met in the corridor quickly, he handed over his camera, and we ran back into the delivery rooms. Lexie arrived at 9.33 a.m., and Jacob at five p.m. At 5.10 I got a text off Robbie: 'Jacob is after Lexie's number.' I pissed myself laughing. I can just picture my girls at fourteen, fifteen, with their blonde hair, and Fowler's little lad chasing them. If Jacob gets Kerry's looks he has a chance; if he gets Robbie's looks, he's not coming near Lilly-Ella or Lexie!

Alex is a brilliant mum to Lilly-Ella and Lexie, and always supportive to me. When Mum and Dad broke up, Alex was a rock. She never pried into the pain I endured, she was just there for me, letting me know how much she cared. All the boxes are ticked for me with Alex. She might not be everyone's cup of tea, I don't know, but I wouldn't change her for anyone. I love her. She doesn't get involved in my career and I don't get involved in hers.

Alex's media career took off because she was getting a bit of stick in the papers about how she dressed. That's such bollocks, that. For me, Alex has always dressed well. And as if someone can be judged solely on what they wear. Alex is a wonderful human being. Anyway, she got fed up with the sniping so we decided to take action. Initially, the idea behind her writing a column in the *Daily Mirror* was to turn her image around; it was an opportunity for people to appreciate the real Alex, to realize that she is a good mum, and a normal person. People think she goes shopping every day. Rubbish. Most of the time it's the same photographs being re-used, or she's taking clothes back for me. I buy a lot of suits and shirts for matches. Now, we have created an image where everyone knows Alex is a nice, normal girl, a Scouser. That column and the little photo-shoots are a small career for her, though I wouldn't describe her as a model. Alex enjoys bits and bobs of work when she gets some free time, but her main priority is to be a mum. And she does a great job. Alex is more into the celebrity world than me. I'm not one for premieres or photo-shoots. My priority is football. If I wasn't playing well, I wouldn't get the attention I do get off the pitch. My number one concern is delivering for Liverpool and England.

When I was younger, I went out golfing, and I hung around snooker halls, and with my mates. A lot of the Liverpool lads were gamblers. Training finished and, bang, straight down the bookies. But for me, betting is pointless. My dad was always interested in the horses, and I used to be fuming with him because he had the racing on the telly, day in, day out. I hated it. Dad loves a little flutter on the horses. He'll say, 'I've got a tip, do you want a little go?' I'll put a couple of hundred quid on it, but I am not a gambler who bets thousands. I can't watch a horse race. It doesn't interest me. If the racing is on the TV when I come in, it is bang off. At Melwood, I see players studying the racing pages, and I think to myself, 'What are they doing?' I wouldn't know where to start. Maybe that's a good thing, because betting can be a dangerous road to go down. Some players go racing after training, or do all that online gambling. Now, the first thing for me after training is race home, get to the girls.

I walk in through the door of our new house in Formby and Lilly-Ella races across the hall into my arms. We have a pool, so I take the girls swimming. I love those girls. I miss them so bad, even when I go away for one night. I pace around my hotel room, holding a photograph of Alex and the girls, thinking of the moment when I'll be back with them, holding them. The family. Together. It means everything to me. I dream of having a little boy as well some time in the future, a son I can take to the park and enjoy kickabouts with. If I do have a son, I would love him to play for Liverpool one day. I want to get a Gerrard dynasty going at Anfield.

20
Millennium Magic

The thirteenth of May 2006 was a good day at the office, a day to tell my children about as they grow older. 'This is our FA Cup final,' I told myself as Liverpool's coach inched through the raucous crowd and into the fantastic Millennium Stadium in Cardiff. 'This is our moment.' I was Liverpool's leader, settled at the club I love. I was in the prime of my life, settled with the woman I love. I had the respect of my peers, having just been named the Professional Footballers' Association Player of the Year – an unbelievable honour. Christ, I was ready for the 125th FA Cup final. My stage, my time. In the build-up to the clash with West Ham United, I played the match through in my head at least three times. I used up a lot of energy thinking about every possibility, reminding myself constantly of the need to take responsibility, to seize the moment. Liverpool expected me to deliver. So did I. As I laced my boots, I looked at the names stitched into the tongues: Lilly-Ella on one and Lexie on the other. Come on, this final's for them. Let's go to work.

I led Liverpool out onto the pitch and into an unbelievable scene. All the fans, from Liverpool and West Ham, were magnificent, cheering twenty-two players as we lined up. We were favourites, a strange sensation. In all our other cup finals, Birmingham apart, Liverpool had been underdogs. Even against Alaves we weren't overwhelming favourites because we weren't flying in the Premiership. In massive Champions League games, against heavyweights like Chelsea or Juventus, Liverpool were never given much hope. I liked that. Going into a game knowing the pressure was on the opposition was fine by me. But this was different. Everybody thought we would steamroller West Ham. I certainly never underestimated the Hammers. They have a terrific manager in Alan Pardew, a good captain in Nigel Reo-Coker, and other decent players.

West Ham were up for this final, all right, as I quickly discovered. Paul Konchesky and Carl Fletcher both clattered me early on. Straight through. Whack. Hide the pain, Stevie, don't complain. Get on with it. I picked myself up, raised also by Liverpool fans singing the stirring 'Fields of Anfield Road', and hurled myself back into the fray. Get stuck in. Had to. West Ham meant business. We knew all about the Hammers but we didn't expect them to be so good on the day, or so dangerous on the counter-attack. Early on we tried to dominate, but we got caught on the break because Pardew had packed his side with pace.

Within twenty-one minutes, we were behind. Carra couldn't do much about the own-goal, diverted in from Lionel Scaloni's cross. Carra had to go for it, because Marlon Harewood was lurking behind him and would have stuck it away. I was gutted for Carra. I knew how much the own-goal would hurt him. Carra's dead proud. If Liverpool had lost that FA Cup final 1–0, he wouldn't have been able to live with it. Defeat would have killed him for years and years. He's such a competitor. In terms of goals scored at either end, Carra's about one goal down overall. Whenever the Liverpool lads wind him up about his goals record, Carra shouts, 'I'm about 350 up if you look at the goals I've stopped.' Carra has an answer for everything. He's right though. No-one could ever point the finger at him because he has been a rock for Liverpool.

We had to pull Carra out of the mess, had to fight back. But West Ham were on fire, and when they scored again, through Dean Ashton, a fear kicked in that I was not going to get my hands on the FA Cup. Ashton's goal was a bad mistake by Pepe Reina, who spilled Matthew Etherington's shot into the striker's path, but none of us Liverpool lads would dream of blaming Pepe. Our Spanish keeper saved us so many times that season. But two mistakes meant we were 2–0 down. Come on, lads! Let's get going!

The players lifted themselves. As we started to play a bit better, inspiring thoughts of Istanbul crept in. Time for another great escape. Pulling one back just before half-time was crucial. I spotted Djibril's run into the box. Have to hit him. Can't waste this golden chance. I took aim and whipped the ball into the box, where Djibril's finish was sensational. He didn't get much credit that season, but he deserves massive praise for that volley, because it got us back into the FA Cup. He had a rough year, playing out of position, and I know he didn't get on with Rafa too well; it was no surprise when he moved to Marseille. Djibril's a bit different. Some of his decisions to do with clothes, cars, tattoos and hair have me shaking my head in disbelief, but as a person Djibril's a great lad, and really caring. He'll do anything for you. I won't miss his colourful clothes, but I will miss his bright personality. I hope he enjoys better luck at Marseille than he had at Liverpool. He will always be remembered at Anfield for that Cardiff belter.

In the Millennium dressing-room at half-time, Rafa made his usual inspirational speech. When the boys went back out, we were even more fired up. Liverpool lagged one goal behind but we had our tails up – let's take West Ham now! But as the second half wore on I worried about whether it was going to happen. Whenever I received the ball in West Ham's half, I tried too hard to push for the breakthrough. That's natural, I know. I was desperate to get that equalizer. We cannot lose, must not lose!

It was Peter Crouch, big Crouchy, who rescued us. After the game the press and everyone focused on my performance in Cardiff, but Crouchy was key. When Xabi lifted a nothing ball into West Ham's box, Crouchy, Fernando Morientes and Danny Gabbidon went up for it. The moment I saw Crouchy stretching his neck, I started jogging into an area where I thought the ball would drop, around twelve yards out. Crouchy got the knockdown; it was bouncing and perfect for a shot. 'Over!' I screamed at Sami, ordering him to leave it. The set was ideal, and I caught it sweetly. Bang. Back of the net, 2–2. In the celebrations, I thanked Crouchy for the set. If Crouchy hadn't been on the pitch, I would never have scored. He's been a good buy for Liverpool, and he has proved a lot of doubters wrong. When Crouchy arrived from Southampton, he was flying in training. Dead confident. Then his belief dipped low because he couldn't find the net, and that was when we played Bare Arse in training. Crouchy's form and goal touch returned, and he now looks a top player for Liverpool. He will work well with Craig Bellamy, our new signing for 2006/07.

What a crazy final it was turning out to be. Liverpool were level for only twelve minutes. When Yossi Benayoun put Konchesky in on the left, there seemed no danger, no problem. We can handle this. I was running in at a decent speed and stretched out my leg into the perfect position to block his cross. But Konchesky mishit the ball. Shit. There were only two places it could go: over the bar or into the top corner. Pepe, off his line, was caught out badly. The ball sailed over him, a freak goal, but an utterly prevent-able goal. Pepe was really disappointed.

At that point, Liverpool looked doomed. A West Ham fan had just notched a winner. Our fans were quiet; their supporters were in party town. A few of our lads' heads were down. West Ham's name was on the Cup. Call the engravers and make it official. It's over. To cap it all, cramp plagued my legs, a season's load of fifty-nine games at full throttle finally catching up with me. Cardiff is a big pitch, and the weather was dead hot, so I was close to meltdown. The clock ran down, and I prepared for the worst. We needed impetus from somewhere.

Rafa, always top man with the subs, sent Didi on, giving me licence to push further forward. We charged all over the place, desperate for the equalizer. I saw Carra bomb on in the left-wing position, making up ground, carrying us towards West Ham's box. We lost possession, but because Cissé went down injured, Scaloni sportingly put the ball out. When we returned the ball to Scaloni, the Argentinian hoofed it back to us. Thanks! I got it and found Riise, who drilled the ball into West Ham's box. I heard the Millennium announcer declare, 'There will be a minimum of four minutes stoppage time.' The countdown had begun: Liverpool were 240 seconds from oblivion.

I was cramping up, nothing left, but I had to be around for the scraps. As the announcer's words drifted away, I hobbled forward. Morientes and Gabbidon fought for Riise's cross and the ball flew back out. Towards me. Oh, God! I stood there, legs stiff as boards, tank empty, thirty-seven yards from goal with this ball coming my way. Everyone raves about what happened next, but they don't realize one crucial thing: if my legs hadn't been riddled with cramp, I would have brought the ball down and tried to build an attack. I was a long way out. Too far to shoot, surely? Come on! Be realistic! There had to be too many bodies in the way. But the cramp made up my mind. I looked at the ball. 'It's set decent,' I told myself, 'so have a go, try to hit the target. Nothing to lose, Stevie.'

I made contact, pouring my few remaining drops of energy into the ball, willing it on its way. People said the ball went in at a decent speed, but it seemed to take ages to travel those thirty yards. My senses were drained, the cramp and the tension taking their toll. Through blurred vision, I saw Shaka Hislop moving. Has he saved it? Has it gone in? Please God. Then I saw the net ripple and stretch. I saw the Liverpool fans leap up. I saw the West Ham fans and players collapse. It was in: 3–3.

My first reaction was of pure shock. I was surprised how well I hit it because of the mess my body was in. All my muscles were pulling. But there was no pain from hitting the ball so hard; there never is when you catch the ball so well. Those two strikes in the 2006 FA Cup final were the best I ever caught the ball. The feeling ripping through me matched the one after my Champions League header, although my second FA Cup final goal was better – my best ever goal. The brilliance of it still hasn't sunk in. I still can't believe I scored from so far out. On the Millennium pitch, I couldn't celebrate properly, I was too shattered. I just smiled and patted the GERRARD on my back. I don't know why, because the lads always cane me. 'Everyone knows who you are!' they shout at me.

Extra time felt like running through wet cement. Everyone was tired, yet West Ham could still have won it when Reo-Coker headed goalwards. Has to be in. Somehow, Pepe appeared from nowhere and pushed the ball away onto the post – an unbelievable save. That one in Cardiff and Jerzy's off Shevchenko in Istanbul were the best two I have ever seen. I was made up for Pepe. It would have been a shame if we lost the FA Cup final on Reina's mistakes, because he had been one of our players of the season. Even then West Ham could have won it, but Marlon Harewood, hobbling badly, missed the follow-up. Football's a harsh business; there's such a fine line between success and failure. Harewood gets the shot on target, West Ham lift the FA Cup, and my heart gets broken. But I didn't feel sympathy for Marlon or West Ham. I couldn't. You have to be hard in football. I don't think Harewood, Reo-Coker or Konchesky would have felt sorry for Carra or Reina if Liverpool had lost.

Football is brutal, and nothing is more brutal than penalties. Such unforgiving tests of nerve. But the moment the final went to a shoot-out, I knew it would be me lifting the FA Cup, not Reo-Coker. No question. The pens were down the West Ham end, an advantage to them as we would get battered by their fans when we stepped up. No problem. Confidence and a feeling of responsibility surged through me. As captain, I wanted to set an example.

'Can I go number one, boss?' I asked Rafa.

'You are number three,' he replied.

As ever, our brilliant manager had a plan. Obviously, I accepted Rafa's instruction and joined my team-mates in the centre-circle.

When Didi strolled forward to take penalty number one, my certainty intensified that Liverpool were on course for a seventh FA Cup. Germans don't miss from twelve yards. Didi is made for big games, daunting occasions, anything that challenges a man's mettle. Nothing fazes him. Ball down, step back, run in, goal. Hislop, no chance.

West Ham had no way back from that, I was sure. Reina would see to that. Pepe arrived in England with an astonishing record of saving pens back in Spain. In two seasons at Villarreal, he stopped twelve out of eighteen penalties, and a keeper doesn't save that many unless he's a master. West Ham's first taker, Bobby Zamora, was up against a goalkeeper with the quickest of reactions, a top professional who had done his research on his opponents.

Zamora hit his kick hard and low towards the corner, but Reina read it. He stretched out his right hand and the ball was stopped. West Ham hearts must have stopped as well. If Zamora could take such a good kick and still not beat Reina, what chance did they have?

Hope then smiled briefly on West Ham. Next up for Liverpool was Sami, which surprised me. Our giant Finn has never been a penalty-taker and his kick was pretty disappointing. At least he showed the bottle to go up there. That's why all the Liverpool lads stood in the centre-circle, arms around each other, showing our unity: we were all in this shoot-out together. Win together, lose together – the Liverpool way. Teddy Sheringham then strode towards the spot, and I knew West Ham would draw level. Teddy's as nerveless as Didi. Bang: 1–1.

Numbers three and four for Liverpool were me, then Riise. We were ready, confident. The pair of us had put in some serious shifts on our penalty technique at Melwood. Three days before Cardiff we thought Rafa might work on pens, but we never did. So me and Riise stayed behind and did our own practice. Unlike his placed effort in Istanbul that missed, Riise kept smashing them in at Melwood.

'If we go to pens in Cardiff, don't be changing your mind,' I told John.

'I won't,' he said. 'I'll never sidefoot a pen again. It's getting smashed.'

I just worked on the same corner, over and over again. Same height, same spot. I'd taken advice off Liverpool's keepers, Pepe, Jerzy and Scott Carson. They showed me the tiny area where a keeper cannot reach the ball, even a keeper with a good spring and great anticipation. Through that practice at Melwood, I kept hitting the mark regularly. Riise shouted over to me, 'Don't change your mind in Cardiff either.' I didn't. That ball was getting buried, just as at Melwood. Bang, past Hislop, job done.

When Konchesky missed, Riise had the chance to make it 3–1. He went for power down the middle. It went like a bloody missile, a bit too close to Hislop's feet for comfort, but still into the net. Brilliant! Riise's quite an insecure character, and if he'd missed again, it would have killed him. His Champions League miss haunted him. Now the ghosts of Istanbul had been smacked away, bang into the net. Cardiff saw the real Riise, such a sweet striker of the ball.

All we needed was for Pepe to save from Anton Ferdinand and my hands were on that lovely Cup. I've met Anton a few times, and he seems a decent guy, but sympathy is the enemy of those chasing victory. I certainly wasn't thinking 'Poor Anton!' when he missed. I was too busy hugging Steve Finnan and the rest of the team. Despite the brutality, penalties are the best and only way to settle finals. We can't go having replays at that stage of the season. Fans would hate it, too. It would be unfair on them to fork out for another expensive ticket.

When Anton missed, Carra was the first to take off in celebration. It was like he was on a Scalextric track, heading straight ahead, then careering off. Fuck you lot, he's thinking, where's my family? I'm off to find my dad! Every time! Carra cracks me up. I love his celebrations. Winning trophies means everything to him and he never hides the emotion. Once he'd waved to his family, he came looking for me. It's a Scouse thing. Sharing the moment of glory means everything to two kids from Scouse estates. After I collected the FA Cup off Prince William, it was a case of you grab one handle, Carra mate, I'll hold the other, and let's go and party.

After I finally laid off spraying people with champagne and was leaving the Millennium pitch, Alan Pardew stopped me and shook my hand. 'I'd hoped you were saving that for the World Cup,' he said with a smile. Top man. Pardew's players were also first-class. They came across, man after man, concealing their agony to say, 'Well done.' Everyone associated with West Ham behaved with real dignity in Cardiff, just like the way I try to be in defeat. If they had won, Liverpool could not have complained. Too many of our players were too disappointing. West Ham were desperately unfortunate to lose. Having played so well, it must have been gut-wrenching to go home without the FA Cup, yet they were all gracious. It really moved me that in their hour of utter desolation, West Ham fans stayed behind to applaud as I lifted the FA Cup. I'll never forget that sporting gesture. I'm Liverpool through and through, head to toe, but I have a place in my heart for West Ham supporters after Cardiff. Fans like West Ham United's make football special. Usually when we do a lap of honour with a cup, the opponents' section is empty. The fans have disappeared, dragging their heartache with them. Not in Cardiff on 13 May 2006. The West Ham fans were tremendous, clapping us as we paraded the Cup. Both sets of fans were brilliant, which made it such a terrific occasion.

Back in the dressing-room we continued to celebrate,

but I was gutted for Harry Kewell, who sat there, ice pressed on his damaged groin. Harry was really emotional, ripped apart with frustration after limping off in another final. I know how bad he felt in Istanbul, so my heart went out to him in Cardiff. It's horrible seeing a team-mate I respect in bits. But the rest of the team were in party mood. 'What a fantastic game!' I screamed.

Everyone raved about the match. The 125th FA Cup final was called the greatest ever, even 'The Gerrard Final'! That meant the world to me. I love the FA Cup. It has taken a few knocks over recent years, and Premiership clubs are perhaps more focused these days on the Champions League, but Liverpool and West Ham put the shine back on the trophy that day in Cardiff. Good. I never knocked the FA Cup. I never underestimated its importance to fans. When Liverpool went out embarrassingly at Burnley in 2005, I was straight in to see Rafa the next day. I was that upset.

'What's the idea of putting out an under-strength side?' I asked him. I was confused, hurt. Explain! 'Rafa, before every season I dream of winning the FA Cup. That's one of our realistic targets every year. The Cup's all I thought about as a kid. Going out of the Cup kills me.'

The Boss sat me down, and calmly talked me through his reasons. 'We are in the Champions League,' Rafa began. 'We have too many games. Our squad is not good enough to deal with them all. Watch. I will prove to you why I have done it.'

And, of course, Liverpool won the Champions League. I won't be knocking at the gaffer's door ever again! Rafa's always right.

In Cardiff, Rafa helped me fulfil my childhood dream of lifting the FA Cup. For that special moment at the Millennium, and for Istanbul, I will always revere the man. My relationship with Rafa is different to the one I had with Gérard Houllier. I was very, very close to Gérard; he was almost family, almost flesh and blood. Benitez is not cold towards me, just a little detached. Rafa doesn't think he needs close bonds with players, even the captain. But respect flows naturally between me and Rafa: he's the manager, I'm a player. Even when all the Chelsea mess was going on, my respect for him remained strong. When I decided to stay at Anfield, I knew me and Rafa had to make our relationship work to carry Liverpool forward. We both had to make more of an effort. Now, after Istanbul, Cardiff and the Chelsea saga, we have a good professional relationship. But it's professional.

Everything Rafa says and does is designed to strengthen Liverpool. Twenty minutes after I lifted the FA Cup, Rafa was downstairs talking to the press and telling them Liverpool could have won it without me. 'I don't think we would have lost if we didn't have Steven,' he said, 'because we have played a lot of games without him.' I'd scored two good goals and banged in a penalty, which was not a bad afternoon's work, but I understood Rafa. The gaffer was not belittling my contribution, as some people thought, he was just saying that the team is everything, that his number eight is simply a cog in the Liverpool machine. Fair enough.

I was not surprised to hear the gaffer's comments. In fact, I'm more surprised when Rafa comes out and pays me a compliment. I know how he works now. He's the complete opposite to Gérard. If Liverpool win and I stick away a dead good hat-trick and do ninety-eight things right and two wrong, Rafa will pull me sharpish. 'Steven, about those two mistakes,' he will say, and then he'll speak to me for ten minutes about them. Nothing about the hat-trick or the ninety-eight good things! Rafa will never, ever mention the goals, the tackles, the passes. Initially, I was gobsmacked by this. 'Doesn't the gaffer like me?' I thought. 'Has he got something against me?' Friends ask me whether Rafa's cold attitude pisses me off, but it honestly doesn't. That indifference is one of the million reasons why Rafa is top man in the coaching world. He doesn't like giving out pats on the back. Sometimes, though, I need that little bit of love, that reassurance during a bad patch. Recently, I've detected a slight mellowing in the boss, a willingness to think about giving a compliment. But even then it's done in such a low-key way I almost don't realize Rafa has made it.

After the FA Cup final, Liverpool threw a party for the players and families, and Rafa was there. I wandered across to him, buzzing with our victory. As I walked towards him, my mind was full of one hope. Go on, just say it, Rafa. Just say, 'Well done, Steven.' For once. Would he? No chance! Our chat once again revolved around things that went wrong on the day; it was nothing to do with how well Liverpool had done to get back into one of the greatest FA Cup finals ever. 'Next season,' Rafa kept saying. 'Next season, we have to do better in the Premiership.' Typical Rafa, always looking forward, never revelling in the moment like me and Carra. Rafa never even mentioned my two goals. Top goals, great goals, rescue-act goals. Not a squeak! I smacked in twenty-three goals that season for Liverpool – not bad for a midfielder. Any other manager would have been all over me. Not Liverpool's gaffer. 'You never hit twenty-five,' he remarked. 'You missed the target by two!' But, a smile! Amazing! Rafa actually smiled! Thank God. I wandered back to the lads, thinking, 'Jesus, that was a compliment off Rafa.'

There I was, on top of the world after the FA Cup final and having scored twenty-three goals over the season, and there was Rafa bringing me back down to earth. Even his tiny compliment was an encouragement to improve. But that's Rafa, always challenging me to push myself higher. Go for twenty-five goals. Go for thirty. Don't relax. And Rafa has helped my performances go to another level. He's such a hungry manager. 'Small details, Steven, small details' is one of his biggest shouts. Leave nothing to chance, even the tiniest detail. I'm getting to like this Spaniard more and more, and my aim is still to get a 'well done' off him before I retire. But then, if he gives me a 'well done', I might need treatment and a long lie-down. My legs would go all wobbly, like that French presenter girl who fainted at the Champions League draw when I was handing the cup back. And it wouldn't be just me who would keel over if Rafa dished out a compliment. Every player in the Liverpool squad would need serious attention off Doc Waller if Rafa went soft on us. His hardness drives me on. I must crack it, though. I want to deliver in games to impress Rafa. I dream of that 'well done'!

21

Frustration in Germany – the 2006 World Cup

Winning's an addiction. As I gently placed my FA Cup medal in the trophy room at the top of our new house in Formby, another burning ambition confronted me. Space was set aside in the room for an even more precious medal.

Three weeks after Cardiff, England landed in Germany as one of the favourites for the greatest prize on earth. This was meant to be England's World Cup, the moment when the so-called Golden Generation ended forty years of hurt and brought the trophy home. Me and Becks, JT and Lamps, Michael and Ashley: England's players were better than at Euro 2004, more experienced and more determined. We arrived in Germany convinced we could win. England expects.

Everything seemed in place for a successful tournament. As the coach from Baden-Baden airport wound its way up through the Black Forest hills towards our hotel, I turned to Carra and said, 'Jesus, it's isolated.' The coach kept zigzagging up these bendy roads. Soon there were no houses, no traffic. Where the hell were we going? Eventually, the bus pulled up outside a castle called Buhlerhohe, our secluded base, with magnificent views over the Rhine Valley. No-one for miles, no-one to bother us. Good. I prefer peace and quiet. Let's leave the noise until match-days. Me and Carra walked to our rooms, which were next to each other. I went into mine and flicked on the TV. We had English telly, and the news bulletins were astonishing. Five days before the big kick-off against Paraguay in Frankfurt, our fans were already flooding into Germany in their thousands. England's unbelievable support reminded the players how much each game means to the nation whose colours we proudly wear. But for now, up at Buhlerhohe, it was good to be away from all the clamour.

Buhlerhohe was perfect. The Football Association had done us proud. They'd even got longer beds in for lanky lads like me, Rio and Crouchy. The food was outstanding, the kit ideal. Nothing was left to chance. When we drove down to the training pitch at Mittelberg the following morning, we found a surface better than any of the World Cup pitches. Determined to give us the very best, the FA borrowed Wembley's top groundsman, Steve Welch, to put in a fantastic new pitch. It was watered every morn-ing, so no wonder our passing was good in training. That Tuesday, 6 June, I glanced around Mittelberg and all the players looked terrific. No excuses, no regrets. Everything was geared up for England to deliver.

We just needed Wayne Rooney fit after his metatarsal break. 'Give us Wayne,' I thought, 'and we'll give you the

World Cup.' Manchester United's manager, Sir Alex Ferguson, kept saying England must be careful with Wayne. But England weren't rushing him, he was just healing quickly. I couldn't help thinking that if Fergie had been English, he might have played it differently. Wazza and I are big mates and I talked to him all the time at Buhlerhohe. 'I'm ready,' he kept telling me. 'I'm ready for Paraguay.' Paraguay! That was our first game, on 10 June. Whenever Wayne saw Sven at Mittelberg or around Buhlerhohe, he told the coach, 'Pick me against Paraguay. I'm flying.' That's what I love about Wayne: he's always so positive. He was just desperate to get back playing.

Speculation about his return was crazy. Every day, Wayne was on the back pages. Will he? Won't he? The saga wasn't fair to Wayne or the other England players, but that's the country we live in. We know what our newspapers, radio and TV are like. Mad at times. Wayne is England's most important player so the attention was bound to be on him, but it was a distraction. Every time we went to dinner, turned on the TV or picked up a paper, there was Wayne. We did lose some of our focus.

Sven was right to take a gamble on the fitness of someone as special as Wazza. If England were to bring back the World Cup, we needed Wayne Rooney. The mistake Sven made was that he should have picked five forwards in his World Cup twenty-three – Wayne plus four others. For a tournament as big and demanding as the World Cup, every team needs five strikers. Minimum. I wanted to be landing in Germany with five forwards, not four. I wanted to be sending this message to the world: we are England, packed with attackers, and we fear no-one. Sven talked about midfielders operating further forward, but that's too specialized. I was gutted when I walked in the Old Trafford dressing-room before the World Cup warm-up against Hungary on 30 May and saw the number 9 shirt hanging on my peg. Number 9? Talk about pressure! That's a recipe for me being destroyed. Get real. I'm an attacking midfielder, not an emergency striker. England required real strikers, footballers comfortable with number 9 on their back, like Wazza, Michael and Crouchy. Sven named them in the squad, but it was his fourth striking choice that stunned me. Not only were England embarking on an arduous World Cup campaign with only four forwards, one of them was Theo Walcott. I almost fell over when I heard.

Now, let's get a few things right about Theo. He's a really nice kid and one day he will mature into a very, very good player. Theo's potential was obvious in training. But as the 2006 World Cup dawned, he represented England's future, not the present. Theo Walcott had no right to be in Germany. None at all. I was gobsmacked to find him on the plane. My faith in Sven has always been strong, but to select a kid who hasn't played any part in a Premiership game, or a competitive international, was clearly a massive gamble.

Could Sven throw him into a World Cup game? No chance. Theo was still a baby. When I was seventeen, I hadn't even played three reserve games. Asking him to come to the World Cup was unfair on Theo. There was no possible way the kid was ready to perform on such a difficult stage. Seventeen-year-olds should never be taken to World Cups, unless they are one-offs like Wayne Rooney or Lionel Messi.

I did warm to Theo. Difficult not to. Initially the Arsenal kid was very quiet around the senior players. That's normal. As the World Cup wore on, though, he came out of his shell and joined in the banter a bit. He worked hard every day in training and was a top professional. But what a bloody gamble! OK, if it had been a World Cup qualifier and England had been killed by injuries to strikers, then take a gamble on a kid. But not the World Cup itself. We were not tourists in Germany, doing a spot of sight-seeing. We were there on business. Theo was not Michael Owen or Pele, teenagers who graced World Cups but had shown their class with their clubs first. Even now, as I get stuck into the new 2006/07 season and the World Cup summer fades away, my mind remains confused as to Sven's thinking. Theo was just not ready. Even if the seven leading English strikers had been injured, it would still have been a risk to take him to the World Cup.

I felt sorry for Theo, but more so for Jermain Defoe and Darren Bent. Jermain and Darren worked hard all season to go to a World Cup, then a kid comes out of nowhere and takes the place they were after. It didn't look right. Darren stayed at home, but at least Jermain came to Germany on stand-by, just in case Wayne didn't recover. Defoe was unbelievable. From the moment England joined up, he was probably one of the best in training. His finishing was sharp. His attitude was spot-on. He never once mentioned any grievance over a kid like Theo being in the twenty-three. When Wayne was confirmed in the squad after flying back for that final scan, Jermain hid his heartache well. Before heading for the airport and a flight back to England, he shook hands with all of us and wished us all the best. Top man. He must have been boiling inside. On the surface, though, he was fantastically professional. Good for him. Jermain went up massively in my estimation as a bloke and a player.

Still, I was punching the air with delight that Wazza was cleared for action. As poor Jermain was upstairs packing his bags that Wednesday, 7 June, Wazza marched back into the Buhlerhohe, stood in reception and declared, 'The Big Man's back!' Typical Wazza! He wasn't being cocky. Wayne just has so much belief in himself. Even before his scan he knew he would be all right. The overhead kicks in training were a statement of intent. The scan was simply a doctor's note confirming what all the players and Wayne knew. He was welcomed back into training on Thursday like a returning hero. But he was still prevented from playing against Paraguay, and it almost killed him to watch it. Football is to Wayne Rooney what oxygen is to everyone else.

Along with all the talk about Wazza, other issues occupied my thoughts. I was just hours away from my World Cup debut, my supreme test. I was desperate to take my Liverpool form into an England game. Everybody was watching. Could I cut it? Could I do in the World Cup what I had done in the FA Cup and European Cup? Questions crowded in on me. Climbing on board the plane out of Lisbon after Euro 2004, I carried a kit-bag full of regrets. Flying into Germany, I kept telling myself, 'No regrets this time, Stevie.' I cranked up the pressure on myself. I paced around my room at Buhlerhohe, saying out loud, 'First World Cup game – make sure it goes well. Remember France at Euro 2004: you were OK until the last five minutes. Have a solid game this time. Ninety minutes, no mistakes.' *No mistakes*.

I couldn't really sleep that week. My mind was jumping with too many concerns to close down for an hour or two. And another worrying distraction soon affected my preparations. On the day Wayne was jetting in and out of Manchester, I went into a tackle with Joe Cole at Mittelberg. Whack. Joe's elbow banged into my hip, and my back went into a spasm. Shit. All the old fears tumbled back into my present. 'That's me out of the group games,' I thought. 'That's another tournament screwed.' Thank God I was in good hands. England's physio, Gary Lewin, examined my back and said, 'It will settle down quite quickly.' Fingers crossed. Touch wood. The doc, Leif Sward, agreed. The next morning an osteopath called Carl Todd arrived from England, and he manipulated my back four times that day. 'You'll make the Paraguay game,' Carl insisted, filling me with belief. But I carried a back problem for the rest of England's stay in Germany.

All that mattered was that the medical lads got me on the field against Paraguay. My instructions were simple in Frankfurt: to hold back when England bombed on. Sven had us playing 4–4–2 without a holding midfielder, so someone had to take responsibility in case Paraguay broke away. 'You are a little bit more defensive than Frank,' Sven told me, 'so don't go up as much as him. Be more cautious.' That sacrificed one of my strengths – storming forward. I craved to play my Liverpool role for England.

Just let me loose, like Liverpool do. No dice. Frank Lampard had the attacking licence. But that was OK. Lamps was worth his place in the World Cup starting eleven. In fact he was one of the main reasons England reached Germany: he'd been immense in qualifying. I had no complaints. Just get on with it, Stevie lad. Frankfurt was my first World Cup match and I was aching to play. Right-back, left-back, anywhere – just let me taste the World Cup atmosphere. I'm twenty-six, it's been too long, let me out there.

The mood in the dressing-room before the game was good. Everyone was up for it. Shouts ripped through the corridors underneath the stadium. Come on! As usual, Paul Robinson didn't shut up from the first minute he marched into the dressing-room until we charged through the door just before kick-off. Everyone buzzed with anticipation. This was it. The World Cup. Our time.

When we walked out of the tunnel, the home of Eintracht Frankfurt belonged to England. What a sight! England flags everywhere. Our fans everywhere. The ticketing problems never affected England. Our boys were out there in force. I wasn't surprised. England fans are unbelievable; I knew they'd pack out the ground. I'd switched on the TV the night before and seen them partying all over Frankfurt, all over Germany really. I'd opened my hotel window in Frankfurt and heard them running through their songbook. Football's Coming Home! Us players now had to make sure it did come home.

We started well. Becks forced an own-goal from Carlos Gamarra early on and we should have made it three or four, but the heat seemed to come straight from the

Sahara. My mouth felt like it was lined with sandpaper. Yet the sweltering conditions affected us only towards the end. Eintracht's pitch was the real reason we never played well. On our beautiful Mittelberg surface, our football was quick. Not here. Frankfurt's pitch was too dry, the grass too long. England tired after the break and Paraguay kept the ball better than us. Yet apart from an unfair booking, I was really, really happy with my individual performance. Collectively, though, we all knew we'd face criticism for our second-half display. But so what? Three points meant one thing: England were up and running.

Next up were Trinidad and Tobago in Nuremberg on 15 June. 'England should win this no problem,' I told myself. Again we failed to impress. In the second half, particularly, I got really frustrated and some of my passing went astray. England did not have the look of potential world champions. For eighty-three minutes, the so-called Golden Generation were held by a team of players from Wrexham, Port Vale and Coventry. We could not break through, until Peter headed in. At last we led. We could relax, and I could take a few more risks. Go on. Push on. Get a few shots in. Back at Melwood I work on my left foot all the time, so when I created a chance in the ninetieth minute I did not hesitate to use my left. I caught the ball really sweet and knew it was destined for the net. In it went. Unstoppable. The feeling of scoring in a World Cup was magical. There was relief, too. People see me hitting the target for Liverpool week in, week out. I felt under a lot of pressure to score for England, so seeing that ball flash past Shaka Hislop was wonderful. As it flew in, all the frustration over missing the 2002 World Cup finally disappeared as well.

Two games, six points, Wayne now back in action – it should have been all sunshine and smiles for England, but the clouds of concern persisted. This time, the press slagged us off for too many long balls. Rubbish. We tried to build up through midfield. The critics just look at Peter Crouch and assume we automatically hit it long. That's unfair on Peter and the rest of the lads. England were not a long-ball side at the World Cup. Sven's tactics were not the problem. It was us, the players, simply not performing as we should do against lesser opposition. Deep down the players accepted that. We talked about it back in Baden-Baden. 'We must play better if we are to win the World Cup,' I said. 'We must take our chances.'

Some tension began to creep into the England camp, partly because we could not spend proper time with our families after each match. The paparazzi and reporters who dogged us in Baden-Baden were a disgrace. So much rubbish was written about the WAGs, as the players' wives and girlfriends became known. People claimed they got more attention than the team. Well, whose fault was that? The bloody paparazzi and the papers for printing the pictures. Why didn't they leave the WAGs alone? Why did they wait around the WAGs' hotel, the Brenners Park, and then stalk the families? I tried once to go for a walk around Baden-Baden with Alex, Lilly-Ella and Lexie. Fucking pointless. Photographers everywhere, following our every step, our every move. Piss off! Even when we tried to relax in the Brenners gardens, the photographers set up camp in a public park opposite and took pictures.

Brenners was like a fortress. When I did visit Alex, we had to stay in our room. It was the only place where we could escape the intrusive photographers. Unfortunately, being in a hotel room with two kids bursting to get out and have a play is hardly relaxing. Even if Lilly-Ella and Lexie had been old enough to understand, how do you explain that no, actually, we can't go to that lovely park outside because there are paparazzi lurking behind every tree? I was livid. Photographers don't stop to think whether they have the right to take pics of me playing with my kids. They just think, 'This will help pay the mortgage.' Snap, snap, snap.

It seemed like a competition for them – 'Let's see who can earn the most money out of Coleen, Posh and Alex'. The WAGs took the kids to a local theme park one day, and the staff there said they had never seen so many photographers, not even when the German national team dropped by. It was crazy. Did the Italian players have their families over in Germany? Yes. Did their media follow their wives and girlfriends? No. So why were the English papers obsessed with the players' families? If I am with my family the night before a massive Champions League game at Anfield, is it an issue? No. I'm left in peace. And some of the stories in the newspapers about the WAGs were ridiculous. Alex went out with the girls one night in Baden-Baden and the bill for the lot of them came to 800 euros – hardly extravagant. In the papers, that bill was inflated to 4,000 euros. The story claimed the WAGs drank sixteen bottles of really expensive champagne. Alex had one glass. The behaviour of the English media during the World Cup was unbelievable. My mum kept getting phone calls from GMTV asking whether she wanted to come on telly. What? Come on!

It really was mad. Newspapers criticized England for allowing the WAGs out to the World Cup, then filled their front pages with pictures of Coleen, Posh and Alex. The WAGs had every right to be in Baden-Baden. Some of the younger players might have become homesick without family and friends about. I remember how lonely I felt at Euro 2000. Why should a seventeen-year-old like Theo not be allowed to see his girlfriend or Mum and Dad for seven weeks? Why can't Becks, Frank, Carra and me see our kids for a couple of days during a tournament? It makes us feel better, train better and play better. Lexie actually fell ill in Germany with a viral infection. Now, exactly how would I have felt if Lexie was back in England and poorly? Shit. I would have been tempted to run for the airport, to go back to help Alex look after our precious new baby. Sven was brilliant. The day I learned Lexie was ill was a day when the players were not allowed down into Baden-Baden. I knocked on his door. 'Lexie's struggling. Can I sprint down to Brenners?' I asked Sven. 'Of course,' he replied. 'I understand completely.' I went down and helped out. If Lexie had been a thousand miles away, I would have been a mess with worry.

If the WAGs had been left at home completely, it would have damaged the squad's morale. Having said that, I did feel they didn't need to be in Germany all the time. Events down in Baden-Baden became a permanent, high-profile side-show to the real England drama. All the talk about the WAGs and the paparazzi was a distraction. Really, the FA should have flown the WAGs in and out. There has to be a happy medium. Before the next tournament, us players need to sit down with the FA and discuss how the family side of things could be organized better. One option is for the WAGs to come out between games. If the WAGs can't go to the match, so what? They can see it on telly back home. Girls don't watch football anyway; they watch their individual fella. At least they have seen their boyfriends two days before a game or two days after. At least we have seen our kids. Probably the best solution is to let the WAGs fly out on the morning of the match, and we see them afterwards. For forty-eight hours after a game, we don't do anything apart from some light stretching. Let the WAGs visit us then. No clever columnist can complain about that.

A lesser frustration surfaced as we prepared for our final Group B match, against Sweden in Cologne on 20 June. One afternoon, after training at Mittelberg, Sven pulled me aside. 'Keep doing what you are doing, Steven,' he began. 'You are doing really well. But I'd like to rest you against Sweden. We're already through. You have a yellow card, and I can't afford not to have you in the last sixteen. What do you think? I think it's for the good of the team that you are on the bench.'

On the bench! God, how I hate those words. 'Yeah, I sort of understand,' I replied, 'but I want to play.'

'I knew you would say that, Steven,' said Sven. 'I appreciate how much you want to play, but I have to make the right decision for the team. Let me have a think about it for another day.'

'OK, boss. If you decide not to play me I'll understand, but I want you to go away thinking I want to play. I've missed enough World Cup games. I want to play in them all.'

I returned to my room and thought hard about the situation. My hunger for involvement against Sweden was immense. Christ, why did that bloody ref book me for nothing against Paraguay? Without that I would be starting against Sweden. I knocked on Carra's door and explained the problem.

'What do you think?' I asked him. 'I have a feeling Sven's going to rest me. I don't want to be on the bench.'

Carra quickly got to the heart of the matter. 'But what if you get a yellow?' he said. 'Just think of the last sixteen, don't think of Sweden. If you get booked again and it goes wrong for England in the last sixteen without you, what will you think then? You'll think, "Why didn't Sven rest me against Sweden?"'

I was torn, so I decided to wait and see what Sven had to say the next day. The boss came straight to the point. 'I'm resting you, Steven. I can't risk losing you for the last sixteen. I know how much you want to play, but I have no choice. We want to finish top of the group. If we need to use you to make sure we get that point, we will.'

'OK,' I said. 'I'm fine with that. Let's go and top the group.'

Sven then added, 'I know Frank's on a booking too, but he hasn't scored in the first two games. I want to give him another chance to get a goal.'

I understood completely. Sven's concern over my booking was really a compliment to me.

Reluctantly, I took my place on the bench in Cologne and watched team-mates like Michael Owen line up.

Michael had been subjected to some flak for his first two performances, so he was right up for Sweden. A feeling swept through me that Michael would score. Definitely. I caught that determined glint in my mate's eye. Been here before, seen it before: Michael means business tonight. I thought back to the Euros where there'd been similar pressure on Michael and he hit back with that great finish against Portugal. He looked focused, sharp and ready to remind everyone of his class.

But then he smashed up his knee barely seconds after the first whistle. I was devastated for Michael, as a friend and also as a player. I felt for his family who were in the stadium, watching their loved one being carried away on a stretcher, his tournament over. Sitting on the bench, I also thought, 'Sven will get hell for this.' Michael's accident exposed the boss's crazy decision to take only four strikers. If only England had travelled to Germany with five forwards, Sven would not have been slated.

England's fans clearly wanted Theo on. Sven was having none of that. His sole aim was to top the group so he couldn't risk anything. There was no possible way the kid from Arsenal was ready. Crouchy came on, and England looked good for a while. Joe Cole gave us the lead with an absolute worldie, definitely a contender for goal of the tournament. At last England were playing good football, living up to our billing as one of the World Cup favourites. Thoughts of Berlin and the final filled my mind. The medal, the parade, the glory.

My day-dreaming was suddenly interrupted when Sweden equalized, through Markus Allback, and we were under real pressure. Sitting along from me was Sven, wearing a worried look. How would he react? England must hang on to the draw to guarantee an easier last-sixteen game.

Sven turned to me. 'Are you ready?' he asked.

Bloody hell. What was all that about not wanting to risk another yellow? 'Yeah,' I replied. 'Of course I'm ready.'

As I stood on the touchline, thinking how brilliant it was to get another cap, I heard a shout behind me. 'Oi, you, post on set-pieces.' It was Steve McClaren, Sven's number two, barking out a final instruction. His order stuck in my head. When Sweden got a corner a minute or so later, I went straight to the post. Thank God Steve reminded me. My first kick was a clearance off the line from Kim Kallstrom.

We had to re-impose ourselves. Come on, Stevie lad, get busy. With Owen Hargreaves buzzing around in midfield, I roamed forward. Look for a goal, look for the win. With five minutes remaining, Joe Cole cut into the area on the right and I made a diagonal run into the box. 'Just find me,' I kept saying, 'just find me.' If the ball came over the last defender, I'd have a chance on goal. Joe read my mind. His cross was perfect, lifted over on time and right on the money. Heading is not my strongest point, but I made great contact with Coley's cross. The ball flew in. Yes! At last, England seemed destined for a first win over Sweden in thirty-eight years. Now we were really on the move in Germany. Just watch us go now!

Then, stupidly, we conceded a very un-English goal. A bloody set-piece. We failed to cut out a long throw-in, Henrik Larsson pounced, and victory was snatched away.

Bollocks. In the dressing-room, Steve McClaren was livid with us. He'd spent hours organizing the players for set-pieces. Every session he'd drummed into us the importance of concentration, and we'd dozed off for a split-second in Cologne and been punished. 'If we defend like that again at set-pieces we will be out of the tournament before we know it,' Steve told us. I felt the mistake was a one-off; we'd actually defended well at set-pieces during the World Cup. Losing Rio to an injury hadn't helped, because he's a big presence at set-pieces. Come on. Be positive. Yes, it was disappointing not to finish the group with a third victory, but we had booked a last-sixteen place against Ecuador rather than in-form Germany. The quarter-finals beckoned.

The following night, Wednesday, 21 June, I was down at Brenners watching Argentina against Holland on the big screen when my text went. The message was from Paul Joyce, the football reporter I trust, from the *Daily Express*. 'What's this about you having a fight with Becks?' asked Joycey. 'There's a rumour going round that Becks decked you!' Bloody hell! News to me!

I immediately called Joycey. 'What the fuck's going on?' I said. 'I never had a slap off Becks or nothing!' Joycey explained that one newspaper was running a story about Becks whacking me in training. I laughed. 'Where do they get these stories from? It's bollocks.' It came as no surprise to learn which paper it was in. The *Sun*.

The moment I put the phone down, my text went again. Becks! He'd obviously been tipped off as well. 'I'm not sure you are aware, mate, but there's a story going around that me and you've had a bust-up. It's a load of shit. Just ignore it. You get these stories in big tournaments.' I texted him back. 'Unbelievable! But who won? I'm not having it that you beat me!' Becks and I swapped a few more texts and just made a complete joke out of it. When I got back to Buhlerhohe, I bumped into Becks and we had another laugh about it.

At breakfast the next day, the FA's press guy, Adrian Bevington, came over to the two of us. 'I'll deal with it,' he said. The FA issued a statement saying the *Sun* story was utter bollocks. Nothing happened between me and Becks. And even if the story were true, why would our own media try to stir up trouble like that in the camp? I know what the reporter would get out of a story like that: a pat on the back off his boss and a 'well done'. Even if it damaged England. And something else bugged me. This was the third time there'd been a ludicrous report about me having a bust-up with a team-mate, and I'd lost every fight! According to one rubbish story, I'd also clashed with Carra twice. My Liverpool team-mate obviously won the re-match as well!

Knockout rounds now awaited England. As the FA were sorting out 'the bust-up', me, Becks and the rest were back at Mittelberg, preparing for our bout with Ecuador. All the players knew we must raise our game. We spoke about that in team meetings with Sven and also among ourselves. During the group stage we showed only in flashes how good we were: first half against Paraguay, last twenty minutes against Trinidad and Tobago, and first half against Sweden. For all the criticism, we still believed we'd go all the way to Berlin.

Stuttgart was the next stop, and Sven gave us a new

shape. After starting three games with 4–4–2, England now switched to 4–5–1. It was a big leap. Me and the other players arrived in Germany thinking we would play 4–4–2 all the way through, but after Michael's injury we went 4–5–1. Even though we'd prepared for 4–5–1 we were still not familiar enough with such a different system. Other World Cup teams stuck with one formation they spent ages fine-tuning. Not us. England changed for the knockout stage of a World Cup, and you cannot expect it to work immediately. Players need time to adapt from 4–4–2 to 4–5–1. England should have practised with a holding midfielder for months before arriving at the World Cup. Come on! The biggest stage of all is no place for bloody rehearsals. I agreed we needed the insurance of an extra man in midfield, though. Most top teams operate with three in the middle, so our 4–4–2 would have been outnumbered in the centre. But we should have changed our system to 4–5–1 before the World Cup, not during it. People argue that 4–5–1 seems negative, but it's 4–3–3 when we have the ball. As a midfielder, I should have three forwards to aim at. The reason why 4–5–1 never worked for England was because when we had the ball, sometimes Wayne came deep, or Joe and David came deep out wide, so we never had any forwards going long. Sometimes I played too far forward in David's position, which meant that David had to cover for me. We were all guilty – me, David, Frank, Wayne and Joe – of 4–5–1 not working.

We were still too good for Ecuador, though. Becks whipped in one of those trademark free-kicks on the hour to see England into the quarter-finals. Thank God for

David. He had been slaughtered in the media, many critics questioning his right to a place, but that goal in Stuttgart showed why David must start. Becks's set-pieces are brilliant, and he offers much more than that. He is so gifted technically, and so competitive, that he can change a game's fortunes in a split-second. Without his stunning free-kick we were destined for extra time and pens. I admire Becks. It's good to play alongside someone who ignores all the criticism and just gets on with helping the team he loves to victory. Other players would collapse under that weight of pressure or simply hide. Not Becks. No chance. He thrives on it. All the players were surprised and disappointed that David got stick at the World Cup. Show me the evidence that Bex under-achieved. Against Paraguay, he forced the own-goal. He played the last pass for the two goals against Trinidad and Tobago. He scored a fantastic winner against Ecuador. 'What else can he do?' I thought. Even in the warm-up matches at Old Trafford, against Hungary in particular, Becks was sensational. Sven and Steve worked on Becks to stay out wide, and he kept delivering frightening crosses at some pace. Becks doesn't need to get behind a full-back to ping in a dangerous ball. Yet still the newspaper snipers accused him of being too static. When Aaron Lennon came on and did so well, pushing opposing defenders back, Becks was slated even more. The press would have loved Sven to drop David for Aaron. Big story! With that, all the journalists could get their pats on the back from their bosses. Fuck off. None of the players wanted Becks out of the team. We love him, and respect him. Ecuador con-firmed Becks's importance. We need experienced players

out there, particularly those like Becks with such an amazing desire to deliver.

I wasn't aware he'd thrown up in Stuttgart until afterwards, in the dressing-room, when he told me. He was
sick with dehydration. Christ, it was hot. We needed
water constantly. The conditions in Germany were the
hardest I have ever played in. We'd met only Paraguay,
Trinidad, Sweden and Ecuador, so people said to me,
'You're mad! How can they be the hardest games you
have played in? You've played against AC Milan!' But
with the high temperatures, and even higher expectations,
those World Cup games were definitely the most gruelling.
Of the four we played in reaching the last eight, the
Sweden match was probably the easiest, because
the temperature dropped, the pitch was moist and we
could play at a high tempo for a while.

When we knew we had Portugal in the quarter-finals,
all the players thought, 'Last four. We're on our way.' Of
course we were worried that we weren't yet firing, but our
confidence never dipped. Portugal were nothing special.
They'd hardly set the World Cup alight. 'We can beat
them,' I told the guys up at Buhlerhohe. Portugal had lost
Costinha and Deco to suspension, and those two were big
players for them. 'I wouldn't swap any of their players for
ours,' I told Carra. 'Why can't we go and beat Portugal?'
We had more time to work on 4–5–1 down at Mittelberg,
too, and slowly the new system was getting better.

As we kicked off in Gelsenkirchen on Saturday, 1 July,
all the lads were convinced the evening would end with
England in the World Cup semi-finals. But almost immediately we had a reality check. Portugal surprised me

how well they kept the ball. They seemed to glow with a belief in their tactics, and their touch. Even without Costinha and Deco, they looked a really settled team. Each player knew his role under Luiz Felipe Scolari. Facing Cristiano Ronaldo and Luis Figo was a nightmare: they were so elusive, so quick at picking up very clever positions. Now you see them, now you don't. It was like chasing ghosts. But Ronaldo didn't hurt us with the ball; he only played in flashes. I looked at Ronaldo and thought, 'There's a kid trying too hard.' I could just imagine what the Manchester United winger was thinking: 'I must be the main man against the English. I play in the Premiership. I must prove how good I am.' So he showed off. Every time Ronaldo got the ball, he tried to beat three or four of us. 'If that's what you want, mate,' I thought, 'that suits us fine. We know how to handle boys like you.' Early on, I chased Ronaldo back and slid in to clear. Everyone raved about the tackle, but it was simple. I knew when to commit because I had watched this Portuguese kid so many times. Once Ronaldo's head is down and he's running, he is not going to release the ball. So I don't have to rush my tackle. Bide your time, Stevie. Wait. Wait. Watch the ball. Now go. Strike. Get the ball. I did that to Ronaldo. He stood there stunned, like a schoolboy who'd had his ice-cream nicked.

Sadly, a dark side stains Ronaldo's game. His part in Wayne's dismissal in Gelsenkirchen was a fucking disgrace. All the Portuguese players should hang their heads in shame for their ambush on Wayne midway through the second half. It was clinical how Portugal set up England's best player. Yeah, let's get Rooney sent off. Aren't we clever? I hate them. When I saw the incident, I thought, 'Well, that's a free-kick for us.' The Portuguese were obviously fouling Wayne. Blatant. Wayne came deep to collect the ball and they were pulling his shirt, pushing him, banging into his ankles from behind. If Wayne had acted like most foreigners and fallen over at the slightest contact, England would have got the free-kick. But we're England. We don't cheat. We take the knocks. We ignore opponents tugging our shirts. Because we don't complain or pull stunts like foreigners, refs just seem to let it go. In the end, Wayne was punished for being too honest. Wazza's strong, and he always tries to stay on his feet, even if defenders like Ricardo Carvalho are fouling him 24/7. It's not in Wayne's nature to go down.

Then I saw Carvalho writhing around on the ground as if his life was coming to a sudden and brutal end. What the hell was going on? The referee, Horacio Elizondo, had blown his whistle. Commotion raged around the Argentinian official. I saw the red card raised. Christ, he's sent one of the Portuguese off. Good. About time. They've been fouling Wazza all game. Tiago even kicked Wayne in the face in the first half. Elizondo had clearly had enough. Brilliant. Last four, here we come. Then, to my horror, I realized it was Wayne walking slowly off. What? The Portuguese were noisily claiming that Wayne had stamped on Carvalho. Utter rubbish. I know Wayne very well. However frustrated he may have been by Carvalho's sly marking, Wayne would never deliberately harm an opponent. Never. It's just not in his nature. He told me afterwards it was an accident, and I believe him. Elizondo screwed up. I hope one day this ref realizes that special talents like Wayne should be protected, not penalized. Players like Ricardo Carvalho are damaging football, not Wayne Rooney. FIFA are always banging on about fair play, but the English are the only ones behaving properly. The world's governing body want footballers to stay on their feet. Wayne did. Yet he's the one who got sent off in Gelsenkirchen. It's bollocks.

Of course Wayne had become frustrated. Up front on his own, he hadn't received the service he expected. He was desperate to score in the World Cup. But the real frustration was having Carvalho and his partners in crime constantly pulling and pushing him. FIFA should be embarrassed about what the Portuguese did to Wayne. Crowding round Elizondo, trying to influence him, calling for a card against an opponent. The behaviour of Scolari's players in Gelsenkirchen was sickening. This synchronized gamesmanship is a foreign disease, and I saw it seven or eight times in Germany. It's disgusting, but it pays off. 'Shall England start doing that?' I thought to myself. 'Shall we start learning how to go down more easily and getting round the referee, conning him into a decision? Or shall I, Wazza and the rest of the England players stay the way we are – honest? Maybe if we can't beat them we'll have to join the cheats.'

That horrific thought only lingered for a couple of seconds. I'm not going to cheat. Even when I got a bit of criticism for winning a cheap penalty against Hungary at Old Trafford on 30 May, I had legitimate reasons. It did look bad, and I'm a bit ashamed I dived, but their right-back, Csaba Feher, was flying into me with a challenge that was definitely dangerous. I saw the two feet and the studs coming in and I thought, 'I either get out of the way or I get hurt.' The World Cup was days away; I couldn't risk getting injured, so I dived for cover. I'm gutted I did it, but I could see my metatarsal being broken by this reckless challenge. But many foreigners dive all the bloody time. I watch them. They are so clever at it I'm convinced they practise in training. Do they get told to dive by coaches? It's coached into them that when an incident like the Rooney one happens, they go to work on the ref. Bang! They are like magnets, straight over to the ref, signalling, keeping their hands behind their back so as not to risk a caution. Fucking Ronaldo was at the front. Go on, ref, go on, send Rooney off. The blame does not rest just with Ronaldo. Five or six of the Portuguese were at it. It angers me. Portugal's deviousness got one of my best mates sent off in the World Cup. England would have won if Wayne had stayed on.

FIFA held meetings up at Buhlerhohe during which their officials stressed to us that any play-acting would be punished. England's players assumed that because all the other teams were getting the same talks, there wouldn't be a problem. Everyone would behave. But the majority of the teams at the World Cup were diving and play-acting. What really pissed all the England players off during the Portugal game was Ronaldo's wink to his bench as Wazza walked down the tunnel. It was a wink that said 'job done'. How could he do that to his Manchester United team-mate? It's unbelievable.

On the bus after the game, Wayne asked me, 'What do you think about the wink, Stevie?'

Simple. 'Honestly, Wazza,' I replied, 'if we were playing

Spain, and Xabi Alonso or Luis Garcia winked at the ref or gave a signal for me to get sent off, I would never speak to them again. Never. No fucking way. I just couldn't. I would be that frustrated at one of my own team-mates.'

Wayne listened to every word. He could tell how angry I was over Ronaldo's behaviour.

'Look, Waz, Ronaldo is trying to do everything to get into the last four of the World Cup, but there is this big thing in football about fair play and respect for other professionals. Ronaldo showed none of that.'

Wayne agreed. He was deeply frustrated with Ronaldo at the time, but he soon calmed down. He sent Ronaldo a text, and seems now to have let it go. Fair play to Wayne for not holding a grudge.

The ten Englishmen who remained on the field in Gelsenkirchen seethed at the injustice, which doubled our determination against Portugal. You can cheat us, but you can't beat us. That was the message coming out from me and JT, Rio and the rest as we resisted everything Portugal threw at us. 'Stick together!' came the shout. Everyone was stirred up. Everyone was screaming encouragement, particularly JT and Rio. Ashley too. I went over to the left to help Ashley as Portugal tried to open England up by going wide. No chance. Ashley and I would not let anyone through. All ten of us were helped by the positive approach from Sven and Steve. I thought the order would be 'hold out for pens'. Sven and Steve thought differently. 'Push on!' came the instruction from the bench. 'Go and win it on the break!'

But as soon as we reached extra-time, my mind turned to pens. I knew I'd be on one. Sven had indicated his main penalty-takers in training. So as extra-time went on around me, I spent half an hour worrying about the only kick that counted – my penalty. Sweat poured even faster off my forehead. Stay calm. Focus. You must get through extra-time. But I was already distracted, the clock only showing how long it was until I had to make that soul-destroying walk from the centre-circle. Nearer and nearer. My pulse raced madly. My head was pounding. Penalties, penalties, penalties. Fuck it. 'Where am I going to put it?' I thought. 'Has their keeper seen my Liverpool pens? Soon find out.'

Elizondo's whistle went, and the teams gathered in two tense groups in the centre-circle. Jesus, I wish I was first up. Get it out the way. The wait's killing me. I envied Frank, taking penalty number one for England. Standing in the line, given support by team-mates, I felt weak with nerves, expectation and pressure. I could hardly watch as Simão scored. Don't worry, Frank will get us level. Go on, Lamps. In training, Lamps had been lashing them in. No problem. He stepped up. Ricardo saved. Shit. The knot in my stomach tightened. I had never felt this bad on a pitch in all my life.

The shoot-out continued its grim course, making heroes and villains. Viana and Petit both missed, Hargreaves stuck his away. Now the spotlight burned on me. Here goes. I broke away from the safety of my friends in the centre-circle. Suddenly I was alone, making my way towards the penalty spot, towards my fate. The journey was only forty yards, but it felt like forty miles. I recalled Sven's advice. 'Count your steps,' he told us in training as we practised pens. 'That will take your mind off the walk.' How could it? Strolling up and taking a pen in front of two men and a dog in training was a world away from this torturous walk in Gelsenkirchen. Even if I counted the steps, what difference would it make? Nothing could hide the fact that in a few seconds I'd be taking a pen in front of a billion or more people.

As I neared the spot, my body went numb. God, I wouldn't wish that walk on my worst enemy. Yet even with all the doubts building, I had belief in my technique. That penalty was going in. I will score. I went through my penalty routine. Set the ball right? Yes, done. Remember all the good kicks in training? Yes. I had hit the target nine times out of ten at Mittelberg. Know where you're going to place it? Yes. Ricardo's good, but if I place the ball exactly where I want, at the spot where Robbo, David James and Scott Carson told me about in training, Portugal's keeper can't stop it.

I was ready. Elizondo wasn't. Blow the whistle! Fucking get a move on, ref! Why the wait? I'd put the ball on the spot, Ricardo was on his line. Why do I have to wait for the bloody whistle? Those extra couple of seconds seemed like an eternity, and they definitely put me off. Doesn't he know I'm on edge? Jesus Christ! I was screaming inside. In training, it seemed so easy: ball down, step back, run in, goal. No wait, no tension. Not here. Not with Elizondo delaying everything. At last he blew, but my focus had gone. The moment I made contact with the ball I knew it wasn't going where I'd planned. It was eighteen inches away from my chosen spot, making it easier for Ricardo. Saved. Nightmare.

A feeling of utter helplessness washed over me. The

walk back to the halfway line was really, really bad. Question after question ate away at me. My FA Cup final penalty had been so good a few weeks before, so where had my accuracy gone? The pressure just got to me. For months, now, it had played on my mind that I would have to take a penalty in the World Cup. I knew we would come up against a shootout in Germany. My nerve, and my accuracy, just went. Shit. But wait. There's still hope. The lads can get me out of this mess. Surely? Even when Helder Postiga tucked his away, I felt Carra could make it 2–2. Sven brought Carra on with a minute remaining simply because he had been deadly in training: one miss from thirty. Carra is not one for hanging about, so he quickly took his pen, which flew past Ricardo. Elizondo hadn't blown, and he pulled Carra back. That was out of order.

When Ricardo got to Carra's second kick, my heart sank. England were going out of the World Cup. Ronaldo would finish us off. The story was set. It had to be Ronaldo, the kid involved in Wayne's sending-off, one of the best foreigners in the Premiership, sending us back home. Empty-handed. Broken-hearted. Ronaldo showed no mercy.

England were down and out. I collapsed in the centre-circle, my body shutting down. I've never experienced such depression on a football pitch. That own-goal against Chelsea in Cardiff was bad, so was getting knocked out of Euro 2004 in Lisbon, but Gelsenkirchen was much, much worse. I sat there with a lump in my throat, fighting back the tears. A few got through. People came across to console me, first Sven, then Steve and Gary Lewin. Becks tried to pull me up. Thanks, guys, for your support, but leave me to my pain. 'It's football,' I told myself. 'Shit happens. Get it out of your system and go and win something else.' And as I sat there, I promised myself that I would seize the next chance to take a penalty, and I'd fucking bury it.

Eventually, I climbed to my feet and joined the rest of the England players in a slow, mournful lap of Schalke's ground to thank our brilliant supporters. They stood and gave us a salute we did not deserve. I felt bitterly that I'd let every one of those magnificent fans down. Every one. They followed us across Germany, lifted our spirits during dark moments. Before each match, when we drove from our hotel, they would be there in their tens of thousands, lining the route, waving at us. We love you. We believe in you. Every game felt like a home game. And how had we repaid them? More heartache.

Why did England screw up? It cannot have been simply down to Portugal's gamesmanship. Everyone called us the Golden Generation. We should have coped. I hate using the word, but we failed. England went out of the World Cup in the quarter-finals, and that stinks. The reasons are scattered around: we didn't keep the ball well, we didn't take our chances, we took some crap penalties. Fucking pens. We practised pens every day for six weeks and missed three out of four in Gelsenkirchen; even the one that beat Ricardo didn't go exactly where Owen Hargreaves intended. England must overcome this mental block over penalties otherwise we will carry on returning early from tournaments. We must use international friendlies to stage practice shoot-outs after the final whistle while the stadium is still full. The England management must consider that. It's the only realistic way of practising penalties. That draining walk from the halfway line. The tension. The feeling that everyone is watching, jeering or cheering. At training, your team-mates are the crowd and you get five goes. Some rehearsal.

The real reason behind England's short stay in Germany is simple. It pains me to admit this, but it needs saying. We were just not as good as we think we are. On arriving in Germany, England were guilty of over-confidence. It was ours for the taking. No-one better than us. Me and the other players placed too much pressure on ourselves by constantly claiming we could win the World Cup. Stupid. We talked ourselves up too much. Never again. In future tournaments, we must learn to be humble. Be calm. We went around Germany blowing our trumpet and returned home mute with embarrassment. I went back to England with only regrets for souvenirs, and I was not alone. I talked to all the other players and we all accept none of us did enough. Nobody came back thinking, 'I was brilliant, the rest were rubbish.' We screwed up together. That's why the mood in the Gelsenkirchen dressing-room afterwards was so terrible. Devastation entered our lives. I have never experienced such a bad atmosphere in a dressing-room. The silence was broken only by the sound of boots being thrown off and the occasional swear-word.

Sven was deeply upset. The media paint him as a cold, unemotional man, but that's wrong. He hurt badly in Gelsenkirchen. The media heaped the blame on Sven, but that's unfair. The players who crossed the white line must share the responsibility with him for England's failure. But I will have another chance with England. Sven won't.

That was it. Game over. I was sad to see him go. I loved working with him. He was always constructive. Sven definitely improved me as a player, developing my positional play and stressing the importance of retaining possession. He always believed in me, and for that I will always be in his debt. I have so much respect for him. Sven kept leading England to quarter-finals but not beyond, and that's one of my biggest regrets. I let Sven down. I just wished I could have scored the goal, or hit the pen, that got England into the semi-finals in Germany. I would have loved to see Sven's face as I scored the winner because he is a great guy.

Of course we knew Sven would get coated for England's failure. He knew it as well. I don't think he was too cautious, as many people claimed, but I did understand some of the criticism towards him. A few decisions were wrong, like not taking five strikers. He certainly shouldn't have brought Theo to Germany. As well as Theo, Sven also didn't seem to have any intention of using certain players. In midfield we had three or four guys who were really, really similar. Sven never showed any interest in playing some of them, so why bring them to Germany? Take those who are going to play.' And another forward would have been nice.

The retreat from Germany took us first to Buhlerhohe to pack. It was late when we arrived at the hotel, but Sven immediately gathered the staff and players together and spoke for fifteen minutes. 'Thank you all for your support,' he said. 'I really believed this was our year. I can't believe we have gone out on penalties again. We should have been last four at least. All the best.' Sven then turned to Steve McClaren, his successor. 'Steve, I wish you all the best.' Sven was all dignity. He went round and shook each player's hand.

The next morning, in reception, as we checked out, I spoke to Sven again.

'Keep doing what you are doing, Steven,' he said. 'Keep enjoying it. See you around.'

'Thanks, Sven,' I replied. 'All the best in whatever you decide to do.'

It was an incredibly emotional moment. I just couldn't find the words to tell him how I felt. I'd worked with him for five years. To lose someone like that was terrible. Sven is one of the best blokes ever. The love is there. He's an interesting guy to talk to, a manager I will really miss. He had some embarrassing front-page moments which didn't help him, but everyone is entitled to a private life. Sven's human. He learned from being England manager that you have to be really, really careful in your private life.

Sven was off, and Becks was stepping down as captain. It was the end of an era. I had no idea David was thinking of giving up the armband. I was in my room at Buhlerhohe on the Sunday morning, getting my stuff packed and thinking about holidays, when Becks came on the telly at a press conference. I assumed he was just going to say a few words, expressing the players' disappointment. I was stunned when he announced he was finished as captain. But, looking back, I feel Becks resigned at the right time. He'd led England at three tournaments and was under a lot of pressure. I'll always remember him as a great captain. Becks loved the job, and I know how much it hurt him to hand over the armband. Watching him read his statement, I was just pleased to hear him say he would carry on playing for England. Becks has so much to offer the squad, whether he is in the starting eleven or not.

But that's now Steve McClaren's decision. I'd watched the FA's hunt for a new manager with interest. I wasn't bothered about whether Sven's successor was English or not. If the foreign candidate was best, then appoint him. But I'm happy the FA decided on Steve. I just hope he believes in me as Sven did. Steve certainly knows my game. He can get the best out of me. I respect him. All those who doubt his credentials should give him a chance. As he tries to steer England towards Euro 2008, people should judge Steve on his ideas and what changes he makes, not on what happened under Sven. Sven made all the big decisions, while Steve did his job really well as coach. Under Sven, Steve took a lot of training, which was second to none. His coaching's top class. I'd come off the training pitch thinking, 'I really enjoyed that.' People claim Steve is a better coach than manager, but that's rubbish. He proved at Middlesbrough he is a good manager as well as a fine coach. He tried to improve me as a player, tried to improve the team shape in certain situations. That's good management. He's honest. Having worked with McClaren, I'm convinced England have the right man. I listen closely to Steve, and 99.9 per cent of what he says is right. He knows his stuff, and he's more in your face than Sven. Noisier. Livelier. He's excellent at speaking in front of the England squad and also very good at one-on-ones. He deserves a go at being England manager. If he hadn't become manager, we might have missed out.

Steve will improve this England team but I'm not making any predictions about Euro 2008. Germany taught me to be more cautious in public. Defeat in the World Cup hit me hard. I had to get away quick. I took Alex off to St Tropez. Just the two of us. Five days' complete break; just what the doctor ordered, although nothing could cure the frustration I felt over England's World Cup display.

On our last night, Sunday 9 July, I couldn't help but turn on the telly to watch the final. Alex didn't mind this intrusion into our romantic break. She was busy packing. So I sat there, and watched France lose to Italy. After the early goals, Italy and France could still have been playing now and not notched a winner. I was still stunned by Zinedine Zidane's head-butt on Marco Materazzi. Even though I idolize Zidane, and understand he got provoked, you simply can't do what he did. It was crazy. France could have done with him in the shoot-out. Watching the pens brought painful flashbacks for me. When I then saw the Italians celebrating, I thought: 'That could have been us.' Neither Italy nor France produced anything special, certainly nothing that would have scared England. It reinforced all my regrets over England's 2006 World Cup campaign.

22
My Future

Someone told me that as I walked past the penalty spot on our sad lap around the pitch that the Gelsenkirchen DJ played 'I Will Survive'. And I will. My future promises so much. Alex and I will marry in the summer of 2007 and I want a son to play football with. There is rebuilding work to be done with England under Steve McClaren. In August 2006, Steve asked me to be England vice-captain, supporting John Terry, and it was an honour I immediately accepted. JT and Steve know they will always have my whole-hearted commitment. There will be more trophies to chase with Rafa and Liverpool. And one day, I'd love to manage Liverpool. I want to stay at Anfield in any capacity. I'm learning under Rafa and looking to do my coaching badges. I just want to help Liverpool. Me and Liverpool Football Club are a love affair that will never, ever end.

23

Athens, Andorra and the Altar

As the 2006/07 season unfolded, it felt like Liverpool's destiny to reach the European Cup final again. It was our calling, as if we were being swept there on a wave that crashed over others.

No-one could claim we enjoyed an easy route to Athens, venue for the final on 23 May 2007. When Liverpool were drawn against Barcelona in the last six-teen, many people thought that was it. Season over. Liverpool would never beat the mighty Barcelona, the team of Ronaldinho, Deco and Lionel Messi. That's what the critics said. My first reaction when we were drawn against the European champions was excitement. Brilliant. Bring it on. Another chance to play in the Nou Camp. Soon, though, that initial buzz faded. Christ, this was some task. Barcelona were the holders, boasting a who's who of the world's best players.

The first leg was at the Nou Camp on 21 February. We had to make sure a candle of hope stayed lit for the second leg at Anfield. To sharpen our concentration, Rafa took the lads to Portugal to train. It made sound sense. There was a ten-day gap between games in the Premiership and the Champions League, and Rafa wanted us away from Melwood, sweating hard in a climate similar to Barcelona. He wanted us away from our families, away from all the expectation swirling around Merseyside. All Rafa thought about was the Nou Camp. Liverpool were on a mission, and nothing could distract us. Rafa was really confident we could get a win, not just a draw, in Barcelona. I admired his belief. I said to Carra, 'I'll take a draw, even a slight defeat, as long as the tie is alive going back to Anfield.' That was the key: we all knew Barcelona would find it difficult in front of the Kop.

With Rafa so bullish, the mood quickly became buoyant among the lads in Portugal despite one or two problems. The set-up there wasn't the best. Liverpool booked the place on the Internet, and it looked lovely. I went on the web myself and checked it out: nice pools, good training facilities, top gym. We were in for a shock. When we arrived, the lads soon realized it was not up to the standard we were used to. The training pitch wasn't the best, and the hotel was damp. But all the lads knew not to complain. Just focus on the Nou Camp. Think of Barcelona. Train hard, get the small details right, and reward will follow in Catalonia.

We worked so well, doing double sessions, that one day Rafa called us together and announced, 'Because you are training so well, go out and have a meal, and enjoy yourself.' The manager is big on team spirit, and he thought a night out would do us good. 'But I want you all back by midnight,' he added. I felt immediately that that was a bit of a mistake on Rafa's behalf. If the manager had just left the time open, the players would have come in at a sensible hour. We went out quite late, which meant we were always going to struggle to meet Rafa's deadline. He should have given us more leeway. The decision came back to haunt him.

As we headed out into the night, the lads briefly complained about the midnight curfew. We soon forgot about it. We were in a great bar, having a top time. When the beers and laughter are flowing it is difficult to remember what time it is. And when the karaoke gets started, all sense gets drowned out. I was partly to blame. The lads were having a great craic on the karaoke, and I should have checked my watch. I'm Liverpool captain, after all. I should have said, 'It's ten minutes to midnight. Listen, we're all going, no matter what. Rafa's orders.' I knew what the response would be from the lads if I suggested we left: they would have turned the volume up on the karaoke and got more beers in. To be honest, I wasn't keen to go home myself. I was enjoying myself. And why not? I'd trained all week, sweated my guts out. Why shouldn't I have a few beers? I was up for staying on for another hour. I'm not really big on karaoke, unless I am in the right company, but I loved the scene. The lads gave me loads of stick for not singing. 'Come on,' they shouted, 'your turn.' Liverpool punters were there, as well as players. In the end, they dragged me up to do a Beatles number. I can't remember which one – I'd had too many by then. Then I went back to my seat, happy to watch the others.

It was a great night. I did notice a bit of handbags

between John Arne Riise and Craig Bellamy over the karaoke, which led to a bigger incident later on when Bellamy hit Riise with a golf-club. But the incident was never as bad as the media made out. Players fall out, and make up in seconds. It happens. Move on. Forget it.

The next morning, Rafa called the players together, and turned to Craig and Ginger. 'I'm not really interested in what happened,' he said to them, before addressing the rest of us. 'You are all out of order for not coming in on time.' He dished a few fines out. We paid up. Craig and Ginger shook hands, and decided not to take it any further. They both deserve a lot of credit for that. Rafa was brilliant. The manager's handling of the situation was spot-on. Some of the other players, me included, intervened as well. 'We have got a big game coming up,' I said to Craig and Ginger. 'Put it to bed.' They did. Time is a big healer. A couple of days down the line, both players had put the incident behind them. The press hadn't, of course. A real storm broke. We saw the headlines, felt the heat, and used it to Liverpool's advantage. All the fuss fuelled our motivation, creating a siege mentality in our dressing-room. Come on, lads, they are all against us. Let's show them. In a funny way, that karaoke-night bonding session in Portugal got us in the right mood to take on Barcelona.

Rafa's game-plan was to shock Barcelona. Do the unexpected. Barcelona felt Liverpool would be really negative: two banks of four, rarely cross the halfway line. Rafa did the opposite: go on the front foot, go for the jugular. Stand firm, and get stuck into them. Even when Deco scored early, we stuck to our tactics. Our plan was to hurt

Barcelona down the sides, in the full-back areas. Bellamy's job was to race down the channels, either side of Barcelona's centre-halves Carles Puyol and Rafael Marquez. All the build-up had revolved around the golf-club incident in Portugal, so when Craig scored, setting up a famous 2–1 win, he celebrated with a golf swing. When I saw it, I had to have a little chuckle. In all the pictures, I'm in the background coming to the celebration, laughing. Inside, though, I had a thought for Ginger. He seemed OK about it, and in the dressing-room afterwards we all joked about it. No wonder we were laughing. We had just beaten the European champions at their place – and Riise had scored the winner off a Bellamy pass.

What made victory particularly special was that Barcelona were a class side. For the first twenty minutes they really made us sweat. That was the first time I had run into Ronaldinho in a competitive game, and the Brazilian didn't disappoint. He was difficult to knock off the ball, and blessed with two good feet that could spirit the ball through a road-block. I felt that when Ronaldinho was in possession, anything could happen. One touch of magic could cast a spell over us. We couldn't afford to let him get going. He never got a chance. Carra was fantastic against Ronaldinho, getting blocks in, blotting him out. Carra was man of the match by a country mile. No surprise: all the way to Athens, Carra was world class.

Back in the Nou Camp dressing-room, Carra, me and all the lads were buzzing. It felt as if Liverpool had won something that night. In a way, we had. We had earned ourselves a massive confidence boost. Barcelona away was such a big game, and no-one expected us to draw, let alone win, but we'd done it. Liverpool had beaten Barcelona. In the showers at the Nou Camp, all the players were singing, shouting and celebrating a famous victory.

I didn't want to throw cold water over the lads, but we couldn't risk any complacency. 'It's not over,' I warned. 'Barcelona will come at us at Anfield. They've got the quality to destroy us.' But they didn't, mainly due to another tactical master-stroke from Rafa. Our tactics on 6 March caught Barcelona out again. Rafa ordered us to play deeper than we had at the Nou Camp. Come and break us down. No chance. Not with Carra barring the way. Eidur Gudjohnsen scored, but it was too little too late. The away goals took us through.

Next up were PSV Eindhoven, and we were really shifting now: 3–0 in Holland, 1–0 at Anfield. Job done. The semi-final draw brought familiar faces: Chelsea. Jose Mourinho. John Terry. Frank Lampard. Joe Cole. The road to Athens had become a trip down memory lane. Two years ago, Liverpool squeezed past Chelsea to reach Istanbul. The same obstacle to the final reappeared. And this tie would be as tough. Both Liverpool and Chelsea were well organized and strong defensively. That's the way both managers like it. Rafa is dead keen on a tight defence. From speaking to the Chelsea lads, I know Jose hates conceding and spends ages in training working on the back-four. We knew one goal could separate the teams, just as it did in 2005.

Also similar to back then, a war of words broke out between the two managers. Rafa went on the offensive about Jose, saying Liverpool fans are the real Special

Ones. No messing from Rafa. Straight in. Bang. Take that, Jose. Rafa's attitude surprised the players. Our manager is not one for talking much in the media, or getting involved with other managers, but he went to town on Jose. By saying Liverpool's supporters were the real Special Ones, Rafa was being really clever. Having to overcome Chelsea's 1–0 first-leg lead, Rafa knew he would need the fans passionately behind us at Anfield on 1 May.

The Kop played their part again, big-time. Chelsea walked into another wall of noise. They also walked into a classic sting. Mourinho's players were caught completely cold by our goal, when I knocked a free-kick to Daniel Agger, who scored from the edge of the area. The move was straight out of Melwood, one we'd practised ever since Rafa arrived. The manager is really big on small details. He analyses the stats, knows that set-pieces settle many matches, and drills us on dead-ball situations, day in, day out. Whatever the occasion, massive European night or modest Carling Cup tie, Liverpool are ready with set-piece weapons. We'd tried the Agger move before, and come really close, but we don't overuse it as opponents will get wise. Chelsea were stunned. Simple as that. They had no inkling of what we'd planned when I pulled the ball back to Agger. Rafa had really done his homework on Chelsea. While watching tapes of them, we noticed that when defending a free-kick in wide areas, they backed off. So if you piled a lot of bodies into the box, distracting John Terry, Ricardo Carvalho and Michael Essien, the pull-back was on. Chelsea very nearly did it to us once. In the Premiership game on 20 January 2007, when we beat them 2–0, Lamps pulled the ball back to Didier Drogba, but he did a fresh-air shot. Agger connected sweetly, and it was off to penalties. We held our nerve, Chelsea didn't. Pepe Reina was sensational, and we were off to Athens. Brilliant.

Chelsea's players were good in defeat. JT grabbed me. 'Go and win it again,' he said. That's John Terry the man for you. A class guy. Frank shook my hand. So did Jose. Mourinho's impressive like that. Whatever the result between us, whether I have beaten him or he has won, Jose always comes across, shakes my hand and says, 'Well done.' I admire Mourinho for that. Everyone talks about the rivalry between Liverpool and Chelsea, between Rafa and Jose, between the fans. I feel the tension rippling between Anfield and Stamford Bridge. Liverpool have had the upper hand on Chelsea in Europe, but they have dominated us in the Premiership. But only one emotion guides my view of Chelsea: respect. Between the players, a mutual respect exists. When I talk to JT, Lamps or Joe Cole at England, they always say the same thing: 'Anfield is a nightmare to play at.' I tell them, 'Stamford Bridge is really tough for us.' Under Mourinho, Chelsea have become a formidable team. It seems to me that if Liverpool are to win a cup, we have to knock Chelsea out on the way. That shows how good Jose and his team are. It's the same in the Premiership. For Manchester United to finish as champions they had to deal with Chelsea's unbelievable threat.

One area where Chelsea and United cannot touch Liverpool is in the amazing noise generated by our fans. I'm not worried that the new stadium planned in Stanley Park will lose that atmosphere. No chance. It's the people who make the atmosphere, and those supporters will never disappear. When I warm up, I watch and listen to the fans. I love their passion, their will to win – qualities you see in Liverpool's home-grown players. I know how much Liverpool means to the fans. Before and after games, I receive text messages from family and friends, all mad about Liverpool. I read the letters in the local papers. The fans' obsession with Liverpool is deep and unending. If the new stadium is built right, the atmosphere will lift to an even higher level. The noise and intensity will be unbelievable. It has been delayed an extra year because the club want to build a Kop, recreating the best parts of Anfield. If Liverpool do have a Kop, with more people in, the atmosphere on big Champions League and Premiership occasions will be out of this world.

Liverpool's new American owners, Tom Hicks and George Gillett, are doing things the right way. They are classy guys, with sharp business minds. I spoke to some rival bidders, the Arab people, who were nice, but it was only a ten-minute chat. Liverpool's board then met Hicks and Gillett and decided to go down that route. The first time I encountered the Americans, I was bowled over by the enthusiasm pouring from the pair of them. Hicks and Gillett are winners. I saw the ambition in their eyes, heard it in their words. They told me and Carra about what they'd achieved in other sports. I sat there, listening and thinking to myself, 'If we can channel all that energy and good ideas into the football side, we'll really take off.' The Americans' passion for their new adventure is obvious. Hicks and Gillett are always popping into Melwood, saying 'hi' and chatting to the players. Top guys. They move quickly, too. When a new contract was mentioned, the Americans were superb, Rick was sharp, Rafa wanted it done, I wanted it done. My adviser Struan had a couple of meetings and it was a done deal. Simple. I admired Hicks and Gillett for that.

When Carra and I talked to Liverpool's new owners, we had one important request: 'Please keep David Moores involved.' He will always be chairman in my eyes. Always. He's a Liverpool fan, and a good friend of mine. He even invited me to a ball at his house recently. David Moores has a great relationship with the players and everyone at Anfield. Thankfully, that bond will continue strong. Hicks and Gillett told me and Carra how much they wanted Mr Moores to stay around. They know what a fantastic job he has done for the club. They realize that he is a committed fan who wears his heart on his sleeve. For me, David Moores will always be the main man upstairs. The Americans understand that.

When Chelsea visited on that memorable European night, the Americans were spell-bound by the Anfield atmosphere. They came into the dressing-room afterwards, clutching bottles of champagne. As Hicks and Gillett stood there in the middle of the room, shaking hands and congratulating us, I saw mischievous looks leap into my team-mates' eyes. I knew what the lads were thinking. Our new owners deserved a celebratory dip in the bath.

'Come on,' someone whispered to me, 'let's throw them in.'

I stole a glance at Hicks and Gillett. They were just standing there, toasting us, laughing, oblivious to any possible ambush. It didn't seem right to bundle them into the bath. They'd only just arrived at the club. The lads decided to let the Americans off on their first visit to the dressing-room. Next time, though, both are going in the bath. No ifs, no buts, no mercy. Straight in.

When the party finished on Merseyside that night, our thoughts turned to Athens, to another final. Again our opponents were AC Milan, but contrasts with Istanbul soon surfaced. The organization of the European Cup final in Turkey had been excellent, but things weren't right on the trip to Greece. I'm no whinger, but Liverpool's hotel wasn't up to scratch. Rafa wasn't happy, and neither were the players. The bedrooms were nowhere near good enough: tiny single beds and a room so small that I could sit on the toilet and have a shower at the same time. It might have been funny if the situation had not been so serious. For a Champions League final, when you know people have gone over to inspect facilities in advance, it was disappointing. While preparing for such a massive event, I didn't want to be distracted by switching rooms, hauling my gear down corridors, and trying to get the air-con to work. It was like Rafa said: the small details must be right. So much is at stake: glory, pride, money, reputations. Everything had been spot-on in Istanbul, but we were let down in Athens. Even the flight home was all wrong, with little leg-room, knees crammed in. Liverpool should travel on bigger planes, where players can move around, stretch our legs. I was disappointed with the whole set-up.

That was frustrating because Liverpool's tactical preparations were perfect. As against Barcelona at the Nou

Camp, Rafa came up with the right game-plan in Athens. We all knew Milan's strengths, the class they had in midfield, so Rafa went 4–5–1 to nullify the Italians' threat. Although Milan set up 4–4–2, their shape quickly became 4–3–2–1 with Gattuso coming into the centre alongside Pirlo and Ambrosini while the full-backs, Massimo Oddo and Marek Jankulovski, bombed on. We swamped the middle. Javier Mascherano got tight on Kaka, doing a really good job and keeping him quiet. The threat is always there with Kaka. Always. When he receives the ball, you must have two men around him. And that gives Milan space in other areas.

Liverpool still controlled the final, without really creating. Many of our best moments in the first half flowed from Jermaine Pennant out on the right. He got in one great cross that I just failed to convert. Jermaine finished the season strongly, showing his terrific potential. At the moment, though, it's just potential. Jermaine needs to deliver week in, week out, season in, season out. How well he does at Liverpool is up to Jermaine. No-one else. Not Rafa. Not the other players. Jermaine possesses every attribute to be a top winger for Liverpool. Touch and pace come naturally to him. Liverpool fans are warming to him because he is going past people and whipping crosses in. He has changed his mentality after getting a bit of criticism. Jermaine's been a lot more focused and professional. Now it's up to him. Jermaine Pennant can be as good as he wants to be. He can hit the heights or slide back. We'll have to wait and see.

For all the efforts of Jermaine and the other players, we couldn't break through. Milan took a flukey lead on the edge of half-time, the ball catching Filippo Inzaghi and sending Pepe the wrong way. How unlucky was that? I couldn't believe it. In the second half, I expected some subs sharpish. We were trailing 1–0 and failing to create real chances. I trust Rafa. The manager clearly had belief in the players who were on, but I was surprised Crouchy didn't come on a bit earlier. Not just Crouchy, any sub. We needed something different.

I partly blame myself. Early in the second half, I missed a chance which I'm still gutted about. Cutting in from the left, and through on Dida, only one thought hammered through my mind: don't waste the opportunity. Few chances had come to us, so I didn't want to shoot with my left foot and regret it. I must use my right, my stronger foot. So I opened up my body to try to pass the ball around Dida with my right. Sadly, I never made a good enough connection. Dida saved. Maybe I should have gone with my left.

When Inzaghi added another, I felt the spirit of Istanbul desert us for good, even when Dirk Kuyt made it 2–1 a minute before the end. The final whistle blew through me like a vicious wind. Frustration ate away at me because Milan were there for the taking. They were. We should have beaten them. I looked around at my devastated Liverpool team-mates, and at our wonderful fans who sang to the end and beyond, and my heart broke in two. Even now, recalling events in Athens, my mind is numb with grief. The pain remains.

Even amid my heartache at the final whistle, I knew I had to show dignity in defeat. A lot was made in the build-up to the final about my criticism of Gattuso in

Istanbul, and I didn't want anyone to feel I disrespect opponents. That's not in my nature. I milk it when I win, but I want people to appreciate that I take defeat well. I saw Gattuso and stretched out a hand.

'Congratulations,' I said.

He was good. No gloating. Just a few kind words. 'Thanks very much. You were unlucky.'

I nodded, and moved away.

However much losing kills me, I always honour the victors. I hate people who go off celebrating and ignore the beaten team. Show some class. Better footballers than me do it, so why shouldn't I? One good thing coming into football now is that most players are starting to take defeat on the chin and not be bad losers. That's good for the game.

Having congratulated Gattuso, Paolo Maldini and the rest of the Milan team, I retreated to the dressing-room. God, it was grim in there. The players were shattered, emotionally and physically. I had to behave as a captain, not as a heartbroken player. 'Listen, lads, we did OK,' I told my grieving team-mates. 'We gave a good account of ourselves. We have not been blown away.' I meant it. In 2005, Liverpool got blown away by Milan in Istanbul. Completely. Although we came back and won on the night, there was only one good team in Istanbul, and it was not Liverpool. 'We can be proud of ourselves,' I told the players in Athens. 'Don't be down and disheartened. Look to the future. Are we moving forward or at a standstill? We all know this team is moving forward.'

I believe Liverpool are heading in the right direction. I've definitely got another European Cup final in me.

Absolutely no question about it. I will be desperately disappointed if I don't win it again. I have to. There's a huge difference between owning one European Cup winners' medal and two. Many players possess one; few have two. My failure to collect another European Cup medal in Athens is a hurt I must live with – until I win it again. Maybe I'm just being greedy. When I was a young lad knocking about on Ironside, if someone had said, 'You'll play in two European Cup finals, winning one and losing the other – do you fancy it?' my reaction would have been to shake their hand so strongly it would have fallen off. Putting all the agony of Athens to one side for a moment, the reality is that Liverpool reached two finals in three years, which is terrific. When our unspectacular domestic form is taken into account, we have been punching above our weight. In truth, Liverpool are still quite a few players away from getting involved in the Premiership race, and continuing to do well in Europe. The future looks bright for the club, though: we've got a good team, an outstanding manager in Rafa, a new stadium being designed, and brilliant new owners. If the Americans hand Rafa the financial backing to strengthen a good team, we can become a great team. Then we can erase the memory of Athens.

Athens left a bad taste in the mouth. The moment I turned my mobile back on, calls and texts came thudding through from family and friends who were at the Olympic Stadium and were horrified by the behaviour of the Greek police. What I heard shocked me. My family and friends were caught up in minor incidents trying to get into the stadium; they were pushed, shoved and tear-gassed. What the hell happened? This was the European Cup final, the pinnacle of club football. Organization should have been miles better. OK, a minority of fans let themselves down, but they might not even have been genuine Liverpool fans. For all I know, they could have been people jumping on the bandwagon pretending to be Liverpool fans, pulling any stunt to get into the European Cup final. I find it hard to believe any real Liverpool fan would snatch a ticket off another Liverpool fan. I have travelled around Europe for years, and our supporters' behaviour has always been spot-on.

The blame game soon began. For me, the people who should look at themselves most closely are the organizers. The Olympic Stadium in Athens was too small and too poorly prepared for clubs the size of Liverpool and Milan. Just think. Champions League finals are only going to be contested by two massive clubs, so why not stage the final in bigger stadiums? If Liverpool had played Manchester United in Athens – which was a possibility until United lost to Milan – I would have been really concerned for both sets of fans. There would have been a bloodbath. UEFA must sit down and discuss the issue of the right venue. A showpiece game such as the European Cup final must be in a larger arena than Athens, with fairer and bigger ticket allocations, proper turnstiles, and double the security.

Frustration became a constant companion for a while. Seeing Steve Heighway leave his post as Liverpool Academy director was particularly disappointing. It still upsets me. If anyone comes in and does a better job, I will be surprised. Watch this space. It won't happen. Steve is impossible to replace. Liverpool can search this country, or any other country, and they will struggle to find anyone good enough to fill Steve Heighway's boots. No-one works better with kids from eight to eighteen. No-one. I will put my life on that. Steve cares for his players, and he's a top judge of a player as well. When I was ten, he looked my parents in the eye and said, 'Your lad will play for Liverpool's first team, if looked after properly.' When Michael Owen was thirteen, Steve told me, 'Michael will get in Liverpool's first team.' Of course, I am biased towards Steve because he helped me. But I just can't understand why he has gone. Over the years he had a bit of criticism, people saying that Liverpool have hardly had any young players coming through since me. But hold on. Tell me which clubs are developing players. All the top sides spend big money on them. Manchester United's best young player is Wayne Rooney, and they spent £27 million on him. Chelsea are buying kids for £5 million. Liverpool Football Club, and me personally, will miss Steve Heighway.

Disappointment dogged me during 2006/07, for country as well as club. England enjoyed a good start under Steve McClaren, but we soon ran into some stormy weather. By the time England came away from Israel on 24 March with a 0–0 draw, we were beginning to feel the anger of England's supporters. Such a point, away from home, would have been considered a decent result if we had been in a better position in our qualifying group for Euro 2008. But we remained in mid-table, and the fans were livid. As we left the field in Tel Aviv, England's fans showed their frustration, giving us a taste of the treatment in store in Barcelona four days later for the tie with Andorra. The main focus of their fury was the manager. McClaren was getting it in the neck big-style.

Guilt gripped me. Questions raced through my mind. Was it just McClaren's fault? No. Can I do more for England? Yes. Players must take responsibility. We cannot hide while the manager dodges the bullets. As we settled into our Barcelona base, Steve told the experienced players to stand up and be counted. He warned us what was in store.

The build-up to Andorra was unforgiving. On the Tuesday, the day before the game, I did a press conference with John Terry and the questions were really, really difficult. Were the players behind McClaren? Had the team let England's fans down? I was running down snipers' alley. The mood was dark and against us. I knew if England didn't score against Andorra in the first five minutes at the Montjuic Stadium, an absolute nightmare awaited. England's fans were waiting to turn. Understandably so. They were following the so-called best players in the country, paying good money and watching shite. A revolt was on the cards.

Stepping out in the Montjuic against Andorra felt like climbing into a pressure cooker. As we struggled to break down Andorra, the abuse was incredible. I was shocked because I hadn't experienced such derision before. It got really personal towards the manager, and the players. 'You're not fit to wear the shirt!' the fans chanted at England's players. That hurt. Footballers often claim they cannot hear such abuse. We can. At the Montjuic, it was inescapable. It grew louder and louder.

I looked around. England's young players were badly affected. There they were, all proud to represent their country, and the team was getting slaughtered by the fans. With all the anarchy in the stands, I found it hard to concentrate on the game, and I had played in more than fifty internationals. God knows how the youngsters were coping. I tried to reassure them, encouraging them to get on the ball. 'You're playing because you are the best in England,' I shouted. 'Go and show it.' I felt for them. At twenty years of age, I would definitely have gone into my shell.

Only a goal would silence our detractors, but Andorra were adding to our embarrassment. No matter how bad a team is – and Andorra were really bad – if they don't move out of position, it's difficult to break them down. Andorra really pissed me off. They were staying down, killing time, stopping our momentum building. I tried to quicken the play, and ended up forcing passes. Be patient, I told myself. Look for the opening. It will come. But it is hard not to hurry attacks and risk things when your own fans are abusing you. I tried to seize the game by the scruff of the neck, make things happen, stop the cruel chants. I struggle to remember playing in a more difficult game against such weak opposition.

With every scoreless minute, the boos worsened. At half-time, England needed inspiration. Badly. As the cat-calls pursued us down the corridors of the Montjuic to the dressing-room, Steve let us regain our breath and then went to work on us. 'Try to raise the tempo,' he told us. 'We need more pace on the pass to move them out of position.' Steve was really good at half-time. He wasn't angry, just stayed calm. He used his experience to help the young players. 'Ignore the atmosphere,' he told them, 'concentrate on the football.' That was good management. The senior players also made little speeches. 'Keep going, don't hide,' I told the team. 'Be patient, blank the noise out.'

Action was needed to match my words. I had to make something happen myself, so I drove into Andorra in the second half, scoring twice and taking the sting out of the fans' venom. For my first goal, set up by Wazza, I made good contact with a half-volley. The moment the ball hit the grass I knew it was in, because the surface was soaking wet and it fair flew into the net. That was a good individual goal. Relief seeped into our bodies. But the dull throb of pain caused by the fans' boos continued. England needed another goal. I played a one-two with Stewart Downing and then Jermain Defoe, and produced a good finish. David Nugent's late goal made it 3–0, and the storm subsided. Thank God. I never want to endure such abuse again.

As we left behind a stadium soaked in rain and the fans' bile, it felt like a watershed for Steve McClaren's England. That had to be the low point. Steve will have learned from that experience. I certainly did. After surviving that, the only way was up for England.

England's next Euro 2008 qualifier came in Estonia on 6 June. Another potential banana skin. Another chance for fans to voice their concerns. Again, pressure mounted on McClaren and the players, but England had too much for Estonia. Joe Cole scored the first and Becks then created finishes for Crouchy and Michael.

Becks' return lifted us. He handled his exile with real

dignity, which hardly surprised me. I expected him to behave with a touch of class. He never moaned. He took Steve's initial decision on the chin and worked hard at Real Madrid to make him change his mind. Becks' performance in Tallinn showed why Steve was right to bring him in from the cold. I was pleased to see him back. Definitely. He still has a lot to offer the team. He looks after himself. He puts quality balls into the box. He's a danger at set-pieces. He works as hard as anyone. People question his age, but Becks is as fit as anyone. When Steve left him out of the squad after the 2006 World Cup, I personally felt he still had something to offer England. The decision was too hasty. At the very least, I believed Becks was a useful squad option. In Tallinn, Becks proved he's a more than useful first-eleven member. He hadn't changed. He strolled back into the dressing-room and immediately resumed his work, helping out the young players, showing everyone his will to win. Becks is a professional. He conducts himself really well. He has achieved so much in life, and in his career, that everyone should look up to him and learn from him. I do.

I did get one medal while on England duty that season: an MBE off the Queen. From where I come from, a housing estate in Huyton, I never, ever dreamed of picking up an accolade like that. I never thought I would be walking up to Buckingham Palace to meet the Queen to get an MBE. I was really flattered and shocked to be invited. Alex came with me, and so did Struan. The ceremony was during England week, so I asked Steve McClaren's permission for the morning off.

Nerves rarely feature in my life now that I am an established England international and European champion. I can handle most situations. But I must admit to feeling nervous stepping through the gates of Buckingham Palace. I had to be on my best behaviour, really polite. Right clothes, right words. Was I going to make a mistake? Was I going to say the wrong thing? Was I going to embarrass myself? Luckily enough, it went perfectly. I bowed in front of the Queen. 'All the best with England,' she said. Fair play to her, she'd done her homework. She knew I was with England and that we had a game coming up. A sense of pride filled me.

I'm not really into the royal family, but I understand the significance of these accolades. At the palace, I met soldiers who had faced unimaginable horror in Iraq, policemen who had been tackling crime for fifty years, and firemen who had fought blaze after blaze. All around me were stories of astonishing bravery. We all gathered in a room for tea before meeting the Queen, and I listened in amazement to all these heroes. Being in the presence of so many special people was pretty humbling. I whispered to myself, 'I must have done quite well at my job to be in this company.' Whenever the pressure of football gets to me, I compare my job to other people's and realize how lucky and privileged I am.

Afterwards, I got a picture of me and Alex outside Buckingham Palace. It was a great day, particularly for Alex. I am not one for all this attention, but I'd do anything for her. Alex has helped me mature over the last five years, and contributed to the success I have had on the pitch. She has given me two beautiful daughters, the most important people in my life. We got married on 16 June, a magical day, and it felt so right. It wasn't a reward for Alex's loyalty, it was just that the time was right. Alex deserved the wedding, because I love her. I hope marriage will now make our relationship even better, taking it to a new level. We are both happy, delighted with the two girls.

Alex is a close friend. I trust her with my life. I lean on her, share everything with her. I'm in love with her. I'm in love with Liverpool. The future looks bright. There are more chapters to be written in my life-story because I've not finished yet. No chance.

Career Record

LIVERPOOL

Debut: 29 November 1998 v Blackburn Rovers (home) – league

First goal: 5 December 1999 v Sheffield Wednesday (home) – league

	Appearances	Goals
League	268	44
FA Cup	20	5
League Cup	17	6
Europe	77	19
FA Community Shield	2	0
Club World Championship	3	1
Total	387	75

(as at end of 2006/07 season)

Honours won:

League Cup	2001
FA Cup	2001
UEFA Cup	2001
European Super Cup	2001
League Cup	2003
UEFA Champions League	2005
FA Cup	2006

Became Liverpool captain: 15 October 2003

ENGLAND

Debut: 31 May 2000 v Ukraine (Wembley)

First goal: 1 September 2001 v Germany (Munich)

Full caps: 57   **Goals:** 12

Under-21 caps: 4   **Goals:** 1

Tournaments played:

European Championships 2000
European Championships 2004
World Cup 2006

INDIVIDUAL HONOURS

PFA Young Player of the Year 2001
PFA Player of the Year 2006
MBE on Queen's New Year's Honours List 2007

Index